Emiott Trust
November 1994

This book is a study of the values and aspirations of the earliest agrarian settlers in the Far West and how they changed in the frontier setting. It compares rural people who settled in the Willamette Valley in the 1840s, the Utah Valley in the 1850s, and the Boise Valley in the 1860s.

Though all three were farming societies, they were remarkably different in values and aspirations. Willamette Valley settlers brought a traditional southern yeoman culture to the Pacific. Utah Valley settlers drew upon Mormon ideology in forming a highly communal society. Those settling the Boise Valley were individualistic, commercial, and acquisitive from the outset. The differences are evident in patterns of migration, of settling upon and using the land, and of their relation to those about them and to the broader society.

The Oregon and Utah settlers tried, with differing degrees of success, to resist the modernizing trends represented by Idaho, but ultimately accommodated themselves to the exploitive and acquisitive values prevailing in the New West of the post–Civil War years. The author explores the reasons for Americans' move away from a culture centering on family and kin and from attitudes that valued and protected the land, not for its commercial worth but as the base of support for future generations.

Interdisciplinary perspectives on modern history

Editors
Robert Fogel and Stephan Thernstrom

**Three frontiers**

Other books in this series

Eric H. Monkkonen, *Police in urban America, 1860–1920*

Mary P. Ryan, *Cradle of the middle class: the family in Oneida County, New York, 1790–1865*

Ann Kussmaul, *Servants in husbandry in early modern England*

Tamara K. Hareven, *Family time and industrial time: the relationship between the family and work in a New England industrial community*

David Rosner, *A once charitable enterprise: hospitals and health care in Brooklyn and New York, 1885–1915*

Arnold R. Hirsch, *Making the second ghetto: race and housing in Chicago, 1940–1960*

Roy Rosenzweig, *Eight hours for what we will: workers and leisure in an industrial city, 1870–1920*

Hal S. Barron, *Those who stayed behind: rural society in nineteenth-century New England*

Jon Gjerde, *From peasants to farmers: the migration from Balestrand, Norway, to the Upper Middle West*

Ewa Morawska, *For bread with butter: the life-worlds of East Central Europeans in Johnstown, Pennsylvania, 1890–1940*

Alexander Keyssar, *Out of work: the first century of unemployment in Massachusetts*

Lance E. Davis and Robert A. Huttenback, *Mammon and the pursuit of Empire: the political economy of British imperialism, 1860–1912* (abridged edition also published)

Reed Ueda, *Avenues to adulthood: the origins of the high school and social mobility in an American suburb*

Allan G. Bogue, *The Congressman's Civil War*

Joel Perlmann, *Ethnic differences: schooling and social structure among the Irish, Italians, Jews, and blacks in an American city, 1880–1935*

Stuart M. Blumin: *The emergence of the middle class: social experience in the American city, 1760–1900*

Gary Gerstle, *Working-class Americanism: the politics of Labor in a textile city*

J. Matthew Gallman, *Mastering wartime: a social history of Philadelphia during the Civil War*

Jeffrey S. Adler, *Yankee merchants and the making of the Urban West: the rise and fall of antebellum St. Louis*

Dino Cinel, *The national integration of Italian return migration, 1870–1929*

# Three frontiers

Family, land, and society in the American West, 1850–1900

DEAN L. MAY
*University of Utah*

CAMBRIDGE
UNIVERSITY PRESS

Published by the Press Syndicate of the University of Cambridge
The Pitt Building, Trumpington Street, Cambridge CB2 1RP
40 West 20th Street, New York, NY 10011-4211, USA
10 Stamford Road, Oakleigh, Melbourne 3166, Australia

© Cambridge University Press 1994

First published 1994

Printed in the United States of America

*Library of Congress Cataloging-in-Publication Data*
May, Dean L.
  Three frontiers : family, land, and society in the American West,
1850–1900 / Dean L. May.
      p.   cm. – (Interdisciplinary perspectives on modern history)
  Includes bibliographical references and index.
  ISBN 0-521-43499-8
  1. Frontier and pioneer life – Oregon – Willamette River
Valley.   2. Frontier and pioneer life – Idaho – Boise River
Valley.   3. Frontier and pioneer life – Utah – Utah Lake
Region.   4. Farm life – Oregon – Willamette River Valley –
History – 19th century.   5. Farm life – Idaho – Boise River Valley
– History – 19th century.   6. Farm life – Utah – Utah Lake Region
– History – 19th century.   7. Willamette River Valley (Or.) –
History.   8. Boise River Valley (Idaho) – History.   9. Utah Lake
Region (Utah) – History.   I. Title.   II. Series.
F882.W6M39      1994
979.5'3041 – dc20                                              93-43560
                                                                    CIP

A catalog record for this book is available from the British Library.

ISBN 0-521-43499-8 Hardback

To the memory of Frank Peter May, 1898–1971
And to Wanda Lowe May Rockhill
With love and gratitude

And Terah took Abram his son, and Lot the son of Haran his son's son, and Sarai his daughter in law, his son Abram's wife; and they went forth with them from Ur ... to go into the land of Canaan.

*Genesis 11:31*

* * *

And it shall come to pass in the last days, that the mountain of the Lord's house shall be established in the top of the mountains, and ... all nations shall flow unto it.

And many people shall go and say, Come ye, and let us go up to the mountain of the Lord, to the house of the God of Jacob; and he will teach us of his ways, and we will walk in his paths.

*Isaiah 2:2*

* * *

And Abram went up out of Egypt, ... and Abram was very rich in cattle, in silver and in gold.... And the land was not able to bear them, that they might dwell together: for their substance was great, so that they could not dwell together.

*Genesis 13:1–6*

# Contents

# Illustrations

GRAPHS AND TABLES

MAPS AND PHOTOGRAPHS

# Introduction

At a 1988 meeting of the Social Science History Association (SSHA), Harvard sociologist Theda Skocpol concluded, after a lively discussion of the role of the state in American political development, that there was a pressing need to "bring the farm back in" through studies of the agrarian people that have shaped so powerfully the cultural landscape of America. She may not have known that an exceptionally able group of scholars had for some time been reaping a notable harvest from that long-neglected soil.[1] Starting in the early 1980s, those attending meetings of the SSHA watched the rural network develop, under the nurturing care of Hal Seth Barron and Robert Swieringa, from a small core of eccentrics into a body whose concerns and questions seemed to occupy an ever more central place in the social history of North America. Theda Skocpol's proposal, offered to a crowd of political and urban historians who had long dominated social history, seemed to those in rural studies the ultimate affirmation of the importance of their once lonely endeavor.

The simple fact is that both Native American and European societies in North America, since their earliest plantation, have been overwhelmingly rural and agrarian. Not until 1920 did the number of urban dwellers in the United States begin to surpass the number of rural

---

[1] A flourishing "rural sociology" movement of the 1920s and 1930s, included seminal work by Charles J. Galpin, *Rural Life* (New York: The Century Company, 1918); John H. Kolb, *Rural Primary Groups: A Study of Agricultural Neighborhoods* (Madison: University of Wisconsin Press, 1921); and James C. Malin, "The Turnover of Farm Population in Kansas," *Kansas Historical Quarterly* 4 (1935): 339–72. See also Lowry Nelson, *Rural Sociology: Its Origins and Growth in the United States* (Minneapolis: University of Minnesota Press, 1969). From the 1940s through the 1970s, however, social historians in the United States concentrated more on cities and on what they saw as the phenomena of urban life – immigrants, machine politics, industrialization, and class formation. In the 1970s European historians, especially those of the *Annales* school in France and the Cambridge Group in England, began to rediscover the rural past, pioneering methods and raising questions that proved enormously fruitful for historians of North America.

1

dwellers.[2] The bitterness of the denunciation of small town America by the pundits of that era – H. L. Mencken, Sinclair Lewis, Bernard de Voto – seems in retrospect an eloquent admission that their rural roots gripped them with a vexing tenacity. So too for the rest of America. The rural mentality was not left behind as easily as the farm. The new urban dwellers brought with them the baggage of three centuries or more of rural life in America and elsewhere, and this did much to shape the character of our urban society.

If Americans seem uncivilized (inept at urban life) compared to Europeans, it is in part because their scant century of experience with urbanity has been too brief and their rural past is too close. It may also relate to theirs being a particular kind of rural past – one that in the Far West began almost within living memory and in what they saw as an unsettled, inexhaustible wilderness. Lewis Fenton, who homesteaded in the western foothills of the Cascade Mountains, east of Sublimity, Oregon, in the 1880s, followed a common practice of clearing not by the laborious chopping and hauling of the giant fir and pine trees that crowded his land, but by boring into their massive trunks far enough to get a fire going, and then tending the fires day and night until the trees fell, after which he burned them on the spot – branches, trunk, and roots.[3] Fenton shared with other rural frontier people the feeling that nature was limitless and human intrusion negligible. His profligate assumption of endless abundance and lack of concern for the particulates his fires raised (he forecast the weather by the lay of the smoke) reverberate today as Portlanders insist upon personal transportation that clouds the air with particulates of another kind, and as huge trucks haul paper cartons, cans, bottles, and plastic packaging to landfills ever farther up the Columbia River. Fenton's cultural descendants still see plenty, though they live in scarcity, and imagine that the air, land, and water have an infinite capacity to supply their needs and absorb their wastes, when clearly they cannot. It may well be that their perspective is in part a residuum of their agrarian frontier past.

Even more fundamental than these attitudes toward natural resources and the environment are the effects of our past on the social character of our society. Since at least the time of Crèvecoeur, many

---

[2] Ben J. Wattenberg, *The Statistical History of the United States from Colonial Times to the Present* (New York: Basic Books, Inc., 1976), p. 11.

[3] Lewis R. Fenton Journal, Oregon Historical Society. One of the most persistent themes in the Fenton journals is his never-ending, and apparently unsuccessful, effort to push back the forest. When he died in 1905, the appraisers of his estate described his property as "wild, uncultivated, and unfenced land, lying in the foothills of the Cascade mountains." See File 2485, Probate Records of Marion County, Oregon State Archives.

observers (Frederick Jackson Turner was perhaps the most timely and eloquent) have speculated on how the act of settling a perceived wilderness might affect human societies.[4] The process is far more complex and subtle than Crèvecoeur or even Turner suggested. The settlers of the new land brought a culture specific to the time and place they were fleeing, then interacted with the cultures they found, the limits or opportunities of the new environment, and ongoing cultural and ideological changes in the home environment. It is my conclusion from this study that there were clear consequences of this process, and that among them was a growing attraction to material abundance as a measure of well-being, and an increasing preference for expansive personal space and privacy in our individual lives, both affecting our ability to sustain a civil society. William Cronon, George Miles, and Jay Gitlin were surely on target in concluding that "We . . . cannot understand the modern United States without coming to terms with its western past."[5]

Though not wishing to suggest that an inappropriate presentism has informed their work, my colleagues in rural studies have similarly, I suspect, understood that not just antiquarian curiosity lies at the heart of their laborious efforts to understand and explain forgotten techniques of butter making, what Pennsylvania farmers raised in the eigthteenth century, or how seventeenth-century New England farm women went about their daily lives. At the heart of it they, like all historians worthy of the name, are engaged in the ongoing labor of helping us to understand ourselves. A few might even admit to harboring a Freudian notion that understanding our past helps us deal more effectively with our present. Knowing our past, we can escape its constraints and learn of other human problems and strategies; we can at once liberate and inform our imagination. These historians are not nostalgically observing America's rural beginnings through a spyglass from afar; as Theda Skocpol put it, they are bringing the farm back in.

There are, of course, many dimensions of our rural past worthy of study. A principal discovery of recent years has been that the roots of American capitalism lie not in cities but on the farm, and a debate has raged over precisely when and how farmers became more commercial

---

[4] J. Hector St. John de Crèvecoeur, *Letters from An American Farmer* (1782; New York, E. P. Dutton & Co., Inc., 1957); Frederick Jackson Turner, "The Significance of the Frontier in American History," the 1893 essay printed in Frederick Jackson Turner, *The Frontier in American History* (New York: H. Holt and Company, 1920).

[5] Willian Cronon, George Miles, and Jay Gitlin, "Becoming West: Toward a New Meaning for Western History," in Cronon, Miles and Gitlin, eds., *Under an Open Sky: Rethinking America's Western Past* (New York: W. W. Norton & Company, 1992), p. 6.

in their orientation, growing crops more for sale in markets and less for consumption at home.[6] Such a transition would probably have altered attitudes toward the land, the family, relations between the sexes, and the status of farmers as independent yeomen, all questions addressed by rural historians and fraught with implications for our society today. Laurel Thatcher Ulrich, Joan M. Jensen, and Elizabeth Fox-Genovese have chosen to focus especially on how women defined and acted their roles in societies where civil power was denied them.[7] Were women more powerful and visible on the eighteenth- and nineteenth-century farmsteads before the "cult of domesticity" began to cloister them in the lace-curtained parlors of middle-class homes? If

[6] Clarence Danhof, *Change in Agriculture: The Northern United States, 1820–1870* (Cambridge, Mass.: Harvard University Press, 1969); Wayne C. Rohrer and Louis H. Douglas, *The Agrarian Transition in America* (Indianapolis: The Bobbs-Merrill Company, Inc., 1969); Michael Merrill, "Cash Is Good to Eat: Self-Sufficiency and Exchange in the Rural Economy of the United States," *Radical History Review* 3 (1977): 42–71; Christopher Clark, "The Household Economy, Market Exchange, and Rise of Capitalism in the Connecticut River Valley, 1800–1860," *Journal of Social History* 13 (1979): 169–89; Winifred B. Rothenberg, "The Market and Massachusetts Farmers, 1750–1855," *Journal of Economic History* 41 (1981): 283–314; James T. Lemon, *The Best Poor Man's Country: A Geographical Study of Early Southeastern Pennsylvania* (New York: W. W. Norton & Company, 1972); Bettye Hobbs Pruitt, "Self-Sufficiency and the Agricultural Economy of Eighteenth-Century Massachusetts," *William and Mary Quarterly* 41 (July, 1984): 333–64; Joyce Appleby, "Commercial Farming and the 'Agrarian Myth' in the Early Republic," *Journal of American History* 68 (1981–2): 833–49; Steven Hahn, *The Roots of Southern Populism: Southern Farmers and the Transformation of the Georgia Upcountry, 1850–1890* (New York: Oxford University Press, 1983); Jeremy Atack and Fred Bateman, *To Their Own Soil: Agriculture in the Antebellum North* (Ames: University of Iowa Press, 1987); Susan Archer Mann, *Agrarian Capitalism in Theory and Practice* (Chapel Hill: University of North Carolina Press, 1990).

[7] Laurel Thatcher Ulrich, *Good Wives: Image and Reality in the Lives of Women in Northern New England: 1650–1750* (New York: Alfred A. Knopf, 1982) and *A Midwife's Tale: The Life of Martha Ballard, Based on Her Diary, 1785–1812* (New York: Alfred A. Knopf, 1991); Nancy F. Cott, *The Bonds of Womanhood: "Women's" Sphere in New England, 1780–1830* (New Haven, Conn.: Yale University Press, 1977); John Mack Faragher, *Women and Men on the Overland Trail* (New Haven, Conn.: Yale University Press, 1979); Thomas Dublin, *Women at Work: The Transformation of Work and Community in Lowell, Massachusetts, 1826–1860* (New York: Columbia University Press, 1979); Linda Kerber, *Women of the Republic: Intellect and Ideology in Revolutionary America* (Chapel Hill: Institute of Early American History and Culture, University of North Carolina Press, 1980); Mary P. Ryan, *Cradle of the Middle Class: The Family in Oneida County, New York, 1790–1865* (Cambridge: Cambridge University Press, 1981); Caroll Smith-Rosenberg, *Disorderly Conduct: Visions of Gender in Victorian America* (New York: Alfred A. Knopf, 1986); Joan M. Jensen, *Loosening the Bonds: Mid-Atlantic Farm Women, 1750–1850* (New Haven, Conn.: Yale University Press, 1986) and *Promise to the Land: Essays on Rural Women* (Albuquerque: University of New Mexico Press, 1991); Elizabeth Fox-Genovese, *Within the Plantation Household* (Chapel Hill: University of North Carolina Press, 1989).

they had no civil power, did they not seize and exercise power in other spheres of the society? The relevance of such studies to our present concern for gender roles, sex discrimination, and equality of opportunity in our society is obvious.

A number of highly skilled historians, including the late Herbert Gutman, John Blassingame, Allan Kulikoff, Steven Hahn, Orville Vernon Burton, and Robert Kenzer, have carefully examined the antebellum South, exploring the gulfs and bridges that separated and connected the planters, yeoman, and blacks who comprised the society.[8] To what degree did poorer farmers emulate and support the slave system that the planters dominated? Did kinship ties hold strong in spite of sharp differences of wealth and status? How did blacks evolve a culture that affirmed and preserved their own identity?

Hahn, Burton, and Kenzer, and for the Midwest John Mack Faragher, have attempted no less than the reconstruction of the essential elements of whole counties or townships over an extended period. Central among their many concerns is that of how some sense of common identity and purpose could have persisted through shattering ideological, political, and economic transformations and despite the incessant wandering that seems the one constant in American society since its founding. Hal Seth Barron has chosen to concentrate on those stolid people who preferred to stay put on their rock-fenced New England farmsteads while their neighbors sold out and moved on to the richer, deeper soils of western New York, the Ohio country, the Great Plains, and eventually the Far West.[9]

This book, however, is concerned not with those who stayed but with those who left, specifically those who, between the 1840s and the 1860s, pioneered what I call the Mountain-to-Pacific Corridor of the Far West, from the present Utah through Oregon. Among them were many who left the South, some who left from the Mid-Atlantic and northeastern states, and others who left England, Ireland, and the Eur-

[8] Herbert G. Gutman, *The Black Family in Slavery and Freedom, 1750–1925* (New York: Pantheon Books, 1976); John W. Blassingame, *The Slave Community: Plantation Life in the Antebellum South* (New York: Oxford University Press, 1979); Allan Kulikoff, *Tobacco and Slaves: The Development of Southern Cultures in the Chesapeake, 1680–1800* (Chapel Hill; University of North Carolina Press, 1986); Charles Joyner, *Down by the Riverside: A South Carolina Slave Community* (Chicago and Urbana: University of Illinois Press, 1984); Orville Vernon Burton, *In My Father's House Are Many Mansions: Family and Community in Edgefield, South Carolina* (Chapel Hill: University of North Carolina Press, 1985); Robert Kenzer, *Kinship and Neighborhood in a Southern Community: Orange County, North Carolina, 1849–1881* (Knoxville: University of Tennessee Press, 1987).

[9] John Mack Faragher, *Sugar Creek: Life on the Illinois Prairie* (New Haven, Conn.: Yale University Press, 1986); Hal Seth Barron, *Those Who Stayed Behind: Rural Society in Nineteenth-Century New England* (Cambridge: Cambridge University Press, 1984).

opean Continent to come directly to the sparsely settled Rocky Mountains and Pacific Coast. Most, however, were American born, and
spent part of their lives in the Sugar Creeks of the Midwest on their
way to Oregon, Idaho, and Utah. And while their story touches on a
good many of the concerns explored by other rural historians, I have
been especially interested in seeing if it might shed light on a problem
that to my mind is of critical importance to Americans today.

There would seem ample evidence, from the flourishing of *Self* magazine to the fluidity of present family structures, that Alexis de
Tocqueville was not far off the mark in his fear, expressed in the 1830s,
that the individualism of America not only makes "every man forget
his ancestors, but it hides his descendants and separates his contemporaries from him; it throws him back forever upon himself alone and
threatens in the end to confine him entirely within the solitude of his
own heart."[10] How does one nourish and sustain a sense of obligation
toward the broader society in a nation founded on an ideological commitment to individualism and attached to the perspective of a rural
frontier way of life?[11] Christopher Lasch and Robert N. Bellah are
among those who have detailed the problems of a society that, in their
judgment, has taken individualism, and a commensurate abdication
of broader community responsibility, to extremes. They see in our
own lives the image of the Lewis Fentons of our past, persons whose
sense of social responsibility extended in time and space only as far
as they could peer through their smoke-shrouded forests.[12]

Fenton was a straggler in a long train of European peoples who in
the fifteenth century began moving into the New World, settling areas
they and we have called frontiers – lands that from their perspective

[10] Alexis de Tocqueville, *Democracy in America*, ed. Phillips Bradley, 2 vols. (New York:
Vintage Books, 1960), 2: 106.

[11] Among the scholars who in the past have been preoccupied with this concern are
Frederick Jackson Turner, *The Frontier in American History* (New York: H. Holt and
Company, 1920); Josiah Royce, *Hope of the Great Community* (1916; Freeport, N.Y.:
Books for Libraries Press, 1967); Robert A. Nisbet, *Quest for Community: A Study of the
Ethics of Order and Freedom* (New York: Oxford University Press, 1953); Richard L.
Bushman, *From Puritan to Yankee: Character and Social Order in Connecticut, 1690–1760*
(Cambridge, Mass.: Harvard University Press, 1965); Michael Zuckerman, *Peaceable
Kingdoms: New England Towns in the Eighteenth Century* (New York: Alfred A. Knopf,
1970); Philip Greven, *Four Generations: Population, Land, and Family in Colonial Andover,
Massachusetts* (Ithaca, N.Y.: Cornell University Press, 1970); Daniel Boorstin, *The Amer-
icans*, 3 vols. (New York: Random House, 1958–73); Mason Drukman, *Community and
Purpose in America: An Analysis of American Political Theory* (New York: McGraw-Hill,
1971); Don H. Doyle, *Social Order of a Frontier Community* (Urbana: University of Illinois Press, 1978).

[12] Christopher Lasch, *The Culture of Narcissism: American Life in an Age of Diminishing
Expectations* (New York: W.W. Norton & Company, 1979); Bellah, *Habits of the Heart.*

had a small, culturally less advanced population and an abundance of unclaimed and underdeveloped resources. I use what some colleagues in studying the American West are now calling the "F" word unabashedly in my title.[13] I do so because I am not persuaded that the concept is useless or (as some insist) an obstacle to historical understanding, simply because colonizing frontier areas did not change people in the ways Frederick Jackson Turner thought. William Cronon, George Miles, and Jay Gitlin argue persuasively that "common social and economic processes repeated themselves as invading peoples 'discovered' and colonized the many Wests that America eventually became." Both frontier and region, they maintain, should be studied "not as isolated, alternative ways of viewing the American past but rather as phases of a single historical process."[14]

I am impressed through this study with the variety, strength, and tenacity of three cultures that were transplanted to the West. Yet in the end I see, in the varied frontier settings, aspects of these cultures amplified – transformed by abundance, by cultural exchange, and by national and international events in ways that made them over time similar in several important respects, though by no means identical. Were Turner to know of this work, he would object to the darkness of my perception of the outcome. Yet we would both agree that the frontier was where it all took place, had much to do with that outcome, and therefore is a worthy object of study.

It is certainly true that newly settled areas offer particularly fertile ground to students of social character, for there they may hope to glimpse societies in the process of being reborn as settlers from different nations, different regions, and often with different social values grapple with the problems of building (or failing to build) a base of common identity and commitment. The study of these processes in

---

[13] Though by no means of one opinion, a number of historians advocate a "New Western history" that abandons the frontier, stresses the importance of considering the West as a region, and emphasizes that region as a particularly promising setting for the study of resource exploitation, cultural and racial interaction, class, and gender in the United States. Richard White's text, *"It's Your Misfortune and None of My Own": A New History of the American West* (Norman: University of Oklahoma Press, 1991), is an eloquent example of this perspective. Also important are Patricia Nelson Limerick, *The Legacy of Conquest: The Unbroken Past of the American West* (New York: W. W. Norton & Company, 1987); Donald Worster, *Dust Bowl: The Southern Plains in the 1930s* (New York: Oxford University Press, 1979), *Rivers of Empire: Water, Aridity, and the Growth of the American West* (New York: Pantheon Books, 1985), and *Under Western Skies: Nature and History in the American West* (New York: Oxford University Press, 1992); and Patricia Nelson Limerick, Clyde A. Milner II, and Charles E. Rankin, eds., *Trails: Toward a New Western History* (Lawrence: University Press of Kansas, 1991).

[14] Cronon, Miles, and Gitlin, "Becoming West," p. 7.

America flowered in the 1960s and 1970s among students of colonial New England, whose research suggested that in Massachusetts and Connecticut a sense of community reached its apotheosis in American life before the forces of individualism supporting and encouraged by the Revolution began to erode it.[15]

There have also been important path-breaking studies of community in midwestern localities, including those of Merle Curti, Don H. Doyle, Kathleen Conzen, and John Mack Faragher. Only a few, however, have focused on the nineteenth-century West – a region particularly rich in its potential for providing insights into the nature and variety of social relationships in rural frontier areas.[16] The very rapid growth, the variety of economic bases, and the polyglot character of the founding populations of the Far West offer a range of fascinating social phenomena that because of rich extant records can be closely examined. This study, then, is in large measure an attempt to identify and understand the operation of the forces during the early settlement of the West that inhibited the development of close human ties and of those forces that encouraged them. If it is indeed true that the social character developed during the settlement period has had an important subsequent influence, as Bellah and associates suggest, then this study may tell us about the meaning for our time of the rural past within us.

Most studies of American communities have examined populations of the East Coast or Midwest, and have either focused on one or a small set of localities (making generalizations questionable) or have offered rather broad, intuitive observations on a very large number. Moreover, they have commonly been preoccupied with urban rather than rural people. Those few that have looked at the Far West have tended to concentrate on unusual and ephemeral populations – those in cattle towns or mining towns – ignoring the much more common and persistent farming people of the West.[17] An important exception is Peter G. Boag's *Environment and Experience*; which appeared after this book was in press.

[15] See Bushman, Demos, Lockridge, Zuckerman, and Greven, cited in footnote 9, and Robert Gross, *The Minutemen and Their World* (New York: Hill and Wang, 1976).
[16] Curti and Doyle are cited in footnote 1. See also Kathleen Neils Conzen, *Immigrant Milwaukee, 1836–1860: Accommodation and Community in a Frontier City* (Cambridge, Mass.: Harvard University Press, 1976) and "Peasant Pioneers: Generational Succession Among German Farmers in Frontier Minnesota," in *The Countryside in the Age of Capitalist Transformation*, ed. Steven Hahn and Jonathan Prude (Chapel Hill: University of North Carolina Press, 1985), pp. 259–92.
[17] Malcomb Rohrbaugh, *Aspen: The History of a Silver Mining Town, 1879–1893* (New York: Oxford University Press, 1986); Robert R. Dykstra, *The Cattle Towns* (New York: Alfred A. Knopf, 1968); Duane A. Smith, *Rocky Mountain Mining Camps: The Urban Frontier* (Bloomington: Indiana University Press, 1967); Ralph Mann, *After the Gold Rush: Society in Grass Valley and Nevada City, California, 1849–1870* (Stanford, Calif.:

In this study, I concentrate on three rural districts surrounding and including the villages of Sublimity, Oregon; Alpine, Utah; and Middleton, Idaho. The three are not only geographically distant from one another but were founded by very different populations. Yet all were profoundly agrarian and rural. The great majority of household heads in all three made their living as farmers. The Sublimity and Middleton people, in addition, lived in the countryside, scattering their homes among the hollows of the rolling Oregon country or along the bottom lands of the Boise River. The Alpine people were different in this regard. Nearly all were Mormons, and most followed a common practice of building their homes in a village center and commuting to farmlands on the outside. Still, they were agrarian and rural in that they made their living off the soil, were few in number, and were isolated in the vast Basin and Range landscape that surrounded them.

Though perhaps other localities could serve the purposes of this project as well, I chose these because they were all reasonably small, had similar growth rates, were not strongly tied to natural resource development, were sustained by farming, and were similarly situated among surrounding towns and cities. The Sublimity area is about fifteen miles south and east of Salem, the county seat and urban center of the region. Alpine is some thirty-five miles south of Salt Lake City and fifteen miles north of Provo, the county seat. Middleton is twenty-two miles west of Boise and six miles northeast of Caldwell, the county seat. Sublimity was settled in the late 1840s, Alpine in the early 1850s, and Middleton in the mid-1860s. None surpassed 1,300 inhabitants by 1910.

As is often the case with rural people, there are few surviving diaries or journals. It is not easy to see into the minds of these folk, though it is their thoughts – their changing views of themselves, their relationships to others and to the land – that we most would like to understand. As a colleague, Paul Johnson, once suggested, the work then becomes archaeological – painstakingly sifting through enormous piles of seemingly trivial bits and pieces in the hope that, through

Stanford University Press, 1982); Robert V. Hine, *Community on the American Frontier: Separate But Not Alone* (Norman: University of Oklahoma Press, 1980); Barbara Laslett, "Household Structure on an American Frontier: Los Angeles, California, in 1850," *American Journal of Sociology* 81 (1975): 109–28; John L. Shover, *First Majority – Last Minority; The Transforming of Rural Life in America* (De Kalb: Northern Illinois University Press, 1976); Kathleen Underwood, *Town Building on the Colorado Frontier* (Albuquerque: University of New Mexico Press, 1987); Larry M. Logue, *A Sermon in the Desert: Belief and Behavior in Early St. George, Utah* (Urbana and Chicago: University of Illinois Press, 1988); Robert Alan Goldberg, *Back to the Soil: The Jewish Farmers of Clarion, Utah, and Their World* (Salt Lake City: University of Utah Press, 1986). Peter G. Boag, *Environment and Experience: Settlement Culture in Nineteenth-Century Oregon* (Berkeley, Calif.: University of California Press, 1992).

empathy and imagination, a satisfying reconstruction of their world might be possible. The crucial bits and pieces for this study include population information from the surviving manuscripts of federal censuses taken between 1860 and 1910, supplemented by agricultural censuses, tax roll information, and probate records. Also vital are newspaper accounts; records of schools, clubs, churches, canal companies, and town councils; credit reports on business; and extant reminiscences, diaries, and journals of inhabitants.

Obviously, in the study of three widely scattered populations over several decades, it has not been possible to gather the richness of detail one sees in Faragher's *Sugar Creek* or Burton's *Edgefield County*. I have studied most of the civil records at ten-year intervals, to match the census reports. There are certainly disadvantages in such an approach but perhaps advantages as well, since successive illuminations at intervals of a decade sharpen the perception of change over time and highlight major transitions that can then be studied more intensively.

It is, of course, not possible in a study of three localities to generalize with confidence to the agrarian society of the broader American West. In fact, one of my more surprising and instructive findings is how different the three societies, all built upon a common agricultural base in the mid-nineteenth-century West, were in their early stages. The people of each town attached different meanings to the land. The size and nature of their networks of close friends and associates varied greatly. Their sense of continuity and place was markedly dissimilar. Their economic environments were dramatically different. The three towns thus present noteworthy points along the spectrum of possibilities for social organization in American rural communities of the period.

While recognizing that generalization in a strict statistical sense is not possible from a population of three, I have tried to place these communities in the larger context of settlement in the American West by gathering data on each town or census precinct appearing in the 1870 federal manuscript censuses for Oregon, Idaho, Montana, Nevada, and Utah. The file contains wealth, occupation, sex, and nativity data for the household heads of each town or precinct, in addition to the year of founding, year of abandonment where applicable, distance to the nearest railroad or navigable waterway, year the railroad was completed to that point, population through 1910, elevation, growing season, annual precipitation, and geographical coordinates.

This body of information helps illuminate the relationship between types of communities (farming, ranching, mining, railroad, commercial, and others) and how they interacted to place a distinctive stamp on both the economic development and social character of the broader region.[18] It opens to view towns in varying stages of settlement, from the newly founded to those approaching three decades since founding. It contains farm towns on railroad lines or navigable waterways, towns close to major commercial centers, towns close to mining or timber camps, and towns remote from all of these.

The broader view of dozens of towns in a variety of situations and stages makes it possible to view changes that many experienced over time by the end of the century, thus giving developmental depth to a file drawn mainly from one census. With it we can answer with considerable reliability such questions as these: What was the proportion of farm towns to mining towns and other types of settlements in the several regions? What was the timing and sequence of settlement for different types of towns? To what extent did agricultural towns in areas remote from railroads tend to cluster around mining towns? Are there major differences among the towns in mean wealth, both by type and by date of settlement? How close is the relationship between rail proximity and mean wealth? How does the presence or absence of nearby mining settlements affect wealth?

The file obviously will be useful for many types of studies, but the principal questions at this stage relate to the social character of farm societies in the early American West. It makes it possible for this book to offer a microcosmic view of community founding and character in three rural districts over an extended period, set against the backdrop of an extensive contextual study that will alleviate the problems of reliability of generalization that have plagued most community studies.

Though the teasing of information from the types of sources I am using is a task that requires attention to methodological and some-

---

[18] See Dean L. May and Jennie Cornell, "Middleton's 'Agri-Miners': The Beginnings of Agriculture in Southwestern Idaho," *Idaho Yesterdays*, 28 (Winter 1985): 2–11, the journal of the Idaho State Historical Society; Dean L. May, "Two Western Towns: A Comparative View," presented at the 1982 annual meeting of the Western History Association; "Wealth, Production, and Community in Two Western Towns," presented at the 1983 annual meeting of the Mormon History Association; "Agri-miners in the North American West: The Nexus of Farming and Mining Cultures," Symposium on Boom and Bust Cycles in Communities of the Canadian and American West, University of Victoria, B.C., August 1987; "When They Left; Time of Migration and Rural Social Character in the North American West," presented at the annual meeting of the Social Science History Association, 1987; "Religion and Social Organization in early Sublimity, Oregon; Alpine, Utah; and Middleton, Idaho, 1860–1880," presented at the annual meeting of the Social Science History Association, 1988; and "Women, Farm Production, and the Meaning of the Land in the Far West, 1860–1880," presented at the conference on Women and the Transition to Capitalism in Rural America, 1760–1940, March 30–April 2, 1989, Northern Illinois University.

times quite technical concerns, I have tried at every stage to remember that the folk of Sublimity, Alpine, and Middleton were not statistics but people. The names in census lists constantly raised questions and concerns about their lives as I entered them into my Macintosh SE. How did the Carlisle family come to know and take in the elderly woman who lived with them in 1910? How did Mary Clymer manage her family alone in what seemed to be so difficult a time for widows? I read in terror Lewis Fenton's diary entries describing the onset of what I knew, but he could not, would be his beloved daughter Vera's last illness at age fifteen. I watched his anguish as death came and as he tried time and again to explain to himself the dimensions and the meanings of his loss. Indeed, I sometimes felt with great discomfort that writing a history is a godlike act, attempting understanding and empathy for people necessarily remote, organizing the chaotic remnants of their lives into patterns that to me have a meaning not always evident to them. Those now living in Sublimity, Alpine, or Middleton may not recognize their ancestors from this account, a matter of concern to me. But I have tried to speak for the dead more than for the living and to see their world, as nearly as I can, as they saw it, which is to say perhaps not always as their grandchildren might wish it to have been. They, like we, were imperfect people in an imperfect world, and to imagine them otherwise is to rob them of the dignity of having taken life as it was.

There is, I fear, no hope of accounting for all the debts and obligations one acquires in pursuing a project such as this. Descendants of the Sublimity, Alpine, and Middleton folk were gracious and generous in sharing memories, admitting me to the homes, barns, fields, and graveyards that are the legacy of the founders. Most important among them were Daraleen Wade of Salem, Jennie Wild of Alpine, and the late Jennie Cornell of Middleton, who offered a near stranger the products of years of observing and collecting the histories of their people. It is not an exaggeration to say that this book could not have been written without them. Thomas W. Steeves, a descendant of Sublimity pioneers, provided materials that enormously enriched the portions dealing with the Hunt family, as did Allan R. Strong, Dennis Smith, and Jill Mulvay Derr for Alpine folk.

Much of the information for this book came from the archives of the states of Oregon, Idaho, and Utah. At the Oregon State Archives, Timothy Backer, Michael McQuade, James Clark, Valerie Klaus Lamphere, and David Wendell were all generous in finding materials relating to Sublimity and Marion County. I appreciated as well the interest Roy Turnbaugh, the State Archivist, and Layne Sawyer, the Deputy Archivist, showed in my work. In Idaho, State Archivist Bill

Tydeman and archivists Karin Ford, Gary Bettis, John Yandell, Guila Ford, and Madeline Buckendorf gave invaluable assistance. A friend and colleague, Judith Austin, editor of *Idaho Yesterdays*, was enormously helpful in ferreting out the odd and esoteric bits of information I was seeking while sharing valuable insights and giving general encouragement to me in pursuing this project. I am grateful to her for permission to incorporate here portions of "Middleton's Agriminers: The Beginnings of an Agricultural Town," originally published in *Idaho Yesterdays* 28 (Winter 1985): 2–11. Merle W. Wells took the time to give advice and offer insights gained from many years of careful research on Idaho history. Edith Hayes shared freely the fruit of her years of volunteer service, indexing newspapers and other sources. The Quondam Folk Arts Coordinator at the Idaho Commission on the Arts, Steve Siporin, did me an enormous service in suggesting Sublimity as an appropriate Oregon district for study. Jeffrey O. Johnson, Utah State Archivist, is a valued friend and advisor whose staff was exceptionally helpful, especially Val Wilson, who went far beyond the call of duty in bringing useful materials to my attention and making them available to me.

The staffs of the Oregon State Library in Salem and the Oregon Historical Society in Portland facilitated my work, especially Rick Harmon, editor of the *Oregon Historical Quarterly*, and Kris White, who made working on manuscripts at the Oregon Historical Society pleasant and efficient, as did Sieglind Smith, Todd Schaeffer, and Kenneth Lomax. Linda Thatcher and Susan Whetstone at the Utah Historical Society; Gregory Thompson, Walter Jones, Paul Mogren, and others at the University of Utah's Marriott Library; Chad Flake at Brigham Young University's Lee Library; and the staff at Harvard University's Baker Library were all efficient and helpful in their support of this study. The Latter-day Saint Family History Library is a remarkable resource. Library Director David Mayfield, Raymond Wright, Lynn Carson, and their always helpful and courteous staff made the library's rich materials available to a researcher who is perverse enough to not wish to look at just one name in a census, but at them all.

The University of Utah Humanities Center granted a fellowship that freed an entire academic year for work on this book while providing occasions for stimulating and useful discussion with other Fellows of the Center. Additional time and funds were made available by the University of Utah Research Committee and the College of Humanities Career Development Committee. The National Endowment for the Humanities provided valuable assistance in a Travel-to-Collections grant, and the Charles Redd Center for Western Studies at Brigham Young University granted funds to help in gathering the 1870 towns file. An enormously fruitful time at the Huntington Library was made possible by a Huntington-Haynes Fellowship.

Though I am by nature a hands-on researcher and uncomfortable delegating work to assistants, excellent work supporting the project has been done by Steven Huefner, Lisa Viperman, Randy Carpenter, Nyman Brooks, Robby McDaniels, John Huber, and Jason Thatcher. Edward M. Sharp was instrumental and timely in making a Macintosh SE available for the project, and with upgrades that John Wagner helped me to acquire, the system served flawlessly and was a (nearly) always obedient and astonishingly efficient servant. Microsoft File and Word, Cricket Graph, and Extatix statistical software were all essential to the project.

Stephen Thernstrom, Robert A. Goldberg, Richard L. Bushman, Laurel Thatcher Ulrich, Walter Nugent, Gregory A. Kemp, Daraleen Wade, and Cheryll May all were generous beyond the call of duty in taking time from very busy schedules to read virtually the entire manuscript and help sharpen it conceptually and stylistically. Martin Ridge, Randall Roth, Maris Vinovskis, Carl Schneider, Tamara Hareven, Hal Seth Barron, Joan Jensen, Elizabeth Fox-Genovese, Allan Kulikoff, Alan Artibese, Merle Wells, Judith Austin, Margaret Brady, Peggy Pascoe, Paul Johnson, Jan Shipps, Leonard Arrington, Charles Hatch, Janet Ellingson, Nancy Fitch, Hugh McLeod, Lothar Hönnighausen, John C. Hudson, and James W. Oberly have all read parts of the manuscript or discussed the project with me, offering (sometimes) encouragement and (always) valuable advice. Numerous students at the University of Utah have provided a willing and helpful forum for discussing my work, and Neil Evans made available a quiet retreat in the Wasatch Mountains that greatly facilitated my final revision of the manuscript. Frank Smith, Camilla T. K. Palmer, and others from the Cambridge University Press staff have been splendidly competent and efficient in seeing the manuscript through to publication. It has been a pleasure to work with them.

John L. Thomas, Barry D. Karl, James T. Patterson, R. Burr Litchfield, Ernest R. May, the late Frank Freidel, and Gordon Wood were mentors and friends at Brown and Harvard universities, though they could hardly have imagined that my career would have turned toward this particular path. I value what they taught me. My friend and spouse, Cheryll, and our friends and children, Timothy, Caroline, and Tad, have patiently endured a decade of my preoccupation with people of another time and place, giving me always their love and support. I shall try henceforth to do better at reciprocating.

# 1    *A long, tedious journey*

During the 1840s, 1850s, and 1860s three streams of migration to the Far West began. The first was to the Willamette Valley in western Oregon; the second to the Salt Lake Valley in what became Utah; and the third to the wooded Boise Valley of Idaho. Some of the migrants eventually settled down to farm in particular districts: Sublimity, west and south of Salem; Alpine, south of Salt Lake City; and Middleton, west of Boise.

In retrospect it is hard to understand why they left. The rich black lands in the Mississippi Valley were not fully cleared of oak and maple when Oregon fever struck, and knots of kin gave up their farms, potentially some of the richest in America, loaded what they could into wagons, and set off to follow the sun to the Pacific. There had been floods in the 1830s, and there was much ague and fever in the lowlands. Yet these alone do not seem enough to account for the flight. They left good land but it was land they sought – more land, and better land. They were a people of the soil.

John S. and Temperance Estep Hunt were among them.[1] Their parents had earlier joined the great stream of migration from the Old South to the lower Midwest. During the third decade of the nineteenth century they, with thousands of Americans from Virginia, the Carolinas, Tennessee, and Kentucky, followed the course of the Ohio north and west into southern Ohio, Indiana, Illinois, Missouri, and Iowa. Temperance and John grew to maturity in Indiana and married there on May 8, 1823, when she was nineteen and he barely twenty. By 1847 they had brought nine children into the world. She followed the common practice of rural women of her time, toiling at gardening, cook-

---

[1] George Washington Hunt, *A History of the Hunt Family* (Boston: McDonald, Gill & Company, 1890). Dates and precise birthplaces are from information gathered by expert genealogist Daraleen Wade from family, census, probate, and other records and assembled into family reconstitution forms or family group sheets.

ing, spinning, knitting, washing, churning, sewing, tending chickens and pigs – and in many other ways meeting the needs of her rapidly growing family. He, in addition to farming, had taken up the trades of gunsmith and wagon maker, and had become active in the Baptist church, where he was a deacon.

The Hunts stood among the settled pillars of the community. But in 1845 they suffered a series of financial reverses and began to cast about for a new start in life. Three of John's brothers – James, Harrison, and William – had preceded him to the Far West. Perhaps the Hunts, like the Benjamin Waldens, who left Missouri for Oregon in 1845, were attracted, as they saw their five sons maturing, by "the great fir and pine forests, land for farms and a chance for growing sons to settle in a wonderful health-giving atmosphere."[2] Certainly, the call of "Oregon, Oregon, Oregon!" resounded repeatedly in their home through an uncle, James Hunt, as well as in the speeches and writings of Thomas Hart Benton, Henry Clay, and General Joel Palmer.[3] All this had its effect. In 1847 the couple, now in their mid-forties, with seven of their nine children, packed up their possessions for a journey to the New Land. (One son, Noah, had died at age eight; a daughter, Hannah, had married.) At a time in life when roots for many begin to run deep, they pulled away to Oregon.

Sixteen-year-old George, the oldest surviving son, became the scion of the family in Oregon and their chronicler. He remembered that "the morning we started it was a novel sight. People came from far and near to see us off, and my father's best friends even then tried to persuade him to remain in Indiana, saying it was folly to start on such a long, tedious journey." The family boarded a steamer that carried them down the Ohio and out onto the Mississippi as far as St. Louis. Another boat carried them up the Missouri to Lexington, and from there they tracked overland to Independence. In Independence they met a young man named Elijah Patterson, who joined them with his one yoke of oxen and one of cows, "which made us a very good outfit." At a place called Indian Grove they met others who were organizing themselves into a traveling "train." The immigrants elected Patterson to be captain and, "we rolled out for Oregon."[4]

[2] "Benjamin Walden," in Sarah Hunt Steeves, *Book of Remembrance of Marion County, Oregon, Pioneers, 1840–1860* (Portland: The Berncliff Press, 1927), pp. 49–50. Steeves's book is a collection of memories of early pioneers gathered during the first two decades of the twentieth century.

[3] Hunt, *Family History*, p. 18. George Hunt remembered that his father received letters from Henry Clay and Thomas Hart Benton, enouraging settlement in Oregon, and a personal visit from Joel Palmer.

[4] Hunt, *Family History*, pp. 19–21.

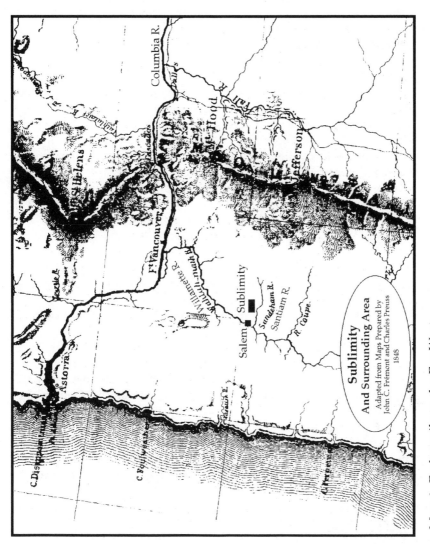

Map 1. Early trails to the Far West.

It was a momentous year along the trails that led to the Pacific. If 1846 had been a year of decision, 1847 was a year of action. The number moving West had climbed gradually between 1843 and 1846 from 1,000 to 8,000. The next year the floodgate burst, and nearly as many spilled toward the West as in all the previous years combined. The Hunts were part of an extended, fragmented caravan some 15,000 strong that strung itself out along the courses of the Platte, the Sweetwater, and the passes and rivers beyond the Divide that summer.[5] Among them were some 2,200 Mormons who had hoped to find refuge in the Rockies in 1846 but had been delayed by poverty, fractiousness, and poor planning.[6] Their scouting company, aware of the great Oregon migration behind them, had on June 16 set up a ferry at the last crossing of the Platte, 794 miles out, which was in operation when the Hunt train reached that point. George remembered that "the Mormons crossed us over North Platte in a rather loose affair called a ferry."[7]

*     *     *

The reasons the Mormons were on the trail that year are very clear. They were seeking refuge.[8] They needed land to survive, but unlike the Hunts, it was not the lure of new land that had tempted them away from the old. Their religion, founded by Joseph Smith in 1830, had made them pariahs in the ebullient atmosphere of Jacksonian America. It did not set well that they believed Joseph Smith had spoken to angels, had found gold plates, and had opened new scripture by translating those plates into the Book of Mormon. Yet their greatest blasphemy was to advocate and doggedly attempt to realize a society where individual freedoms would be compromised by the needs of the broader community. "Gathering" after conversion to form communities of fellow "Saints," as they were called, in the Midwest, they alienated and angered people like the Hunts everywhere they settled.[9]

---

[5] John D. Unruh, Jr., *The Plains Across: The Overland Emigrants and the Trans-Mississippi West, 1840–60* (Urbana: University of Illinois Press, 1982), pp. 84–5. I have rounded Unruh's figures, which give the illusion of a precision not possible given the fragmentary nature of the records.

[6] Richard E. Bennett, *Mormons at the Missouri, 1846–1852: "And Should We Die. . ."* (Norman: University of Oklahoma Press, 1987), offers the best description of the flight of the Mormons from Nauvoo, Illinois, and their sojourn on the Missouri.

[7] Hunt, *Family History*, p. 22.

[8] The refuge theme was given its earliest and best development by Marvin S. Hill, *Quest for Refuge: The Mormon Flight from American Pluralism* (Salt Lake City: Signature Books, 1989). Also see Wallace Stegner, *The Gathering of Zion: The Story of the Mormon Trail* (New York: McGraw-Hill, 1964).

[9] The family of Nancy Smith was offended by the presence of Mormons near their home in Missouri, recalling that "there were phases of the Mormon religion that did not

Their closeness was cliquishness; their communalism threatened individualists; their bloc voting was undemocratic.

Bitter persecution had forced successive flights from New York State in 1831; Jackson County, Missouri in 1833; Kirtland, Ohio, in 1838; Caldwell County, Missouri in 1839; and finally, Nauvoo, Illinois, in the early spring of 1846. Now they were fleeing settled America altogether and seeking a home where, as a hymn written on the trail put it, "none shall come, to hurt or make afraid." During the spring and early summer their wagons pulled out of Winter Quarters, the log cabin city north of present Omaha, where they had wintered in 1846 and 1847. They called their traveling groups "companies," the term expressing a sense of enduring connectedness quite unlike the "train" in which the Hunt family traveled, with its suggestion of temporary coupling.

Following a revelation given by Brigham Young on January 14, the Mormon companies were divided into groups of ten, fifty, and a hundred wagons, with a captain presiding at each level. The revelation commanded that each company was to "bear an equal proportion, ...in taking the poor, the widows and the fatherless," and before departure was to "prepare houses, and fields for raising grain, for those who are to remain behind this season." It sternly warned against excessive individualism. "If any man shall seek to build up himself, ...he shall have no power, and his folly shall be made manifest." The authority by which the instructions were given and the newfound identity of those joining the exodus were affirmed in the assertion that "I am he who led the children of Israel out of the land of Egypt; and my arm is stretched out in the last days, to save my people Israel."[10]

Among the Mormons heading West that spring was William S. Wordsworth. Born in 1810 in New Jersey, he was an early convert to the new faith. Nearly six feet tall, 180 pounds, and with a stentorian voice, Wordsworth was a likely choice for scout and bodyguard in the advance company of Mormons. He thus was among those who in early June had established the ferry the Hunts were to use in crossing the North Platte. The Hunts and Wordsworth probably did not meet

coincide with the Methodists, so when a large party of near relatives came by, in 1846, with covered wagons, on the way to Oregon, Mr. Smith began to think of the great west. Widowed while on the trail, Nancy Smith in 1850, married the, by that time, widower, John S. Hunt." See "Nancy Scott Wisdom Smith Hunt" in Steeves, *Book of Remembrance*, pp. 109–111.

[10] The travel organization followed the practice of ancient Israel as described in the book of Exodus, as well as earlier Mormon practice. The revelation is printed in the Mormon scripture "Doctrine and Covenants," Section 136.

that summer, but they certainly did cross paths. A thousand miles from Independence, at Fort Bridger, their trails diverged forever.

Wordsworth's company veered southwest from Fort Bridger down Echo Canyon, following the dim tracks left in 1846 by the Donner party. They toiled up East Canyon to the summit of Big Mountain, careened down its sharp southern slope, and then followed Big Mountain Creek until they climbed westward over Little Mountain. From its summit they dropped into Emigration Canyon, which after eighteen crossings of the creek brought them into the Salt Lake Valley. Family legend reports that during the journey Wordsworth had become an aide to the ailing Brigham Young; if so, he may have been with the Mormon leader on July 24, when he looked out upon the Valley and announced that it was the place, at least for the present, where the Latter-day Saints would settle.

Wordsworth camped that winter with some 1,930 others along a creek at the northern end of the Salt Lake Valley, some 800 miles in any direction from the nearest settlements of white Americans. Over the next few years he would help establish several settlements that became home for many of the thousands of Latter-day Saints in America and Europe eagerly awaiting news that the pioneer companies had found a gathering place in the Rocky Mountains.[11]

\*   \*   \*

While the Mormons were settling down to a cold, wet winter in their isolated valley, the Hunts were approaching the Boise River. From Fort Bridger they had veered northwest, following the Bear River along its circuitous course, until an escape from the southward bend led them northwest to the Portneuf Plain and Fort Hall. From there they followed the Snake River, tracing its arc across the sagebrush plains of southern Idaho and then pulling away from it north to strike the Boise near the present city.

The Oregon-bound generally found the Boise Valley a joy and a relief after traversing a barren, rocky country. John C. Frémont wrote that his expedition's 1843 crossing from the Snake to the Boise was "extremely rocky, with hard volcanic fragments and our traveling very slow."[12] Basil Nelson Longsworth recorded his contrasting im-

---

[11] A highly readable account of the Mormon migration to Utah is Wallace Stegner's *The Gathering of Zion*, cited above; the best of recent scholarly studies is Eugene E. Campbell, *Establishing Zion: The Mormon Church in the American West, 1847–1869* (Salt Lake City: Signature Books, 1988). See also Bennett, *Mormons at the Missouri*, and Leonard J. Arrington, *Brigham Young: American Moses* (New York: Alfred A. Knopf, 1985).

[12] Brevet Capt. J. C. Frémont, *Report of the Exploring Expedition to the Rocky Mountains in the Year 1842, and to Oregon and North California in the Years 1843–44* (Washington: Blair and Rives, 1845), p. 170.

pression of the Boise Valley itself ten years later, on August 18, 1853. "This morning early we ascended a long hill and after driving three or four miles, one of us saw Boise River [the 1,500-mile mark]. One of our oxen was quite sick and would not eat. About 1:00 we struck the river which is a beautiful river forty or fifty yards in width. The water has a rapid current and is as clear as crystal and quite full of fish." After frequent references to the valley's "very rich growth of grass," Longsworth concluded, "There is a very good soil along Boise River, the bottoms being from two to four miles wide and mostly covered with a heavy growth of grass. There might be thousands of tons of pretty fine hay made here."[13]

It was, of course, the trees that gave the "broad green" valley its name – "the Riviére Boisée" [wooded river], as Frémont wrote; some called it the Bigwood. Stately, abundant trees had a special meaning to farmers of the time, signifying fertile soil and sufficient rainfall – the promise of good crops. In the Midwest they had generally cleared and planted among the trees even when nearby open prairie lands were not taken. Frémont's party was delighted that the river banks were lined with "varieties of timber – among which are handsome cotton woods. Such a stream had become quite a novelty in this country and we were delighted this afternoon to make a pleasant camp under fine old trees again."[14] The lush, wooded banks of the Boise River were the first sign on their whole dust-dry journey that the West might really offer in some places the arboreal paradise they had hoped to find. Yet attractive as the Boise Valley was, no one chose to settle there. This was Shoshoni and Paiute country, and they were, after all, Oregon-bound, so the trains picked their way along down the river, departing from it here and there to cross dry benches where travel might be shortened. Some twenty-five miles downstream the westering waters flowed through lush black bottom lands, then cut sharply south through a mile-long dark-hued basalt canyon. The immigrant road climbed up on a bench to avoid the canyon, descended to a good ford at its mouth, and then followed along the river north and west until the Boise fed into the Snake near Fort Boise, a Hudson's Bay Company outpost.

[13] Basil Nelson Longsworth, *Diary of Basil Nelson Longsworth, March 15, 1853 to January 22, 1854, Covering the Period of His Migration from Ohio to Oregon* (Denver: D. E. Harrington, 1923), p. 26.

[14] Frémont, *Report*, pp. 172–3; James Clyman, *Journal of a Mountain Man*, ed. Linda M. Hasselstrom (Missoula, Mont.: Mountain Press Publishing Company, 1984), p. 117. John Mack Faragher describes such attitudes toward timbered areas in a midwestern frontier settlement, in *Sugar Creek: Life on the Illinois Prairie* (New Haven, Conn.: Yale University Press, 1986), esp. pp. 62–3.

From there immigrants crossed a fourteen-mile desert to the Mal-
heur, which they followed northward to "Farewell Bend," where the
Snake, their intermittent guide and chief sustenance since Fort Hall,
turned away to the north. Alternating barren stretches with refresh-
ment at the Burnt River and the Powder, they came into the lovely
Grande Ronde Valley. (There George Hunt remembered trading a big
buffalo rifle they had brought with them to an Indian for a no doubt
much-needed good horse.) After a tough climb over the Blue Mountains, the travelers descended the Umatilla or the Walla Walla River
to Marcus Whitman's mission on the Columbia, soon to be destroyed
in a late November uprising of the Cayuse.[15] Reaching the waters of
the famous river was a major milestone, for they could follow its
course as far as The Dalles. There, prior to 1847, travelers had reached
the end of the trail for wagons, as there was no road through the
Columbia Gorge to Fort Vancouver at the mouth of the Willamette
River. The long wait for canoe or barge transportation through the
Gorge was alleviated that year, however, when John Barlow opened
a toll road that made wagon travel possible over the Cascades and
into Oregon City.

The enormous journey, some 2,000 miles, commonly took from four
to five months, two months longer than the Mormon trail to the Great
Salt Lake (1,031 miles), a full month beyond the wooded Boise (1,500
miles). Small wonder that they felt, as they stumbled into the Willamette Valley, that in their ordeal they had "seen the elephant." Yet
many concluded, as did Samuel Hancock in 1845, that the game was
well worth the candle. They had found a virtual paradise, "beautiful
prairies, . . . abundantly timbered and water[ed] so all were soon comfortably settled, the land producing all necessary vegetables, while
venison could be procured easily and in abundance, and those who
had cattle were constantly increasing their stock."[16]

The great adventure of Americans in the Far West began like this
not just for the Hunts and Wordsworths, but for the thousands and
tens of thousands that they represent, a people all bringing their own
extravagant expectations – visions of how their lives would be different in the New Land; but also a people laden with traditions – time-
honored assumptions about how to situate themselves on the face of
the land, how to relate to one another, how to manage the myriad

---

[15] In November 1847 the mission would be decimated by a measles epidemic and a
retaliatory Indian raid that would result in the death of Marcus, Narcissa, and twelve
others.

[16] Unruh, *The Plains Across*, p. 341; Samuel Hancock, *The Narrative of Samuel Hancock,
1845–1860*, intr. Arthur D. Howden (New York: Robert M. McBride & Company,
1927), p. 40.

personal, familial, and public tasks that make life possible. And beyond this, these were a people who could not know how the New Land itself might open or obscure the hopeful visions they carried in their minds and the habits they carried in their hearts; or how successive waves of change would wash in from the broader world, reordering the materials from which their new society was being pieced together. These forces would play upon each other over the formative decades, evolving societies that were distinctly different from one another and from those left behind.

*   *   *

The Willamette Valley is a broad plain that flanks the river of that name originating in the Diamond Peak area of the Cascade Mountains and flowing north between the Cascades and the Coastal Mountains to enter the Columbia at present-day Portland. It is twenty to thirty miles wide and a hundred miles long. Air masses from the tropical south and the northern Pacific converge there, drenching the land with forty to fifty inches of rainfall each year. The temperatures are moderated by the sea, with summer highs rarely above the seventies and winter lows seldom below freezing. One guidebook, which the Hunts may well have carried in their wagon (it was published in Indiana the year before they left), offered this description to potential immigrants.

> On the lower Willammette, the country near the River is broken,
> and covered with dense forests of Pine. Further back from the
> River, it is diversified, with open woodland and groves of heavy
> timber; and still further, there are beautiful plains, lying between
> the streams, separated by belts of timber, and extending back to
> the Mountains. On the upper Willammette the country is more
> open and level and is diversified with groves of Oak, Pine, and Fir,
> and broad and fertile plains, covered with luxuriant crops of
> grass.[17]

Whether navigating up the Willamette River from Fort Vancouver or struggling up over the Barlow road, the gathering point for American immigrants of the late 1840s to Oregon was Oregon City. The infant American settlement was strategically located on the falls of the Willamette, twenty miles upriver (south) from its confluence with the Columbia. The bustling town was an outgrowth of fur trading in the area that dated back to 1825. In that year John McLoughlin founded Fort Vancouver, the Hudson's Bay Company headquarters in the

---

[17] Overton Johnson and Wm. H. Winter, *Route Across the Rocky Mountains, with a Description of Oregon and California* (Readex Microfilm Reprint, 1966; Lafayette, Ind.: John B. Semans, Printer, 1846), p. 42.

West, the first enduring white presence in the valley. As trapping became less profitable, two distinct groups of former trappers chose to retire to farming. French Catholics settled on a plain well south of the fort between the Champoeg and Pudding rivers. American trappers were encouraged by McLoughlin to settle on the Tualatin River, a short distance southwest of the fort. A third and strikingly different white presence appeared in 1834 when Jason Lee and other Methodists began founding Indian missions south of the French settlement near the site of present Salem.

As tensions arose between the United States and Britain over possession of the jointly occupied Oregon country, promoters and politicians – men such as Jason Lee and Thomas Hart Benton – helped enlist the farming folk of the Mississippi River Valley in the cause of Oregon. In 1842 Elijah White headed up the first immigrant train worthy of the name to travel from the states to the Northwest, somewhat over 100 persons. Some of its members were hired by McLoughlin to help build a milling center on the falls of the Willamette, perhaps with the intent of keeping them well south of the Columbia, where he hoped the eventual boundary between the United States and British Canada would be established.

The enterprise quickly grew into the town of Oregon City, and by October 1844 was already recognized by newly arrived James Clyman as "the Seat of government & the main commercial place for all the settlments of the Teritory of Oregon."[18] Nearly 800 persons came to Oregon during the "Great Migration" of 1843, and a census in 1845 reported that the rising flow of immigrants had brought the population south of the Columbia to some 2,000 persons. The next year the U.S./Canadian boundary was established along the forty-ninth parallel – a compromise line well south of the southern border of Alaska, the boundary blustering Americans had hoped for, but comfortably north of the Columbia, the border preferred by the Hudson's Bay Company officials.

The certainty that the valley would be American helped open the flood of immigration that carried the Hunts in 1847. Some 4,000 came to Oregon that year, and another 1,300 in 1848. In 1849 California diverted all but 450 of the Americans traveling to the Pacific, but in 1850 the flow to the Willamette rebounded sharply to 6,000. Some 3,600 arrived in 1851; in 1852, 10,000; in 1853, another 7,500; and in 1854, 6,000. Between 1840 and 1855 some 46,000 made their painful way from the states across the plains to Oregon.[19]

[18] Clyman, *Mountain Man*, p. 131, entry for October 13, 1844.
[19] Unruh, *The Plains Across*, pp. 84–5.

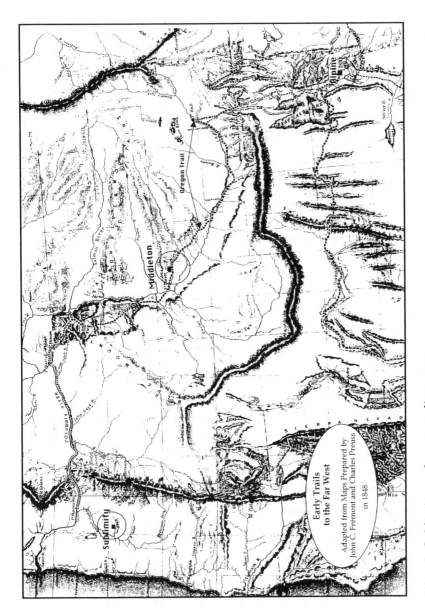

Map 2. Sublimity and surrounding area.

Always arriving tired and spent in the fall, many immigrants of the 1840s and 1850s wintered in Oregon City, many earning money as craftsmen until they could assess the neighboring country and identify a promising site for a land claim. They then began distributing themselves among the "broad and fertile plains" bordering the Willamette – French Prairie, the Tualatin Plains, Howell's Prairie, Waldo Hills, or other districts that were being named and known as white settlement proceeded. The Reverend George H. Atkinson described some aspects of the settling process in 1847:

> An immigrant will come in during the autumn, put himself up a
> log house with a mud & stick chimney, split boards & shingles,
> break eight or ten or twenty acres of prarie and sow it with wheat.
> You call upon him the next year & he will have a fine field ripe for
> the sickle. His large field will be well fenced with newly split fir
> rails. There will be a patch of corn, another of potatoes, & another
> of garden vegetables. Outside a large piece will be broken for the
> present year's sowing. His cattle & horse & hogs will be on the
> prairie, thriving and increasing without care.[20]

Some sixteen miles east of the Methodist Mission at Salem, between the Pudding and Santiam rivers, the largely open prairie land begins to break into gently rolling hills that grow in pitch as the eastern sections rise to become the foothills of the Cascades. There were scattered thickets of Douglas fir, hemlock, spruce, and incense cedar in the 1840s, leaving much of the land clear enough to plow, though toward the east these coalesced to form the dense rain forests of the Cascades. Cutting north through this region was the well-worn Klamath trail, used for centuries by Indians in traveling down the valley to the Columbia. To this spot in 1844 came an American settler, Daniel Waldo, seeking high land, well up from the river bottoms, where he feared the fevers that had been such a plague along the Mississippi and Missouri. James Clyman found him there in May 1845:

> Visited Mr Waldows settlement  the day proved showery and
> disagreeable  Mr. Waldow has made his selection in the Hills
> deviding the waters of the Moleally and the Santiam rivers and
> was last season the only person in the colony who cultivated the
> settlement is now around him extending their farms in all
> directions over the most beautifull tract of country sinking and
> swelling in regular rounded forms of all immaginary verieties
> finely interspersed with groves of oak and Firr Timbr and

[20] "Diary of Rev. George H. Atkinson, D. D.," *Oregon Historical Quarterly* 40 (December 1939): 349. The entry is for July 15, 1847.

numerous springs of never failing clear water in many insances
bursting out neare the top of the hills.

    Mr Waldow has a fine stock of the best blooded cattle I have yet
seen in the Teritory[21]

Others followed, and the rolling countryside came to be known as
the Waldo Hills. To those who had toiled past Scott's Bluff or Devil's
Gate or marveled at their first sighting of Mt. Hood, the view from
the foothills looking across rolling, patchily forested landscape towards the west was perhaps more picturesque than sublime. Yet such
fine distinctions did not bother James Denny, one of the settlers in the
southern part of the Waldo Hills, who in 1852 suggested that a proposed post office be named Sublimity. John and Temperance Hunt
made a claim six miles north of Denny in 1848. Three years later their
son, George, found land four miles south of them and squarely within
the Sublimity district. His descendants still occupy some of the land
he settled on.

     \*    \*    \*

The Wordsworths had been in the van of perhaps 30,000 Latter-day
Saints in the United States and Europe (chiefly England and Wales)
who in 1847 awaited breathlessly the news that the Camp of Israel
had alighted and a new gathering place had been found. That call was
not long in coming. Brigham Young and a select company headed
east from the Salt Lake Valley on August 26, arriving in Winter Quarters on October 31. By December 23, the twelve apostles had drafted
a "General Epistle to the Saints Throughout the World" in which they
urged all to gather to the new-found Zion in the Rockies:

    We found a beautiful valley of some twenty by thirty miles in
    extent, with a lofty range of mountains on the east. . . . The soil of
    the valley appeared good, but will require irrigation to promote
    vegetation, . . . The climate is warm, dry, and healthy; good salt
    abounds at the lake; warm, hot, and cold springs are common; mill
    sights excellent; but the valley is destitute of timber. . . .

    The Saints . . . [are] making all their exertions tend to their
    removal westward. Their hearts and all their labors are towards
    the setting sun, for they desire to be so far removed from those
    who have been their oppressors, that there shall be an everlasting
    barrier between them and future persecution.[22]

---

[21] Clyman, *Mountain Man*, p. 164, entry for May 9, 1845. Spelling and (lack of) punc-
tuation as written by Clyman and printed by the editors.

[22] December, 23, 1847, "General Epistle from the Council of the Twelve Apostles to the
Church of Jesus Christ of Latter Day Saints Abroad, Dispersed throughout the Earth,"
*Millennial Star* 6 (March 15, 1848): 81–8.

Their praise was extravagant, reflecting their hopes for the Great Basin more than the realities. The Saints had landed squarely in the middle of what geographers now call the Wasatch Oasis. Though surrounded by formidable deserts, the Salt Lake Valley is one of several that run in a north-south line along central Utah, flanking the western edge of the Wasatch Mountains and (south of Utah Valley) the mountains of the High Plateau section of the Colorado Plateau. These mountains rise sharply from the valley floors, thrusting moist westerly air currents up to a chilling 10,000- or 12,000-foot elevation, where they give up their burden to fall on the Wasatch as rain or snow. Thus though the valleys may have only fifteen inches of rainfall (one-third that of Sublimity), the mountains capture moisture, store it as snow, and feed it to the valleys below through canyons and streams during most of the summer growing season. Where land is level enough for the plow, it can be irrigated by an elaborate system of dams and ditches.

Still, farming in such a setting is a constant, costly labor, requiring the building of irrigation works prior to planting and continuous subsequent attention. In many localities the mountain stream feeding the ditch dwindles to a trickle by mid-July, so that water must be carefully allocated by the "water master" to the users. During the heat of the summer, a farmer might be granted a two-hour period of water use once a week at three o'clock on Tuesday mornings. In July and August temperatures average in the mid-nineties, and many days the heat rises to above 100° F. In January the temperature often drops to well below zero. The only trees in the valleys – principally box elder and cottonwood – lined the banks of the streams that flowed from the eastern mountains. Clearly, this was no Oregon. The Willamette Valley is a mild land that wants to be a forest. Utah is a harsh land that wants to be a desert.

Unlike the Willamette Valley, there had been no white occupation prior to 1847, though a few months before the Mormons arrived, trapper Miles Goodyear had built a cabin and stockade on the Weber River, calling it Fort Buenaventura. The Mormons bought him out shortly after their arrival. They thus reduced for a time the cultural complexity and competition among whites that had remained in the Willamette Valley as a legacy of the long presence of the fur trade and the British-built Fort Vancouver. Utah had been unequivocally Mexican territory, part of Upper California from the Adams-Onis Treaty of 1819 until the Mexican War of 1846. Its status was not resolved until the Treaty of Guadalupe Hidalgo was signed on February 2, 1848 (the winter Wordsworth and other Mormons were shivering in their pioneer fort in the Salt Lake Valley), and twenty months after the Americans and British signed the treaty that fixed the northern boundary of Oregon Territory. Hispanic explorers, trappers, and traders had crossed through the territory since the mid-eighteenth century, but they did not find permanent settlements or leave an enduring imprint.

Salt Lake City thus instantly became an Oregon City for many immigrants to Utah – the initial destination and orientation place, from which they moved after finding an opportunity in one of the settlements. Yet, whereas immigrants could go in almost any direction from Oregon City and find arable land, the Utah settlers had to space themselves out in discrete clusters – seeking the few sites that combined mountain stream with reasonably level terrain, often an alluvial fan at the mouth of a canyon that was geologically the product of the stream flowing through it. The Mormon settlements thus became quite literally small oases scattered across an expansive desert region. The orchards and fields always gave way abruptly to rabbit brush and sage at the edge of the highline canal. This was the land the Wordsworths and their fellow Mormons found – more notable for isolation than opportunity. Yet it was refuge that they sought. The counsel of church leaders would resonate strongly across the empty spaces, and commitment to the common good would prove essential to collective survival. It was, as Brigham Young often put it, a "good place to make Saints."

The gathering of both American and British Saints to this western haven was an ongoing task that occupied much of Brigham Young's time and attention until completion of the transcontinental railroad in 1869. Church leaders incorporated the Perpetual Emigrating Fund Company (the PEF) in 1850. Its officers shortly began to charter whole vessels from Liverpool, stationing Mormon agents in New Orleans, Boston, New York, Philadelphia, St. Louis, and Council Bluffs, Iowa, to greet immigrants, organize them into companies, book upriver steamboat passage, order teams and wagons, and thus speed them "homeward to Zion." To the 1,930 who came to Utah in 1847, some 2,400 were added in 1848; 1,500 in 1849; 2,500 in 1850; and 1,500 in 1851. Then as the Missouri River settlements were being closed and emigration from Britain was increasing, 10,000 made the trek to Utah in 1852 (the same as the number to Oregon that year); another 8,000 in 1853; 3,200 in 1854; and 4,700 in 1855. From 1847 to 1855 some 36,000 traveled overland to Utah, 10,000 fewer than had traveled to Oregon since overland travel to the Pacific began in 1840.[23]

---

[23] Unruh, *Mountain Man*, pp. 84–5. Unruh relied on B. H. Roberts for the 1847 count, which subsequent research has shown to have exaggerated the population some-

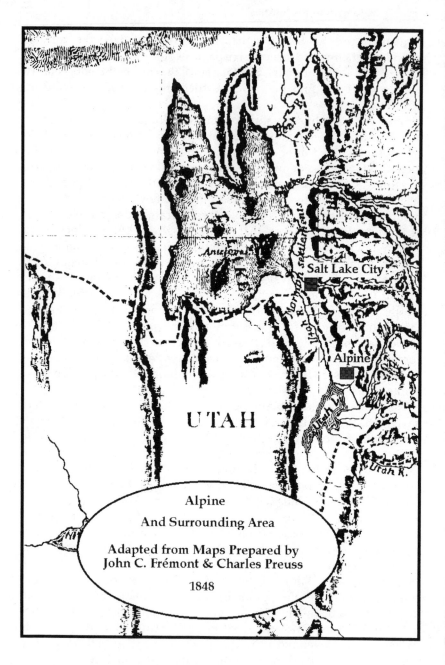

Map 3. Alpine and surrounding area.

Despite terrible cholera epidemics on the Mississippi and Missouri rivers in the early 1850s, this migration was accomplished with relative harmony, speed, and efficiency, thanks in large measure to the common ideological commitment of the travelers and the great stress church leaders had placed on communal and cooperative enterprises.

The new settlers rapidly took up the available farmlands in the Salt Lake Valley and began to spread beyond it. The first winter, a salient was made in Bountiful, just north of Salt Lake City. The next year, colonists moved up onto lands recently purchased from Miles Goodyear at the site of present-day Ogden, thirty-five miles north of the city. In 1849 Tooele was founded 28 miles to the west and Manti 100 miles to the south in central Utah's Sanpete Valley. Also that year, an incursion began into an important Ute homeland directly south of the Salt Lake Valley, when Provo was founded in Utah Valley. Shortly thereafter, a crescent of satellite towns sprang up in Utah Valley, scattered east of Utah Lake from Lehi in the north to Payson in the south. By 1850 the incoming population had occupied the available niches in the Salt Lake Valley and was spilling out into the valleys north and south along the western front of the Wasatch Mountains.

Among those looking toward the south was William Wordsworth. In July 1850 he and seven other men crossed into the Utah Valley to seek out farmland they could claim. All the land at American Fork Creek was taken, and Wordsworth rejected the land around lower Dry Creek (the Lehi area) as too arid. He returned again in September with six others, and the men explored north and east until they found a narrow triangle of alluvial lands nestled in a pocket where the north-south running Wasatch intersects a westering spur known as the Traverse Mountains. There was more water there closer to the mountains, and the soil was rich and dark.

The census marshal that fall found twenty-nine persons in the "Mountainville" settlement in seven households, fourteen males and fifteen females. Among them was William Wordsworth, who listed his occupation as fisherman. Other families arrived later in the year, those who couldn't finish their cabins setting up housekeeping in dugouts or wagon beds along Fort Creek and upper Dry Creek – streams flowing from the Traverse Mountains to the North and the Wasatch Mountains to the east. In 1853, however, the counsel of general church leaders and fear of Indian attack encouraged the people to rearrange their settlement to conform to a pattern followed uniquely by Mormons in the West. Log homes, which originally lined the stream

what. Here I use the more recent and likely more accurate research of Eugene Campbell, *Establishing Zion*, p. 14. Thereafter his figures are reasonably accurate.

banks, were moved to a fort enclosure and then later to a platted village site. The fields surrounded the town, and civic buildings occupied the center of the settlement. In 1855 Mountainville was incorporated under the more lofty name Alpine City. By that time, however, many of the founders, disappointed by the shortness of the growing season, had left. The Yankee Wordsworths, Shermans, and Clydes were gradually replaced by Strongs, Nashes, and Healeys, all representing the British Saints who were streaming into Utah too late to claim prime lands and thus forced to move to newer, more marginal areas.

Catherine Kemp Nash was one of these, born in Melksham in Wiltshire County, England, in 1813. Catherine's parents were not married until she was sixteen, and, following the custom for children born out of wedlock, her surname was that of her mother. Of her life prior to age thirty-two, little is known. Three children were born to her, the first when she was but fifteen, all recorded on parish registers as illegitimate. Her lot was apparently one of poverty and exploitation as she worked at dairying in order to maintain her family. Then in 1845 her life changed. She came in contact with Mormon missionaries and was converted to their faith. The PEF advanced her a sufficient supplement to her meager savings to pay for passage to Utah.

Full of hopes and expectations, Catherine and her family – Worthy, seventeen; Ephraim, fifteen; Isaac, ten, and an eleven-year-old nephew, Albert Marsh – set sail on an American ship, the *Jersey*, on February 5, 1853, from Liverpool. The 314 Mormons on the 849-ton vessel were organized by George Halliday, a Mormon Elder, into several "districts" (following the pattern of church organization in England and other missions), each presided over by a designated district president. Single men were located at the bow of the ship, women at the stern, and married couples provided a watchful buffer amidships. Each president organized the members of his district to ensure efficient food preparation, cleaning and sanitation, and sleeping arrangements. He called his district members to daily prayers and organized regular planning meetings where they addressed common problems.

The regimen paid off, and the *Jersey* docked in New Orleans, forty-four days out from Liverpool, with but one death (a woman of advanced age) and no significant illness. Elder John Brown met the ship and arranged the group's steamboat passage 1,373 miles upriver to Keokuk, Iowa. There they were outfitted for the overland journey, traveling as part of the Jesse W. Crosby company that left Kanesville, Iowa (Council Bluffs), on July 1 and arrived in the Salt Lake Valley in early September.[24] Shortly thereafter she moved with her family to

[24] See Conway B. Sonne, *Saints on the Seas: A Maritime History of Mormon Migration,*

Alpine, where she eked out a living making butter and cheese and selling it in rail and mining camps up the nearby American Fork Canyon. She was but one of many British Saints who by 1860 had heeded Brigham Young's call to Zion and were supplanting the American families of Alpine as the principal population of the village.[25]

* * *

It is evident that the settlers of Sublimity and Alpine (the broader farming districts, not just the village centers) engaged in a "nesting" process that lasted for several years as they looked at one site, then another, often laying some claim to a parcel of land – a cabin, fence, or plowed field – then selling their improvements or abandoning them in favor of pastures elsewhere. Elijah Bristow, who settled in 1846 on a land claim in Lane County, Oregon, well south of Sublimity, advised a friend in 1857 that there were still opportunities, as "This country is like all other new country, settled up with characters who will never be contented in any one place very long at a time."[26] Many in Oregon and a few in Utah were struck with gold fever, taking advantage of their early presence in the Far West to troop off in 1848 and 1849 to California in the hope of getting to the diggings before argonauts from the states. The oldest of the Hunt boys, George, at eighteen "bought his freedom of his father" and joined the rush to the mines in 1849.[27] Though some of the Oregonians and Utahns were captured by the allure of the golden land, a surprising number returned to their farms, reportedly richer, if not wiser. All of this shuffling about in the early frontier period makes the first decade particularly difficult to study, and perhaps misleading were such a study possible, for we would be seeing the two societies in an exceptional period of dislocation. It is thus perhaps not a loss to our deeper understanding of these rural people that Sublimity and Alpine first appear as identifiable districts of any dimension in the 1860 census, sixteen years after Daniel Waldo began white settlement in the Sublimity area and ten years after William Wordsworth's party pioneered Alpine. By this time the nesting

*1830–1890* (Salt Lake City: University of Utah Press, 1983), pp. 76–7; 150. The Nashes' journey was particularly well documented by fellow passengers Frederick Piercy, an artist and diarist, and James Linforth in James Linforth, *Route from Liverpool to the Great Salt Lake Valley* (Liverpool and London: Franklin D. Richards, 1855). The definitive study of British Mormon migration to the United States is P. A. M. Taylor, *Expectations Westward: The Mormons and the Emigration of Their British Converts in the Nineteenth Century* (Ithaca, N.Y.: Cornell University Press, 1966).

[25] Biographical information on Catherine Nash from Merma G. Carlisle, ed., *Alpine: The Place Where We Lived* (Nash family publication, n.p., n.d.), pp. 1–5.

[26] Elijah Bristow to Zachary C. Fields, April 7, 1857, Letter Book, Huntington Library

[27] Hunt, *Family History*, p. 38.

period was largely over, the California fever had run its course, and the rural people visited by census takers had begun to form firm attachments to their new homes.

There were, of course, continuing disruptions, the effects of which are vital to our understanding these people's lives. Yet they occurred as impositions upon a society in place, not as the mass dislocation that characterized the settlement period. Important among these were the continuing gold and silver rushes across the West, which, beginning in the early 1860s, peppered the Utah landscape, and some parts of Oregon, with new communities dramatically different from the Alpines and Sublimitys that were already in place. These affected the established rural farm districts in complex ways, stimulating the demand for foodstuffs while at the same time draining away part of the work force needed to produce them. From the late 1850s well into the 1860s, the mines drew a tide of gold seekers to a succession of sites in the northwest – the Fraser River of British Columbia (1858), the Clearwater (1860), the Salmon (1861), and the Boise (1862), in Idaho; and Grasshopper Creek (1862) and Alder Creek (1863) in Montana. The frantic wandering had the unintended consequence of stimulating agricultural settlement in interior regions that otherwise might have long gone unsettled by farm folk. It may also have had the effect, as we shall see, of changing the value system of the society dramatically, stimulating the hope of quick wealth and drawing thousands from farming settlements in the Midwest to join a frantic chase from mining district to mining district that in itself eroded enduring societal attachments.

One of many "Yonsiders" (people from the yonder, or western side of the United States) who followed the mining strikes east from the coast was the recent widower Elijah Bristow. In 1862 he left his Lane County, Oregon, land claim, a small general merchandise store in Eugene (and his four motherless children to the care of his sister), to join the crowds rushing to the central Idaho mines. He often reported encountering friends from the Willamette Valley as he bought and sold claims, attempted to sell socks and other supplies, and tried to keep up with the flow of men chasing rumors of new strikes. He spent nearly a year in Florence and Black Hawk Gulch, then moved south to Placerville, on the headwaters of the Boise, admitting to a friend in the summer of 1863 that "I am getting very tired and weary of this kind of life, But I am Here and will not leave until I can bring Money enough to clear me of Debt."[28] By 1864 he was home in Eugene and boasting to friends that he and a partner had cleared $9,000 the pre-

---

[28] Elijah Bristow to Willard Jones, July 29, 1863.

vious year.[29] It is likely that waves of such migrants, enduring these experiences time and again, would settle eventually, with more changes in their lives than just the size of their purses.

Some miners, like Bristow, returned to the communities they had left. Others, disappointed in their quest for quick wealth, had occasion to look again at farming opportunities they had passed by in their earlier migration to the Pacific. Among the latter were Robert, John, and Alexander McKenzie of Auburn, (eastern) Oregon, who in 1864, as Bristow was returning to the Willamette, joined a stream of gold seekers retracing their route along the Oregon Trail eastward in a rush to the mining district then being opened in the Boise Basin. The three brothers did not go directly to the mines, however, but decided to build a cabin on the bottom lands of the river above the mile-long basalt canyon they and thousands of others had passed a decade or more previously en route to Oregon. Times had changed. The bustling mining camps in the Owyhees were but sixty miles to the southeast (a two- to three-day haul), and those of the Boise Basin were about the same distance east and north. Boise City had grown up around Ft. Boise, a military camp established in 1863. Faced by an invasion of armed whites, the Indians had moved from the valley. Flour was fetching thirty-three dollars per 100 pounds and eggs two dollars a dozen, suggesting that there was at least as much gold in the bottom lands along the river as there was up in the Owyhees or the Boise Basin.[30] The lands the Oregon-bound had passed by in the 1840s and 1850s now seemed less remote, the farming prospects more promising, and the 1862 Homestead Act a happily timed beneficence. Robert McKenzie settled in and sent for Emmaroy, his wife, who joined him the next year. The U.S. census marshall found them still there in 1870, between the Patrick Ayerses and George Perkel: Robert, aged thirty-three; Emma, his wife, twenty-two; six-year-old William; and little Elizabeth Alice, aged four. The farming had apparently been profitable. The McKenzies had three hired hands and Robert McKenzie reported his worth at $2,700.[31]

[29] Elijah Bristow to Henry G. Bristow, January 31, 1864.

[30] The prices were reported in the *Boise Tri-Weekly Statesman*, December 26, 1863.

[31] The account of the McKenzies is from Morris Foote, comp., *One Hundred Years in Middleton* (Middleton, Idaho: *Boise Valley Herald*, 1963), pp. 10–14; and from the manuscript of the U.S. Census for Ada County, Idaho, 1870. There was no Middleton census precinct in 1870, but the census taker's route has been followed, linked to land records and to those living within the boundaries of Middleton, as used in this study, thus identified. Middleton, in this study, consists of people who lived on a strip of land about three miles wide bordering the Boise River on both sides and extending west from present Blessinger Lane eight miles to where the river enters the canyon

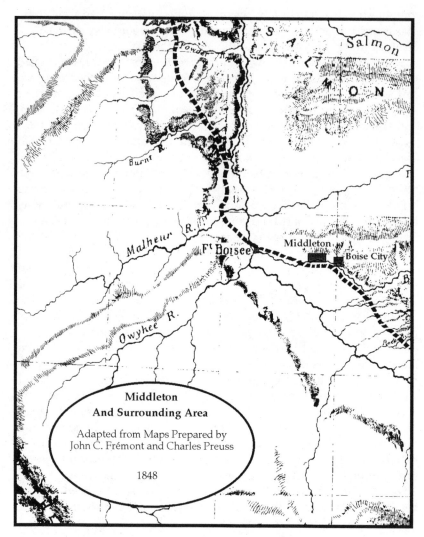

Map 4. Middleton and surrounding area.

Few Yonsiders, however, followed the lead of the McKenzies in settling the Boise Valley. More commonly, the early settlers were from the Midwest, such as Junius B. Wright and his bride (unnamed in his memoir), who traveled from Iowa to the Boise Valley the same year

– specifically, residents of Sections 2 through 6; 7 through 11; 14 through 18; and the north half of 19 through 22 in Township 4 North, Range 3 West and Sections 1, 2, and 10 through 12 of Range 4 West, Canyon County Survey. The village center is in Section 6.

the McKenzies were coming east and wintered very near them, along the Boise above the canyon. The next spring he set out for the mines, but four miles upriver met Moses Fowler, who had built a cabin and cleared some land. Fowler invited Wright to stay and help farm. "This proved to be a pleasant and profitable venture," Wright later wrote. "We sold, during the summer and fall, $1,700 worth of farm products. Peddlars came every week or two to buy what we had to sell and take it to the mines."[32]

The Lewis Spangler family, Confederate sympathizers from Missouri, arrived at about the same time. One of their daughters became fatally ill as they entered the Boise Valley and was treated by Junius Wright. The family claimed land along the river and immediately put it into production, raising cattle, poultry, vegetables, and other crops to market in the mining camps. Spangler became involved temporarily in politics, taking a position as justice of the peace, while the older two of his three boys worked on nearby ranches and in the mines. For a time, at least, they too were part of the pioneering population of the district.[33]

Also from the Midwest was William Montgomery, a native of Illinois, who came to the Boise Valley with his bride, Caroline, probably a year before the Wrights. On January 9, 1865, he filed in Boise a claim for a town site that he said he had chosen on July 23, 1863, and named Middleton. The eight blocks were surveyed and marked, including a public square, and the village quickly acquired a store, a saloon, and a mill, serving as the commercial center for most of the farmers scattered along the lower Boise until the competing upriver towns of Eagle and Star and the downriver town of Caldwell were built up in subsequent decades.

Though there were flat bench lands well up from the river, these were arid and covered with sage. The first farming was in the two- to four-mile-wide strip of bottom lands that had been combed and leveled by the river over centuries and flooded by it every spring. The bottoms were wooded, covered with brush, and often cut through with sloughs, but the topsoil was deep, soaked by the spring rise, and subirrigated by the low water table throughout the season. In some seasons a boat was as necessary a vehicle as a wagon. Moreover, the climate was mild, a finger of coastal air poking far inland here, and keeping winters mild and summers usually below 90° F. Precipitation was not abundant, an annual average of 11.5 inches per year, but the Boise River carried a strong, reliable stream from an extensive mountain watershed, so the bench lands offered the promise of great ex-

---

[32] Junius B. Wright Reminiscences in Idaho State Archives, Boise.
[33] Mary R. Luster, *The Autobiography of Mary R. Luster* (Springfield, Mo., n.p., 1933).

pansion beyond the river bottom when irrigation canals were built. The earliest farms, however, lined the river and stopped at the benches, imparting a linear pattern to settlement that dispersed the population widely. It was to this land that the McKenzies, the Wrights, the Spanglers, and the Fowlers came, expecting to mine but settling for a time instead to farm.

Three societies had moved to the West over three successive decades. The Oregonians began their departure from the states in the mid-1840s, drawn by the promise of rich and abundant land for farming. Some ninety-seven families settled in the country around Sublimity town, and there began an attempt to bind their family destiny to the land.[34]

The Mormons left the states in the late 1840s, and the emigrants from England who ultimately settled down in Alpine arrived in the early to mid-1850s, eager to gather with the Saints and do their part in building the Kingdom of God on earth. Alpine City, as the fifteen families who lived there in 1860 called it (it began and remained the smallest of our communities), became in many ways an instrument for accomplishing this and, at the same time, a local manifestation of the Mormon dream to build a refuge – a holy city in the desert.

The fifty-nine families who settled Middleton came in the 1860s. They left a country torn by civil war and strife and were drawn to the Boise Valley by the hope of quick wealth. They found relief from the chaos of war in the search for gold and silver, whether in the mountains or the river bottom soils. Their fixation on material well-being would do as much to shape their society as did the Mormons' quest for community and the Oregonians' quest for family continuity. Many in all three societies would achieve for a time some measure of what they had dreamed of, and their descendants would be deeply imprinted by those founding visions of dynasty, community, and wealth.

---

[34] "Families" here are census households. The data are from counts by the author of the 1860 U.S. manuscript censuses for Sublimity and Alpine and of the 1870 census for Middleton. The 1860 census precinct of Sublimity was much larger than that of later decades. The author has reconstructed, insofar as possible, the route of the census marshall and has included only those families that were in the townships he subsequently defined as Sublimity. Sublimity, for the purposes of this study, consists of all of the residents of Township 8 North, Range 1 East; the first six sections of Township 9 South of that range; Sections 1, 2, 3, 10, 11, 12, 15, 14, 13, 22, 23, 24, 27, 26, 25, 34, 35, and 36 of Township 8 Range 1 West; Sections 1, 2, and 3 of Township 9 South of that range; and Sections 6, 7, 18, 19, 30, and 31 of Township 8 South Range 2 East. Alpine's population was unambiguous and remained so, the census district coinciding with the town and nearby farmsteads in all decades.

# 2   *His own customs are the best*

Those who settled around Sublimity were principally yeoman farmers from the Ohio, Mississippi, and Missouri river valleys, with roots in the Old South. They were seeking farm land, enough to sustain themselves and their descendants for generations to come. The Alpine settlers by 1860 were mostly from England, converts to Mormonism, and refugees from the world's first industrial centers. They sought order and community. The people who came to Middleton were of the same stock as those who settled Sublimity, though a generation distant. They were fleeing the ravages of America's Civil War and seeking wealth in Idaho's hills.

The people of early Sublimity, represented by George and Elizabeth Hunt, spoke of their lives with words and phrases still used by their descendants. And yet, they were on the far side of a divide American rural society has long since crossed. Their words were freighted with far different meanings and associations. They used our words but not, in the deepest sense, our language. Like rural people since the beginnings of settlement in America, they married, bore children, worshipped, planted and harvested, and marketed any surplus. Yet all that was most important to them – families, neighbors, land, the products of farms – seem to have had different meanings. The means and ends of their lives were remote from our own. Even the educated elite who lived and worked among them found these farm folk difficult to understand.

One was the Rev. George Henry Atkinson, graduate of a New England theological school, who in 1847 concluded that he would devote his life to missionary service, seeking Christian salvation not for Africans or Asians, but for Americans settling the Oregon country. "I do not love F[oreign] Missions less," he explained to an uncle, "but I love H[ome] Missions, if possible, more. It has been a painful struggle to give up the hope of doing something in person for the degraded

African." Protestant missionaries, he concluded, were as critically needed in Oregon as in Africa.

> Upon the Missionaries is to depend the welfare of those
> settlements. They must give the education & exert the moral &
> religious influence which is to save the people. . . . If vices once
> become popular there will be rapid destruction of character, the
> people are generally ignorant. . . . There are none of the strong
> restraints, which we feel in New England.

Arriving in Oregon City in 1848, Reverend Atkinson began a ministry in the burgeoning frontier town. His concerns reached beyond Oregon City, however, to include rural people, such as those of Sublimity, and twice a month he would turn over his pulpit to an Episcopal minister and travel into the country. Yet he made little progress and concluded by 1850 that there was not much hope for those in the farming districts:

> They cannot or will not appreciate a style peculiarly New England.
> Every man believes that his own customs are the best. So that the
> Missourian is proud of Missouri and would reproduce many of the
> characteristics of its people here. A Kentuckian would do the same.
> So would one from North Carolina and another from New York,
> and another from Mass, and Vermont. It is impossible not to cross
> the opinions, prejudices, or to disturb the feelings of some. There is
> as yet no homogenousness in Society as a whole.[1]

It is certainly true that the Oregon frontier, true to our common notions of the early West, attracted a wonderfully varied set of people from all parts of the United States. Sublimity settler John Matoon had been born in Massachusetts; his wife, Ophelia, was from New York. John Downing was a native of Pennsylvania; his wife, Temperance, John S. Hunt's youngest daughter, of Indiana. Counting wards, boarders, and hired hands, members of John Downing's household as of 1860 had been born in Pennsylvania, Indiana, Illinois, Iowa, and Oregon.[2] The 592 persons living in the small farming district of Sub-

---

[1] George Henry Atkinson to Josiah Little, December 31, 1841; June 15, 1847; and to Josiah Hale, December 27, 1850, George Henry Atkinson Collection, Huntington Library, San Marino, California.

[2] By 1860 the Downing household contained the parents and two surviving children, Edwin and Albert (a twin of Albert had died in 1858), as well as a niece, Mary Riches, eight; Margarette Henline, perhaps a domestic; and hired hand, F. Hunt, eighteen, likely Temperance's brother, Thomas Benton Hunt; and William King, eighteen, probably John Downing's nephew. These and the subsequent data are taken from the author's tabulation of information in the manuscript federal census, schedule 1, for the years indicated. The Sublimity 1860 census was taken by D. B. Hamnal, Assistant Marshall, beginning on July 11, 1860. As noted in Chapter 1, Sublimity, for the purposes of this study, consists of all of the residents of Township 8 North, Range 1 East;

limity in 1860 had been born in twenty-four of the then thirty-three states and in four foreign countries.

But, as Reverend Atkinson suggested, Sublimity was by no means a microcosm of the rest of the country. If we eliminate most of the Oregon-born by looking at the 225 adults over twenty, more were born in Missouri (thirty-eight, or 17 percent) than in any other state, with Kentucky not far behind (thirty, or 13 percent), followed by Tennessee (twenty-five, 11 percent). Already a pattern seems evident, with 41 percent of the adults in the population coming from these three states.[3] The Hunts were not typical in this respect, though the family had North Carolina roots and though Wayne County is in the lower third of Indiana and more oriented toward the South than the Northeast. Fifty-seven percent were from a state that was either southern or had received during the previous generation a strong stream of settlers from the South.[4]

The Hunts were part of the next largest portion of the population, 26 percent having been born in Ohio, Indiana, Illinois, and Iowa, though it is likely that most of them were of southern ancestry as well.[5] Six percent of Sublimity's adults (thirteen) were from the Mid-

the first six sections of Township 9 South of that range; Sections 1, 2, 3, 10, 11, 12, 15, 14, 13, 22, 23, 24, 27, 26, 25, 34, 35, and 36 of Township 8 Range 1 West; Sections 1, 2, and 3 of Township 9 South of that range; and Sections 6, 7, 18, 19, 30, and 31 of Township 8 South Range 2 East. The 1860 census precinct of Sublimity was much larger than that of later decades. The author has reconstructed, insofar as possible, the route of the census marshall and has included only those families that were in the townships he has defined as Sublimity.

[3] The 1850 census for all of Oregon, as tabulated by William A. Bowen, shows 28 percent Missourians in the state as a whole; 8 percent from Kentucky; and 4 percent from Tennessee, the three states accounting for 35 percent of the non-Oregon born reporting population of 9,294. Ten percent were from the Mid-Atlantic states, 5 percent from New England, and 49 percent from the South Atlantic, Gulf, and South Central states, including Missouri and Arkansas. Another 32 percent were from the North Central States, including Iowa. Thus Sublimity parallels to some degree the 1850 Oregon population, but shows a notably smaller concentration from New England and the Midwest and more from the South. See William A. Bowen, *The Willamette Valley: Migration and Settlement on the Oregon Frontier* (Seattle: University of Washington Press, 1978), p. 25.

[4] From Alabama, Arkansas, Kentucky, Maryland, Delaware, Missouri, North Carolina, South Carolina, Tennessee, or Virginia.

[5] This estimate is consistent with the findings of John Mack Faragher in his study of Sugar Creek in central Illinois. Three-quarters of the heads of household who settled in the Sugar Creek area before 1840 were from Kentucky, Tennessee, or Virginia or Carolina upcountry regions. Fewer than one in ten came from a state north of the Mason-Dixon line. See John Mack Faragher, *Sugar Creek: Life on the Illinois Prairie* (New Haven, Conn.: Yale University Press, 1986), p. 45. Don H. Doyle found that New Englanders made up only about 7 percent of the early population of the urban center

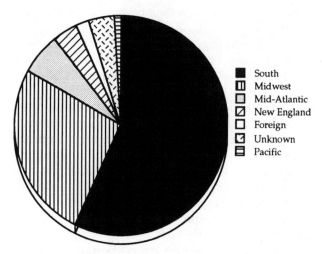

Figure 2.1 Sublimity, Oregon. Birthplaces of early settlers.

Atlantic states. (This included Pennsylvanians John Downing and his brother George, neighbors to the west of the Hunts.) Small wonder that the people did not appreciate the New England style of Reverend Atkinson, as only 4 percent (nine) were from the Northeast. The remainder were made up of one or two each from California, Oregon, Germany, Prussia, and England.

Reverend Atkinson's description of cultural chaos overstated the case. Seven or eight of every ten persons who might have stopped by John Hunt's home to chat or have him fix a shotgun hammer would likely have spoken one of the dialects of the South, and in their habits and traditions would have imparted a southern tone to the society. And more than this, they were rural southerners – people of the soil. Eighty-eight percent of those identifying themselves to census marshalls by occupation were farmers or farm laborers. These are eloquent facts and keys to understanding the social character of the population.

Hunt's friends and patrons did not, moreover, represent proportionately all levels of the hierarchical southern society. The extremes at the top and bottom of the hierarchy were notable for their scarcity in Sublimity. Few of the gentry came to Oregon. One local man, Daniel Delaney, sold his east Tennessee plantation and nearly all his slaves

of Jacksonville, Illinois, in *The Social Order of a Frontier Community: Jacksonville, Illinois 1825–1870* (Chicago: University of Illinois Press, 1978). See also John Barnhart, "The Southern Influence in the Formation of Illinois," *Journal of the Illinois State Historical Society* 32 (1939): 358–78; and William O. Lynch, "The Westward Flow of Southern Colonists Before 1851," *Journal of Southern History* 9 (1943): 303–27.

in 1843 in preparation for his move to Oregon but brought with him a domestic servant, eighteen-year-old Rachel Belden. Benjamin Stanton, a native of Tennessee, after a sojourn in Missouri, brought to Oregon a black servant named Ed. Chisholm Griffith of Kentucky, and later Missouri, reportedly kept "colored servants." According to family lore, Philip Glover, born in Maryland, left a home in Missouri because of his opposition to slavery, but he nonetheless brought with him a servant, Travis Johnson.[6] These people, however, are exceptional. Most slave-holding planters, the elite of southern society, were understandably not attracted to a country that had shown a strong current of opposition to slavery, as indicated in laws passed by the provisional territorial governments in 1843 and 1844. Although the issue was kept alive, it was finally resolved decisively in an 1857 referendum that, by large majorities, approved provisions in the state constitution barring both slavery and free blacks from Oregon.[7]

The clear message that blacks were not welcome in early Oregon ensured that few planters, free blacks, and, of course, very few slaves would come to the territory. Sublimity followed that pattern.[8] The great majority in the district were white southern farmers who had long been – as expressed in 1857 by one Georgia agent to his client – "wanting to go to the west . . . where tha can get land cheap."[9]

The evidence suggests, further, that they were principally yeomen

[6] Sarah Hunt Steeves, *Book of Remembrance of Marion County, Oregon, Pioneers, 1840–1860* (Portland, Ore.: The Bernelff Press, 1927), pp. 30, 192–3, 184–5, 189–90, 260. Not all of these people lived within the district I have designated in Sublimity, but all were in the broader area.

[7] Slavery was prohibited in the 1843 Organic Laws of the provisional territorial government and again in 1844, when a law was passed providing that any black slave brought into the territory should be freed within three years of arrival, but that no free Blacks could remain for more than two years, thus barring both slavery and free blacks. The law was repealed the next year, but the controversy continued. A referendum on slavery was held in 1857 in connection with consideration of a territorial constitution, with decisive majorities against slavery and against allowing free blacks to enter Oregon. Of 10,372 votes cast, 2,645 – about a third – were in favor of slavery, 214 of them from Marion County (1,269 votes cast). Yet 8,640 of 9,721 voters favored a ban on free Blacks entering the territory. Both provisions were made a part of the constitution under which Oregon entered the Union in 1859. See T. W. Davenport, "Slavery Question in Oregon," *Oregon Historical Quarterly* IX (1908), 227–8.

[8] Rachel Belden, her husband Nathan; Ed; who lived with Benjamin Stanton; Travis Johnson, and the "colored servants" in the Griffith household. These are all reported in Sarah Hunt Steeves, *Book of Remembrance*, but they do not appear in the appropriate household listings for the 1860 census.

[9] Quoted in Steven Hahn, *The Roots of Southern Populism* (New York: Oxford University Press, 1983), p. 68, from Michael Frix to John Dobbins, Gordon County, June 15, 1856; A. N. Edmundson to Dobbins, Gordon County, March 31, 1857, in Dobbins Papers, Reel 2, Emory University Archives.

– families who had taken pride in their independence gained through owning and operating their own land or shops in the South and Midwest – or, in some instances, tenants who managed to save enough to seek the same opportunity in the West. Moreover, they were not all young couples. There were many like the Hunts – families headed by mature parents hoping to find in the West opportunities for their growing sons that could not be afforded back home. The median age of Sublimity's married couples and single heads of household in 1860 was 38 years (as many older as younger than 38); the mean, or average, was nearly forty (39.5). Most were already well into parenthood at the time of migration. Only one of the 1860 parents had been born in Oregon; most of the rest, as Atkinson ruefully observed, bringing with them cultural baggage from the South and Midwest. What did this cultural baggage consist of? How were the rural people of Sublimity different from the New England style that George Atkinson feared would never wield its restraining influence in Oregon? Fortunately, the lives of pre–Civil War southern people have been closely studied by contemporary observers and subsequent scholars. While a full description would be the work of another book, a number of traits that became salient in Oregon emerge from these studies.

\* \* \*

Some 80 percent of those who lived in Sublimity in 1860 were people who had roots in societies long dominated by an agricultural planter class jealous of its accustomed right to control the wealth, politics, religion, and social life of the region.[10] Anglo-European settlement had begun in 1607 at Jamestown, Virginia, and despite terrible death rates, the flow of new immigrants continued until other colonies were established along the Chesapeake and down the coast from Virginia: Maryland, the Carolinas, and Georgia. During the first half of the seventeenth century, as the native populations were being decimated by disease, deprivation, and conquest, the English colonists distributed themselves among the many inlets and natural harbors lining the Chesapeake Bay and its tributaries, dispersing themselves widely amid the forested landscape, and claiming as much land adjacent to and extending back from their ship landings as possible. One native Virginian, Robert Beverly, wrote that many colonists hoped to be "Lord of a vast, tho' unimprov'd Territory," an ambition facilitated

---

[10] A comprehensive and tightly reasoned discussion of the evolution of the hierarchical system dominated by the southern gentry is found in Allan Kulikoff, *Tobacco and Slaves: The Development of Southern Cultures in the Chesapeake, 1680–1800* (Chapel Hill: University of North Carolina Press, 1986). The following discussion relies heavily on Kulikoff's analysis.

by "the many Rivers, which afforded a commodious Road for Shipping at every Man's Door," but which also limited the sphere of social interaction. "To this Day they have not any one Place of Cohabitation among them, that may reasonably bear the Name of a Town."[11] The ship landing became their principal link to the outside world – connecting each plantation not to local regional trading centers, but to London, Manchester, or Liverpool.

With settlement so far-flung, each farm or plantation came to constitute in some measure a world unto itself. The fields of the most successful, vast by English standards, surrounded a house and outbuildings that after the turn of the eighteenth century came to emulate the country estates of the gentry in England – tall, imposing, ordered, and testifying eloquently to the power and social standing of their possessors. There were a few hamlets, usually at the crossings of rutted, primitive roadways, where an Anglican church (the only legally recognized religion), an inn, a tavern, or a blacksmith shop might form the nucleus of a settlement. But the great bulk of the population consisted of farmers who lived on their lands. Only a few times a year did ships tie up at the plantation wharf, and the time between shipping and payment, or between orders and delivery, could be a full year or more. They thus had to develop a considerable degree of self-sufficiency, producing on their farms much of what they consumed.

The isolation moved them toward self-sufficiency in educational, social, and religious matters as well as production. The distances between dwellings made it difficult to maintain schools for the general populace, and the wealthy provided the rudiments of an education for their own children in their homes. At least monthly attendance at divine service in the parish church was required by law, and there was much business talk and socializing before and after the service. But the powerful family rituals marking vital events of birth, marriage, death, and burial commonly took place on the plantations rather than in the church.[12] Even the monthly court day at the county courthouse did not seriously challenge the home as the principal place of socializing. During the seventeenth century, the community of family

---

[11] Robert Beverley, *The History and Present State of Virginia*, ed. Louis B. Wright (Chapel Hill, N.C.: The Institute of Early American History and Culture, University of North Carolina Press, 1986), pp. 57–8.

[12] Indeed, as Dell Upton has pointed out, the parish church was designed for one purpose and one purpose only: divine worship. Though forbidden by the church, it was common, especially among the gentry, even for baptisms to take place in the home. Dell Upton, *Holy Things and Profane: Anglican Parish Churches in Colonial Virginia* (Cambridge, Mass.: The Architectural History Foundation, MIT Press, 1986), pp. 10, 173.

and close kin replaced for many the community of village and parish that many of the settlers had known in England, whether in production, marketing, religious practice, or other social interaction.

During the early years of the eighteenth century, Chesapeake society was sorting itself into increasingly differentiated social ranks. At the top, a class of wealthy planters had emerged, such as the Byrds and the Carters, perhaps one man in twenty. These were seen by themselves and others to be gentlemen – a gentry that expected and received deference from the rest of society, governing the region through wealth and political power, often in a spirit of noblesse oblige and in what they deemed to be the best interests of the society as a whole. Close to them in kinship and in social standing, but remote in lifestyle, were the yeomen – independent tillers of relatively small farms or craftsmen/farmers, like John S. Hunt – about half the white men. Next were nearly as many poor whites – sometimes tenants, sometimes itinerants – who had little or no property. Beneath all whites were a few free blacks, and beneath them a great number of black slaves, by midcentury approaching half the population in some counties.[13]

The images that the Hunts and people like them held of the planter's life were distorted by their own particular place in the society. Since the yeomen families most commonly lived in a small frame house, with few if any windows and plank or even dirt floors, they were no doubt powerfully impressed by the stately Great House, and the way it stood as the center and symbol of a self-contained social world.[14] Since yeomen rarely had enough land to promise a viable farm to all their sons, the expanse of the gentlemen's holdings opened for them an enduring vision of estates seemingly sufficient to sustain family identity and fortune for generations. Because yeoman men and women experienced life as an endless round of plowing, planting, harvesting, feeding, milking, spinning, weaving, baking, and cleaning – all labors they, with few exceptions, performed themselves – they were struck by the leisure whites enjoyed on the plantation.[15] Rarely did the yeomen have the opportunity to glimpse the myriad mana-

---

[13] Kulikoff, *Tobacco and Slaves*, pp. 262–3.

[14] Rhys Isaac, *The Transformation of Virginia 1740–1790* (Chapel Hill: The Institute of Early American History and Culture, University of North Carolina Press, 1982), pp. 66–9.

[15] Elizabeth Fox-Genovese has noted that it was common for the first slave in those yeoman households that could afford servants to be a domestic, who could relieve the wife of the burden of work that was the lot of rural women. Elizabeth Fox-Genovese, *Within the Plantation Household: Black and White Women of the Old South* (Chapel Hill: University of North Carolina Press, 1988), p. 166.

gerial duties and interpersonal and financial tensions that were integral to the plantation system. In other words, yeoman men and
women were profoundly imprinted by a superficial visual image of
plantation life, particularly those aspects that resonated as the antith-
esis of conditions in their own hard lives, but they had little notion
of the problematical structure of human relationships that undergirded it.

The yeomen held aspirations informed by their distant vision of
planter society. Even for the many who went over the mountains and
settled along the Ohio and its tributaries, the images that informed
their cultural aspirations lingered – family identity, the Great House,
acres and acres of land, and the leisure to live as a gentleman. Four
generations after the Hunt family had left North Carolina, George
Washington Hunt's daughter, Sarah, set out in 1920 to find their family roots. Motoring from town to town in North Carolina and calling
Hunts in phone directories, she was thrilled to find in Oxford a post-
card showing the William Hunt mansion and proceeded immediately
to the place. "Imagine, if you can," she wrote,

> a most beautiful old, square built house with wide Ionic pillared
> porticoes or porches on all four sides, reaching clear to the roof . . .
> bordered by two rows of fine old elms, oaks, etc.
>
> The family were all out on the porch enjoying the cool evening
> shades, with two large dogs resting on the steps. . . . Mr. Hunt,
> paper in hand, advanced to meet me in genuine southern style.
>
> I introduced myself, . . . and immediately these hospitable
> southern folks accepted me . . . and made me feel at home with
> them.

Though disappointed to learn that the resident family were not kin,
it had almost seemed for a moment that Sarah Hunt had come home.[16]
It would be easy to underestimate the power of such images to persist
among yeomen in spite of geographical and temporal removal from
plantation country.

Yet the small, independent farmers of the South had habits and
customs inherent to their own social and economic world, a world
where, as Steven Hahn put it, "production and consumption focused
on the household, in which kinship rather than the market place mediated most productive relations, in which general farming prevailed
and family self-sufficiency proved the fundamental concern."[17] The

[16] Sarah Hunt Steeves, "The Family of Hunt," typescript in the possession of Thomas
W. Steeves.
[17] Hahn, *Roots of Southern Populism*, p. 29. Hahn's study is of a particular set of yeomen,
those of the Georgia upcountry, especially Jackson and Carroll counties.

world of the yeomen, so defined, had a logic of its own, spinning out from a central premise they shared with the gentry – the overriding importance of maintaining and perpetuating the family through time.[18] The logic of this premise powerfully affected relationships with others in the society, reinforcing geographical factors that limited social interaction principally to kin and close neighbors.

At the same time, as Hahn found, it severely limited the role of yeomen in production of staple crops, such as tobacco, cotton, or rice. Crops on the farms of yeomen before the Civil War emphasized grain, hay, pasture, and livestock and clearly aimed to provide first a sufficiency of food and fiber for the household. The pressing need to provide for the family caused the women, who produced much themselves, while processing what the men produced, to become adept at a far greater variety of skills than did the mistresses of plantations. Elizabeth Fox-Genovese concluded that they not only could load and shoot a rifle, but were "more likely to know how to spin, wash, make soap and candles, and weave."[19] If the family-centered character of their society expanded the variety of skills both women and men had to master, it at the same time contracted their world of exchange. Most production was for household processing and use. Surpluses, when they existed, were usually traded within a localized network, severely thinning their links to the national and international markets so vital to the lifestyle of the gentry.[20]

It has often been remarked that the yeomen were surprisingly supportive of the hierarchical society of the South and the slave system upon which it was built. More accurately, they were ambivalent, pas-

---

[18] The central importance of the family- and kin-centered character of yeoman society is also stressed in Robert C. Kenzer, *Kinship and Neighborhood in a Southern Community; Orange County, North Carolina, 1849–1881* (Knoxville: University of Tennessee Press, 1987), and in Orville Vernon Burton, *In My Father's House Are Many Mansions: Family and Community in Edgefield, South Carolina* (Chapel Hill and London: University of North Carolina Press, 1987). James E. Davis concluded that household structures on the early American frontiers replicated those in the East, and that a "fundamental" observation was "that it was, after all, the *household* that formed the basic economic and social unit in the wilderness." James E. Davis, *Frontier America: 1800–1840: A Comparative Demographic Analysis of the Settlement Process* (Glendale, Calif.: The Arthur H. Clark Company, 1977), p. 99. Most men and women of the period I have studied regarded their central purpose of perpetuating a lineage as a cooperative endeavor informed by some measure of mutual consideration and respect. Thus, I prefer the term "familial" to "patriarchal," seeing it as more descriptive of the affective relationships among members of most households and less freighted with the connotations of oppression and mutual hostility often associated with the term "patriarchal."

[19] Fox-Genovese, *Within the Plantation Household*, pp. 167, 206.

[20] This thesis is argued persuasively in Hahn, *Roots of Southern Populism*, esp. pp. 15–49.

sionately devoted to many of its central features and symbols – its family-centeredness; the independence ensured by possessing an expansive private domain; the ease, extravagance and sociability of the Great House. And yet they were offended by much that sustained it – the pretensions of the gentry, the deference the gentry expected as their due, and the very presence of the blacks, whose deference the yeomen expected but did not always enjoy. This was true for the common farmers who continued to live among the gentry in the South, as well as for the Hunts and others who moved west. Though they did not live in the Great House, they nonetheless subscribed to many of the values sustaining it, and in their hearts they harbored a quiet hope that one day their children might live there. The deep draughts they and their parents had taken of the heady brews of republicanism and evangelical religion stiffened their determination to eliminate wherever possible those conditions that had kept them subservient. But paradoxically, they were also driven to replicate, when opportunity presented itself, at least part of the lifestyle of the elites among whom they had lived. For most, the best hope of seeing that opportunity realized lay in the prairies and plains of the West, what they commonly called (inadvertently telling us what was most important about it to them) "the new land."

As elites began taking an increasing share of farmlands, opportunities for the sons of yeomen began visibly to diminish. In such circumstances the Hunts, and tens of thousands like them, did not regret greatly their decision to leave. They loaded their worldly goods into wagons and rolled away from the domain of old planters and the upcountry regions of Georgia, the Carolinas, and Virginia, climbing over the mountains and rafting down the Ohio and Mississippi to Kentucky, Tennessee, and Missouri, and even to Indiana, Illinois, and Iowa.[21]

They took few slaves to the West because they had few, and in some instances because they opposed slavery as a moral evil or as an economic liability. And they took with them a thin-skinned resentment of the airs of planters, or of any elites at one end of the social scale, and of blacks at the other. They hoped to escape the hierarchical character of the old society; but at the same time they expected that they

[21] See Eugene D. Genovese, *The Political Economy of Slavery: Studies in the Economy and Society of the Slave South* (New York: Pantheon Books, 1965); and Gavin Wright, *The Political Economy of the Cotton South: Households, Markets, and Wealth in the Nineteenth Century* (New York: W.W. Norton and Company, 1978), pp. 26–37. Steven Hahn found yeoman farms in upcountry Georgia shrinking at the same time that staple agriculture began to penetrate the economy during the 1850s. Hahn, *Roots of Southern Populism*, pp. 83–5.

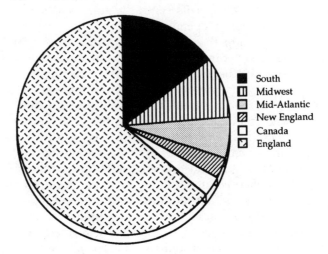

Figure 2.2 Alpine, Utah. Birthplaces of early settlers.

could build in Oregon their own plantations and live as the gentry
had lived. Like most of humankind, they were not reflective and did
hold themselves to consistency, even, or perhaps especially, in the
most fundamental dreams that drove them to seek new lives on the
frontier.

\*    \*    \*

Though their paths crossed on the Oregon trail, the world from which
the Sublimity settlers had come was remote from all but a few of those
who settled in Alpine. Both groups came to the West at about the
same time, with the hope off changing their lives for the better, yet
fixed in habits of thought and action that shaped and constrained the
society they would build in their new setting. The first Alpine settlers
– the Wordsworths, Shermans, and Clydes – were American born,
though most did not stay long. By 1860 their places had been taken
by people like the Nashes, Healeys, and Strongs, a folk who, like the
distant ancestors of those who settled Sublimity, were native English
men and women, but whose voyage across the Atlantic followed that
of the Chesapeake settlers by as much as two centuries. They left a
very different England than the one the first American Hunts had
known.

By 1860 there were more English-born adults in Alpine than American. Twenty-one of thirty-three adults in the town (64 percent) shared
with Catherine Nash and her sons English birth. Five had been born
in parts of the United States bearing a strong southern stamp, four in
Tennessee and one in Missouri. Three were from the Midwest – In-

diana and Illinois. There were but two from the Mid-Atlantic states, and one each from New England and Canada. Strolling down the streets of Alpine on a Christmas Day in the 1860s, you would likely have smelled puddings steaming in most houses and heard English accents in two of every three homes you might pass. There were four times as many adults in the town of English birth or recent background than from any other country or state of the United States – two English-born adults for every American-born. Yet like the Sublimity settlers, those from Alpine thought of themselves by 1860 as a rural agrarian folk. Everyone who reported an occupation in 1860 told the census marshall they were farmers. In doing so, they were avowing an identity new to most, and one that effectively obscured their pre-Alpine lives.

What, then, were these people – farmers all – like, and how were they different from the farmers of Sublimity? Charles Dickens boarded an emigrant ship, the *Amazon*, chartered by English settlers bound for Utah as it was preparing to embark from London on June 4, 1863, and wrote of his impressions. The emigrants, he observed,

> came from various parts of England in small parties that had never seen one another before. Yet they had not been a couple of hours on board, when they established their own police, made their own regulations, and set their own watches at all the hatchways. Before nine o'clock, the ship was as orderly and as quiet as a man-of-war.

He noted the busy and determined scribbling of letters to post before sailing, the singing of a choir, the "universal cheerfulness," the abundance of children, and confided to the shipping agent his impression that "it would be difficult to find eight hundred people together anywhere else, and find so much beauty and so much strength and capacity for work among them." Though "there were many worn faces bearing traces of patient poverty and hard work, . . . there was great steadiness of purpose and much undemonstrative self-respect among this class." The passengers, as near as he could tell, represented "most familiar kinds of handicraft trades," including farmers and farm laborers, "but I doubt if they predominated."[22] Dickens's eye was quick. In a short visit he noted that this was a family migration of parties from several parts of England, hitherto unacquainted.

---

[22] Charles Dickens, *Great Expectations* (New York: The F. M. Lupton Publishing Company, n.d.). The set of journalistic essays titled *The Uncommercial Traveler*, originally published between 1860 and 1869 in Dickens's weekly magazine, *All the Year Round*. The portions cited here were bound in the Lupton edition of *Great Expectations* on pages 449–706, the section quoted from previously, pp. 631–43. The *Amazon* was unusual in that most Mormon-chartered ships sailed from Liverpool.

He described them as a literate, self-confident working people – and a people unusually decorous and orderly.

Though none of the *Amazon* passengers, so far as I can determine, came to Alpine, the English-born who did were much like those Dickens described. Family records show that sixteen of thirty-eight native English left for the United States from the three counties of Lancashire (six), Staffordshire (five), and Derby (five).[23] Four were last in Devon prior to migration, and there were two each from Herefordshire, Northampton, Nottingham, Warwickshire, Wiltshire, Worcestershire, and the Channel Island of Jersey. One each was from Shropshire, Lincolnshire, and Gloucestershire.[24]

[23] In this they varied somewhat from the general pattern of emigration from England to Utah, which, of course, is not surprising in so small a sample. P. A. M. Taylor reported that of 12,618 who emigrated between 1850 and 1862, the great majority were from Lancashire (2,250, or 18 percent), as was also true of Alpine (6, or 16 percent); the other areas of great emigration were London (1,301), Yorkshire (1,203), and Warwickshire (1,178), of which only Warwickshire was represented in Alpine. There were large numbers in the general emigration from Gloucestorshire (654), Lincolnshire (443), Staffordshire (411), Nottinghamshire (407), and Worcestershire (395) but few from the other counties represented in Alpine. P. A. M. Taylor, *Expectations Westward; The Mormons and the Emigration of Their British Converts in the Nineteenth Century* (Edinburgh: Oliver & Boyd, 1965), p. 248.

[24] I have gathered these data from "family group sheets" or family reconstitution forms in the Latter-day Saint Family History Library in Salt Lake City. Each sheet provides a demographic history of the family, with dates and places of parents' births, marriage, and deaths and the place of the birth of each child. I have considered the last place of residence prior to departing from England to be that of the vital event chronologically preceding a vital event showing a residence in the United States, though, of course, in many instances there could have been intervening moves that were not linked to vital events. A two- or three-year period between births or longer periods between a last child's birth and a parental death would provide ample opportunity for additional moving. Only the parents of each family are included in this file, and as polygamy occurred in this population, men are listed with only one of their wives, though additional wives are listed as well.

The file was drawn by compiling a list of household heads mentioned in the 1860 consensus and nonredundant household heads mentioned in the 1870 census and then drawing from the Patron's section of the Family History Library the family group sheets that could be positively linked to those families. I was able to find thirty-six completed family group sheets of fifty-seven households in my master list, or 67 percent. I drew names from both censuses in order to have a file of sufficient numbers to justify some level of generalization, assuming that the characteristics of those arriving later would not differ greatly from the characteristics of those arriving earlier. This commonality cannot be asserted with statistical precision because of the low numbers involved, but a comparison of the 1860 and 1870 lists reveals no dramatic differences. Both show a preponderance of emigrants from northwestern England, and both show considerable dispersal within that region. They came from the same region but did migrate as family or neighborhood groups, and apparently had little

The family records give us important information about this migration to Alpine. Most immigrants came as married couples, often with children, as did those of Sublimity. Twenty-two of the thirty-eight were married at the time they left England. (It seemed to Dickens that "nearly all" on the *Amazon* had children.)[25] But they did not come as broader kin or neighbor groups, as the settlers of Sublimity did. No more than four had lived in the same town prior to emigration, two couples from Pinxton, Derbyshire – George and Catherine Clark and John and Mary Healey. Our data show, as Dickens maintained, that they came from many towns and had little acquaintance prior to migration. Yet the great majority were from Lancashire and other counties close to the ports of Liverpool and Manchester, in north-west England.

This once rural, even rustic, region had become by the turn of the nineteenth century the first in the world to experience rapid industrialization and urbanization. And the most dramatic part of that transformation, with all its attending dislocations, had taken place within the half-century prior to the departure of the Alpine settlers (on average born in 1830, median 1828). Though the process by which Lancashire and the surrounding districts became industrialized is complex, and the precise linkage among the dynamic forces is debated among economic historians, the main elements seem clear enough. Lancashire and portions of the adjoining counties had been sparsely populated prior to the sixteenth century, when settlers began to clear and plow lands that had never been cultivated. Because of this relatively late clearing, the open field system and many other vestiges of feudalism were never fully operative in the region. There were few gentry, there was little influence from manorial overlords, and the predominant group was landowning yeoman farmers. (In this sense, the society began, perhaps, more like that of New England than of East Anglia.) In time the local custom of partible inheritance divided the yeoman landholdings into parcels too small to provide an adequate living, and by the second quarter of the sixteenth century many families began to convert their homes into small family spinning and weaving shops in order to augment their income.[26]

---

in common prior to migration other than their regional and social place in English society and their Latter-day Saint faith.

[25] Dickens, *The Uncommercial Traveler*, p. 633.

[26] In New England the common strategy for dealing with the same problem was for sons to move to the less settled regions of the West, with consequent undermining of paternal authority and family solidarity. See Philip J. Greven, Jr., *Four Generations: Population, Land, and Family in Colonial Andover, Massachusetts* (Ithaca, N.Y.: Cornell

This dual farming/manufacturing economy characterized large portions of the region, with 50 to 88 percent of the adult males reporting textile occupations in several Lancashire localities during the second half of the eighteenth century. As the century wore on, cotton came increasingly to supplement and then replace linen and wool as the principal fiber. All of Britain imported just under 4 million pounds of cotton in 1772, nearly 42 million pounds by 1800, and an astonishing 452 million pounds by 1841.[27] By 1790 the Lancashire port of Liverpool had become the main British entrepot for this trade. While the cotton trade grew, the domestic factory system was changing to a "putting-out" system, whereby households did not operate as independent shops but were supplied fiber and machines by a merchant who paid a set price per piece of goods produced. This minimized risks but reduced the independence of the home textile producers, and often led to specialization and fragmentation of the production process. By the 1820s, spinning machines and the power loom began to eliminate home weaving, removing both spinning and weaving to factories strategically situated for use of water power, or increasingly within easy reach of coal to power the boilers of steam engines.

These changes transformed the accustomed world of the people of northwest England. They found it necessary to alter long-practiced modes of organizing production. The home was no longer a family workplace, where they could control the rhythms of their labor. Some moved to rapidly growing towns and cities or watched their old neighborhoods become crowded, losing the stabilizing complementarity of the farming/manufacturing dual economy. Increasingly they became subject to severe seasonal and business cycle fluctuations in income.[28] Many, angered and frustrated by what was happening, organized labor unions and cooperatives, struck out to smash machines, and in other ways attempted to stem or control the tide of change.[29]

The majority of those who became the farmers of remote Alpine,

University Press, 1970); and Kenneth A. Lockridge, *A New England Town: The First Hundred Years; Dedham, Massachusetts, 1636–1730* (New York: W. W. Norton, 1970).

[27] Peter Mathias, *The First Industrial Nation: An Economic History of Britain, 1700–1914* (New York: Scribner, 1969), p. 486.

[28] John K. Walton, *Lancashire: A Social History, 1558–1939* (Manchester: Manchester University Press, 1987), pp. 10, 11, 12–15, 62, 104, 109–10, 124. The description in this chapter of the society from which the Alpine folk came relies heavily on Walton's study. More of those who came to Alpine were from Lancashire than from any other county, and nearly all of those not from Lancashire were from surrounding counties that experienced similar social and economic changes at the same time as Lancashire.

[29] The development of a working-class mentality in England is described in the classic study by E. P. Thompson, *The Making of the English Working Class* (New York: Pantheon Books, 1964).

Utah, grew up in the middle of all this. Before they left for America, they had been among the first generation of industrial workers the world had known, and thus they became twice pioneers – first, helping to define new sets of relationships between workers and the factory production system, with its wide-ranging impacts on every aspect of their society, and second, trying to build a society, literally from scratch, in the arid American West.

It is difficult to tell, except in a few cases, from precisely where in the rapidly changing social system the future Alpine settlers were drawn. P. A. M. Taylor's sample of male emigrants bound for Utah, as listed on ships' passenger lists and shipping books, offers some insights. Taylor's data do not tell us all we would like to know, but they make it clear that emigrants to Utah were principally from the ranks of skilled and semiskilled laborers, but people who did not own their own workplace – especially miners (15 percent), metal and engineering workers (10 percent), and textile workers (9 percent) – 55 percent of the whole group working in these and similar occupations. Another 32 percent were general laborers or domestics. There were at the top of the scale a few who likely owned some property and perhaps their own workplaces – shopkeepers, professionals, and clerks – some 7 percent of the sample, and a small minority of farmers (5 percent). Very few were agrarian rural people. The great majority were workers in the new industrial economy of England, owning little property, suffering by some accounts a declining standard of living, and in any case reeling from the social dislocation and unpredictability of incomes that attended industrialization.[30]

The future settlers of Sublimity, Oregon, had one important link to the new industrial economy rocking the world of future Alpiners. Since the 1660s, hogsheads of Virginia and Maryland leaf had been loaded from piers along the Chesapeake onto vessels bound for Liverpool and Manchester. By the early 1700s, many of those same vessels

---

[30] The issue has been highly controversial, with some studies claiming increased real wages between 1820 and 1850 and others insisting that living standards nonetheless declined. See Peter H. Lindert and Jeffrey G. Williamson, "English Workers' Living Standards during the Industrial Revolution: A New Look," *Economic History Review* 36 (February, 1983): 4, 13; but also see R. S. Neal's refutation in *Writing Marxist History: British Society, Economy, and Culture Since 1700* (New York: Basil Blackwell, 1985). Walton, after a careful review of the relevant literature, concluded that because of income discontinuities, poorer urban housing and diets, and increasing employment of women and children in factories, there were serious declines in the living standards of Lancashire working people in the late eighteenth and early nineteenth centuries. He maintains that despite this situation, the people were remarkably resilient, and maintained coherence in family life and essential institutions. Walton, *Lancashire*, pp. 170–80, 196–7. Taylor, *Expectations Westward*, p. 150.

were maximizing their profits by calling in West African ports on their voyage out to take on blacks, whom they carried to the Caribbean and the Chesapeake to be sold as slaves.[31] After 1800, yeomen of the American South had watched the dramatic rise in shipments of cotton to Lancashire ports, where machines – some tended by the future settlers of Alpine – spun the fiber into thread, wove the thread into cloth, and bleached and dyed the cloth for export throughout England and the world.[32]

Being yeomen, the future Sublimity settlers supplied but a small proportion of the cotton bales bound for the mills of Lancashire, but their social world, as we have seen, had been increasingly fixed and sustained by the reign of "King Cotton." The centrality of cotton after 1800 revived the moribund and archaic slave system, stifling industrial growth, rigidifying the social structure, limiting opportunity for the yeomen, and marking the region in the eyes of much of the world as a barbaric atavism. Ironically, at the same time, as historian John K. Walton, observed, "it was cotton, above all, which transformed Lancashire in the eyes of the outside world from provincial backwater to herald of a new economic system and social order."[33] The ancestral setting of the Hunt family was as much a product of the new agricultural system based upon cotton as was the world of the Healeys the product of the new industrial system that made it into cloth. And the unsettling, antipodal changes cotton brought to the two regions propelled many in both out. For the Sublimity folk, the problem seemed simple and obvious. They could never hope to pry loose from their rigid world enough land for their growing sons to claim a patrimony. It was time to seek for new. For the Alpine folk the situation was far more complex. All things – the home, the family, the purposes and products of one's labor – all were awash. They sought new ways of capturing and staying the bewildering flux that their world had become.

*   *   *

Dickens hinted that those on the *Amazon* perhaps had already found coherence and clarity – not so much in the promise of far-away Utah as in the meeting houses, streets, and homes of their native towns. He wrote, "I have seen emigrant ships before this day in June. And these

---

[31] P. G. E. Clemens, "The Rise of Liverpool, 1665–1750," *Economic History Review* 29 (May, 1976): 211–25; and Roger Anstey, *The Atlantic Slave Trade and British Abolition, 1760–1810* (London: Macmillan, 1975).

[32] Stanley D. Chapman, *The Cotton Industry in the Industrial Revolution* (Basingstoke, UK: Macmillan, 1987).

[33] Walton, *Lancashire*, pp. 103–4.

people are so strikingly different from all other people in like circumstances whom I have ever seen, that I wonder aloud, 'What *would* a stranger suppose these immigrants to be!'" The answer to Dickens's rhetorical question was, of course, that they were converts to the Mormon faith. Dickens was witnessing not the beginning, but the culmination and natural consequence for them, of one last, thoroughgoing transformation – a transformation catalyzed not by international markets, technological innovation, and reorganization of manufacturing processes, all vast and impersonal forces, but by their own decisions after being convinced that the Mormon missionaries brought a message of truth and hope. The Mormon elders taught that God had spoken and called a prophet to establish in America one last dispensation of gospel truth. For many the message resonated strongly, and they chose to make it the instrument by which they would shape for themselves a new sense of purpose and even a new identity. Dickens saw that transformation was already well along. He candidly admitted that,

> I went on board their ship to bear testimony against them if they deserved, as I fully believed they would; to my great astonishment they did not deserve it; and my predispositions and tendencies must not affect me as an honest witness. I went over the Amazon's side, feeling it impossible to deny that, so far, some remarkable influence had produced a remarkable result, which better known influences have often missed.

The "remarkable influence" Dickens observed seemed clearly to differentiate these emigrants in his mind from the ordinary lot of the English working classes. "By what successful means, a special aptitude for organization had been infused into these people, I am, of course, unable to report. But I know that, even now, there was no disorder, hurry or difficulty." He was struck by the order, discipline, and cheerfulness of those on board, quoting a report from the *Edinburgh Review* that "The Select Committee of the House of Commons on emigrant ships for 1854 . . . came to the conclusion that no ships under the provision of the 'Passenger Act' could be depended upon for comfort and security in the same degree. . . . The Mormon ship is a family under strong and accepted discipline, with every provision for comfort, decorum, and internal peace."[34]

[34] Dickens, *The Uncommercial Traveler*, pp. 634, 643, 639, 643. Dickens no doubt underestimated the British working classes. Walton's research suggests that the family remained strong, even as it was transported to urban settings, and experienced great increases in the proportions of women, children, and men working outside of the home. Reasonable stability within urban neighborhoods and a plethora of working-men's organizations, such as the Friendly Societies, countered disintegrative forces.

Something seemed to have wrought a similar transformation within the individual lives of the British working classes who converted to Mormonism, bringing them personal discipline, comfort, decorum, and some measure of internal peace. Catherine Nash, the Wiltshire dairymaid, had had three children born out of wedlock before her conversion to Mormonism in 1845. Eight years later she embarked with her family and a homeless nephew on the *Jersey*, settling in Alpine in 1853. There she established herself, working hard at her old trade to provide for her children. The family within a short time gained a respectability and station in the community they had never known in her home town of Melksham. "Kitty" Nash, as she was known, never married. When she died, she left a comfortable two-story brick home, considerable progeny, and a reputation that would endure for over a century in the town as a hardworking, wholly admirable entrepreneur and provider for her family.[35]

Family historians of Richard and Jane Fields Carlisle record that "when in 1849, they heard the Gospel preached by Joseph Edward Taylor, they found a plan of life that they had been looking for." Carlisle, once a worker in Nottingham lace mills, had settled to the life of a gamekeeper and farm laborer and had long been dissatisfied with organized religion. Under the "plan of life" Mormonism offered, Carlisle was promptly ordained into the priesthood and made "presiding elder" of the local congregation. In 1851 he, Jane, and five surviving children (all but his oldest son, who joined them later) left for Utah, though Jane died en route in St. Louis. Richard settled in Alpine about 1855, later marrying Maria Crook. He became a pillar of the community, serving as alderman in the first city government and remaining active in church and community affairs until he died in 1879 at age eighty-one.[36]

William Strong had worked in factories since childhood. After his conversion to Mormonism at age sixteen, he joined the fellow worker

Still, the fact remains that the society had undergone great changes in a short period, and stress accompanied the uncertainty that such rapid change occasioned. Moreover, Dickens claimed to be offering a comparative perspective, that is, he found passengers on this particular ship remarkable compared to those on other emigrant ships he had seen, as did the Select Committee of the House of Commons. See Michael Anderson, *Family Structure in Nineteenth-Century Lancashire* (Cambridge: Cambridge University Press, 1971); P. H. J. H. Gosden, *The Friendly Societies in England, 1815–1875* (Manchester: University Press, 1961). This literature is summarized in Walton, *Lancashire*, pp. 196–7.

[35] Merma G. Carlisle, ed., *Alpine: The Place Where We Lived* (np., nd.), BYU Archives, Provo, Utah.

[36] Betha S. Ingram, ed., *The James & John Healey Family History* (Provo, Utah: privately published, 1963), pp. 6, 12, 26–32.

who had converted him in quietly preaching his new faith among other apprentices and operatives of the Griffiths and Hopkins tin plate manufacturing firm. They converted sixteen other workers in the same factory, five of whom left for America before Strong. Strong was ordained a priest shortly before sailing. After helping to pioneer an infant settlement in Utah, the young man who began life polishing spoons in Birmingham for a penny a day became one of Alpine's leading citizens.[37]

It is difficult to know with certainty what it was in the message of the Mormon elders that attracted people like Catherine Nash, Richard Carlisle, and William Strong. The famous March 30, 1851, Sunday census of religion in England and Wales shocked established clerics with the news that they were losing the poor in the cities. Church attendance was higher in rural areas than in cities of 10,000 or more, and urban working people were the least likely to attend.[38] Yet Mormonism had reaped its greatest harvest among urban workers.[39] Nor did it attract solely the "seekers" and those from sects on the radical fringes. Malcolm R. Thorp found that more were converted from Methodism than any other religion (25 percent of 280 in his sample), with the Church of England not far behind (21 percent). The third largest pool of converts (15 percent) was from folk who read the Bible, said prayers, and believed that God could intervene in human affairs but had not joined any church.[40] What could account for the Mormon harvest in so unlikely a field?

Mormon missionary work had begun in England with spectacular success in 1837, when apostles Heber C. Kimball and Orson Hyde landed in Preston, Lancashire, and began immediately to preach their gospel.[41] The excitement they felt in their message was captured in Parley P. Pratt's Hymn, written while on his mission to England.

---

[37] Bill and Carolyn B. Strong, *The Ancestors and Descendants of Clifford Oscar Strong and Fern Paxman Miller*, Vol. III (n.p., privately published, n.d.), pp. 291–2, 294–5; 327–8.

[38] James Walvin, *English Urban Life: 1776–1851* (London: Hutchinson & Company, 1984), pp. 104–8. See also W. R. Ward, *Religion and Society in England, 1790–1850* (London: B.T. Batsford, Ltd., 1972).

[39] P. A. M. Taylor, "Why Did British Mormons Emigrate?" *Utah Historical Quarterly* 22 (July 1954): 260.

[40] Malcolm R. Thorp, "The Religious Background of Mormon Converts in Britain, 1837–52," *Journal of Mormon History* 4 (1977): 51–65, esp. 60.

[41] The story of the opening of Mormon mission work in England is ably told in James B. Allen, Ronald K. Esplin, and David J. Whittaker, *Men with a Mission, 1837–44: The Quorum of the Twelve Apostles in the British Isles* (Salt Lake City: Deseret Book Company, 1992). See also Thomas G. Alexander's valuable biography of Wilford Woodruff, *Things in Heaven and in Earth* (Champaign: University of Illinois Press, 1991).

The morning breaks; the shadows flee
Lo, Zion's standard is unfurled!
The dawning of a brighter day
Majestic rises on the world.

. . . . . . . . . . . . . . . . . . . . . . . . . . . . . . . . . . . . . . . .

Angels from heaven and truth from earth
Have met, and both have record borne;
Thus Zion's light is bursting forth
To bring her ransomed children home.[42]

Stirred by such sentiments, the missionaries in less than a year had converted 400 in Preston and 1,500 in the surrounding country. Conversions continued at a rapid rate, and the apostles, headed by Brigham Young, arrived in 1840 to take up the mission. That year they began publishing the *Millennial Star*, distributing it widely among the growing communities of Latter-day Saints. The core doctrinal messages, repeated time and time again in the *Star*, and in numerous tracts and pamphlets, including Parley P. Pratt's widely distributed *Voice of Warning*, were that God, through personal and angelic visitations to Joseph Smith, had restored the true gospel and the authority of the priesthood, which now resided exclusively among the Mormons.[43]

God had also brought forth scriptures long hidden from the world, especially the Book of Mormon. The book, which Smith said he had been inspired to translate from gold plates given him by an angel, tells the story of two migrations of Semitic peoples who had been instructed by God to escape the corruption of the Old World and come to the New. The book detailed God's dealings with them in America, including a moving description of a visitation of Christ after His crucifixion. The Book of Mormon affirmed that America is a "land choice above all others" and promised that America would be the seat of Christ's millennial reign. Thus God had opened the last and most glorious of the great religious revelatory epochs or dispensations, the Dispensation of the Fullness of Times. This dispensation was to be characterized by great polarities, as widespread catastrophes and cor-

---

[42] *Hymns: Church of Jesus Christ of Latter-day Saints* (Salt Lake City: Deseret Book Company, 1975), No. 269.

[43] Pratt's *A Voice of Warning and Instruction to All People* . . . was first published in New York in 1837, with the first British edition appearing in Manchester in 1841. Except for The Book of Mormon and twentieth-century use of Joseph Smith's 1837 account of his first vision, "Joseph Smith's Own Story," it continued throughout the mid-twentieth century to be the most widely distributed missionary literature of the Mormons. It was printed in some eighty-eight editions before 1930, including Danish, Dutch, French, German, Icelandic, Spanish, and Swedish translations. See Chad J. Flake, ed., *A Mormon Bibliography, 1830–1930* (Salt Lake City: University of Utah Press, 1978).

ruption would sweep the world, while at the same time the Jews would return to Palestine, and God would gather the faithful to America – a new covenant people destined to iterate the key teachings of all previous dispensations as they prepared to meet Christ at His return and assist in His reign.

This is the core of the doctrinal message that Mormon missionaries brought to Britain, beginning in the late 1830s. Moreover, it was clear that a serious conversion required action as well as belief. Converts entered an organization structured through a complex set of priesthood offices. Smith and Oliver Cowdery wrote that they had been ordained to the Aaronic Priesthood through an angelic visitation of John the Baptist in 1829, and subsequent revelations described the duties of the three offices within that priesthood of deacon, teacher, and priest. Later the ancient apostles, Peter, James, and John, ordained Smith to the higher or Melchizedek priesthood, with offices of elder, seventy, and high priest.[44] Subsequently, all male converts were ordained to these priesthoods, usually beginning as deacons and advancing from office to office and from lower to higher priesthood. Some were ordained to be bishops, to care for temporal needs of the Saints, and later to preside over congregations. In 1835 Smith began to select and ordain apostles, twelve of them designated as a quorum equal in power and authority to the First Presidency, the latter consisting of Joseph Smith and two or more counselors. He also ordained his father to be a patriarch, an office that was to continue in the Smith family. The patriarch gave blessings to church members that amounted to a personal prophecy of their potential in life and an indication of their descent, through lineage or adoption, from ancient Israel.

Priesthood officers, usually elders in the missions, presided over congregations called "branches" (or, in Mormon areas of the States, "wards," presided over by Bishops). Several branches formed a conference or district, headed by a presiding elder. (In the United States, several wards comprised a "stake," which came to be presided over by a stake president and high council of twelve high priests.) Regular General Conferences of all saints were held – in April and October in the States, and at these and other designated times in the mission field.

The priesthood offices provided the basic structure for an elaborate hierarchy that administered proselytizing and pastoral care. The first *Millennial Star* had a long article on the duties of membership and of holders of each priesthood office. A principal duty of the apostles seems to have been to ensure consistent and orderly exercise of those

[44] Doctrine and Covenants, Sections 13, 20, 42, 84.

offices. Typical of dozens of such entries was an 1840 letter from missionaries in Herefordshire, who reported that "before leaving the Saints, we considered it wisdom to set in order the church, and organize them into Branches, and Conferences, that they might be properly represented before the General Conference." The minutes of a conference held in Stanley Hill, Castle Froome, Herefordshire, record that "the President, followed by Elder Richards, then proceeded to give such instruction to the Saints concerning the order of the Church and the several duties of the members, as the Spirit directed."[45]

Frequently the *Star* not only instructed the Saints in the functioning of the various offices, but printed stern reminders that all were to respect and be obedient to those having authority, such as the letter of apostle David W. Patten:

> Therefore brethren, beware concerning yourselves, that you sin not against the authority of this dispensation, nor think lightly that those whom God has counted worthy for so great a calling, and for whose sake he hath made them servants unto you, that you might be heirs of God, to inherit so great a blessing, and sit there with the ancient of days, even Adam, our father, who shall come to prepare you for the coming of Christ, our Lord.[46]

Debating with a Primitive Methodist minister on the Isle of Man, apostle John Taylor emphasized the exclusiveness of the Mormon priesthood. "He [Taylor] did not believe that the church of Christ was divided into sections. The Holy Spirit did not inspire one party with one opinion and another party with another opinion; God was not the author of confusion; there was one God, one faith, and one baptism." A hymn called "I'm a Saint" affirmed, "I fear not old priestcraft, its dogmas can't awe, I've a chart for to steer by that tells me the law."[47]

Thus Mormonism offered workers of northwest England beliefs and doctrines emphasizing the importance of authority and order, and, perhaps more important, church leaders implemented a program whereby poor and dispossessed males were given priesthood office – ordained to positions in an elaborate hierarchy of authority that all were urged to respect and follow. The Mormons undercut the authority of the established Church of England priests not by preaching, as did most dissenters, that converts shared in a vague "priesthood of all believers," but by laying their hands upon the heads of ordinary people, endowing them with clearly delegated priesthood authority

---

[45] *Millennial Star* 1 (March 1840): 83, 88.
[46] *Millennial Star* 1 (September 1840): 127; reprinted from *Elder's Journal* (July 1839): 39.
[47] *Millennial Star* 1 (November 1840): 179; 12 (April 1850): 128.

they claimed came directly from God and from no earthly institutions. Women, too, were brought closer to priesthood authority by the fact that it was exercised not by a cleric who was socially and culturally remote, but by their own husbands, fathers, or sons. The high responsibility of holding priesthood office was brought home by Brigham Young in his observation that "Christ, Himself, had to be given the priesthood to qualify him to minister," and he underscored the general blessing of having the priesthood among the Saints by ensuring them, using words applied to ancient Israel in Exodus 19, that "ye are a chosen generation, a royal priesthood, a holy nation, a peculiar people."[48]

There was another part of the Mormon elders' message, however, that was to be of transcendent importance to the new communicants. That was the doctrine of the "gathering." As indicated earlier, the messages concerning the corruption of the world and the signs of the times were always accompanied with the admonition to flee the world – "Babylon," as they called it – and gather with the Saints. The 1839 letter from apostle Patten concluded, "the time is at hand, therefore, gather up your effects, and gather together upon the Land which the Lord has appointed for your safety." Joseph Smith in 1831 had designated Jackson County, Missouri, as the new Zion and gathering place, but in 1833 mobs drove the Mormons from the county and in 1838–9 from Missouri altogether. The new city of Nauvoo, Illinois, became the first American Zion to which British Saints were urged to gather. It was from there that Francis Moon, one of the early British converts, wrote counsel to his countrymen back home. He assured them that "the gathering of the people of God has been a subject of great importance in all ages of the world. – The children of Israel must be delivered from the bondage of Egypt." Continuing the metaphor, he urged them to gather so that they might escape the coming tempest and offer a sacrifice in a sanctuary built with their own hands.

> And when you bid your native land farewell, when you forsake father and mother and what you may call friends, and set your face towards the Land that the Lord has blessed, may the same principles that bore up the mind of Moses in his afflictions in the wilderness yield comfort to you, for he chose rather to suffer with the people of God than to have the pleasures of sin.[49]

Four years later, in 1844, Joseph Smith was assassinated. For the next three years there was confusion as to who his ultimate successor would be and, with increasing pressures to leave Illinois, where a new

[48] *Millennial Star* 1 (January 1841): 221.
[49] *Millennial Star* 1 (February 1841): 252–3.

Zion might be. In 1847 Brigham Young led an advance party to the Great Salt Lake Valley, and upon his return to the temporary Mormon settlements on the Missouri River, he resolved both issues. That winter he sent out the famous apostolic letter announcing that a new gathering place had been found, and shortly thereafter was confirmed as the new prophet and successor to Smith. Having presided over the British mission during its most fruitful period, he was well acquainted with the Saints there and felt strong affection for them.

> To the Saints in England, Scotland, Ireland, Wales, and adjacent
> islands and countries, we say, emigrate as speedily as possible to
> this vicinity, looking to and following the council of the presidency
> at Liverpool; . . . Tell [converts] to flee to Zion, – there the Servants
> of God will be ready to wait upon them, and teach them all things
> that pertain to Salvation, . . . Should any ask, where is Zion? tell
> them in America; and if any ask what is Zion? tell them the pure
> in heart.[50]

The gathering henceforth took upon itself a new and positive dimension, for its object was no longer just to escape the world and be with the Saints. Under a new Joshua, the Saints were moving into a promised land. They now were entrusted, as a spiritual obligation, with the task of erecting the bricks and mortar of Zion in a remote region hitherto unsettled by whites. And in that process, the skills of the British Saints were of vital importance. As Brigham Young put it in an 1849 letter to Orson Pratt, then presiding over the British mission:

> We want a company of Woollen Manufacturers to come with
> machinery, and take our wool from the sheep, and convert it to the
> best clothes. . . . We want a company of Cotton Manufacturers,
> who will convert cotton into cloth and Calico. . . . We want a
> company of Potters, we need them, the clay is ready, and dishes
> wanted.[51]

In 1850 the Territorial Legislature of the New State of Deseret incorporated the Perpetual Emigrating Fund Company, founded to oversee emigration and to raise funds for the gathering of poorer Saints, who were expected to repay the advance after their arrival. Increasingly, local church leaders were preoccupied with the evacuation of the British Saints. As the tasks of establishing savings accounts for emigration, administering PEF funds, and organizing and implementing the emigration itself became dominant, the purview of priesthood officers in

[50] "General Epistle from the Council of the Twelve Apostles to the Church of Jesus Christ of Latter Day Saints Abroad, Dispersed throughout the Earth," *Millennial Star* 10 (March 15, 1848): 81–8.
[51] *Millennial Star* 12 (April 1, 1850): 141.

Britain was extended. In 1851 apostle Franklin D. Richards made it clear to the presidencies of the various conferences that "you are appointed to preside over all the affairs of our Conferences, both of a temporal and of a spiritual nature."

Thus the Mormons offered to the working men and women who eventually made their way to Alpine salvation, in its many dimensions, and a structure to propel them toward it. But if we know what the Mormons said, can we hope to know what the people heard? How and why did they receive the message? At the most evident and conscious level, they listened, studied, prayed, and believed that the spirit confirmed the validity of what they had been taught. Yet, at another level, it is hard to avoid the suspicion that Mormonism helped the converts toward a sense of control over the deep and perplexing problems of their new industrial world. That is to say, the promise of Mormonism to effect authority, unity, order, and predictability in their lives – a "plan of life," as the Carlisles put it – resonated deeply. William Chandless, a non-Mormon adventurer and journalist from England, visited Salt Lake City in 1856 and inquired of several of the converts from his homeland their reasons for entering Mormonism. In his immediate Salt Lake City neighborhood he found "a cabinet-maker, a carpenter, a tinman, a Nottingham stocking-weaver, a Cornish miner, and a Yorkshire tailor."

Chandless found that the cabinet maker "had a good opinion of Mormonism, and a better of himself; he prophesied vast success to the Church, and hinted at his own rise in it. . . . He was a restless, ambitious temperament, and if he had not been a Mormon, would certainly have been a Chartist, and an unfavourable specimen of that." The carpenter believed in Mormonism "with a child-like simplicity, . . . but did not else trouble his head about the matter: he had come to Salt Lake because he was told, and if ordered elsewhere, would go as a matter of course: that was the history of his mind." The tailor "must have become a 'saint' when oblivious to the outer world, and on that one point remained intoxicated ever since, for he professed a special admiration of the Book of Mormon." The miner, he found, was illiterate and had joined Mormonism because he was angered by a payment that he could not afford required by the established church for the funeral service of a brother. "He heard of a strange set of men called Mormons, who charged nothing for their services in religion; he was baptized at once without enquiry into doctrine."[52]

If we read past Chandless's light treatment of the religious convic-

[52] William Chandless, *A Visit to Salt Lake; being a Journey across the Plains and a residence in the Mormon Settlements at Utah* (London: Smith, Elder and Co., 1857), pp. 210–13.

tion of his erstwhile countrymen, we can discern some clues as to what may have attracted them to the new faith. The cabinet maker obviously saw himself as part of an emerging new order, and gained self-esteem from that understanding and his expected role in it. The carpenter, and perhaps the tailor as well, had hoped to find an authority not deriving from the ecclesiastical elites of England to help them in understanding and ordering the rapid changes affecting their world. Once converted, they were willing to let their fortunes be determined by church leaders who offered a prescribed program for their lives, but who also endowed them with the authority to take an active role in shaping and implementing that program for their own families and for those of others as well. The miner was incensed at an established religion that charged money for access to God and embraced Mormonism as a rejection of the venality of traditional authorities in his native Cornwall.

If we consider the rapid pace of change that industrialization had brought – its unremitting breaking down of the old order – another dimension of the appeal of the new religion would seem understandable. Once there had been an order where one's station was reasonably clear and well defined through social position and livelihood. But urbanization and factory work had within living memory changed all that. Would not some of those marginalized by such processes find solace in an organization that undercut the old regime and promised to place them squarely in the van of world history? Men once had presided in their homes over the family production of food and yarn or cloth to sell for cash. Now a foreman called the tune, and in a factory that paid well at times but often cut them off for long periods without the means of survival. In such circumstances, would not some feel a loss of control and authority and be attracted to a church claiming authority legitimized by God? To those who resented the power factory owners and capitalists wielded – the establishment that most directly touched their lives – would not the promise of being personally endowed with this "restored," superior authority be wonderfully tempting? To people who experienced industrialization as physical and social dislocation, would not the promise of a divinely guided order be great? In a society wracked by the cries of Luddites, Chartists, Owenites, and others, would not some long for a clear, strong voice that rose above them all to promise unity and harmony?

Add to all this the commandment to gather – to leave the entire confusing scene behind and start life anew, where "the Servants of God will be ready to wait upon them, and teach them all things that pertain to Salvation" – and the forces that drew the Nashes, Healeys, Carlisles, and Strongs to Alpine seem obvious enough. Religious teachings – heard, embraced, and deeply felt at that level – nonetheless were voiced in words and phrases that could as aptly have been applied to deep-seated economic, social, and indeed cultural anxieties. At the heart of the matter were fundamental oppositions of chaos and order, fragmentation and unity, dissension and harmony. These people cried out for new authority to endow them with new identities and heard, in the message of the Mormon elders, an answer to their prayers.

Thus deep, unarticulated discontents reinforced the good news that God had spoken from the heavens and sent new prophets to convey His word, giving tens of thousands a determination to put their own lives on a new course. This was the mechanism that had wrought the "remarkable influence" so mystifying to Dickens, who, expecting to see on the Amazon the dregs of British industrial society, found instead "the pick and flower of England." Small wonder that, as these people boarded their respective vessels, "they feel that this is not their home, and their eyes and expectations are westward."[53] It was common for them to sing a favorite hymn as their ships pulled away:

> The harvest is great, and the laborers are few;
> But if we're united, we all things can do;
> We'll gather the wheat from the midst of the tares
> And bring them from bondage, from sorrows and snares.
>
> We'll go to the poor, like our Captain of old,
> And visit the weary, the hungry and cold;
> We'll cheer up their hearts with the news that He bore
> And point them to Zion and life evermore.
>
> O Babylon, O Babylon, we bid thee farewell;
> We're going to the mountains of Ephraim to dwell.[54]

So, twice fired – in the furnace of overwhelming industrial change and then in the kilns of religious renewal – a stream of English workers set out for Utah, eventually to find a niche in the mountains of Ephraim indeed – in Alpine, Utah. The settlers of the Oregon town of Sublimity were bringing to the Far West a different culture – unremittingly rural – and in many respects archaic and backward-looking; those of Alpine were bringing an urban culture direct from the hotbed of the Industrial Revolution, but much modified by their conversion to Mormonism. Once in Alpine they seemed, perhaps understandably,

---

[53] *Millennial Star* 23 (December 1861): 141.
[54] *Hymns: Church of Jesus Christ of Latter-day Saints* (Salt Lake City: Deseret Book Company, 1975), No. 344.

to look in both directions. Those who settled Middleton represent yet another society, thoroughly American yet from an America that had been through fires of its own since the Hunts loaded their wagons and took leave of Indiana and the Nashes bid farewell to Wiltshire to make a new home in Alpine City.

* * *

Middleton settlement took place in a rush, within two years of the discovery of gold in the Boise Basin in August 1862. The McKenzies, Wrights, and Montgomerys were not atypical. The McKenzies were among the nine Yonsider (Oregon or California) families that helped settle the area. Robert had been born in Pennsylvania, Emma in Wisconsin, but they had come to Middleton by way of Oregon. Robert came first, with his brothers Alexander and John, arriving in 1864 and promptly taking advantage of the 1862 Homestead Act to file a claim on land four miles west and south of what would be Middleton village. The next year his wife and infant son joined him, and he settled down to a life that alternated freighting and farming, both clearly tied to the lucrative business of servicing mining camps.[55]

Junius Wright was a native of Virginia; his wife, Elizabeth, was from Indiana. They came to Idaho from Monterey, Iowa, a small village five miles above the Missouri border. Wright recalled that with the coming of the Civil War, "roving bands of Bushwhackers and horse thieves were troublesome along the border, stealing horses for the Southern Confederacy, recruiting for Gen. [Sterling] Price's army and often committing murder." In 1863, as the war continued to cause distress and tension along the border states, "the news spread all over the United States that rich gold mines were discovered in Montana and Idaho." This news, under the circumstances, had a powerful effect. "The turmoils of war and politics had become irksome and the new Gold excitement was a great relief to the people of the Middle West. Thousands were trekking to the Gold Mines." The Wrights decided that "it was a good time now to take our long delayed honey moon trip." They headed west in a buggy, planning to visit Utah and the mines of Montana and Idaho until the war was over and then return to Iowa.[56]

Of William Montgomery, born in Illinois, we know much less. He is one of the many hundreds of pioneers who had a moment of dis-

---

[55] Martha Knight, "The McKenzie Story," in Morris Foote, compiler, *One Hundred Years in Middleton* (Middleton, Idaho: *Boise Valley Herald*, 1963), pp. 10–14.

[56] Junius B. Wright, "Autobiography," section titled "Our Honey Moon," manuscript in Idaho State Archives, Boise, Idaho, pp. 1–6. The Wright memoir was written in sections, each numbered separately.

tinction in being first, but then, after staying a few years, disappeared from local memory. His principal Middleton connection lies, according to his own account, in identifying a site for the town on a likely hot, muggy July 23, 1863. The new settlement was to be on government land just north of the Boise River, twenty-two miles downstream from Boise City, and was to be named Middleton because it was about midway between Boise City and Fort Boise, near where the river flows into the Snake. It was a year and a half, however, before Montgomery got around to surveying the site and recording the plat with county officials in Idaho City. As the next decade began, Montgomery was living in the town with his wife and two young children. They apparently ran a boarding house, for seven others, including one married couple, were in the same household. Before the 1880 census, however, Montgomery had moved on, perhaps never to see the fruit of his moment of entrepreneurial glory. Even in this act of disappearing from the place after a brief sojourn, he was not atypical, as we shall see.[57]

Seven years almost to the day after Montgomery picked his town site, census taker Stafford Mowry made his rounds on the lower Boise, riding from farm to farm along paths that the wagons of the Oregon bound had imprinted on the land, recording in a flowery hand what Middleton's early settlers were like. As he entered the district I have chosen to call Middleton, he reached family number 124 of his census. There, about four miles upriver (east) from Middleton town, he found a farm family that had arrived in 1867 from Oregon – Alexander Blessinger, thirty-two, born in Pennsylvania; his wife, Maria, from Illinois (they had married in Oregon); three-year-old Laura, born in Oregon; and the baby, Charles, born in Idaho. Fifteen-year-old Charles Crosby, also from Oregon, lived with them and worked as a farm laborer. Blessinger told county tax assessors that year that his sole worth was $145 in personal property, but when Mowry called, he claimed $1,500 in land and buildings and $200 in personal property.[58]

Stopping next at the Herons, Swalleys, and Seaveys, Mowry continued, crossing out of Middleton district at times and then back again, until he had visited fifty-two families in the greater rural district, including the Montgomerys and five other households in the town center. His Middleton peregrination ended eight miles downriver from the Blessingers with the David Dodd, Elijah Frost, and George Ligget

[57] Foote, *One Hundred Years*, pp. 14–15; and Middleton Centennial Book Committee *Middleton: In Picture and Story* (Nampa, Idaho: Downtown Printing, 1989), pp. iv, 2.

[58] U.S. manuscript census, schedule 1, population, 1870; and Foote, *One Hundred Years*, p. 71.

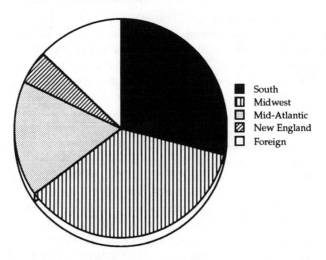

Figure 2.3 Middleton, Idaho. Birthplaces of early settlers.

households. If Mowry was a gregarious sort, who enjoyed summer rambles and front porch visits, it must have been for him pleasant work.

He found a people that bore at first glance a resemblance to those who had settled Sublimity almost two decades before. As in the Oregon district, most of the adults had been born in the American South and in the Midwest. Yet, unlike Sublimity, those from the two regions were fairly evenly balanced – 28 percent from the South (Sublimity, 56 percent) and 35 percent from Midwest (Sublimity, 25 percent). There was no single group in Middleton that could by sheer numbers dominate and attach its own peculiar character to the place, as the southerners did in Sublimity and the English in Alpine. Twenty-three of the Middleton settlers had been born in Ohio but nineteen in Missouri; seventeen in Pennsylvania but twelve in Indiana. No other of the twenty states and seven foreign countries represented in the town had more than ten of their native sons and daughters present there. Ohio was geographically and culturally distant from Missouri, as was Pennsylvania from Indiana, and these polarities bespeak a strikingly diverse and fragmented character in the whole population that, as we shall see, seems to have entered many aspects of life.

Powerful events had transformed the lives of stateside Americans in the score of years that passed between the 1840s, when the Hunts departed, and the 1860s, when the Wrights went west. New transportation networks – first canals, then railroads – broke down isolation and opened steady accessible markets for the products of inland farmers. In 1818 transportation costs pushed western flour to $2.48 more per barrel in New York than in Cincinnati. By 1858 the price difference was only $0.28.[59] At the same time, cities were growing rapidly, a growth fed partly by the expansion in America of the factory system of production that earlier had so greatly affected the lives of the Alpine settlers in their native England, and partly by the mushrooming of western milling and trading cities like Rochester, New York, Cincinnati, and Chicago. Those dwelling in cities of both types needed flour from wheat they could not grow and demanded milk, eggs, meat, and vegetables – the high prices they paid for food inducing farmers to allocate ever more of their produce to commercial sale.

A major component of this urbanization was the growing influence of New England on the northern Midwest. The new canal and rail systems linked the two regions, speeding Indiana wheat to New York bakeries and drawing a growing stream of settlers down from the Northeast, who proceeded to take up lands along the hitherto sparsely settled southern shores of Lake Erie and Lake Michigan. Their acquisitive and commercial mentality gradually began to dominate the older yeoman culture that two decades before had followed the courses of the Tennessee and Ohio rivers to found the "Egypt" and "Hoosier" sections of southern Illinois and Indiana (and had fed the migration to Sublimity).[60]

The more commercial orientation of the new Yankee population accelerated the trend toward commercialization on all the farms of the Midwest, with even yeoman moving toward efficient production of staple crops to be sold for cash to exporters. John Mack Faragher found that in the Illinois prairie town of Sugar Creek, "increasingly, during the 1840s and 1850s, farm owners oriented their work to the production of agricultural commodities, . . . convinced that transportation development offered the best way to break into the market economy." Even in the Georgia upcountry, a stronghold of subsistence farmers, there was by the 1850s a discernible trend toward staple ag-

[59] James M. McPherson, *Ordeal by Fire: The Civil War and Reconstruction* (New York: Alfred A. Knopf, 1982), p. 8.

[60] The early settlement of the lower Midwest and the later influx of settlers from the Northeast into the upper Midwest are described in Richard Lyle Power, *Planting Corn Belt Culture: The Impress of the Upland Southerner and Yankee in the Old Northwest* (Indianapolis: Indiana Historical Society, 1953). See also Henry Clyde Hubbart, *The Older Middle West: 1840–1880* (New York: D. Appleton-Century Company, 1936). Especially insightful is Andrew R. L. Cayton and Peter S. Onuf, *The Midwest and the Nation: Rethinking the History of an American Region* (Bloomington: Indiana University Press, 1990).

riculture.[61] Nationwide, between 1820 and 1860, the proportion of farm products sent out for commercial sale rather than used on the farm doubled.[62]

Sharpening these long-term changes, as Junius Wright's narrative suggests, was the cataclysm of the Civil War.[63] Farmers throughout the Midwest expanded production to fill a brisk demand for the food, fiber, and draft animals needed by the Union armies. In the lower Midwest, rural people supplied a highly lucrative trade with the South in foodstuffs in 1860 and 1861, and thereafter smuggled a considerable flow of their produce downriver to the Confederacy, as well as to suppliers of Union armies.[64] The new center of the midwestern grain trade, Chicago, underwent convulsive growth, and even older cities serving the lower Midwest, such as Cincinnati and Indianapolis, prospered as never before. The wartime prices for the farm goods fixed the farmers' attention on markets and the commercial potential of their land; with increasing demand and a reduced work force, it stimulated the use of machinery to make all the land pay. In consequence, there were subtle but important alterations in the meaning farmers attached to the land and in the purposes of agrarian productive enterprise. In the two decades from 1845 to 1865, the character of midwestern rural society shifted in a manner that left places like Sublimity and Alpine – remote from rail links to the East and far from the fighting – in a different world.

Though an economic boost for much of the Midwest and Northeast, the war was a societal bane, wrenching the lives of individuals in painful and lasting ways. Verbal and at times physical battles over secession and the justice of the war tore at the social ligaments of Maryland, southern Pennsylvania, western Virginia, Kentucky, Tennessee, Missouri, Kansas, and even extensive sections of Ohio, Indi-

---

[61] Hahn, *Roots of Southern Populism*, p. 85; Faragher, *Sugar Creek*, pp. 177–8. See also Clarence Danhof, *Change in Agriculture: The Northern United States, 1820–1870* (Cambridge, Mass.: Harvard University Press, 1969); Allan Bogue, *From Prairie to Corn Belt: Farming on the Illinois and Iowa Prairies in the Nineteenth Century* (Chicago: University of Chicago Press, 1963); Hal Seth Barron, *Those Who Stayed Behind: Rural Society in Nineteenth-Century New England* (New York: Cambridge University Press, 1984).

[62] McPherson, *Ordeal by Fire*, p. 9.

[63] See the provocative piece by Maris A. Vinovskis, "Have Social Historians Lost the Civil War? Some Preliminary Demographic Speculations," *The Journal of American History* 76 (June, 1989): 34–58. I am grateful to a colleague, L. Ray Gunn, for calling my attention to this article.

[64] Trade with the South increased dramatically in 1860 and 1861 and goods continued to be smuggled south throughout the war. Hubbart, *Older Middle West*, pp. 155–60, 218–3. E. Merton Coulter, "Effects of Secession on the Commerce of the Mississippi Valley," *Mississippi Valley Historical Review* 3 (December 1916): 275–300.

ana, Illinois, and Iowa. Neighbors castigated one another as "Black Republicans" or (the worst verbal abuse in the North or South) "Abolitionists," or as "Copperhead" traitors to the Union. The acrimony partisans brought to the public debate ate at the ties of consensus that had been the basis of public order and coherence. It led to secession in Tennessee; to internal warfare and violent faction in Virginia, Missouri, Maryland, Kentucky, and Kansas; and to discontent among the yeomen of lower Ohio, Indiana, Illinois, and Iowa, who resented the power of the arriviste Yankee majority in northern portions of their states.

In 1861 and 1862, as the war revealed itself to be real and deadly, the debate took new forms. Peace factions arose in all the midwestern states, and after initiation of the draft in July 1862, resistance became widespread and violent. In Ohio, the "Holmes County insurgents" – gangs numbering as many as fifty men – intimidated and openly defied draft authorities. Noble County newspapers reported an organized "conspiracy" to persuade soldiers to desert. Draft resisters were active in as many as nineteen Indiana counties as mobs burned draft records and attacked, abused, and in some instances killed draft officers. In Illinois draft officials had to be protected by federal troops. A riot in Danville resulted in five deaths. The killing of an antiwar activist in Keokuk County, Iowa led to widespread fighting and terrorism.[65] All this turbulence caused many to cast about for a possible distant haven.

A more direct instrument of upheaval was the course of the war itself. During the summer of 1861, young farm boys from throughout the Midwest volunteered and marched away in spirited companies to join battle with the secessionists. The early optimism quickly faded as the lethal combination of traditional tactical maneuvers and high-technology weaponry decimated regiment after regiment. The character of the war was revealed in all its horror at the Battle of Shiloh on April 6–7, 1862. Some 75,000 Union troops faced 45,000 Confederates near the Shiloh country church in west Tennessee. In two days of seesaw fighting, *each side* suffered more than 1,700 killed and 8,000 wounded. A Union soldier wrote, "The dead and wounded lay in piles. I gave water to some poor wounded men, and then sought food in an abandoned camp near us." A Confederate survivor was sickened by what he saw. "O it was too shocking too horrible. God grant that I may never be the partaker in such scenes again."[66]

---

[65] Hubbart, *Older Middle West*, pp. 194–8.
[66] This and other battles of the war are described in McPherson's *Ordeal by Fire*, esp. pp. 225–9. The quotes are from pp. 228–9.

Though Shiloh saw the greatest wartime carnage in the Western Hemisphere prior to that time, six subsequent Civil War battles would surpass it in the number of dead and wounded. By the end of the war, more than 3 million men had born arms, over 2 million in the Union forces and nearly 1 million in the Confederate. In the South, 61 percent of all white men between thirteen and forty-three served in the Confederate military, and in the North 35 percent in the Union armies. People from the towns and villages of the North lost 360,000 of their young men; from the South, 258,000. One of every six Yankee boys who went off to the war would die; one of every four Southrons.

Faced with such odds, it is not surprising that many deserted their units. Despite the possibility of summary execution if caught, 200,000 deserted from the Union military and 104,000 from the Confederate, in both cases approximately one in ten.[67] In addition to the ravages of formal battles, guerrillas, outlaw gangs, and renegades roamed along the border areas of the Midwest, pillaging and murdering those they deemed their enemies in the conflict. It was precisely such turmoil that led Junius Wright and his young bride to flee their southern Iowa home in 1863.

Those who fled the wartime dislocation, whether private citizens, draft dodgers, or deserters, were thereby expressing an attitude concerning their relationship to the rest of their society. They had decided that the threat the war posed to their personal lives was too great to be endured further. For them, not duty, honor, patriotism, or a desire to continue close in association with family and accustomed friends could outweigh the promise that in the West they would be relieved of the stress of war. The decision to head west for such people was in some measure an expression of individualism, an avowal that personal safety was more important than societal approbation or connection. The migration was in this sense selective. It was selective in other ways as well.

As is common in most frontier areas, the population heading west in the 1860s was dominated by young men. The sex ratio in Idaho in 1870 was 580 – that many men for every 100 women. A typical Idaho town of 116 had but 13 females.[68] These circumstances helped for a

---

[67] The data were gathered by Vinovskis from various sources. Vinovskis calculated that in the Civil War there were 182 military deaths per 10,000 of the population. In comparison, in Vietnam there were 3 military deaths per 10,000. See Vinovskis, "Civil War," pp. 36–9.

[68] Data calculated by the author from information in the manuscript of the 1870 U.S. census and from the printed population schedules of the same census.

considerable time to impart a certain asocial character to the new settlements in the Rockies, reflecting a common aspect of heavily male
societies, and at the same time reinforcing a disposition toward the
pursuit of personal rather than the societal aims embedded in family
and community life. The Rev. Daniel S. Tuttle, Episcopal missionary
bishop to Montana in the late 1860s, traveled throughout the Rocky
Mountains ministering to his flock. Silver City, Idaho, he described as
"a rough, rocky barren mountainside." Idaho in general, he felt, "does
not seem to me to be as rich or as homelike as Montana. Less land is
cultivated; The towns are smaller and poorer." Writing to his wife
from Idaho City on a Sunday afternoon, he complained that "I can
hardly think and write, for hundreds of men and boys are shouting
their best in exultation over the winning horse coming in. The street
is a fair specimen of pandemonium. My imagination must be laid
under tribute for me to think it Sunday."[69]

The migration west in the 1860s, then, was selective, bringing a
people perhaps more prone to be individualistic in any case, and a
people who, because of imbalance in age and sex ratios, were prone
to feel less obligated to the broader society and less restrained in personal behavior by societal norms. But the migration began during the
war and continued after it ended. It is likely that the warfare had the
added effect of altering the value systems of many of the men in
combat, reordering in some measure their sense of their own primary
purposes and goals in life. A reaction to the Vietnam War seemed to
have turned many Americans in the 1980s toward the pursuit of personal material well-being, afflicting many veterans with a distinctive,
disorienting postwar syndrome. What might the cultural consequences of the Civil War have been – a war fought for four years on
American soil, with sixty-one times as many war deaths per 10,000 of
the population as Vietnam?[70]

Historian Merle Curti concluded that in Trempealeau County, Wisconsin, the war increased the level of activity in community affairs,
diminishing prewar distinctions between older and newer settlers,
ethnic groups, and income groups. He suggested further that the war
"must have stimulated a sense of unity," but he did not present evidence to support that supposition.[71] Don Harrison Doyle found that
in Jacksonville, Illinois, the initial patriotic fervor was quickly replaced

[69] D. S. Tuttle, *Reminiscences of a Missionary Bishop* (New York: Thomas Whittaker, 1907),
pp. 133, 150, 152, 158.
[70] Vinovskis, "Civil War," p. 37.
[71] Merle Curti, *The Making of an American Community: A Case Study of Democracy in a
Frontier County* (Stanford, Calif.: Stanford University Press, 1959), p. 136.

by a hostility between those supporting and opposing the war so strong that the community suspended celebration of the Fourth of July between 1861 and 1865. Despite a stimulus to the beef and woolen industries and to manufacturing generally, the war did not change the fundamental character of the town.[72] John Mack Faragher concluded that in Sangamon County, Illinois, the conflict ultimately "demonstrated important continuities in the social and cultural life of the countryside" and "confirmed the community of feeling."[73] Robert Kenzer found that in Orange County, North Carolina, the war "compelled both the soldiers and civilians ... to become part of a larger world." Yet its social and economic consequences were short-lived, and within a decade the county returned to its old structures and relationships, centered in family, kinship, and neighborhood.[74]

The general theme of continuity offered by these studies, one suspects, is to a degree an artifact of their particular perspective. Studies of the same locality before and after the war fail, by definition, to follow those whose lives were so disrupted that they fled the community altogether, a numerically large and telling indicator of broader changes in societal values. In addition, the demographic data these scholars rely upon offer only oblique insights into possible changes in the meanings society attaches to its central elements. Families, after a "demographic fault" caused by war deaths and migration, returned in time to sex ratios and to household structures that looked much like those of prewar times; but did the role and meaning of the family in the society remain the same?

Gerald Linderman has studied the letters and diaries of soldiers on both sides and concluded that their participation in the war dramatically altered their values. At the outset, a traditional set of soldierly values prevailed, emphasizing manliness, godliness, duty, honor, and even knightliness, all undergirded by the central quality of courage – "heroic action, undertaken without fear." The meanings attached to these terms were not trite and trivial, but went to the very core of the perceived relationship between the individual and the broader society. The brutal realities of the war were to make short work of such idealism. It became evident, for example, that the once-sought honor of bearing the regimental colors led more often to death than to glory. By 1863, not even special incentives could draw out volunteers for the assignment. Jacksonville, Illinois, hoping like many communities to avoid conscription, offered bounties to those who would reenlist. In

---

[72] Doyle, *Frontier Community*, pp. 232–59.
[73] Faragher, *Sugar Creek*, pp. 225–8.
[74] Kenzer, *Kinship and Neighborhood*, pp. 96, 127.

1862 a $50 bounty attracted enough to quickly fill the quota. By 1865 a $500 bounty drew out only 40 volunteers for a quota of 113.[75]

Officers who early in the war courageously led their men into battle died in great numbers, a fact not lost on the rank and file, who as the war progressed found themselves under the command of less well-trained and experienced men. One veteran remembered that by 1864–5 "The soldiers naturally distrusted the efficacy of prayer when they found that the most devout Christians were as liable to be shot as the most hardened sinner, and that a deck of cards would stop a bullet as effectively as a prayer book." The obvious lesson the survivors took from the daring charges at Antietam, Fredericksburg, and Gettysburg was that courage bore an inverse relationship to survival and none to victory.

Despair and resignation affected soldiers on both sides as the war ground on. Avoiding conflict came more and more to be seen as an understandable reaction of youth to battle than a cause of humiliation and shame. General George Meade's decision in late 1863 to call off a Union charge against impossible odds was hailed by his men as an act of courage. At the beginning of the war, the side of courage had lain in the audacity to go against the odds. The tedium of the trenches, the familiarity with death and carnage, and the total war against civilians all had their erosive effects, obliterating conventions of war etiquette and honor. An Illinois officer told his men toward the end of the war that "Everything must be destroyed . . . all considerations of mercy and humanity must bow before the inexorable demands of self-preservation."

After being discharged from duty, the survivors became increasingly convinced that the disillusioning and dehumanizing character of their ordeal could not be understood by those at home. They commonly spoke of the war only with other veterans, and some reported being treated by civilians with condescension or even contempt. For over a decade many did not list their war service in biographical indexes, and until the 1880s it was rare for either veterans or civilians to refer to the war at all. Linderman concluded that by 1865 most would have embraced New York Congressman Roscoe Conkling's cynical early view that war "is not a question of valor, but a question of money; . . . it is not regulated by the laws of honor, but by the laws of trade."[76]

[75] Doyle, *Frontier Community*, pp. 234–5.
[76] Gerald F. Linderman, *Embattled Courage: The Experience of Combat in the American Civil War* (New York: The Free Press, 1987), esp. pp. 159, 168, 214, 264, 273. The erosive effect of the war on traditional values among the people of Missouri, the state that

The cumulative effect of the ordeal was a narrowing of the social conscience, the core of new attitudes brought home by over 2 million veterans to hamlets and towns all across America. The old values of duty and honor became obligations more to self than to comrades or the broader society. Piety had declined in an all-male society that spent more time at poker than prayers. Greed and the search for material well-being had been elevated to new levels. Historian Michael Fellman, studying changing values among Missourians ravaged by the war, concluded that "Accompanying this psychic numbing was a bottomless greed – for food, for clothing, for ornaments, for self-service at the expense of all others, and above all, for money."[77]

Most of Middleton's settlers had been touched in some measure by these events. The Spangler family left Illinois in 1864 partly to avoid the ravages of war that had devastated their Missouri/Illinois border habitat. One son had been killed while fighting for the Confederate army, another had run away to join the Confederate cause, and yet another was of draft age. They accordingly decided to head West "before the draft caught us," traveling with others who "were probably impelled by the same motives. West of Missouri were mostly territories and it seemed like going to another country." On the trail they happened to meet their son, David, who had deserted from the Confederate army and was planning to go west without the family's knowing it.[78]

In 1864 a large train of 100 wagons headed west from Missouri, a number of the emigrants having served there under Sterling Price, commander of the Confederate troops in the state. Some thirty families from the train settled in a district hence known as "Dixie" a few miles downriver from Middleton.[79] The Henry K. Hartley family came to Middleton from Missouri in 1864. Thomas Wheatley left Fremont County, Iowa, on the Missouri border that same year. Pleasant Latham, born in Kentucky, came to Idaho in 1861. The Rev. Benjamin F. Morrow left from southwestern Missouri in 1864. Indiana, Illinois, Iowa, and Missouri were the last known stateside residences of the families of Bryce Shipley, Adam Manley, Robert Clark, John Eggleston, Charles Wilson, Pleasant Latham, Silas Fowler, Lewis Kelso, Ma-

supplied the largest number of Middleton settlers, was the principal theme of Michael Fellman, *Inside War: The Guerrilla Conflict in Missouri during the American Civil War* (New York: Oxford University Press, 1989).

[77] Fellman, *Inside War*, p. 59.

[78] Mary R. Luster, *The Autobiography of Mary R. Luster* (Springfield, Mo., n.p., 1933), pp. 39, 54–7.

[79] Caldwell, Idaho *Tribune*, May 6, 1953, clipping in Jennie M. Cornell, "Pioneers of Canyon County, Idaho," Book 2.

thew Kennedy, William Dryden, John Stapleton, and Elijah Frost, all present in the Middleton area by 1870. These people left no reminiscences or other personal accounts that might give insight into their motivation. But it seems likely that the war had touched them deeply and was among the forces driving them west.

This may have been the case especially for the large number of young men identified in 1870 by Stafford Mowry, the census taker, as farm laborers, many more, in fact, than were listed as farmers (seventy-three laborers, forty-one farmers). Most of the hired hands (sixty-two) were unmarried, and all but seven had been of draft age during the war. Three (4 percent) had been born in states of the Confederacy; twenty-seven (37 percent) were from the border states of Missouri, Maryland, Kentucky, and Iowa; another sixteen were from the old Midwest; and five were from Pennsylvania. Seven were from New York, Michigan, Wisconsin, or the West Coast, and fourteen (20 percent) were foreign born. There was, as we shall see, more than one reason for so many footloose young men to be cutting hay and threshing wheat in the raw, isolated Boise Valley at this particular time, but one cannot discount the possibility that a good many had deserted their military units or had come west to avoid the draft.

The Civil War – the rancor of partisanship, the scourge of battles and border raids, the threat and actuality of conscription and death – all were strong solvents to the feelings that had attached people to accustomed lands, neighbors, and even kinfolk, strong enough even to counter the prospect of record prices for their crops. The war not only eroded attachments, it drove many away from their homes in search of haven and a fresh start. It gave them a reason to leave, but other events suggested where they should go.

In 1860, during the year of Lincoln's election, Elias Pierce, one of thousands of peripatetic miners who since 1849 had crisscrossed the mountains and deserts from California to British Columbia to Colorado to Nevada, discovered gold on the Clearwater River in northern Idaho. His discovery prompted a rush of prospectors to the Idaho Rockies, men who, oblivious to the war, worked their way south, discovering the placers of the Boise Basin in August 1862. The wave of new strikes then moved west into eastern Oregon and east to Montana, prompting rushes to both regions. The news, as it reached the eastern press, had a remarkable effect, coming, in the suggestive words of Middleton's Junius Wright, as "a great relief to the people of the Middle West." The vision of new opportunities in the remote Rockies offered distraction and a real alternative to the turmoil of the war – a relief indeed. Mark Twain, who in July 1861 had discreetly broken off a brief career as a Confederate soldier to travel as secretary to his Unionist brother Orion to Nevada, was in the van of a small army already predisposed to seek relief from the war in the distant gold and silver fields of the West. A census taken late in 1863 counted 20,000 in the Idaho territory, where virtually no whites had lived in 1860. Tax collectors found as many in Montana the next year.[80] Much of this traffic came west by way of Salt Lake City, the only substantial city in the intermountain area. Brigham Young took note of their passing in an October 1863 General Conference of the Latter-day Saints, possibly attended by the Nashes, Carlisles, or Healeys of Alpine. Young urged his followers to be hospitable to "the stranger that passes through our country in search of gold, or in search for safety. ... Hundreds and thousands who are not Latter-day Saints are ... passing through from the east to the regions north and west of us, ... all through necessity; they are fleeing from trouble and sorrow.[81]

They were, indeed. And more than that, they were seeking to ease their distress in the excited anticipation that over the next ridge, in the next hollow, might lie the bonanza that would compensate for all they had endured. The transportation revolution had created new markets, leading them to attribute meanings to the land and its products that were only peripheral to those of the preceding generation. Northerners had streamed into the heartland, adding to the growing acquisitiveness and commercial orientation of the region. The Civil War accelerated these changes, while at the same time visiting upon the people a scourge of faction, hostility, and destruction. It helped to narrow the social vision, eroding obligations to kin and community, setting many out on their own in a quest for personal satisfaction. The gold fields offered haven from the scourges of war and, more than this, the possibility of vast fortunes. The Hunts and Downings – Sublimity folk – had gone west in the 1840s, seeking land enough to fulfill their visions of an unending family identity. The Alpine folk sought refuge from the perplexing dislocations of industrialization and association with others of their new-found faith. The purposes of the Middleton people who headed west in the 1860s were centered not in family, or in community, but in securing a personal horde of gold and silver. And if wealth was not to be found in the streams, perhaps the virgin lands would do the trick.

[80] Rodman W. Paul, *The Far West and the Great Plains in Transition, 1859–1900* (New York: Harper & Row Publishers, 1988), pp. 24–30, esp. p. 30.

[81] Brigham Young Sermon, October 6, 1863 in *Journal of Discourses* vol. X (Liverpool: Daniel H. Wells, 1865; repr. 1966), p. 248. A colleague, Gordon Thomasson, kindly called my attention to this reference.

# 3    *These savage desert regions*

The decade of the 1860s is crucial to understanding the social character that ultimately triumphed in the Far West. The pioneers of Sublimity and Alpine had brought values in many respects at odds with those on the ascendant in America. Their dreams were different from those of the settlers that would follow. The 1860s saw the beginning of a new migration, a stronger, more sustained flow, represented in this study by those who settled Middleton. They were a people whose values had been altered dramatically by the Civil War and by an increasingly commercial and market-oriented rural America. The new farm and mining folk intermingled, in fact, were one and the same, and with common hopes and values built a new West.

As the 1860s approached, George and Elizabeth Hunt of Sublimity had lived there the better part of a decade.[1] They and many of their neighbors had become affixed to the lands they expected would long remain the focal point of family coherence and identity. Sublimity folk could speak with unambiguous meaning of the "Hunt Place," a choice of words rich in its implications, sharing that concept as one of many markers of their landscape. By 1857 George and Elizabeth claimed 640 acres from a Donation Land Grant. They told tax assessors in that year their land was worth something over $2,000. Yet George farmed on that extensive spread no more than thirty-five acres, raising small amounts of wheat and oats, enough to feed the family and sustain his hogs, sheep, horses, and cattle. He had established a thrifty farm, adequate to his needs and aspirations, but it was by no stretch of the imagination a commercial operation.

[1] An early version of this chapter was prepared for the "Rural Villages in the Twenty-first Century Symposium," July 20, 1990, sponsored by the Mountain West Center for Regional Studies, Utah State University, the Charles Redd Center for Western Studies, Brigham Young University, and the Utah Endowment for the Humanities. Portions also were included in the annual Critchlow Lecture at Weber State University in November 1991.

Photo 1 "Estate" of Jesse Looney, typical of Sublimity area farmsteads of the 1870s. (From *Historical Atlas Map of Marion & Linn Counties* (1878; reprint ed., Salem, Oregon: Marion County Historical Society, 1981, p. 34. Used

Photo 2 Home of George Washington Hunt, north of Sublimity, Oregon, as it was in 1992. (Photograph by the author.)

James Healey had been in Alpine six years by 1860 and, following the custom of most of the villagers, made his living on a small parcel of land that lay outside the village, seven acres, worth $60. As with George Hunt, his products were few – small amounts of rye, oats, potatoes, butter, and hay – barely enough to keep himself, his wife, six children, and eight cows through the hard Alpine winters. Neither he nor his neighbors would likely think of his farm land as an iden-tifiable "Place" in the landscape. The parcel was out of town and hence out of sight. But they *would* think of his house in Alpine town this way. His lands made him a living, but his house, set amid grid-surveyed streets lined with the lots and houses of others, not amid the fields he worked, was the symbolic center of family identity.[2]

[2] The 1860 tax rolls for Utah County are in the archives of Utah State University. A friend and colleague, Charles Hatch, discovered them there and made them available to me. The 1870 list, also at Utah State University, shows Healey with seventeen acres of land and, in the 1880 list, with twenty acres. Photographs of the Healey house in Alpine are included in the printed family history, but none of farmlands. See Betha

Photo 3 Alpine Main Street looking south, 1870s. (Used by permission of Jennie Wild.)

In 1860 no Anglo-Americans yet lived on the lands in the Boise Valley that during the next decade became known as Middleton. Only Utah, Nevada, Oregon, and Washington were populated enough to be seen as civil jurisdictions in the whole vast stretch of American country north and west of the central Rockies. The future Idaho and Montana were still vaguely defined parts of the surrounding states and territories. The settlements in the Mountain-to-Pacific Corridor – from Utah, Nevada, Montana, and Idaho, through Oregon to the Pacific – contained fewer than 100,000 Anglo-Americans, averaging 5 persons per square mile.[3] Yet the 1860s were to see dramatic changes,

---

S. Ingram, ed., *The James & John Healey Family History* (Provo, Utah: privately published, 1963).

[3] When final boundary adjustments were made, there would be 515,955 square miles in the territories that became the states of Utah, Montana, Nevada, Idaho, and Oregon. Some 99,595 Americans were visible to census takers in 1860, or 5.2 per square mile. In the present study, I have not gathered data on California, which was in some senses a world unto itself, with a Hispanic presence dating into the eighteenth century. Utah and Nevada had, of course, been Spanish and then Mexican territory prior to 1848, but Hispanics had established no missions or settlements in either. The incursion of Anglo-Europeans into this region was like that into the Oregon country – a people of European descent moving onto the lands of Native Americans who had had no persistent prior experience with other European peoples. The territory of Washington had been created by 1860, but I have not included it because it duplicates to a considerable degree the character of the Oregon population.

This chapter centers, then, on Utah, Montana, Idaho, Nevada, and Oregon as they appeared in the 1870 census. I and my assistants have gathered a file of information on each of the 667 cities, towns, or census districts in these territories and states, including aggregated wealth and occupational information from the manuscript census on all heads of household or other persons with wealth or others whose occupation made them likely to possess wealth. We have added the population of each census precinct in census years through 1910 where this could be reasonably determined, as well as sex ratios, proportion foreign born, number attending school or who could not read or write, distance to nearest early railroad or water transportation route, year railroad was completed to that point, year the settlement was founded, year abandoned if relevant, average annual precipitation, average annual temperature, elevation, and latitude and longitude coordinates.

The unit of analysis is the town or precinct, which means that all of this information, when available, has been entered into the file for each town or precinct reported in the 1870 census in each of the five states or territories. In population centers with several precincts, such as Salt Lake City or Salem, all precincts have been combined into one aggregate for the locality. Throughout the text, I commonly refer to these population centers as "towns," the term people of the time used for them. But the reader will understand that these are in some cases villages, towns or cities; in others mining or railroad or army camps; and in still others farming districts, sometimes covering a whole valley or even a county. Properly speaking, they are census precincts, except where I have aggregated the data from several precincts that are part of a single city.

Photo 4 William Johnson Strong home in the 1950s. A common house type in Alpine City. (Used by permission of Jennie Wild.)

as a flood of newcomers pushed into the region, carrying new ideas and values.

Accounts by two well-known early travelers to the Far West frame the decade of the 1860s, suggesting a transformation powerful in its consequences for the social character of the region.[4] The flamboyant British adventurer Sir Richard Burton traveled from St. Joseph, Missouri, to San Francisco in 1860. He found his journey a grueling test of endurance. His Concord coach left St. Joseph on August 7. At first, riding across the northeastern corner of Kansas, his party was in a country "unusually well populated."[5] Three days later, they reached the Platte River near Fort Kearney and began to leave civilization be-

---

[4] For an excellent overview of the period, see Rodman W. Paul, *The Far West and the Great Plains in Transition: 1859–1900* (New York: Harper & Row, 1988).

[5] Kansas had a population of 58,892 in 1860 living in some 155 towns or precincts, somewhat more than that of Oregon at the time. Nebraska territory, which included most of present Wyoming, had 28,841 inhabitants in fifty settlements, about 72 percent of the population of Utah, but nearly the same number of settlements.

hind. Making their way up the Platte, they crossed a land broken only by wretched, flea-infested stage stations that served meals of hard biscuits, bacon, or tough game washed down with watery coffee. Fort Laramie offered brief respite in "cool comfortable quarters," but the night after they left the fort, Burton and the other men in the coach slept in a station barn "hardly fit for a decently brought-up pig."

Nineteen days after leaving St. Joseph, Burton's stage entered Salt Lake City, the first settlement of any significance (8,236) since the party had struck the Platte (indeed, outside of Sacramento and San Francisco, the largest established city in the entire Far West).[6] After a three-week stay, Burton traveled on across central Utah to Nevada, edgy about possible attacks from warring Gosiute Indians. His stage arrived at Egan's station in eastern Nevada just days after angry Gosiutes had burned the buildings and killed the staff, their grim remains evident among the charred ruins. The western Nevada camp at Fort Churchill (349) and the town of Carson City (714) offered the only glimpses of settled life during the month-long trip from Salt Lake City to the foot of the Sierras. Had Burton chosen instead to travel to Oregon, he would similarly have found nothing but an occasional fort or way station until reaching the Willamette Valley. Throughout his journal the theme of desolation repeats itself again and again. The whole vast region was to Burton an unremitting wilderness – a physical, social, and (most depressingly for such an epicure) culinary wasteland – with only two or three real oases in 2,000 miles.[7]

Seven momentous years later, a young Episcopal priest, Daniel S. Tuttle, traveled from Albany, New York, to Salt Lake City. In 1866, when still twenty-nine, he had been elected missionary bishop to the Rocky Mountains. His friends made light of the refined New Yorker's being sent to "these savage, desert regions," and he himself confessed that "I did not grasp the topography of it; my ideas concerning it were very hazy." He was surprised to learn that "Montana and Nevada are not the same place, nor exactly the same region, indeed that they were a thousand miles apart." (They are but 180 miles apart in a direct line from border to border.) Having resolved that initial con-

[6] Denver had reached 4,749, and the mining boom town of South Park had swollen temporarily to 10,610. No other settlements in the upper American West surpassed Salt Lake City in population except for Sacramento and San Francisco.

[7] Sir Richard Burton, *The Look of the West, 1860: Across the Plains to California* (Lincoln: University of Nebraska Press, 1963), pp. 26, 112, 115, and passim. The population figures are from the printed returns of the Ninth U.S. Census of 1870. The Burton book cited is a photomechanical reproduction of the travel portions of Burton's *The City of the Saints and Across the Rocky Mountains to California* (London: Longman, Green, Longman and Roberts, 1862), edited and with a foreword by Robert G. Athearn.

fusion, he began systematically "to find out all I could about Montana, Idaho, and Utah," a vast area (he was again misinformed), covering 340,000 square miles and inhabited by but 155,000 persons.[8]

Yet the West of the late 1860s was far less a savage, desert region than it had been seven years before when Richard Burton crossed it. Bishop Tuttle's journey was accomplished with comparative ease. He left Albany, New York, by train on May 23, 1867, and in three traveling days reached North Platte, Nebraska, near the western terminus of the Union Pacific Railroad, then hastening its construction westward to meet the Central Pacific. Indian raids on stages and settlers in the area delayed his departure, and he set out in a convoy of four stages with armed escorts on June 9, arriving without incident at Denver on the 12th. His party left Denver by stage on June 26 and arrived in Salt Lake City a week later. Though nervous about Indians during the stage portion of his journey, he experienced little discomfort other than being dusty and tired from the long ride. His entire journey from Albany to Salt Lake City had taken fourteen days, compared with Burton's nineteen days from St. Joseph. The uncomfortable, anxious stretches from North Platte to Denver and from Denver to Salt Lake City seem in his narrative deviations from a relatively uneventful norm.

The experiences of Burton and Tuttle emphasize the important point that Willamette Valley and Utah Valley, the homes of such families as the Hunts and Healeys, had begun as distant, isolated pockets of Anglo-American culture. When Americans began to settle the Sublimity area in the late 1840s and when Alpine was founded in the early 1850s, the crossing of the continent commonly took more days than did the crossing of the Atlantic for the colonists of Jamestown or Plymouth colonies. But during the 1860s, thousands of Americans moved out of the Midwest toward the setting sun. As they settled in the valleys stretching from the Rockies to the Willamette, they peppered the "waste places" that Burton had found so tedious with hamlets and villages. This change was already evident to Bishop Tuttle when he came to Idaho in October 1867, devoting his pastoral attentions to settlers in Boise City and "a farming district up and down the valley."[9] While on that visit he may well have passed through the infant settlement of Middleton one of hundreds of new towns resulting from

---

[8] Daniel S. Tuttle, *Reminiscences of a Missionary Bishop* (New York: Thomas Whittaker, 1906), pp. 30, 31, 101. The bishop had in fact been misinformed on both counts. The 1870 census takers found but 114,968 in the three territories, whose area has since been determined to be 309,878 square miles.

[9] Tuttle, *Reminescences*, p. 145.

the great American diaspora of the 1860s. These new farm towns were not distant outposts, as the Sublimity and Alpine areas had been, but integral to a mosaic of settlement that by 1870 was touching all but the most inhospitable lands and foreshadowing clearly the West that later generations would know.

Middleton was one of these new settlements, and to it in 1864 came Junius B. Wright. We have seen that he found the turmoils of the Civil War "irksome" and the promise of adventure and wealth in the West a "great relief." He and his wife headed west in a buggy, planning to visit Utah and the mines of Montana and Idaho until the war was over and then return to Iowa.[10] But when Wright found that the mining camps were paying scarcity prices for farm commodities, he staked out a homestead claim in the Boise Valley and settled down to farming. Within a few months of his arrival, nearly all the bottom lands along the lower Boise had been claimed and were being put into production.

The gold and silver mines, then, were a powerful magnet pulling recent immigrants as well as Americans from all parts of the United States to the Far West. But, as Wright suggested, it was not the lure of gold alone that persuaded these hardy souls to leave kin, neighbors, and well-established farms to brave the perils of overland travel to what they, like Burton, thought of as a savage and desert region. The British adventurer had completed his journey to the West Coast and was just easing into the comforts of San Francisco when the news arrived that Abraham Lincoln had been elected President of the United States. On December 20, 1860, South Carolina began the secession process, and by mid-April 1861 the first shots were fired in a war that shocked the world in its brutality and devastation. Continuing for four years, until April 1865, the war wreaked widespread physical destruction, threatened millions with the draft, and frayed traditional societal ties to a thread. The Wrights were not alone in choosing the occasion for an extended trip to the West to see what prospects the gold and silver fields might offer.

Another important spinoff of Lincoln's victory in 1860 was the passage of legislation that led to the building of the transcontinental railroad. With the southern states withdrawing from the Union, opposition to a railroad crossing the central part of the country was removed and the U.S. Congress promptly passed a bill authorizing its construction, which Lincoln signed in July 1862. Knowledge that a

---

[10] Junius B. Wright, "Autobiography, " section titled "Our Honey Moon," manuscript in Idaho State Archives, Boise, Idaho, pp. 1–6. The Wright memoir was written in sections, each numbered separately.

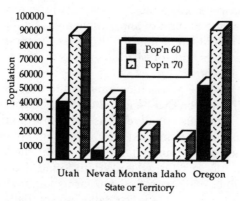

Source: U.S. Census, 1860, 1870

Figure 3.1  Population in 1860 and 1870, Mountain-to-Pacific Corridor states.

railroad was being built linking the Midwest to the Pacific no doubt eased reservations potential emigrants would have had about leaving for so isolated a region, and as Bishop Tuttle found, the actual construction itself, as it proceeded, accelerated travel and increased the flow of immigrants.

Thus, during the 1860s, three factors – the pull of gold, the push of war, the promise of a railroad – had propelled tens of thousands out of traditional and familiar haunts and into the Far West, a region that the people of Sublimity and Alpine had had pretty much to themselves. In these states and territories the population increased 157 percent during the decade, whereas the general population increased 26 percent. The 1870 census described in columns and numbers the powerful changes suggested by Burton and Tuttle as they wrote of their travels across the region. In 1860 Burton could have found only 53 settlements in all of Utah and 23 in Nevada, and had he headed that direction, 131 in all of Oregon – 207 for the entire corridor. By 1870 Bishop Tuttle (having taken up residence in Salt Lake City) could have counted 667 settlements in the region, a 222 percent increase; 174 in Utah, 117 in Nevada, 79 in Montana, 60 in Idaho, and 237 in Oregon. In absolute numbers, Utah added the greatest number of settlements, 119; Oregon, 106; Nevada, 96; Montana, 79; and Idaho, 60.[11]

[11] The 1870 count for Idaho and Montana, starting from an 1860 base of zero, represents, of course, the number of settlements they added to the region. The text should make it clear that these comparisons are from counts of towns, precincts, or districts for each state or territory in the printed U.S. Census for 1860 and for 1870. They are thus different from the following data, which are based on dates of founding for those settlements that survived to be seen as identifiable districts in the 1870 census.

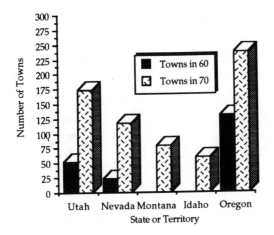

Source: U.S. Census, 1860, 1870

Figure 3.2 Number of towns in 1860 and 1870, Mountain-to-Pacific Corridor states.

But where do the people of Sublimity, Alpine, and Middleton fit into this rapidly changing world? A baseline that highlights the distinctive qualities of our three towns might be a settlement that is a composite of all the 667 towns of 1870. This imaginary town of Allton, as I call it, would have been founded in 1862. Located at 42°01' north latitude and 114°14' east longitude, barely north of the parallel that marks the northern boundary of Utah and the southern boundary of Oregon, and about ten miles west of the Nevada/Utah border, it would have been on the west fork of a stream called Goose Creek (where, in fact, there are no Anglo-European towns today, nor ever have been). The elevation would be 4,667 feet, the annual precipitation a rather arid 14.5 inches, and the average annual temperature a chilly 47.8° F. Residents would have had to haul goods to and from the nearest railroad, completed in 1880, about twelve miles away.

Who lived in Allton, and how did they make a living? There were 383 persons in 85 households, about 4.5 per household. The town was heavily male, which delighted saloon keepers and managers of hurdy-gurdy houses but caused the local minister to set his jaw. Of the residents, 142 were women, giving a somewhat unbalanced sex ratio of 180, that is, 180 men for every 100 women. Nearly a third were foreign born. About 156 held down jobs of one kind or another, 37 of them farming or ranching, 48 mining, and 50 working at service jobs, such as barbers, masons, teachers, clerks, or sheriffs. Two were rail workers, one was a lumberjack, three were in the military, and nine were unskilled laborers. Each household head had goods valued at about $2,125, some $1,091 worth of real property and about $1,034 in personal property.[12]

Allton, thus, was a fairly lively, affluent, wide-open town, more like Helena than Sublimity or Alpine. Sublimity had nearly twice the population of Allton, Alpine somewhat more than half, Middleton about two-thirds. Sublimity and Alpine both had larger households, with 6 and 5 persons, respectively, in each house, but Middleton was below the mean, with 4.2 persons. The sex ratios also varied widely, with Sublimity balanced at 99, and Alpine having somewhat more males than females at 106, but the sexes in these farm towns were more evenly balanced than in Allton, which had 180 men for every 100 women, and far more than in the farm town of Middleton, which had 187. The foreign born were generally concentrated in the mining districts, with the predominantly mining territories having proportions of foreign born ranging from 38 percent in Montana to 52 percent in Idaho. Yet only 14 percent of the Middleton population was foreign, and but 10 percent of the Sublimity people. Alpine ranked with the mining districts in this regard, with 43 percent of its whole population being foreign born, and, as suggested in the case of Sublimity, a good many more of its adult population. It is no surprise to find that occupationally our three towns, selected because they were agricultural districts, were heavily dominated by farmers, with Alpine 62, Sublimity 71, and Middleton 93 percent farm people. Yet, whereas Sublimity and Alpine are close in household size and sex ratios, suggesting a familial society such as we might expect to find in Arcadia, Middleton, even more agricultural, is in these respects closer to Allton, with its heavy mining population.

Middleton was different in part, one suspects, because it was a product of the 1860s, a period of booming growth in population and even more rapid proliferation of new settlements – three where one had been before. The growth was enough to shorten greatly the travel time from settlement to settlement and reduce the dependence of overland travelers on the miserable stage stations. Small wonder that the West did not seem as empty and trying to Tuttle as it had to

[12] See Appendix Table A.1, which summarizes the data from this file. Population, household, occupation, and wealth data are based on aggregate figures as printed in the *Report of the 1870 Census*. Other data are based on information gathered for each town from the manuscript census and from geographical dictionaries, atlases, place name books, climatological maps, and other sources for each state or territory. All Oregon towns are included in the file, but complete information has been gathered only on Marion County, thus weighting the data reported in the table from "Year of Railroad" through "Longitude" toward the areas south and east of Oregon.

Burton. Yet, the advent of the Middletons of the West heralded more than just growth in numbers. Our evidence suggests that the social character of the new West diverged sharply from that of the old. It thus becomes important to examine more closely how these new settlements came into being.

Data on the year of founding for 1870 towns and census districts provides an illuminating profile of how that process took place geographically and chronologically. Not surprisingly, they show Marion County settlement concentrated in the 1840s and 1850s, five towns being settled there before 1851, seven during the next decade (which saw Sublimity's founding), and only two during the 1860s, when Middleton was founded.[13] In the territories of Utah, Montana, Nevada, and Idaho, thirty of the 1870 settlements were founded before 1851 – all but three of them in Utah. During the next decade – 1851 through 1860 – eighty-two new settlements were added, sixty-seven of them in Utah. But the 280 new settlements made in the 1860s more than tripled the number added in any previous decade, and for the first time they were rather evenly divided among the four states – seventy-four in Utah, fifty-one in Idaho, seventy-one in Montana, and eighty-four in Nevada.[14] The 1860s were thus the formative decade for the Rocky Mountain region. The structure of future settlement and the pattern of population distribution across the landscape, barely evident in 1860, were recognizably in place by 1870.

The pace of settlement in the four states and territories was not even. Most remarkably, we see in Figure 3.3 a pattern that provides evidence for the power of the Civil War/mining forces and the impact of the transcontinental railroad in settling the Mountain West. New settlements in the four Mountain states were reasonably steady at the start of the decade – twenty-one in 1861, nineteen in 1862, and twenty-four in 1863. Then, just when we would expect that war weariness

---

[13] Date of founding is, of course, a problematical concept. In this study, I have gathered the information from geographic and place name directories, considering for each locality the first evidence of a substantial population as the date of founding – for example, the building of a mill or the establishment of a post office. Many Utah settlements have preserved accounts of their founding, with lists of founders and rather precise dates, which gives them greater reliability. But I am satisfied that nearly all the rest are accurate within two or three years. The year of founding could not be ascertained for two 1870 Marion County settlements, seven in Montana, six in Utah, eight in Idaho, and sixteen in Nevada. The data include in the Utah count one settlement made in the 1850s that later became part of Idaho, thirteen made in the 1860s that later became part of Idaho, and four during the same decade that later became part of Nevada.

[14] These figures do not account for all of the 1870 towns, as they consider only those for which the year of founding could be determined.

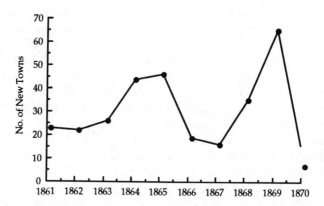

Figure 3.3 Mountain-to-Pacific Corridor states. New towns founded by year, 1861–70.

would show its erosive effects, they nearly doubled to forty-two in 1864, and the next year, as the war was drawing to its end, forty-four new settlements were added. With the war over, there were but seventeen new settlements in 1866 and fourteen in 1867, but 1868 saw nineteen new settlements in Nevada alone, bringing the total to thirty-three, and 1869 saw the greatest single year of growth in the decade, sixty-three new settlements, including twelve rail camps in Utah. The railroad boom was short-lived, however, as there were only four new settlements in the four states and territories in 1870.

Each state or territory, however, had a distinctive pattern of growth. Throughout the decade new settlements were added to Utah gradually, with no year seeing fewer than two founded or, if we discount the twelve temporary Box Elder County railroad camps of 1869, more than fourteen.[15] The greatest increment in the decade was in the three year period from 1862 through 1863, when twenty-seven settlements were added, but this is notably less than earlier similar spans. For example, thirty-three settlements (including Alpine) were added in 1849 through 1851 and forty-two in 1859 through 1861. The twenty-seven settlements made in the peak years of the 1860s were but 16 percent of all Utah 1870 settlements whose founding date we know. The central point, as Burton and Tuttle well understood, is that Utah, like Oregon, was settled early and its population centers were well in place by 1860. At the beginning of the decade it, like Oregon, constituted an agrarian island in the West, though the social character of the Utah farm people was strikingly different from that of the Oregon

[15] The year 1869 shows twenty new settlements in Utah, but twelve were railroad camps listed as separate precincts, containing only a few people each, all but three of them disappearing by 1880.

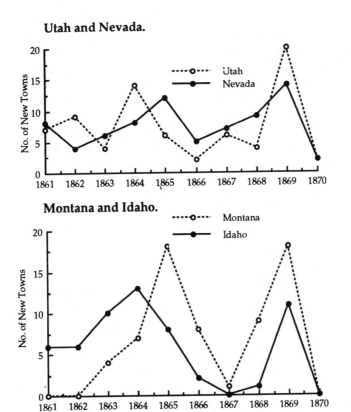

Figure 3.4 Mountain-to-Pacific Corridor states. New towns founded by year, 1861–70, Utah and Nevada; Montana and Idaho.

folk and from that of the Middleton farmers who were to come.

The other Mountain states were relative neophytes. Idaho saw six localities added in each of the years 1861 and 1862 but did not take off until 1863. The three-year span that saw the most settlements added was 1863 through 1865, when thirty-one were founded, 60 percent of all the Idaho settlements (fifty-two) for which we have date of founding through 1870. Montana lagged behind Idaho by one year, its greatest three-year span being 1864 through 1866, when thirty-three settlements were founded, 46 percent of all those founded in the territory throughout the decade. The greatest proliferation of settlements in Nevada was railroad driven, with forty settlements added in the years 1867, 1868, and 1869, 40 percent of all the settlements added prior to 1871. Eight of the forty were founded the same year the railroad reached their site and were likely creations of the Central Pacific Company. Nearly half (eighteen) of the forty were built on a railroad

line, but these new settlements were not just hell-on-wheels railroad
camps. In only one were the majority of the household heads in rail-
road-related occupations. Ten were commercial centers, their household heads employed in a variety of service occupations. Fourteen
were new mining towns, but nearly as many – thirteen – were farm
towns or towns where farming was mixed with railroading, mining,
or ranching as principal occupations of household heads. It is perhaps
more an indicator of change in self-perception than in actual means
of earning a livelihood that in a region later known for its ranching,
only four of the new towns were dominated by persons who called
themselves ranchers or who were clearly associated with the livestock
industry.[16]

[16] Typing of towns by occupation is complex and difficult. In this study, I have assigned
the occupational listing for household heads to one of eight categories – farming,
ranching, mining, service, timber, army, nautical, or other. Occupational designations
clearly related to a principal category were coded with it. For example, a farm laborer
was considered a farmer; a herder, a rancher; a woodcutter, a part of the timber
industry. "Service" or commercial industries included crafts, trades, government
workers, and professions that could not be clearly linked to one of the other categories. Those called "laborer" with no reasonable indication as to the type of labor they
engaged in were coded "other." However, when one or more laborers lived in a
household headed by a person whose occupation would likely have required hired
help, they were coded under the same category as household head. For example, in
a community comprised almost entirely of farmers, laborers living in a household
headed by a farmer were assumed to be farm laborers.

Having summed the total in each occupational category for each census precinct
or settlement, we calculated the proportion in each occupational group. A given town
might be 40 percent farmer, 30 percent service, 15 percent rancher, 10 percent miner,
and 5 percent other. Then the entire community was typed according to the following
rules. At least 30 percent of all reporting occupations had to be in one category for
the town to be typed as exclusively that. In addition, the dominant category had to
account for a percentage twice as great as that of the next occupation below it. For
example, a settlement would be typed as "f" for farming if 30 percent were farmers
and no more than 15 percent were in any other single category, *with one exception*:
The service industries were assumed to be driven by the producing industries, so that
a town that was 30 percent or more farmer and had no more than 15 percent in any
other occupation was assumed to be a farming town, even if the service component
was as high as 29 percent. In such an instance, it seemed reasonable that the farm
culture dominated even a large service sector, providing its reason for being. Hence,
a settlement could be 30 percent farmer and 28 percent service and still be typed as
a farm town. If, however, the service component was as large as the dominant component, the town was classed as mixed. If it was 30 percent farmer and 30 percent
or more service, it was typed as "fs" for farming and service or commercial. If no
producing industry was 30 percent or more of the occupations in the community, but
service was, then the locality was classed as "s" only. If no occupational group, including service, was 30 percent or more, then the town was typed with the two or
three principal occupational designations in order of magnitude. Thus "fxr" would
be a settlement where farmers, rail workers, and ranchers predominated in that

The Nevada numbers raise an important question. Though Nevada is thought of as principally a mining, railroading, and ranching state, the number of new farming towns added in peak growth years was nearly as high as those in any other category. Mining was obviously an important agent in bringing agricultural settlement into being. As we have seen, Utah and Oregon settlement began earlier and as isolated farming commonwealths, making their experience less relevant. Nevada also was settled early but had very few towns before 1859. Its first scattered population centers, formed when it was still part of Utah territory, included districts dominated by persons in both farm and service occupations. There were in Nevada before 1859 seven farming, four mining, and four service localities. In 1859, with the discovery of the Comstock Lode, mining became central to the economy. Yet from that year to the end of the decade, farm towns kept pace with mining towns. Throughout the decade 1861 through 1870 more farm than mine towns were added. Forty-one were dominated by farming or ranching or with strong components from these sectors, while thirty-three mining or strong mining component towns were added.

Montana and Idaho did not develop as strong a farming sector by 1870, but nonetheless they show a similar pattern. In the Montana of 1863, three mining and two service towns were founded, the first in the territory. The next year farming began as one of seven of the towns founded, though dominated by miners, reported a large minority of farmers. In 1865 five farm and two ranching settlements were made, and in 1866 three more. Two more followed in 1869. By the end of the decade, 20 percent of all Montana settlements were driven by farming or ranching or had a strong component from those sectors.

In Idaho there was a two-year lag between the founding of the first settlements (eight mine towns, three service towns, and one army post in 1861) and the appearance of farm towns.[17] But in 1863, five of ten towns added were farming or had strong farming components. The total by the end of 1870 was ten, during a period when forty-one mine towns came into being, one of these with a sizable farming population. About 17 percent of all settlements made in the territory during the decade were farm towns. It is clear that farm towns followed mine towns closely in Nevada, Montana, and Idaho, lagging at the longest two

order, but none was 30 percent or more of the whole occupational group. Similarly, "sfx" would be a locality dominated by service people, farmers, and rail workers in order of magnitude. Following these rules, a single or mixed occupational type was coded for each town or precinct.

[17] We have not included here the fourteen farm towns founded by Mormons in northeastern Idaho, which in 1870 were still counted as Utah settlements.

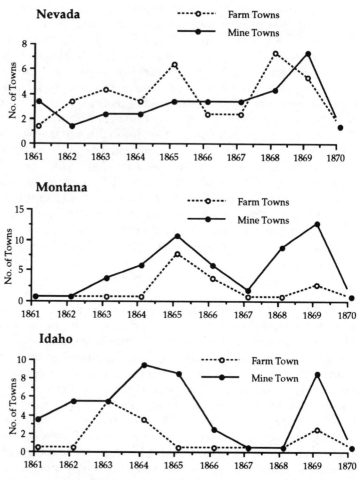

Figure 3.5 New farm and mine towns, 1860s. Nevada, Montana, and Idaho.

years behind mine towns. By the end of the decade, 63 farm towns had been founded in the three territories during a time when 118 mining towns were established, one farm town for every two mining towns.

By plotting the number of new farm and new mine towns for each year of the 1860s, as in Figures 3.6 and 3.7, one can see clearly that the foundings of both town types were closely related. The $R^2$ statistic in Figure 7.2 summarizes the data points on the graph, telling us that, knowing about the founding of a mine town, one could, on average, predict the founding of a farm town with 62 percent accuracy. Thus, there was, throughout the Mountain-to-Pacific Corridor, a strong tem-

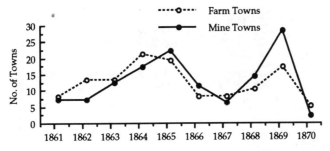

Figure 3.6 New farm and mine towns, 1860s, Mountain-to-Pacific Corridor states.

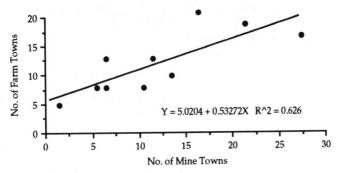

Figure 3.7 Relation of new farm and mine towns by year, 1860s.

poral relationship between the two types of towns. When a mine town was founded, the odds were 6 in 10 that a farm town would be founded in the same year.

There was, in addition, a very strong geographical relationship between the two town types. Figure 3.8 shows average estimated distances from mine to farm towns founded in the 1860s by state. In all of Utah, Nevada, and Montana, the hauling distances by wagon from average mine town to average farm town were a reasonable fourteen to fifty-two miles. Such drives were not only common but uncommonly short; the heavily traveled route from Silver City and the Boise Basin districts to Middleton was about fifty miles. The average Idaho haul was a longer ninety-six miles, due to the fact that north-central Idaho had numerous mine towns, while agriculture was limited by the terrain to the Boise Valley and Snake River Plain in the southern part of the state. Given that the Montana Trail from the Wasatch Front to the Montana mining districts was 400 to 500 miles, and heavily

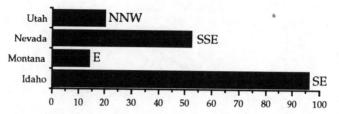

Figure 3.8 Mean proximity of farm and mine towns by state or territory, 1870.

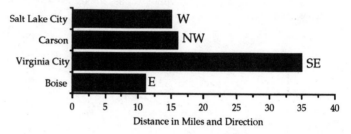

Figure 3.9 Mean proximity of farm and mine towns by district, 1870.

used throughout the 1870s, these average distances seem short, even as roughly estimated minimums. They are based on averages for all towns in the entire state or territory, a perspective that tends, as we see when comparing Figure 3.8 to Figure 3.9, to stretch average distances. Since mine towns were usually in mountainous terrain, while farm towns had to be located in the valleys, it would seem that wherever mine towns were established, farm districts sprang up on the closest available arable lands.

Figure 3.9 gives us a closer look at the relationships between the two types of towns in the region, by focusing on four areas, all but the Salt Lake area about 100 miles from east to west and 140 miles from north to south. (The Salt Lake area is seventy miles from north to south.) It shows that within these concentrated mining areas there were always farming districts founded at about the same time and usually one day's drive or less from the mining towns.[18]

Middleton would thus seem to be reasonably typical in its relationship to nearby mine towns. It was founded in 1863, the year after the Boise Basin strikes were made, about fifty miles from the nearest farming districts, on the closest lands that could readily be farmed. And,

[18] See Appendix tables A.2 and A.3, which explain the method of estimating mean distances and direction.

as we shall see, the Middleton example suggests that outside of Utah, the region was not a mosaic of discrete farming and mining communities culturally and socially distinct from one another. There was not one flow of people who came in the 1860s to farm and another to mine. The allure of quick wealth led thousands, already frazzled by the dislocation of war, to the West during the decade. But many as they arrived found mining hard, unglamorous, and unrewarding. Like J. B. Wright of Middleton, they found they could do about as well farming as mining, and settled down to the agrarian pursuits they had known in the East.

Yet, in so doing, they did not create placid rural districts that contrasted sharply with the hard, commercial acquisitiveness of the male-dominated mine towns. As we shall see, the early farm towns exhibited the same unbalanced sex ratios, small household sizes, low persistence rates and commercial orientation as the mining towns.[19] Farming and mining cultures bled into one another as dozens of young miners hired out to farmers in the summer and as dozens of farmers grew staple crops to supply the camps, worked seasonally or periodically in the mines, and freighted produce to the mine districts. In all these respects, the new farmers of the West were radically different from the early Oregon and Utah farm populations. They were, simply put, already capitalists when their plows first broke the sod of the Boise, Gallatin, or Ruby valleys, motivated by the hope of making profits and amassing money.

This was less the case in Sublimity and Alpine, where at first farming was not as oriented toward market sale of staple crops. George Hunt, possessed of 640 acres, farmed but 35 because no other perception of the uses of land made sense to him. It was his cultural predisposition to aim first at raising enough to care for his family, then to market whatever surplus was possible, but always keeping enough acres in reserve for his sons to do the same as they came of age. John Healey, born a Derbyshire coal miner, produced barely enough for his family on his seven acres because stark necessity, imposed by a severely limited supply of arable land, offered few alternatives. He knew that no more than one son could hope to farm in Alpine, and that some might not be able to make a living as farmers at all. Junius Wright took up his homestead in Middleton with a shrewd eye on the high prices miners in Idaho and Silver City were paying for flour, eggs, and butter. He quickly put into production all that he, hired

---

[19] Data relevant to this argument are in Dean L. May, "Middletons Agriminers: The Beginnings of an Agricultural Town," *Idaho Yesterdays* 28 (Winter 1985): 2–11, and also are incorporated into a more extended discussion in Chapter 5.

hands, and any equipment he could acquire could care for and proudly reported making $1,700 the first season. A physician by trade, he did not intend to stay in Middleton long enough for the lands there to provide a livelihood for his sons, and his farming there was in any case a momentary opportunity for amassing capital, by no means a way of life.

It is perhaps indicative of a broader change in societal values that in 1860 the census had begun seeking information on the value of real and personal property held by each individual. Those entrusted with the census had long concerned themselves with who the household head was, as indicated by age, birthplace, and race, as well as the number of persons in each family, but by midcentury they were becoming increasingly interested in the names of all family members, the birthplaces of parents, and how much wealth the family controled – new and portentous indices of identity and place in American society. The response the Hunts and Healeys gave to the questions concerning their wealth in 1870 was probably not seen by them to be of great interest or importance, but it may have been seen differently by the Wrights. In any case, all dutifully answered the questions asked of them and probably did not reflect long on what the new set of questions said about how their world was changing.[20]

George W. Hunt, now thirty-nine, was by far the wealthiest, reporting that the 640 acres he owned in the Sublimity area were worth $12,000 and his personal property $1,000. He was notably more wealthy, at least in land, than the average head of household in Sublimity, who reported $4,709 in real estate and $1,319 in personal property. James Healey, forty-five, in Alpine for some seventeen years, claimed $1,000 in real estate and $500 in personal property, somewhat more than the town average of $657 and $428. Middleton's Junius Wright had done better. At age thirty-four, and after but six years in Middleton, he owned $5,000 in real estate and $1,000 in personal property, compared to a community average per head of household of $1,440 and $1,393. The ranking in wealth of Hunt, Wright, and Healey

---

[20] These data are only rough indicators of wealth. They are commonly reported in units of $100, and often no wealth under $100 is reported. Many, who clearly must have had some cash to pay for rent, groceries, or other basic expenses, are reported without wealth. The data are computed from total wealth values reported on county and state levels in the printed report on Wealth and Industry of the Ninth U.S. Census. Town and individual-level data are from the manuscript census. Because of the problematic character of census wealth reports, I have attached significance only to very wide disparities in values. In Chapters 5 and 7, I use tax roll and other indicators of wealth, the data for individuals and communities varying somewhat in specific amounts, but not in ranking or magnitude of difference.

was paralleled in the ranking of average wealth for each community, with household heads in Sublimity worth $5,990 in total wealth, those in Middleton $2,883, and those in Alpine $939.

Middleton's affluence is remarkable when we consider the relatively short time since settlement. Especially revealing are differences in the balance between real estate and personal property. The Sublimity farmers had, on average, land worth $3,269 more than the average Middleton farmers, but their personal property was worth $74 less. It would seem that this great disparity in the ratios of real to personal property identifies the Oregon farmers as persons who felt no strong need to maximize the productivity of their farms. As we have seen, the George Hunts owned great farms but were content to farm but a small portion of them, and were consequently relatively poor in personal possessions. The average Alpine farmer owned land worth but half that of the Middleton farmer, and his personal property was worth less than a third. Poverty overshadowed Alpine farmers – their small tracts of land, not their keeping some in reserve for the next generation, inhibiting accumulation of personal wealth.

Sublimity and Alpine followed trends in their broader regions, but Middleton did not. In Oregon, the average household had $1,549 worth of land and $1,238 in personal possessions. Utah families averaged $527 worth of land and $412 in personal property, very close to the situation in Alpine. Middleton folk were more wealthy than Idahoans generally, perhaps because they had settled one of the first farm districts of western Idaho, close to two lucrative mining markets and Boise City. Others did not fare as well, averaging $581 worth of real estate and $1,015 in personal property. This reversal of the ratio of real to personal property is common in mining and service localities, but its occurrence in towns where most reported themselves to be farmers argues eloquently for the intermixing of farm and mine societies in the regions populated during the 1860s. A similar pattern is evident in Montana districts, where real estate averaged $590 per family but personal property an impressive $1,561. In Nevada, which had almost an even balance between farm and mining towns, the average householder had $1,787 in real estate and $1,365 in personal property.

These figures use the number of household heads as the numerator, a procedure that indicates wealth per active producer and thus relates to how much had been produced in the respective states and territories. Another perspective is gained, however, if we ask how many people had to share the wealth. In this latter instance, we use total population as the numerator, and as mining communities had fewer families and fewer nonproducers, it is no surprise to find the ranking

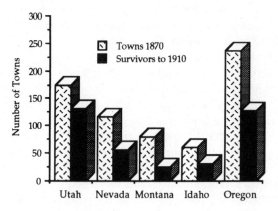

Figure 3.10  Towns, 1870 and survivors to 1910.

changed. If personal property per capita were our best approximation for standard of living from these data, people of our time might most have preferred to live in Montana, where there was $535 per person. Nevada was a distant second, at $317; Idaho next, at $278; Oregon third, at $252; and Utah a dismal last, at $82 per person. Alpine's James Healey family was even poorer, its nine members sharing $500 in personal property, some $56 each.[21]

Yet, as we have intimated here, Oregonians and Utahns, coming to the West earlier and with different motives, may have had measures of personal well-being that the new settlers of the 1860s could not fathom. Again, we are looking at town-level data, not individuals, but it may be worthwhile to ask of these towns, as has often been done of individuals, how many survived into subsequent decades. In the whole region, 382 of the 667 towns of 1870 – 57 percent – were still identifiable as precincts in 1900 and 373 in 1910. One can see this glass as half empty or half full, but given the vagaries of changing census districts, renaming of towns, and the austere character of great portions of the region, we are impressed with the high level of persistence over four decades, affirming the importance of the 1860s as a crucial

---

[21] Standard of living is, of course, difficult to estimate, even when records are generated for that purpose. The reasoning here is that the value of personal property approximates better than the value of real estate the degree to which homes, furnishings, vehicles, commodities, and other possessions make for a comfortable life or living standard. It may also be true for farmers that given equal values of real estate and time on the land, a relatively high proportion of total wealth in personal property would suggest a strong propensity to maximize production and invest in consumer goods – in other words, perhaps a more materialistic orientation.

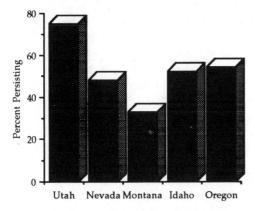

Figure 3.11 Percentage of towns persisting, 1870–1910.

formative period for both settlement and laying the cultural foundation that would come to characterize the West.

But this persistence was not uniform throughout the region. Oregon, Idaho, and Nevada were just below the regional average, with 54, 52, and 48 percent of their 1870 towns persisting into 1910. Montana had but 33 percent persisting over the same period. A remarkable 75 percent of all 1870 Utah towns persisted into 1910. There would seem to be a paradox here. Montana, the richest per capita territory of 1870, saw the fewest of its towns persist into the second decade of the twentieth century. Utah, the poorest, saw the most persist. And this would not seem to be just an effect of Utahns having had a longer time than Montanans to "nest in" before 1870, for Idaho had barely a year longer than Montana, and its towns survived nearly as well as those of Oregon, the oldest of the states or territories in the region.

It is important to remind ourselves that we are here speaking not of people who did or did not move away; we are speaking of towns or settlements, corporate entities that endured as such whatever wandering the George Hunts, James Healeys, and Junius Wrights may have been inclined to do. The cultural importance of this difference is profound, for it would seem that the identity and sense of place shared by a people must surely be highly correlated with the persistence of markers they recognize on the land. And of these markers, none could be more compelling than a living, human community. Three out of four such communities endured in Utah. In the rest of the West barely more than half survived, and in Montana but a third.

The imprint of the 1860s was strong throughout the region. New settlers came, etching the new lands with roads, farmhouses, and towns. Yet the novelty consisted not just in the fact that there were now many where previously there had been few, that Sublimity and Alpine were no longer so remote and isolated. The places the new settlers left, the timing and purposes of their leaving, and the attractions they found in the West all combined to make these people different from those who had preceded them.[22] The missionary bishop of Montana chose to settle his family in Salt Lake City rather than Virginia City, where "if I leaned on, or trusted in, this community, ... I would now be plunged in the lowest deep of despair," or Helena, where, seeking solitude in his room, he was disturbed by "feet moving, chains clanking, teamsters shouting more noisily than other days (because the miners from the gulches all round come in to-day. . . . ) Anything but a calm, quiet Sunday is this."[23] It was more the cultural than the physical imprint of these new people that shaped the new American West in the last quarter of the nineteenth century. Sublimity and Alpine were settled early by people of different background and purpose, and many in these communities stayed for a time culturally distant from the new settlers. Yet even they eventually imbibed much of the New West that the acquisitive farmer/trader Junius Wright represented.

[22] The suggestion here is similar to that of Louis Hartz in *The Founding of New Societies* (New York: Harcourt, Brace & World, Inc., 1964), in which he argues that the culture of new societies is deeply imprinted by the timing and character of the out-migration from the old ones. Hartz maintains (p. 3) that "when a part of a European nation is detached from the whole of it, and hurled outward onto new soil, it loses the stimulus toward change that the whole provides. It lapses into a kind of immobility." I suggest here that, similarly, when frontier areas are settled, they are strongly imprinted by the cultural modes prevailing at the time of migration among those who made up the main currents of the migratory stream. Sublimity, Alpine, and Middleton thus represent three different cultural strains. Cultural geographers have long recognized the importance of the founding peoples as shapers of culture in new societies, and the momentum of cultural patterns is a main theme in historian David Hacket Fischer's highly influential *Albion's Seed: Four British Folkways in America* (New York: Oxford University Press, 1989) and in Andrew R. L. Cayton and Peter S. Onuf, *The Midwest and the Nation* (Bloomington: Indiana University Press, 1990).
[23] Tuttle, *Reminiscences*, pp. 141, 184.

# 4    *The heirs of my body*

Sublimity people migrated as families and neighbors to the West, these kin/neighbor groups comprising most of their social world. They performed virtually all the important rituals of life, as well as schooling, production, exchange, and provision of welfare services, within their kin/neighbor groups. The early Sublimity area was a mosaic of such groups scattered across the rolling countryside.

Alpine people had severed contact with kin and neighbors when they converted to Mormonism and migrated to the West. But Mormonism offered them a new set of connections and a new identity, redirecting social ties outward to fellow Saints in the broader community of Alpine town. The vital duties of life were attended to not by a neighbor/kin group, but by fellow townspeople.

The ties of Middleton's settlers had likewise been torn – by the Civil War and by their eagerness to escape the havoc it created in their lives. Yet they were not able in the Far West to form new connections, remaining relatively isolated and distant from kin and from a sense of broader community. Their social world was thin and incomplete. In the three societies women played different roles, shaped in part by the ideas of family and community distinctive to each.

When John and Temperance Hunt and seven of their children clambered into wagons to head out for the Pacific in 1847, they were by no means cutting themselves off from kith and kin. The family was leaving partly in response to the importuning of John's brother, James, that they join him in Oregon.[1] Two other brothers, Harrison and William, had preceded them as well, and no doubt all three were on hand to welcome the John Hunts as they rolled into the Willamette Valley

[1] "George W. Hunt," biography drawn from his "Hunt Family History" and personal memory of Sarah Hunt Steeves, printed in Sarah Hunt Steeves, *Book of Remembrance of Marion County, Oregon, Pioneers, 1840–1860* (Portland: The Berncliff Press, 1927), pp. 96–101.

Photo 5 George W. Hunt and family members, 1890s. George Hunt's centrality in the photograph is clear. The women also seem hierarchically arranged. The one on the upper right is probably Elizabeth Hunt, and left of her are the couple's surviving daughters, Temperance and Sarah, in order of age. The children are likely theirs; the boy is honored by being placed next to his grandmother. The photograph clearly communicates the importance to them of family continuity across generations. (Used by permission of Georgia Wetteland.)

and helped them to settle in. The Hunts traveled in a wagon train headed by Doctor (his given name) Smith and his wife, Nancy Scott Wisdom Smith, she a native of Virginia. Doctor Smith died on the journey and was buried near the Green River. Nancy, now twice widowed, was a plucky woman, remembered by her family as "high-spirited, beautiful, and talented." Despite the devastating loss of her husband, she persevered, shepherding her six children on toward Oregon. Nonetheless, it must have been a great relief when she was met on the Columbia by her oldest son, Dick Wisdom, and his in-laws, Anson Kimsey and Vania Simpson, all of whom had preceded her to the Willamette Valley.[2]

Settling into a log cabin in the Sublimity area, Nancy Smith suffered much privation in her efforts to care for her family. Her descendants tell of an occasion when she asked to borrow a cow for the milk from Daniel Waldo, the first citizen of the area.[3] Waldo was a man who "took great pride in the idea that he was not a proud man," and he resented the fact that a woman in such reduced circumstances always wore a prim white collar fastened at the neck with a small gold brooch. He told her he would lend her the cow when she removed her collar. The widow snapped back that "my collars have cost me nothing, having been made from old linen shirt bosoms and embroidered with ravelings, and I absolutely refuse to take them off. He may keep his cow."[4] She and her children endured the remainder of the decade in poverty and pain. But in 1850, her neighbor and friend from the wagon train, Temperance Hunt, died, and the next summer the widower John Hunt and Nancy Smith were married. A month later, in August 1851, John's oldest son, George W. Hunt, now twenty, married Elizabeth Smith, his new stepmother's daughter. The younger newlyweds at first took up a claim near the sawmill of George's uncle, Harrison Hunt, but gave it up and settled on a farm north of Sublimity.

The intertwining of families continued. John Downing, a native of Pennsylvania, also set out for Oregon in 1847. His train came up to the Hunt train on the trail, and during an evening frolic the tall, dark-haired young man attracted considerable attention by nimbly dancing a jig on a wagon bed. Among the onlookers was John Hunt's daughter, thirteen-year-old Temperance ("Tempa") Hunt. Two years later, John Downing and Tempa Hunt were married at a ceremony in her father's home. The newlyweds settled on a Donation Land Claim that John took up just west of Tempa's older brother, George. In 1852 John Downing's brothers, James and George, and a sister and her husband, Harriet and Thomas King, joined him in Oregon, and in the 1870s

---

[2] Moses Ira Smith Narrative, quoted in *Steeves, Book of Remembrance*, pp. 118–27, esp. p. 124.

[3] Credence is given to the family memory by the fact that the Mountain Man, James Clyman, made special mention of the fine herd of cattle Daniel Waldo had in 1844. "Mr Waldow has a fine stock of the best blooded cattle I have yet seen in the Territory." James Clyman, *Journal of a Mountain Man*, ed., Linda M. Hasselstrom (Missoula, Mont.: Mountain Press Publishing Company, 1984), p. 164. Waldo lived several miles north and west of the area we have called Sublimity.

[4] Reported to Sarah Hunt Steeves by Hannah Townsend or Elizabeth N. Hunt, in Steeves, *Book of Remembrance*, pp. 109–12.

two more brothers, William and Alexander, came west. The Hunts and Downings had become by 1860 the core of a neighbor/kin cluster that came to be known as "Whiteaker," one of many such scattered across the Oregon countryside.

Numerous other examples could be given of the pervasive role of the family in migrating to and settling the Oregon country. Joel Palmer, who came to Oregon in 1845, observed that there were in each train "four or five wagons generally from the same neighborhood, or they were relatives and assisted each other."[5] These same people, as William Bowen found in his study of the 1850 Willamette Valley, usually settled close to one another in Oregon.

Sublimity settlers likewise tended to congregate in family groups. In 1860 thirty-one of ninety-seven heads of household (32 percent) shared a surname with at least one other family in the district. Sixteen shared a surname with two or more household heads.[6] Not only did the same surnames occur frequently, those of the same name commonly settled close to one another. Thirteen of the twenty-seven families sharing surnames were found by the census takers to be but one household distant from another family of the same name (essentially next-door neighbors). Seventy percent of all those sharing surnames lived within four households of another family of the same name. The median distance of families sharing surnames with the nearest neighbor of the same name was two households.[7]

---

[5] Joel Palmer, "Conducting the Wagon Trains Flanking Mt. Hood and Cariboo," Bancroft Library ms. P-A 58, p. 25, quoted in William A. Bowen, *The Willamette Valley: Migration and Settlement on the Oregon Frontier* (Seattle: University of Washington Press, 1978), p. 24.

[6] Though it is obvious that there were many in-laws and other kin who did not share surnames, noting patterns of repeating surnames as an indication of the degree to which family clusters were present in the society permits comparision with other communities, such as Middleton, for which extensive family histories and genealogies have not been produced. The counting of repeated surnames thus provides a minimal index of the number of family clusters that can be readily compared from community to community.

[7] The data are from Manuscript Schedules of the U.S. Census of Population for 1860. Household distance is, of course, determined by the numbers the census takers assigned to households. It is possible for near neighbors to have distant household numbers, as when census takers doubled back after working to the end of parallel lanes or roads. But close numbers would always identify near neighbors. In other words, these data probably minimize the actual geographical closeness of some of the same-surname families. Previous work assessing household connections through census list proximity includes Frank L. Owsley, *Plain Folk of the Old South* (Baton Rouge: Louisiana State University Press, 1949); Fabian Linden, "Economic Democracy in the Slave South: An Appraisal of Some Recent Views," *Journal of Negro History* 31 (April 1946): 140–89; and Robert C. Kenzer, *Kinship and Neighborhood in a Southern Community:*

Photo 6 John Downing and brothers in 1885. Seated: William, John and Samuel. Standing; James, Alexander, and George. (Used by permission of Daraleen Wade.)

Photo 7 Temperance Hunt Downing, first wife of John Downing, probably taken in the early 1870s, when in her late thirties. She died in 1876 at age forty-two. (Used by permission of Daraleen Wade.)

Thus it is no surprise to find that John and George Downing lived next to one another, or that John S. Hunt, his brother James, and James's son, Nathan, all were located on adjoining properties. Clearly,

*Orange County, North Carolina, 1849–1881* (Knoxville: University of Tennessee Press, 1987). See especially Kenzer, *Kinship and Neighborhood*, pp. 155–60.

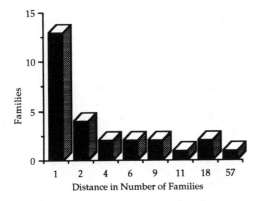

Figure 4.1 Sublimity, 1860. Distances of families from nearest family of same surname.

a high proportion of Sublimity folk followed the old southern pattern of forming in their new setting what historian Robert Kenzer called "isolated, self-contained, rural neighborhoods." Their time-honored folkways were brought intact to Oregon and played a major role in shaping the social landscape of Sublimity. Migration to Oregon did not break down traditional social structures. They were maintained in some measure on the trail and re-created in the new setting.[8]

John Shotwell Hunt was forty-eight when he and the proud widow Nancy Smith married. He had six children under the age of sixteen. She was fifty-one and brought to their new household four of eleven children she had borne during her two previous marriages. Elizabeth, Nancy's daughter by Doctor Smith, was but fifteen when she married George Washington Hunt one month after their parents' marriage. Her husband was twenty. Their first child, Temperance, was born ten months later, on May 17, 1852. Five more children followed: Josephine, born in late 1853; Georgianne in 1858 (the long spacing suggesting possible intervening miscarriages); Melancthon in 1860; Jeptha in 1862; and Sara, nine years later, in 1871, when her father was forty and her mother thirty-six.

They apparently named their first child after George's mother and his sister, Tempa, who in 1849 had married John Downing when she

---

[8] Kenzer found the North Carolina countryside of the same period settled in "isolated, self-contained rural neighborhoods" where "from birth to death, residents' lives were shaped not only by the households in which they lived but also by the kin network of the neighborhood." The Oregon pioneers obviously continued, to the degree possible under the circumstances of migration and new settlement, the social patterns their families had long established. Kenzer, *Kinship and Neighborhood*, pp. 9–22.

was seventeen and he twenty-one. John and Temperance did not have a child for six years. Edwin was born in 1855, and three years later twins came, only one of them, Albert, surviving. The other was buried unnamed on the George and Elizabeth Hunt family farm. Two years later Alice was born, followed in four years by Marion Thomas. Then came John Herbert in 1867 and Harry, the last of seven, two years after that. He was but seven when his mother died, in 1876 at age forty-two. The next year John married Jennie Carpenter, who helped him to raise his four minor children and bore him yet another child, Everett, in 1878.[9]

The course of these couples' lives, full of power and meaning for those descended from them, was much like that of their neighbors in the Sublimity area. Most adults in the community married, and if the marriage was severed by death or divorce, were not slow to marry again. Seventy-four percent of the women above fifteen years were married, and 67 percent of the men above nineteen were married.[10] Eighty-nine (92 percent) of the ninety-seven households had a married couple at the core, eighty-two of them with their own children (and, as we shall see, frequently those of others) in the household. The other households consisted of six men living alone and three dwellings with two or more apparently single men living together.[11]

Marriage and the formation of families thus were clearly common

[9] Information on these families was supplied by Daraleen Wade of Salem, a granddaughter of Everett Downing. Throughout the study, I have relied on information in family reconstitution forms for most Sublimity families compiled and generously made available by Mrs. Wade.

[10] There are several instances in Sublimity of women marrying at age fifteen, suggesting that women above sixteen were likely to be married. Men married later, rarely before twenty, so I have used men above nineteen as the marriageable pool. The youthful marriage of George and Elizabeth Smith Hunt and others was probably hastened by a desire to increase land holdings through the additional 320 acres a married couple could claim under the Donation Land Claim Act if the claim was filed prior to December 1, 1851.

[11] These data are obviously gathered by the author from the Manuscript Schedules of the U.S. Census of Population for 1860. The 1860 census does not specify marital status or relationships of household members. Households headed by an adult man, followed by an adult woman near the same age, and one or more children of the same surname and descending order of ages were assumed to be families headed by married couples. Persons of the same surname but breaking the descending age order pattern were assumed to be kin living in the household, not part of the nuclear family. Children with other surnames were listed as "other youth" unless it could be absolutely determined that they were kin, such as siblings, stepchildren, or cousins. Similarly, adults with other surnames living in the household were assumed not to be related unless a clear link could be established. As the text suggests, it is altogether likely that a good many of these were kin of the couple that formed the core of the household.

episodes in the life course of Sublimity people. In addition, many of these families reached out to include more than the core couple and their children. A full half of the eighty-two couples with children had taken others into their homes as well. These extra household members were not commonly lodgers or hired help (neither likely in a community with thirty-five unoccupied dwellings and a production pattern not strongly keyed to markets). Only four were designated in the census as hired hands, and but one was clearly a lodger – a schoolteacher boarding with a family. Seven of the households had taken in persons who were likely kin (persons sharing the surname of the family), five adults and two children. Twenty-four families had others living with them who were possibly kin – persons who did not share the same surname but were not designated as lodgers or hired help. Twelve of these were other adults, eleven were children (under eighteen), and in one household there were both adults and children not sharing a surname with the family head. Five households consisted of two nuclear families living together.

Obviously, the households in Sublimity stretched themselves to provide a wide range of social services. They took in orphans, sheltered young working adults without families, and cared for the aged and the infirm. Yet most of the nonnuclear family residents were kin. The John Downings represent a common pattern. The nuclear family in 1860 consisted of John, thirty-three, Temperance, twenty-six, and their two sons, Edwin, five and Albert, two. They had also taken into their home eight-year-old Mary Riches, a niece of Mrs. Downing. Margarette Henline, sixteen, a neighbor girl, was temporarily helping Mrs. Downing (Tempa was about to give birth to their third child, Alice). There were, in addition, two "farm laborers," F. Hunt and William King, both relatives of the Downings. The Downing household suggests that though the social world of these people did not commonly extend far beyond the neighbor/kin clusters, within that world people were fairly fluid, the young and the aged floating freely from household to household as their own needs, or the needs of the families within the cluster, required. The frequent presence of nonnuclear family members helped raise the average household size in Sublimity to a substantial 6.1 persons.

There was an additional reason for the large household size, however – the high fertility of Sublimity women. There were two or three children under 10 years of age in Sublimity for every woman aged 16 to 45 (2.38), giving the district a high child-woman ratio for a mid-nineteenth-century rural community. In comparison, rural people in Sugar Creek, Illinois, had had 2.45 children per adult woman in 1830, but only 2.23 in 1840 and 2.08 in 1850, the decades during which many people from rural Illinois emigrated to Oregon.[12] Apparently in the Willamette Valley, the paucity of young women lowered the age at marriage, with early and sustained childbearing pushing the child-woman ratio up. Though there were in the whole district 114.2 men for every 100 women, the sex ratio in the crucial age group of 20 to 30 was 166.7, giving women who wished ample opportunity to marry. In Sublimity there were twenty- eight single men in that age group, but only seven single women. Most young men of Sublimity could hope to find a bride in the district only if they considered women as young as sixteen as possible mates (twenty-four unmarried women aged sixteen to twenty-nine to twenty- seven men aged twenty to twenty-nine). Thus it is no surprise to find that the average married woman was more than 4 years younger than her husband, 37.1 years (median, 35.5) compared to the husband's 41.7 (median, 40).

It is nonetheless probable that the abundance of children can be attributed to more than unbalanced sex ratios and the opportunities young people found for making a living on the lush Oregon frontier. Couples seem to have aimed at a family size that would ensure clan survival but not overwhelm the family resources. Simple and reasonably effective techniques of limiting childbirth were known and available, even to rural people at the time. The cessation of childbearing by sisters-in-law Temperance Downing and Elizabeth Hunt at ages thirty-five and thirty-seven, well before the normal onset of menopause, supports this observation.[13] And, as we shall see, other rural people of the time, a few hundred miles east, in Middleton, Idaho, had far fewer children, whereas those living toward the Rockies, in Alpine, Utah, had many more. Perhaps the most fundamental reason

[12] See John Mack Faragher, *Sugar Creek: Life on the Illinois Prairie* (New Haven, Conn.: Yale University Press, 1986), pp. 88, 253–4n. Faragher has calculated child-woman ratios from data printed by James E. Davis in *Frontier America, 1800–1840: A Comparative Demographic Analysis of the Frontier Process* (Glendale, Calif.: Arthur E. Clark Co., 1977), p. 169, that show ratios (normally reported standardized to a base of 1,000) for northern backcountry areas of 2,550 in 1830 and 2,091 in 1840. The 1860 ratio in Sublimity of 2,385 (children under ten years per 1,000 women aged sixteen to forty-five) shows that on the Oregon frontier, as on other frontiers, the general late-nineteenth-century pattern of fertility decline was reversed.

[13] Abstinence, withdrawal, the vaginal sponge, spermicidal douches, and the rhythm method were all used. Rubber condoms were available by 1850, though usually associated with prostitution and hence shunned by married couples. See Norman E. Himes, *The Medical History of Contraception* (New York: Gamut Press, 1963); James Reed, *From Private Vice to Public Virtue: The Birth Control Movement and American Society Since 1830* (New York: Basic Books, 1978); Linda Gordon, *Woman's Body, Woman's Right: Birth Control in America* (New York: Penguin Books, 1990); and Carl Degler, *At Odds: Women and Family in America from the Revolution to the Present* (New York: Oxford University Press, 1981).

Sublimity women had many, but not too many, children was cultural. They and their husbands saw one of life's major purposes to be the perpetuation of their particular family or clan. It was this cultural imperative that led them to undertake the costly and often dangerous move to Oregon. As they understood before they left the East, the new environment would favor its realization, for in Oregon there was land enough to provide a sacred center that henceforth would be known as the Hunt or the Downing place, a matrix that would ensure the continuation of their seed into the future.

\* \* \*

Alpiners were similarly moved by cultural predisposition, but at play in this case was a mix of an English working-class culture and an adopted religious one that nonetheless had incorporated many elements of the rural New England in which Mormonism had been founded. The resultant hybrid was in 1860 still mutable and not fully articulated. Yet the frontier they entered, though austere compared to the Willamette Valley, had its way of facilitating the realization of deep cultural desires as well. This was evident in the experience of William Johnson Strong.[14] Strong's father, a factory worker in Birmingham, England, died in 1839, when William was seven years of age. Their father's death made it necessary for he and his twin brother, Enoch, to take jobs in a spoon factory, helping to support the family, while their mother labored as a button maker. A Baptist Sunday school provided their only education. At fourteen, William apprenticed himself to a tin plate manufacturer, where he met Edmund Warren, a Mormon. By the next year, Strong had been converted to the new American religion. He was baptized July 23, 1847, one day before William Wordsworth, the first settler of Alpine, entered the Salt Lake Valley in faraway Utah in the company of Brigham Young.

Through Edmund Warren, Strong met Eliza Brown Dyer and her fourteen- year-old daughter, Julia, and he and Julia began an extended courtship. Julia's "very happy, and loving family" had been shattered when her mother was converted to the Mormon faith in 1845. Her father, Gideon Dyer, a respectable police officer, was angered by his wife's conversion but nonetheless agreed to attend a Mormon meeting to please her. There his worst suspicions were confirmed. He was offended by the "humble" people he saw there and found the meeting place, a room above a saloon, hardly a fit setting for worship. After the meeting he gave Eliza an ultimatum that she either abandon "Joe

---

[14] Biographical information on the Strongs is from Bill and Carolyn B. Strong, *A Proud Heritage . . . The Ancestors and Descendants of Clifford Oscar Strong and Fern Paxman Miller* (Privately published, nd.), pp. 291–6, 327–31.

Smithism," as he called it, or he would abandon her. She stubbornly clung to her new faith, and (in the words of his descendants) Dyer "kissed his little daughter goodbye and left one night, never to return." Julia, whose pain at the loss of her father one can well imagine, remained with her mother, moving from Windsoredge, Gloucester, to Birmingham, where they found lodging in the house owned by Edmund Warren. Her mother tried in vain to locate her husband, hoping to persuade him to return, but also remained firmly attached to her new faith. Julia was baptized at age fourteen, one month after the young tinner, William Strong.

The Dyers raised funds sufficient to "gather" to Utah in 1851, and William and Julia, both nineteen, agreed that they would marry when he could join her there the next year. His yearning to be with Julia was compelling, however, and on December 17, 1851, he secretly booked passage for America. On January 8 he went to work as usual, but there feigned illness and left directly for Liverpool, without even going home to bid farewell to his mother and twin brother. His descendants recall that this "sudden and painful departure" was "one of the most trying periods of his life." In particular, the abandonment of his mother and twin brother, "was a most severe ordeal and was always painful for him to think about." At the docks in Liverpool he boarded the *Kennebec*, a ship bound for America, joining the 333 Mormon immigrants among the passengers. His master sent police officers who searched the vessel's passenger list in an effort to find the truant apprentice, but he had registered under his mother's maiden name, and they were unable to locate him. During what a fellow passenger called a "long, rough voyage" to New Orleans (sixty-four days, from January 10 to March 14, 1852) he was in the midst of the "brothers and sisters" of his new faith, but we know of no blood relatives or friends from Birmingham aboard the vessel.[15] After a passage upriver to St. Louis on a side wheeler, *The Pride of the West*, he and Julia were reunited and the two were married there by Daniel Sutherland, a Mormon elder, on April 4, 1852. Julia's mother was the only family member present.

They began their overland journey in June, traveling in a company led by a venerable Mormon elder, Abraham O. Smoot. After arriving in Utah they found lodging in Provo, in the Utah Valley, fifty miles

---

[15] Information on the *Kennebec* passage is found in Conway B. Sonne, *Saints on the Seas: A Maritime History of Mormon Migration, 1830–1890* (Salt Lake City: University of Utah Press, 1983), pp. 31, 48, 50, 56, 103. The George and Hannah Hobson May family was also aboard the vessel, their son, James, describing the voyage as quoted. See James May, "Reminiscence," LDS Church Archives, Salt Lake City, Utah.

south of Salt Lake City, sharing a house with the family of Apostle George A. Smith. Smith's jurisdiction extended beyond the city of Provo, and in September 1852 he formally organized a bishop's ward in the settlement of Alpine, the homes of its residents forming an enclosed fort some eighteen miles north of Provo. It was no doubt Smith who introduced Mrs. Dyer to Isaac Houston, for she was married to Houston seven months later, on April 13, 1853, under her maiden name, Eliza Brown, and moved to Alpine. In September 1854 William and Julia moved from Provo to Alpine to be closer to her mother, and there, knowing only Julia's mother and new stepfather, they began to construct a community of friends and family to replace those they had left behind in Birmingham.

The lives of William and Julia Strong, unlike those of the Hunts and Downings, had been buffeted by a series of disruptions before they came to the West that all but severed the social networks they had known in their youth. William's most memorable experiences with his father, John Strong, were in a factory, not a home, as the young child carried lunches to his father's workplace, which the father then shared with him. But that relationship ended with John's death in 1839, and at age seven the boy himself began factory work to help sustain the family. His conversion to Mormonism was instrumental in his meeting Julia, a coreligionist, and at nineteen he severed his family ties to gather with Julia and other Mormons in Utah. From the time he converted to Mormonism, his confidants and associates were people with official church positions: Edmund Warren, who converted him and introduced him to the Dyers; John W. Young (Brigham's son), who ordained him a priest six days before the sailing; Josiah Higbee, the leader of the Mormon community aboard the emigrant ship; Elder Daniel Sutherland, who married them in St. Louis; Abraham O. Smoot, captain of their overland wagon company; and Apostle John Taylor, who recommended them to George A. Smith (Joseph Smith's cousin) in Provo. Clearly, any kin-based social networks that might have survived British industrialization were shattered by Strong's conversion to Mormonism, and new networks, linking him to the church and its hierarchy of leaders, were being forged.

Similarly, the family associations of Julia Dyer were disrupted by her mother's conversion to Mormonism, her father's abandoning them, and their subsequent impoverishment, probably leading to their move to Birmingham, which distanced them from their former friends and associates. There a fellow church member, Edmund Warren, provided lodging. Their gathering to Zion put them, as it did William, from that time forth in the company of saints. Eliza was no doubt startled to find awaiting her in St. Louis a letter from her husband,

Gideon Dyer, who apparently had kept himself secretly informed of her situation. He offered her and Julia passage back to England if they would abandon Mormonism, but by this time Eliza was resolute in her new course. In Utah she lived with William and Julia until she met Isaac Houston through Apostle Smith. After their marriage she moved with Houston to Alpine. As with James, we see the ties of association broken again and again, but then gradually reattached to new strands within the Mormon community, often through the agency of church officials. In such circumstances, the power of church leaders to reshape cultural values and practices through example and exhortation was immense.

The Strongs and Dyers were not alone in such experiences. Only one surname appears more than once in the Utah town, whereas in Sublimity there were twenty-seven families that shared a surname with at least one other, and a number sharing names with two, three, and even four other families. Though Alpine was much smaller than Sublimity in 1860, with but fifteen households, the difference is at least highly suggestive. The numerous clusters of kin that dotted the Oregon landscape in 1860 were simply not present in Alpine. There the severing of family associations through industrialization, conversion to Mormonism, and migration to the American West had created a social world radically different from that of the Willamette countryside. For those who came to Utah, old networks of association had been dissolved and new ones were being formed. Alpine people were even more prone than Sublimity people to marry and form families in Zion, but the kin groups, dismembered by conversion and emigration, could not bear the manifold social burdens or play the same central role that they did in Sublimity.

As we have seen, William and Julia Dyer Strong, like others, had few kin in Alpine when they moved there in 1854. They brought with them their first child, William Frederick, who had been born in Provo in 1853. Their second son, named for Enoch, the twin brother William had left behind in England, was born in Alpine in December 1855, and babies continued to arrive about every two years until 1872: Don Carlos in 1857, Julia Clara in 1859, Davis Johnson in 1862, Samuel Oscar in 1864, Orlando Henry in 1866, Eliza Emeline, in 1867, Estella in 1870, and Frank in 1872. Julia turned forty a month before the baby, Frank, was born, and bore no more children after that. She apparently nursed each child until about one year of age, the only birth breaking the two-year pattern being that of Eliza (known as Emma), born eleven months after Orlando, who died the day of his birth and was buried in the Alpine town cemetery.[16]

---

[16] Family vital events are from a "family group sheet" or family reconstitution form

Alpine was apparently on hard times when the U.S. census was taken in 1860, with eight of twenty-three houses in the town unoccupied. And even though there were no neighborhood clusters of kin, every individual in the population, with one possible exception, lived in a household as part of a nuclear family or as close a relative to the resident family. All the homes had a married couple at the core, and there were children in all but that of one aging couple, John and Elizabeth Oker. Nine of the households consisted of parents (or, in the case of Catherine Nash, one parent) and their children only. Mormons at the time practiced polygyny, or plural marriage, and one man, John Wesley Vance, twenty-nine, first married to Angelia (Ann) Vale in 1854, had in 1859 married a second wife, Rhoda Freestone, fifteen. Vance, his two wives, and three children by Ann all lived in the same home. At least one and perhaps five other heads of household in Alpine would eventually marry a plural wife (a maximum six of fifteen), but William Strong was not among them. Four families had taken persons of different surnames into their homes – all but one close relatives. Two were mothers-in-law, including Julia's mother, widowed and now living with the Strongs again. Another was an older woman, perhaps an aunt of the mother in the household. The last was a younger child, probably a granddaughter of Davis and Mary McOlney. There was no one in the settlement living alone, nor were there any all-male or all-female households. There were no borders, lodgers, or hired hands.

Although the population in 1860 was too small to allow us to generalize with great confidence, the Alpine households were apparently more limited in function than those of Sublimity. Whereas in the Oregon district half of the eighty-two couples with children had taken at least one other into their household, in Alpine four of fifteen (about a quarter) had done so. Moreover, the guests in Sublimity households, although mostly kin, represented a great variety of life-situations – those in advanced age, of diminished mental ability or with mental illness, orphans, household helpers, hired hands, teachers, and young men or women who, because they were kin, were not precisely paying lodgers but were not living with their parents.

prepared by descendants, Reed C. and Louise Bateman Roberts, from family records in the possession of Betha S. Ingram, of American Fork, Utah, and filed in the "Patrons Section" of the LDS Family History Library, Salt Lake City, Utah.

Nursing inhibits conception, a phenomenon called "postpartum amenorrhea," the spacing of Julia's children providing strong evidence that she nursed for about a year after each child and used no artificial means of contraception. Since Orlando did not survive, she did not nurse after his birth, and became fertile more quickly than after her other births.

Perhaps in part because there were no neighbor/kin clusters, there were fewer nonnuclear people in Alpine households, and they were less varied in their life situations. Two were parents of the household heads, one probably was an aunt, and one probably was a grand-daughter. In Sublimity the neighbor/kin clusters had rigid outer boundaries, but the population within the cluster was known, had commonly accepted rights and obligations, and was hence more fluid, moving from household to household as needs made such movement advantageous to the movers or the settled. The Alpine people seem to have been more rigidly attached to one household, the homes less open to life-course drift.

Perhaps one reason for the more fixed character of Alpine house-holds was that the houses were small, yet contained nearly as many persons as the larger Sublimity homes. In 1860 the settlement con-sisted of some twenty-three houses, mostly log, facing each other in a square and surrounded by a city wall, built on the advice of church leaders to protect the community in case of Indian unrest. On average these cabins housed 5.7 persons (median, 6), just slightly fewer than the number in Sublimity homes.[17] The Strong home, west of the north-east corner of the fort wall, held a family of six – William, twenty-eight; Julia, twenty-seven; William F., seven; Don C., four; baby Julia, eleven months old, and Eliza Houston, aged forty. William and Julia were young among household heads in the town, which averaged forty-one years (median, thirty-eight) for men and thirty-three years (median, thirty-three) for women. The married men were about the same age as those in Sublimity, the women three or four years younger.[18]

Julia's fertility reflected that of the town. There were but 69 men for every 100 women in Alpine, but there were well over 3 children (3.36) for every adult woman, far more than were ever recorded in Sugar Creek or Sublimity.[19] As noted, there were few plural households in Alpine, and thus the patriarchs there were not depleting unduly the pool of marriageable women. Yet there were six unmarried women in Alpine over fifteen, four of them widows (31 percent of nineteen women over fifteen) and but one unmarried man (6 percent of six-

---

[17] The Sublimity household size averaged 6.1; the median was the same as that of Al-pine, 6.

[18] Married men in Sublimity averaged 41.7 years (median, 35.5) and women 37.1 years (median, 35.5).

[19] As noted earlier, the child-woman ratio commonly used by American historians is the number of children under ten divided by the number of women aged sixteen to forty-four times 1,000 (i.e., children per 1,000 women). The highest ratio in Sugar Creek was 2,452; in Sublimity, 2,380.

teen). The sex ratio for this pool of eligible men and women was 17 (men for every 100 women); that for the same group in Sublimity was 157. The extreme predominance of marriageable women in Alpine must have been a consequence of a random imbalance in so small a population, as sex ratios in the entire territory were reasonably balanced and thus did not, as in Oregon, and even more in the neighboring Mountain states, inhibit marriage and births.[20]

The behavior of Alpine people, then, suggests that children and family were valued, as they were in Sublimity. Alpine women had more children than their Sublimity counterparts, and a greater proportion of the pool of marriageable men and women was married.[21] Yet family in the broader sense of in-law, cousin, and intergenerational interaction hardly existed at all in early Alpine, while it was very nearly a hallmark of Sublimity society.

When descendants of Alpine people wrote their family histories, they took great pains to place them in the context of the town. Jennie Adams Wild compiled some 268 life sketches and reminiscences of Alpine people, titling the four typescript volumes *Builders of Alpine*.[22] The James and John Healey family history, after a brief review of their British origins, turns on page 9 to the history of Alpine, concluding that "The Healey family played a very important role in settling and building up of the community of Alpine. . . . Much of their time was spent in service to their fellowmen in making Alpine a better place to live. They have left a wonderful heritage to the people of the community and to their descendants, the Healey Family."[23] (Note how the narrative clearly emphasizes community above family.) The Strong family history likewise begins with a brief introduction, but moves on page vii to a history of Alpine.[24] Time and again, these documents

---

[20] Lee L. Bean, Geraldine P. Mineau, and Douglas L. Anderton discuss the effects of unbalanced sex ratios on fertility in *Fertility Change on the American Frontier: Adaptation and Innovation* (Berkeley: University of California Press, 1990), pp. 43–9. See also Jack E. Eblen, "An Analysis of Nineteenth-century Frontier Populations," *Demography* 2 (1965): 399–413; and the seminal article by Richard A. Easterlin, George Alter, and Gretchen Condran, "Farms and Farm Families in Old and New Areas: The Northern States in 1860," in Tamara Hareven and Maris Vinovskis, eds., *Family and Population in 19th Century America* (Princeton, N.J.: Princeton University Press, 1978), pp. 22–84. It would seem that the religious motivation for immigration to the West was selective in favor of females (as in Utah), whereas the material motivation for immigration was selective in favor of males (as in other western states).

[21] Eighty percent in Alpine; 70 percent in Sublimity.

[22] Note the contrast with Steeves," *Book of Remembrance*, which stresses the pioneers in a broad county setting, not as town or community builders.

[23] Betha S. Ingram, ed., *The James & John Healey Family History* (Provo, Utah: privately published, 1963), pp. 9–10.

[24] Strong, *Ancestors and Descendants*, pp. vii–xii.

make it clear that in the view of the descendants of early Alpine settlers, their family story was nurtured in and took its meaning from their connection to the town. Almost never do they speak, like Sublimity folk, of family-owned fields and pastures as the matrix from which their race sprang, but rather of Alpine town. For Sublimity folk the center of the world was the family farm – the house, its surrounding fields, the neighborhood cemetery. These made up their physical world and set the bounds of their social world – all intertwined with extended family in memory and meaning. Theirs was a family-centered society, and as such they produced enough children to perpetuate themselves. Yet their end was family perpetuity, not countless progeny, and their fertility pattern suggests that they understood that the two aims could work counter to each other.

The center of existence for Alpine people was the community. It was their belief, rooted in Mormon ideology, that a numerous progeny was a blessing beyond reckoning. Church leaders on every possible occasion lauded the rewards of parenthood and the joys of rearing children, their preachments imparting a strong pro-natalist bent to their society. The most solemn Mormon rituals, uniting men and women for eternity, promised a progeny to rival that of the ancient biblical patriarchs. They were taught and understood that they should have as many children as God would give them, and they responded with remarkable diligence and stamina. Yet, why all these children? What was the purpose of such a progeny? They saw the bearing of many children as in large measure their contribution to the building up of Zion – bringing as many spirits as possible into the ordered, harmonious world of Mormon belief and behavior, where they could assist in helping prepare the world for Christ's return.[25] Shortly before her death, Caroline Henrietta Lind Adams, whose third child was born in Alpine, called all her twelve children (she had done her part) to her bedside. She gave them advice, bid them farewell, and then sang a song to remind them that life's purposes transcended the personal and even the familial – one of the oldest of Mormon folk narratives.

> Now let us rejoice in the day of salvation.
> No longer as strangers on earth need we roam.
> Good tidings are sounding to us and each nation,
> And shortly the hour of redemption will come.

[25] Larry M. Logue reviews Mormon sermons and statements advocating marriage and large families in *A Sermon in the Desert: Belief and Behavior in Early St. George, Utah* (Urbana: University of Illinois Press, 1988), pp. 44–5; 72–3. Logue's data make it clear that "natural" fertility was the practice in St. George, i.e., that child spacing does not indicate efforts to limit the family to a certain normative size.

We'll love one another and never dissemble,
But cease to do evil and ever be one.
And when the ungodly are fearing and tremble,
We'll watch for the day when the Savior will come,

When all that was promised, the Saints will be given,
And none will molest them from morn until even,
And earth will appear as the Garden of Eden,
And Jesus will say to all Israel, "Come home."[26]

She took the solemn occasion to remind the crowd at her bedside that they were not just her children, but also her contribution to the ongoing task of building the Mormon Zion, and that they should take up the charge with zeal. Sublimity was a pro-familial society, Alpine a pro-natal one. Both valued marriage and family, but for different ends: one to sustain a close community of kin, the other an extended community of Saints.

\* \* \*

When Junius B. Wright and his bride came to Middleton in 1864, they knew no one else in the Boise Valley. He had been born in Cascade, Pittsylvania County, Virginia, in 1836, the sixth of eight children, and in 1851 his parents migrated by wagon through Kentucky to the lower Midwest. He graduated from a course of medical training in Keokuk, Iowa, in 1859 and in 1860, at age twenty-four, "hung out my shingle in the village of Monterey, Davis County, Iowa, notifying the people that I was a practicing Physician."[27]

During the summer of 1861 Wright met a young lady from Bloomfield, Iowa, and decided that she "might be a prize worth catching. She was the niece of a prominent lawyer and politician of the State, and a lieutenant-colonel in the union army. Her social environment was all that could be desired and though she was only a little past 16 and I was 26 I thought her apparent good qualities would give me an opportunity of training her up so she would be able to take the prize in any field of endeavor."[28] They were married on December 24, 1862. During the Civil War, Wright served in a home guard unit, the Monterey Blues, defending the local area against border ruffians, but as we have seen, he found the wartime period "squally" and, when he

---

[26] *Hymns: Church of Jesus Christ of Latter-day Saints* (Salt Lake City: Deseret Book Company, 1948), No. 118.

[27] Section titled "Our Honey Moon" in Junius B. Wright, "Reminiscences," Idaho State Archives, Boise.

[28] "Our Honey Moon," pp. 2–3, Wright, "Reminiscences."

heard of gold discoveries in Idaho, persuaded his wife that it was "a good time now to take our long delayed honey Moon trip."

The Wrights traveled by buggy across Nebraska and Wyoming to Idaho's Boise Valley. Stopping near the canyon narrows above present-day Caldwell, they built a sixteen-foot-square cabin in which to spend the winter of 1864–5. When a pair of mule drivers came through, looking for winter lodging, he and Elizabeth curtained off a sleeping area for the men. Wright's rambling and digressive memoir is richly detailed as he describes contact with a number of people during the winter, purchasing hay, hunting deer, and exploring the region. But not one of the people he met that winter was kin or a former acquaintance.

When spring came, the couple loaded their furniture and headed out again, "like Abraham of old not knowing whither we were going," thinking perhaps "of going on to Boise and stopping or perhaps go[ing] on into the Boise Basin to the mines." The first night out they camped near the Moses Fowler farm at Middleton, and the next morning Fowler proposed that they stay for a summer. The two agreed that "we would run the farm and divide the proceeds."[29] Wright had concluded by fall that the climate and prospects in the area were good. He went into partnership with a young man from Missouri, and together they purchased a 160-acre claim with a cabin a half mile west of the Fowler place.

The narrative continues, describing a winter at the mining town of Silver City, "a very prosperous mining camp," as part of a series of glowing success stories. "Bob Noble herded sheep for 35 dollars a month, saved his wages and invested in sheep and died a millionaire." A neighbor, Jacob Plowhead, "raised three nice boys that have added much to the personnel of Canyon County and promoted its prosperity." Before 1870 Wright sold his farm and built a hotel in Middleton center. "The country was gradually filling up with people. With Hotel revenue combined with the increasing income from medical practice, I thought I might be able to keep the wolf from the door."[30] Wright describes his role in the opening of new lands and the building of canals, mills, railroads, and housing developments. Yet he never refers in the narrative to his parental family, or the birth of his sons, nor does he mention them or his wife by name. (We know from other sources that her name was Elizabeth Jones.)

In addition to these inadvertent but eloquent expressions of his val-

[29] "Honey Moon Continued," pp. 9–12, Wright, "Reminiscences."
[30] "Honey Moon Continued," pp. 13–14, and untitled sections, Wright, "Reminiscences."

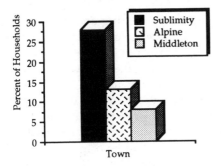

(Source: U.S. Manuscript Census, 1860, Middleton, 1870. Sublimity had ninety-seven households, Alpine fifteen [making the percentage less stable as a comparative measure], and Middleton, fifty-three.)

Figure 4.2 Percentage of households sharing a surname with one or more other households, 1860/1870.

ues, Wright offers a few explicit observations on the role and place of the family in early Middleton. "The valleys," he writes, "were mostly filled with settlers, mostly old bachelors from Missouri, California, and Oregon. A few families among them. Of course, girls over 15 were Scarce and Cowboys were plenty. Any kind of a girl was called handsome."[31] The notes taken by Stafford Mowry, the census taker who made his rounds in the Middleton area in the summer of 1870, confirmed Wright's impression.[32] The settlers of Middleton were a disparate people, more so even than those of Alpine and much more so than those of Sublimity. Residents of but four households shared a surname with another family: Pleasant Latham and William C. Latham, apparently brothers, and Moses Fowler (Wright's partner the first summer) and his brother, Silas. They represent 8 percent of the fifty-three households in the area. (It is interesting that both the Fowler and Latham families had a Tennessee/Kentucky background.) The two Lathams had adjoining places, but the Fowlers were six farms from one another.

Clearly, in Middleton, as in Alpine, there was virtually none of the neighbor/kin clustering that was so common in Sublimity. The absence of such a settlement pattern is no great surprise in Alpine, peopled largely by British converts to Mormonism, all recent immigrants to the United States. But, as we saw in Chap. 2, Middleton's founders were rural people, a good many from the same parts of the United

[31] "Tom Johnson's Courtship," p. 1, Wright, "Reminiscences."
[32] As noted in earlier chapters, Middleton's founders are first visible in the 1870 census, rather than in the 1860 census, which opens Sublimity and Alpine to our view.

States as those of Sublimity, the principal difference being that most
came West a decade or more later – during and just after the Civil
War, drawn by the hope of finding gold or silver. Sublimity was
founded in 1850, and we first capture it in the 1860 census; Middleton
in 1863, our first fix on its people from the 1870 census. Whereas the
Oregon settlers had three extra years of nesting in before their first
census, Middleton folk had seven years before 1870, making it unlikely that the difference in time since settlement could account for
such dramatic differences. Both Oregon and Middleton settlement began in time to take advantage of federal land grants – the Donation
Land Act for the Oregon settlers, the Homestead Act for those of
Idaho – ruling out land availability as a significant influence on the
settlement and social patterns. It would thus seem that the Civil War
combined with the mining booms to precipitate a profound cultural
quake, rending such fundamental societal habits as how people related to kin and neighbors and how, on the new lands of the Far West,
where they could do as they pleased, they distributed themselves on
the landscape. Sublimity was an extension of an old rural America,
Middleton of a new one.

A consequence of that change is the difficulty of reconstructing the
life courses of Middleton people. Many descendants of Sublimity and
Alpine pioneers have carefully researched and preserved their family
histories, finding and compiling records of events vital in the lives of
their ancestors. Very few Middleton people have done so. Middleton's
local historians have made a prodigious effort to gather information
on early settlers. But their product is generally brief and anecdotal,
reporting census information about specific families as they appeared
in 1870 or 1880, listing the first farmers in a district, the names of
millers, blacksmiths, pastors, city officers, the founders of stores and
saloons, or the builders of canals.[33] Sometimes there is information
about where the people came from and where they were bound for
when they left Middleton. But this researcher, with extensive local
connections, newspaper advertisements, and diligent perusal of local
and state archives, has found only an occasional completed family
history of early Middleton settlers. It is evident that Middleton people
have not perceived their past genealogically, as the Sublimity and Al-

---

[33] The principal sources are Morris Foote, comp., *One Hundred Years in Middleton* (Middleton, Idaho: *Boise Valley Herald*, 1963); Middleton Centennial Book Committee *Middleton: In Picture and Story* (Nampa, Idaho: Downtown Printing, 1989); and, most
important, materials gathered over many years by Jennie (Mrs. Vance) Cornell and
kept in numerous files and binders in her extensive collection. The Cornell collection
has information from many sources – newspaper clippings, interviews with descendants, census lists, and others, not all of them identified.

pine people have done. And though one generally wishes to avoid drawing conclusions from negative evidence, where we have other rural districts from the same period to compare with, their local archives yielding an abundance of material, we have to consider seriously the possibility that the near absence of such materials in Middleton is telling us something about the social character of the people who lived there.

We know from the 1870 census that Junius B. Wright, thirty-four, of Virginia was married to a woman named Elizabeth, twenty-four, born in Indiana, and that they had a four-year-old son, Erastus. Other sources indicate that the Wrights left Middleton in 1875, opening a drugstore in Boise for a time, and then moved their business to the town of Caldwell when it was founded in 1883. Wright eventually made his way to the Portland, Oregon area, where he died at age 102, in 1938. Though several sources refer to another son, they do not mention his name. Apparently the Wrights had only the two children.[34]

W. N. Montgomery, who platted the town site, was living in Middleton in 1870 with his wife, Caroline, their son, Ora, five, and their daughter, Rosa, two. He and his family were gone by 1880, and Middleton preserves no memory of their subsequent whereabouts. Moses Fowler and his first wife, Emmaroy, apparently had no children, but by 1870 they had taken in her mother, Mahala Douglas, her blind brother, William, and Elizabeth Fowler, apparently his sister or a sister-in-law of the core couple. Her family had been part of the stream of migration entering the Midwest from New England, the birthplaces revealing that they followed a common migratory track, proceeding from Vermont to New York to Indiana before taking the great leap to the Far West. The household was unchanged in 1880, except for the addition of a nephew, but shortly thereafter, Emmaroy died and Moses married Emma McKenzie, widow of Robert McKenzie, one of the very first settlers in the area. Fowler was living alone at age sixty-eight in 1900 but died three years later. Emma was not counted in the 1900 census but appears again in 1910, living alone except for a boarder.[35]

The unfixed character of these family structures was typical of early Middleton. Only 54 percent of the adult population was married, 78 percent of the women (Sublimity, 74 percent) and but 44 percent of the men (Sublimity, 67 percent). There were in the area sixty-seven unmarried men over nineteen, and but eleven single women over fifteen. Small wonder that every single girl was avidly courted! A good

[34] "J. B. Wright," in Cornell Files, Middleton Idaho.
[35] U.S. Manuscript Census, 1870.

many young men were living with families as hired hands or did not live in families at all. Only seven of fifty-three households (13 percent) consisted of a couple and their children only, and but 72 percent had a nuclear family at their core (Sublimity, 92 percent; Alpine, 100 percent). Of these, 74 percent had persons other than the family in the household, all but two of them with surnames other than those of the core couple. Twenty-eight percent of the fifty-three households consisted of apparently unrelated people, mostly men, batching together.

There were on average but 5 persons in the Middleton homes, considerably fewer than in Alpine or Sublimity (5.7 and 6.1). And far fewer of these were children. For each of the 45 adult woman in Middleton there were between 1 and 2 children (1.75), whereas in Sublimity there were between 2 and 3 (2.38) and in Alpine more than 3 (3.36). The Wrights and the Montgomerys, each family with two children, were typical of Middleton people. They were also typically youthful, for the average age of women in their childbearing years (16–45) was 29.2 in Middleton compared to 28 in Sublimity and 30.4 in Alpine. Part of the reason for fewer children under ten in Middleton per adult woman is that the married couples there were younger and more likely to be just starting their families. Yet these age differences are not great, and the 1910 census, which reports the number of children ever born, suggests that there were differences in fertility that cannot be accounted for entirely by age structure. Looking at women in each of the three communities who were over fifty-five in 1910, and who thus had entered their childbearing years in 1870, the same ranking appears. Sublimity women averaged 6.3 children each, Alpine women 6.9, and Middleton women 5.1. Again, given the possibility in all three societies of some degree of control over fertility, it would seem that the differences must be accounted for in part by varying preferences in family size, reflecting more general societal attitudes toward the bearing of children and the role and purposes of family in human societies.[36]

When the Hunts, Smiths, and Downings came to the West, they did so as families and settled in family clusters. The boundaries of the nuclear family were highly permeable for those of the larger family group. Family was at the core of the social vision. The Strongs, Healeys, and Nashes came as fragments of larger family groups, beginning

---

[36] It would seem possible that Middleton's population, coming west more recently, departed from an America that was more likely to see deliberate family limitation as acceptable. The evidence suggests, however, that the earliest of these populations to come West, the Oregonians, did limit family size in a way that the Utah people did not.

in their new setting the process of reattachment, a process in which church leaders, church aims, and the local church community played central roles, and family was valued as a support to these broader entities. When the Wrights and Montgomerys fled from war to the promise of wealth, they came as isolates – couples or individuals making up a society where family in the larger sense was even more diminished than in Alpine, and where potential moorings were few and frail. The meanings and purposes of family were thereby confined to immediate genetic affinities and loyalties, sharing neither Sublimity's extension of spheres of frequent contact and interaction with an extensive group of kin nor Alpine's with a broader community of fellow believers. The Middleton families, compared to those of Sublimity and Alpine, seemed to live for the most part within themselves.

*    *    *

The different meanings the three societies attached to the family had a direct bearing on the role and place of women. In some respects, those we have seen seem representative of women in each of the societies. Nancy Scott Wisdom Smith Hunt, twice widowed, shepherded her flock of youngsters alone from the Green River to Oregon, there refusing to be humbled by Daniel Waldo and eventually joining her family to that of John Hunt. Eliza Brown Dyer, unshakably converted to her new faith, resolutely refused to yield to her husband's ultimatum, leaving all she had known to take herself and her daughter, Julia, to the Mormon Zion. Her new neighbor in Alpine, Catherine Nash, mother in her native Wiltshire of three illegitimate children but then converted to Mormonism, somehow scratched together the means to bring her boys and a nephew to Alpine, where she began a new life as a contributing and respected member of the community. Elizabeth Jones Wright, who, though unnamed by her husband when he recalled his life in Middleton (and described as an object to be trained up to his liking), nonetheless accompanied him in a buggy all the way from Iowa to the Boise Valley, where she managed in primitive circumstances the myriad domestic tasks vital to their household. Since the women in these farming districts left little introspective writing, it is necessary to interpret their scattered anecdotal accounts and reminiscences in the light of the broader social and economic structures of the three frontiers.

We have seen that the Sublimity folk distributed themselves thinly across the landscape, aggregating in neighbor/kin clusters that admitted little of the social world beyond that visible from the front stoop of their stately frame houses. Habits brought with them from the South and Midwest encouraged the forming of intense family and close neighbor ties, these constituting, to all appearances, the com-

Photo 8 Catherine Kemp Nash. Photograph of a tintype. (Used by permission of June Pack.)

munity in which the greater part of their lives was played out. It was true for them, as for Steven Hahn's upcountry Georgia yeoman, that "families seemed particularly inclined to locate near one another" and that "when family did not reside nearby, yeomen reached out to other farmers in the area, creating bonds of community." The breadth of those bonds as created in Oregon was limited and local. There is little evidence of a wider identification with the civil jurisdiction and trading center of Sublimity, but rather with local farm districts, such as Whiteaker, McAlpin, or Victor Point.[37] Even worship took place prin-

---

[37] Steven Hahn, *The Roots of Southern Populism: Yeoman Farmers and the Transformation of the Georgia Upcountry, 1850–1890* (New York: Oxford University Press, 1983), esp. pp.

cipally in family/neighborhood groups, a pattern of considerable importance to women. Moreover, as we shall see in subsequent chapters, their world, again like that of Hahn's upcountry yeomen, was one where the household was the setting of most production and consumption, where much of the trade and barter took place within the kin/neighbor group, and where each household's first preoccupation was to assure that it could produce enough to sustain its members until the next harvest.[38]

Alexis de Tocqueville's description of a rural society he thought American farmers had never known seems to capture perfectly the aspirations of many of Sublimity's founders. "The family represents the estate, the estate the family, whose name, together with its origin, its glory, its power, and its virtues, is thus perpetuated in an imperishable memorial of the past and as a sure pledge of the future."[39] All of this would seem to have profound implications for the Sublimity women. If indeed this was initially more a generation of dynasty founders than of empire builders, women become central to the enterprise. Production and exchange, like fighting and conquest, can theoretically be accomplished by either sex alone. But dynasty founding cannot. G. W. Kennedy has many woman protagonists in his memoir, *The Pioneer Campfire*, a series of anecdotes about adventures crossing the plains and pioneering the Willamette Valley. The anecdotes stress the women's courage, stamina, and entrepreneurial talents, as well as their domestic skills.[40] Sarah Hunt Steeves, daughter of Sublimity pioneer

52–3; Burton, *In My Father's House Are Many Mansions: Family and Community in Edgefield, South Carolina* (Chapel Hill and London: University of North Carolina Press, 1985); and Robert Kenzer, *Kinship and Neighborhood in a Southern Community: Orange County, North Carolina, 1849–1881* (Knoxville: University of Tennessee Press, 1987).

[38] These two points are elaborated upon in subsequent chapters. The discussion of what constitutes sufficient production for subsistence and for market has produced an extensive literature. See Bettye Hobbs Pruitt, "Self-Sufficiency and the Agricultural Economy of Eighteenth-Century Massachusetts," *William and Mary Quarterly* 41 (July 1984): 333–64; Carole Shammas, "How Self-Sufficient Was Early America?" *Journal of Interdisciplinary History* 13 (1982): 260–2; James A. Henretta, "Families and Farms: Mentalité in Pre-Industrial America," *William and Mary Quarterly*, 3rd Ser., 35 (1978): 3–32; Michael Merrill, "Cash Is Good to Eat: Self-Sufficiency and Exchange in the Rural Economy of the United States," *Radical History Review* 4 (1977), 67–8; and James T. Lemon. *The Best Poor Man's County: A Geographical Study* of Southeastern Pennsylvania (New York: W.W. Norton & Company, 1972).

[39] Alexis de Tocqueville, *Democracy in America*, 2 vols. (New York: Vintage Books, 1961), I: 53.

[40] Tabitha Brown, for example, saved part of a pioneer train when she set out ahead of the starving main party to seek help. Enduring great privation, she kept the ailing man with her on his horse until they were able to catch up with the party in front of them. She later founded a school that grew into Pacific University. Kennedy's

George W. Hunt, wrote, in tones disparaging to men, that among the pioneers "there were men of vicious habits who wanted to get away from all law and order. There were lazy men who had to be prodded all along the way with threats of being left behind on the plains, to become the prey of Indians." They and their families were rescued from the consequences of their frailties and vices by strong women. "Had it not been for their good wives . . . , this threat would have been carried out in many cases."[41] Women seem unusually evident and valued in the surviving accounts of settlement in Oregon.

The voices of the Oregon women did not go unheard. The Nancy Hunts and Temperance Downings were present and active in the social activities of their small kin/neighborhood communities. Yet most such activities took place in family parlors or one-room neighborhood schoolhouses – spaces where female influence was traditionally strong. This was especially evident in religious observances. On a tour of rural districts in the Willamette Valley in July 1848, the Rev. George H. Atkinson found many families holding services in their homes. Pastors of the Disciples of Christ described in the 1850s "little country organizations here and there over the land" and estimated that in Oregon there were "about 1200 disciples, but in a most disorganized condition."[42] Local lore indicates that Oregon women shared with their husbands family worship both in the home and in the ephemeral neighborhood religious groups that characterized the region. G. W. Kennedy's mother and a neighbor lady from Missouri joined in sponsoring a preaching service by the itinerant Rev. Joseph Hines. Kennedy recalled that "Our cabin, being large, was for years the preaching place for the neighborhood." The West Union Baptist Church, a small rural congregation, counted equal numbers of men and women members in 1844 and 1856.[43] The surviving accounts describe an unstructured, family-centered religious life that predated the coming of organized religion and in which men and women participated together, partly because the observances took place in homes or local

mother's ability to "shoot the head of a squirrel" made the children feel secure in their log home while their father fought in the Cayuse War of 1855–6. The mother of one pioneer family clubbed a cougar attacking her child to death with a hand spike. See G. W. Kennedy, *The Pioneer Campfire* (Portland: Clarke-Kundret Printing Co., 1914), pp. 30–7, 51, 59–159, and passim.

[41] Steeves, *Book of Remembrance*, "Preface."

[42] "George H. Atkinson, D.D., 1847–58," *Oregon Historical Quarterly* 40 (1939): 172, 177–8; C. F. Swander, *Making Disciples in Oregon* (C.F. Swander, 1928), p. 40.

[43] Kennedy, *The Pioneer Campfire*, pp. 152–4, 159, 52; Orin Oliphant, ed. "Minutes of the West Union Baptist Church," *Oregon Historical Quarterly* 36 (1935): 253, 371.

schools and under family auspices and initiative, rather than at the instigation of ordained male pastors or church officials.

Women also occupied an important place in the economy of Sublimity. The farms were vast, but as Chapter 5 explains, they produced principally for household use and consumption, which required women, as planners and administrators of household economies, to assume a significant role even in field decisions, such as which crops to plant and when, and how much of which crops to market. In Marion County women would have been partly or principally involved in the production annually on an average farm of 116 pounds of butter, 36 pounds of cheese, 61 pounds of potatoes, and 4 pounds of honey, and in processing 136 pounds of meat and 47 pounds of wool, and caring for seven cows.[44] In addition, they prepared meals requiring the growing and harvesting of garden produce; baked biscuits and bread; made, washed, and mended clothing; and cleaned homes and yards. In short, virtually everything produced on the farm involved the woman in an important role at some point in the process. Even the exchanges of commodities made necessary by seasonal scarcities were negotiated principally by women of the neighbor/kin group, trading eggs for butter and flour for peas. The less commercial orientation of the economy thus placed women in a pivotal role in this society's perception of its purposes and in its efforts to nurture those bearing the family name into the future.

Sublimity women had considerable influence *within* the home – for this folk the social world of most meaning to most persons of both sexes. Yet, when they moved beyond the family and close neighbor/kin group, their influence quickly diminished. More than a third of those over eighteen in Sublimity in 1860 could not read or write (35 of 94; the corresponding figure for men was 15 of 151, or 10 percent). Such women no doubt felt disadvantaged in situations requiring them to deal with those outside their neighbor/kin group. The tax lists of 1862 and 1871 record only two land parcels in women's names (in both instances widows), in spite of the Donation Land Act, which made it possible for wives to claim the same amount of land as their husbands and an 1866 Oregon law permitting women to own personal and real property in their own name. As noted, there are virtually no surviving accounts of formal women's activities outside the home un-

---

[44] U.S. Census, *Agriculture in 1860*, pp. 120–1. Obviously, the amount of production per farm is an estimate, as it was in the original reporting to census takers. The role of women in the production of these commodities, especially butter, and the manner in which that activity linked them to commercial farming are principal themes in Joan M. Jensen, *Loosening the Bonds: Mid-Atlantic Farm Women, 1750–1850* (New Haven, Conn.: Yale University Press, 1986).

til the 1880s. Apparently Sublimity's good wives rarely ventured beyond the kin/neighbor group that defined their social world.

Alpine farmers were like those of Sublimity in producing mainly for the family and for a narrow local market. Their small plots were barely adequate to feed the many mouths, limiting the possibility of surpluses for sale. But in Alpine the taking of land was more an economic necessity than an effort to acquire a base for perpetuation of a dynasty. Family, for these people, was detached from land and came to be inextricably bound up in community. And interaction with that community greatly amplified the sphere of women beyond that of the Sublimity neighbor/kin groups.

The key institution in Alpine was the church – the motivating and driving force behind politics, cooperative economic endeavors, and the center of social life. Neighbors and kin in Alpine likely met more often in the meeting house than in their parlors, the favorite meeting place of Sublimity folk. The lines of a poem written by an Alpine native express it well. "A church arose of sturdy native stone, and five hundred people proudly called it home."[45] Whereas Sublimity settlers dispersed themselves into expansive physical space, Alpine settlers contracted into a compact settlement surrounding the church, which they saw as their home. Whereas the structure of Sublimity was made up of fairly autonomous clusters of neighbors and kin, that of Alpine society comprised the whole population of the village.

What did this mean to the Alpine women? Men filled all positions of ultimate power in their society. Any man deemed worthy by the male church hierarchy could be ordained to the lay ministry which gave him the responsibility of presiding in the home, as well as in most administrative offices of the church. Women could not. But the picture is not simply one of unalloyed male domination. Women, upon marriage, were given powers of priesthood with their husbands. Many were ordained in a priesthood ritual empowering them to anoint and bless others during childbirth, as well as to act as midwives.[46] Catherine Nash was given a "patriarchal blessing" in 1855 by Emer Harris, a church patriarch whose calling was to give blessings to men and women at their request, specifying the lineage and the

[45] La Von Alice Brown Carroll, "Alpine," in Jennie Adams Wild, *Alpine Yesterdays* (Salt Lake City: Blaine Hudson Printing, 1982), p. iv.

[46] Linda King Newell, "A Gift Given, a Gift Taken: Washing, Anointing, and Blessing the Sick Among Mormon Women," *Sunstone* 6 (November/December 1981): 26–7. The following discussion was prepared for a conference on "Women and the Transition to Capitalism in Rural America, 1760–1940," held March 30–April 2, 1989, sponsored by Alan Kulikoff and Northern Illinois University with funding from the National Endowment for the Humanities.

future promise of their lives. In blessing Catherine Nash, a single parent, the patriarch dwelt upon her matriarchal lineage: "Thou art a daughter of Sarah of old," an ancestry that made her "entitled to the holy priesthood which has come down through the lineage of thy father even unto thee and therein entitled to the blessing confirmed upon Sarah and Rebecca of old which is an innumerable posterity." Apparently aware of her difficult early life, he said, "Thou hast seen trouble in thy former days, but thy latter shall be better than thy former, and the fruit of the earth shall be given to you here-after until thou shalt be satisfied therewith." He concluded by assuring her that "thou shalt enjoy the comfort of the Holy Priesthood in connection with thy family and thou shalt have power to administer to thine own family by the laying on of hands in the name of the Lord and they shall be healed from their infirmities" (referring to a healing ritual performed by Mormon priesthood holders).[47] The blessing was remarkable in affirming the importance of Catherine Nash's descent from biblical matriarchs and her right to exercise priesthood power.

A number of Alpine women occupied important (but never principal) positions in the church and in other community organizations. Yet Mormon theology taught that neither men nor women could achieve ultimate celestial happiness unless they married (obviously a condition more limiting for women than for men, who had more opportunity to take the initiative in such matters). But the vision of a patriarch and matriarch presiding over a family into eternity was deeply cherished, their offspring constituting an enduring blessing of incalculable magnitude. So compelling was this image that male church leaders praised and affirmed the potentially revolutionary theology in Eliza R. Snow's hymn.

> I had learned to call thee Father,
> Through thy Spirit from on high;
> But until the key of knowledge
> Was restored, I knew not why.
> In the heavens are parents single?
> No; the thought makes reason stare!
> Truth is reason, truth eternal,
> Tells me I've a mother there.
>
> When I leave this frail existence,
> When I lay this mortal by,
> Father, Mother, may I greet you

[47] Merma G. Carlisle, ed., *Alpine: the Place Where We Lived* (np., nd.), BYU Archives, Provo, Utah.

> In your royal courts on high?
> Then at length when I've completed
> All you sent me forth to do,
> With your mutual approbation
> Let me come and dwell with you.[48]

Thus, ultimate perfection required the cooperation of men and women in forming a family.

The sense that they stood with their husbands at the head of a dynasty extending into the future was as strong among them as among women at Sublimity. Yet they presided with their husbands not so much over a physical domain, identified by particular houses and stretches of land, as over a progeny extending into a celestial future. They did not expect, as did the Sublimity parents, that their children could remain physically close to the family home in this life, but they had not the slightest doubt that they would all share a mansion in the next.

Though clearly men held the key administrative offices in this society, women may have felt themselves more a part of that power structure because the men presiding over congregations and conducting meetings were husbands or close neighbors, not a minister from elsewhere. Any man of the village might be called to preside in the local church. In some respects, formal church organization represented in Alpine an extension of the family organization. Indeed, one couple, Thomas and Margaret Vance McCullough, presided over the congregation and the women's organization for over a quarter of a century, commonly being called by local people the "father" and "mother" of the ward. Both men and women participated in the religious activities the McCulloughs directed.

Alpine women occupied roles in the home and family economy similar to those of Sublimity. Yet they were much more inclined to undertake the tasks of organizing and administering voluntary associations outside the home. Nurturing was their principal responsibility, but the church callings and organizations extended their nurturing work to the entire community, an undertaking no doubt facilitated by the fact that all could read and write. They headed and staffed church-related volunteer societies for children and young women. Elsie Edge Booth was chosen president of the first Primary organization in 1879 and presided over the organization until her death seventeen years later. (The organization provided weekly religious instruction and social activities for all the children in the village.) The Young Women's Retrenchment Association was organized in 1875, its president and

---

[48] *Hymns*, No. 139.

her staff, all women, teaching domestic skills to teenage girls in weekly meetings and providing a regular set of social activities, often coordinated with a similar organization for young men.

The Relief Society, for adult women, was organized in 1868 to direct relief and welfare efforts of the community. That year they raised funds to purchase a loom "to broaden manufacturing of the young people" through donations, in the cash-poor economy, of butter, wool, eggs, wheat, and honey. They also organized a women's choir and appointed a visiting committee to make regular visits to all families in the village needing assistance. In 1874 they attempted "to take hold of the raising of silk for making bonnets and hats." In 1877 they built a granary to hold the wheat they gleaned from the surrounding fields, using it to provide for the poor and a surplus for women's activities in the town.[49] Margaret Vance McCullough, wife of the bishop and mayor, was president of the organization for twenty-four years until 1902. Moreover their work in the community often took them into more secular realms, such as theater groups and choral societies. Public space in Alpine was not exclusively male space; men and women mingled in the home and neighborhood, as in Sublimity, but also in most spheres of the broader society.[50]

Alpine women, like Sublimity women, were the chief planners and administrators of household economies, and thus consulted with the men when decisions were to be about how much of what to plant and to market. Yet the fact that their husbands in a sense commuted to work in the fields outside of town made the domestic hearth, including garden and barnyard animals, more exclusively their domain. The women's production of vegetables, butter, and eggs from backyard gardens and pens accounted for much of the tiny marketable surplus their hardscrabble farmlands produced. Payments of tithes and contributions to community fund-raising efforts were often made in eggs and butter – principally the products of the women of Alpine. In all of Utah County, women would have been partly or principally involved in the production annually on an average 1860 farm, of 91 pounds of butter, 11 pounds of cheese, and 70 bushels of potatoes and

---

[49] The Relief Society Granary was preserved, and local citizens took the initiative to have it added to the National Registry of Historic Sites in 1990, indicating that local people consider it and the activities of the women who built it important in their collective past.

[50] Wild, *Alpine Yesterdays*, pp. 84–86, 89, 95–7, 191–205. The opening of public space to women may have favored the decision in 1870 by the territorial legislature to give women the vote. Several early Utah women traveled east for medical training and returned to practice in the territory. Utahns were the first in the United States to elect a woman state legislator, mayor, and all-woman city council.

in processing 94 pounds of meat, 25 pounds of wool, and 5 gallons of sorghum molasses. They also produced home manufactures worth $24 and cared for four milk cows.[51] The range of a woman's domestic authority and labors was expressed in another folk poem from Alpine titled, with deliberate irony, "The Good Old Days":

> She made all our dresses we didn't wear slacks,
> Our undies were made from Star Flour sacks.
> She'd carry water from outside to boil and scrub our clothes clean,
> And all through the day her kitchen would smell of soap and
>     steam.
> The irons she used to iron our clothes,
> Were heated with care on top of the stoves.
> With spit test of oven, she baked beautiful bread,
> Pies cakes and cookies, she kept us well fed.
> She made lots of butter in that big wooden churn,
> We would wait for the magic to happen as each would take a turn,
> She gathered the eggs, and she milked the cows,
> She shut up the chickens and watered the sows.
> She fed the calves and set the old hen,
> And chased the sheep back into their pen.[52]

In Utah generally, though less so in Alpine, where there were few polygamous families, the burden of managing the household was especially heavy for plural wives. Often economic survival required them to work as principal providers for their families. The frequent absences of the husbands led them to assume a degree of independence otherwise known in Sublimity only among widows. Yet, in these cases, their authority to act came principally from their relationship to their absent husbands. Their function was very close to that of "deputy husbands" – acting with patriarchal authority in the absence of their spouse – described by Laurel Thatcher Ulrich among women of northern New England.[53] The number of polygamous men and men absent on missions (including, in the latter group, a good many from Alpine) probably made this responsibility more widespread and more frequently exercised in the Utah town than in Sublimity. The result was that many Alpine women had to exercise considerable autonomy for extended periods, making a multitude of decisions and carrying out tasks that husband and wife commonly did together. The inde-

---

[51] U.S. Census, *Agriculture in 1860*, pp. 180–1. Sublimity women produced 116 pounds of butter, 36 pounds of cheese, 61 pounds of potatoes, 4 pounds of honey, processed 136 pounds of meat, 47 pounds of wool, and cared for seven cows.

[52] Louise B. Whitby, "The Good Old Days," in Wild, *Alpine Yesterdays*, p. 202.

[53] Laurel Thatcher Ulrich, *Good Wives: Image and Reality in the Lives of Women in Northern New England, 1650–1750* (New York: Alfred A. Knopf, 1982), pp. 35–50.

pendence thus gained may ultimately have been liberating, as some writers have suggested.[54]

In sum, Alpine exhibited a curious mix of the characteristics of proto-capitalist rural life and modern urbanity. The men and women who headed families had a strong sense of continuity and eternal purpose in their lives that related to their roles as parents. Their physical survival depended on what they could get a small, indifferent plot of land to yield, but that land had little meaning beyond its power to provide a meager livelihood. They pursued their lives in a shared social space that involved them in a rich variety of communal activities and expression, similar in nature but transcending in scale the narrow family/kin networks and rootedness in particular lands seen in Sublimity. Their rootedness seemed to make it possible for them to build a critical mass of communal attachment that eluded another set of contemporaries – farmers tilling rich, well-watered bottomlands along the Boise River some 400 miles to the northwest.

In early Middleton, neither the land, as in Sublimity, nor the community, as in Alpine, provided a base for social organization and cohesiveness. Women were nearly as rare in the farming as in the mining districts of the territory, and neither family nor community was a vital institution for the founding population. Early visitors found that Middleton people interacted principally at the local flour mill (at times it served as the post office), the saloon, the race track, and at dances. The mill and saloon were parts of the male domain, excluding one third of the adult population by virtue of their sex. The race course was also principally a male space, devoted to intense competitiveness and a certain recklessness, neither qualities high on the list of late-nineteenth-century female virtues. Dancing was the one public activity that offered the whole adult community some opportunity for social interaction.

If Sublimity society can be represented by small nodes of neighbor/kin groups that dot the landscape and Alpine by an extensive, tightly woven community net, early Middleton would seem to be a series of points spread along the Boise River with but a few faint lines connecting families into neighborhoods or a broader community. Middleton seemed in some measure to have realized what Tocqueville feared might happen in America. "Where family pride ceases to act, individual selfishness comes into play. When the idea of family becomes vague, indeterminate, and uncertain, a man thinks of his pres-

---

[54] See Cheryll L. May, "Charitable Sisters," in Claudia L. Bushman, ed., *Mormon Sisters: Women in Early Utah* (Cambridge, Mass.: Emmeline Press, Ltd., 1976), pp. 225–39.

ent convenience; he provides for the establishment of his next generation and no more."[55]

The effects of these conditions were important to the women of Middleton in several ways. As farmers came to specialize in chickens, hogs, or vegetables, their intent to make a living thereby apparently inhibited the need or opportunity for women to duplicate the effort in backyard gardens or pigpens. It would be misleading to list for Middleton, as we have done in the case of Sublimity and Alpine, the commodities traditionally produced by women. Most of the butter, cheese, and eggs of Middleton was produced by men and their hired hands on a few specialized farms. Where household needs had a smaller claim on overall production, there was less place for women in production and production decisions. The men kept informed on what prices horses, hay, or potatoes were bringing in Silver City and decided what to produce on the basis of that information – information gained in settings where women were seldom present and had little voice. The demands of women for household needs could be met through exchange – a more efficient process than attempting to raise on each farm the full range of commodities needed by the family.

Thus the manner in which these rural women related to agrarian economic activities was dramatically different. Production and consumption were becoming separate enterprises, mediated only by the transfer of money allocated from one activity to the other. Rather than being partners in production on the family farm, Middleton women were becoming principally consumers, who purchased goods needed by the household from profits earned through primarily male production enterprises.[56] Though they had long played a vital role in *family* economic life, they as yet had no clearly defined and accepted role in *public* economic life – selling commodities in the marketplace and buying foods and household goods there. Their early reluctance to enter this world may explain in part the phenomenal rise of the mail order catalog industry in the last quarter of the nineteenth century. It was not just that the catalog offered a much greater range of goods than the local storekeeper could stock. New opportunities to make purchases by mail permitted the redefined economic responsibility of women to take place in the same setting as did the old, in the home, and without having to enter a traditionally male public

---

[55] Alexis de Tocqueville, *Democracy in America*, 2 vols (New York: Vintage Books, 1961), I: 52.

[56] Jeanne Boydston's work on this matter is helpful. See *Home and Work: Housework, Wages, and the Ideology of Labor in the Early Republic* (New York: Oxford University Press, 1990).

space, the streets and shops of the village. Increasingly restricted in
their role as producers, these rural women began to concentrate exclusively on housekeeping and mothering, their principal economic
activity reduced to that of making consumer decisions for the purchase of the many items they had once helped to produce.

Had there been in Middleton a well-developed community, these
women might, as in Alpine, have become involved in churches or
other voluntary associations and found a sphere where at least moral
authority could be exercised in spite of the limitations imposed by
new purposes and means of production and marketing. A few, such
as Cordelia Foote, who helped to found a Baptist gathering in Middleton village in 1886, did. But most lived on isolated farmsteads scattered some eight miles along the bottoms on either side of the Boise
River, making such association difficult and rare. Neither the close
neighbor/kin nodes that characterized the social landscape of Sublimity nor the community orientation of an Alpine were available to
them.

Perhaps predictably, the Idaho women seem as obscure in public
memory as they were few in numbers. It is as if the exclusively commercial character of farm production there diminished the need for
women and the very record of their presence. On the largely self-
sufficient and subsistence farms of Oregon, women had clear and
needed work outside the house but within the farm economy. Alpine
women had similar responsibilities, but they also worked outside of
the household in various community endeavors that took them early
into public, male space. In the commercial farming society of Middleton, women's roles outside the home were more limited. Isolated
physically and socially, they turned inward, mirroring a society that
was becoming increasingly market oriented, valuing land principally
for its commercial potential – a society that formed few and weak ties,
whether to neighborhood or village. Perhaps bringing with them values that had been drastically altered by the cataclysmic national events
of the 1860s – the Civil War and the lotterylike allure of the local
mining booms, they formed a materialistic and individualistic society
far more familiar to our times than one can discern either in Sublimity
or Alpine.

In such a society, women became in some senses more free. Many
chores related to family production were no longer required. Their
new role as consumers propelled them with greater frequency into
male space and into new types of work, permitting in time a new
sphere of independence. But at the same time, their role in production
decisions relating to the family enterprise was diminished, eroding for
a time their economic authority and their power in their traditional

domain. Moreover, the new direction transformed communities of personal affinity into communities of exchange, creating a new type of personal isolation unknown in Sublimity or Alpine. The different meanings and purposes of family in the three societies had shaped powerfully the role and place of the women whose labors had brought those families into being. Those meanings were eloquently expressed in narratives left at life's most crucial transition by persons who had lived in Sublimity, Alpine, and Middleton.

In 1890 George Washington Hunt, who had come to Sublimity with his father, John S. Hunt, in 1847, wrote his last will and testament. In the document he designated a plot of land to be "set apart and dedicated" as a family cemetery. He ordered further that all his lands remain forever in possession of the "heirs of my body," an evocative phrase he used three times in that short document. At perhaps the most crucial moment of life, when contemplating what its fundamental purposes had been, George Hunt saw two gifts he could leave to future generations – his body, as perpetuated through his descendants, and his land. And the two were to be inseparable. For Hunt and his Sublimity neighbors the family was not only the central institution of society, it was central to the purpose of life itself.[57]

When Alpine's Caroline Henrietta Lind Adams considered what her deathbed legacy would be, she chose to sing a hymn to her twelve children. The text reminded them that in Mormonism the family had found community and refuge. ("Now let us rejoice in the day of salvation. No longer as strangers on earth need we roam.") They were to commit their future lives to that community even if it meant personal sacrifice. Failing to honor the communal vision would be a grievous sin. ("We'll love one another and never dissemble, but cease to do evil and ever be one.") But fidelity to that vision would prepare mankind for the millennium and bring it eternally into the family of God. ("When earth will appear as the Garden of Eden, and Jesus will say to all Israel, 'Come home.'")[58] In her parting words there were no references to land or even family, but instead powerful admonitions to perpetuate the Mormon community and its sustaining religious vision.

James Spangler, who spent part of his childhood in Middleton when

---

[57] Probate Case Files, No. 2168, Marion County Court House, Salem, Oregon. Hunt's instructions were specific: The lands left to his children "shall descend to the heirs of their bodies only and in case there shall be no heirs of any one of their bodies the land of that one without said heirs shall revert to the other heirs of my body." All of his surviving children, sons and daughters, received, through his and his wife's wills, equal 160-acre portions.

[58] *Hymns*, No. 118.

his family sought refuge there from the Civil War, died in 1934. He was a man, his sister recalled, who, like J. B. Wright, "was ambitious to gain wealth and very early began to accumulate. . . . He was dutiful and helpful to the home folk but always had the larger profits for himself." Though once he had been a wealthy man, the Great Depression had by 1934 taken his fortune. His sister wrote that "nature was kind and he never quite realized that he was no longer Bank President nor Farmer Jim as he preferred to be called. The shock of the first big bank failure obliterated his mentality for present events." Mary Spangler Luster, writing in the eighty-first year of her own life, was nonetheless shaken by the death of her brother. "Jim's death leaves me the last of the ten whose story I have told. . . . I can not quite tell you how my heart sunk and the wave of loneliness that overcame me when I realized the last link was broken and no one was left who knew the story with me." Not assured that her progeny would continue the clan on family lands, or comforted by the thought that offspring would perpetuate an enduring community of Saints, she understood that she alone had escaped to tell us – ensuring her immortality not by dynastic or communal continuity, but by writing, in her eighty-first year, the shortly-to-end story of her family's odyssey to Middleton.[59]

[59] Mary R. Luster, *The Autobiography of Mary R. Luster* (Springfield, Mo.: np., nd.), pp. 192–3, 196.

# 5    *The soil to our posterity*

This is Sublimity's chapter. There, the land was to support and sustain the family for generations hence. It ensured continuity into the future and would tie future kin to the past. Most settlers thus claimed large tracts but farmed little, content to feed their families, sell a small surplus, and save the rest for children and grandchildren.

For Alpine people land had no special meaning. Their tiny farms provided a bare subsistence, but not much more. There was too little to hope to leave a patrimony to their abundant progeny. Family destiny was intertwined with that of the town, not of particular parcels of land.

Middleton's settlers saw land as a resource to be exploited for its commercial potential. They claimed tracts that could be farmed efficiently and produced staple crops for sale in the market. A mine or a mill would have done as well. And the land was readily abandoned as opportunities diminished and new ones arose.

In 1927 Sarah Hunt Steeves explained why her parents and their neighbors had come to the Willamette:

> To these pathfinders there was gold to be had in sunny California; the great cattle ranges of Idaho held out the promise of wild, untrammeled life, with easy money; but to those early pioneers who came with their families to the valley of the Willamette, the desire for land upon which to build homes, with the better opportunity for their growing sons, was the idea uppermost in their minds.[1]

T. T. Geer, a son of 1847 pioneers and a contemporary of Steeves, sounded a similar theme in comparing Oregon's first settlers with those of California. There was nothing among the Californians, Geer said, "that bound them to the country; they were not and did not

---

[1] Sarah Hunt Steeves, *Book of Remembrance of Marion County, Oregon, Pioneers, 1840–1860* (Portland: The Berncliff Press, 1927), p. 11.

intend to become landholders." In contrast, the Oregon settlers "had in view the acquisition of lands," and having arrived in the Willamette, they "settled down to the cultivation of the soil at once and the erection of homes."[2] In emphasizing the appeal of the land as a homesite, Steeves and Geer seem at first glance simply to have been repeating the most common cliché of western settlement. But a closer look suggests that they understood their parents well. Steeves made it clear that the early Sublimity folk had not been devoid of options. They had deliberately chosen the Willamette Valley over the "gold . . . in sunny California" or the "wild untrammeled life" and "easy money" Steeves imagined Idaho settlers enjoyed. As she saw it, her grandparents and parents sought the Willamette lands because they offered important advantages over other forms of wealth. They provided opportunities for "growing sons," and thus would be the bedrock of a particular, and to her mind superior, society. The vision she and Geer evoked would have been applauded by Thomas Jefferson, America's most influential advocate of agrarian life, who died just a few years before their parents were born.

It was in fact Thomas Jefferson who had sponsored the 1804–6 expedition of Meriwether Lewis and William Clark up the Missouri to the Columbia that first opened the Willamette area to American consciousness. They concluded in a widely read report, that the valley was

> the only desireable situation for a settlement on the western side of the Rocky mountains, and being naturally fertile, would, if properly cultivated, afford subsistence for forty or fifty thousand souls. The highlands [i.e., Sublimity country] are generally of a dark rich loam, not much injured by stones, and though waving, by no means too steep for cultivation, and a few miles from the river they widen at least on the north side, into rich extensive prairies.[3]

Six years later, Alexander Ross, one of the traders working for John Jacob Astor's American Fur Company, concluded that "as regards agricultural purposes, Bellevue Point and the valley of the Wallamitte were the most favorable spots we met with," though Ross's good news was not published before 1849.[4]

[2] T. T. Geer, *Fifty Years in Oregon* (New York: The Neale Publishing Company, 1912), pp. 18–19.

[3] Nicholas Biddle, ed., *The Journals of the Expedition under the Command of Capts. Lewis and Clark . . . to the Pacific Ocean*, 2 vols. (New York: The Heritage Press, 1962), 2: 422. The Biddle edition of the Lewis and Clark Journals, the first published, appeared in 1814 and was widely read by Americans of the period. Their description of the "highlands" is recognizably Sublimity country.

[4] Alexander Ross, Foreword by James P. Ronda, *Adventures of the First Settlers on the*

By that time Oregon fever had become an epidemic, and a small army of self-appointed evangelists was preaching the virtues of the Willamette as zealously as Henry Ward Beecher the evils of ale. Many, such as Missouri Senator Thomas Hart Benton, Protestant missionaries, Jason Lee and Marcus Whitman, and Boston school teacher Hall J. Kelley, saw the question in geopolitical and georeligious terms. More than the richness of Willamette, soils they stressed the proximity of Astoria to Canton (and thus the missionary and commercial potential of the region to the United States).[5] Kelley, for example, had as a youth read Nicholas Biddle's version of the Lewis and Clark journals and in 1817 was struck by something of an Oregon epiphany. "The word came expressly to me to go and labor in the field of philanthropic enterprise and promote the propogation of Christianity in the dark and cruel places about the shores of the Pacific." He published his "Geographical Sketch of . . . Oregon" in 1830, before he had been there, outdoing Lewis and Clark in his praise of the region. "The top soil is a deep black mould; the forests are heavy and extensive; and the trees are of vast dimensions; and vegetation, generally, is luxuriant to a degree unknown in any other part of America; and we can add, that there are physical causes to render the climate the most healthful in the world."[6]

All along the valleys of the Mississippi and Missouri, farm folk, like the Hunts and Downings, read the newspapers, tracts, and pamphlets, listened to the lectures and sermons, and, although not ignoring talk about foreign trade and markets, took the message most important to them – that the Willamette offered abundant fertile land in a healthful climate. In the mid-1840s, news spread that the U.S. Congress was considering granting a full section free to American families willing to settle along the Northwest coast, and the call of Oregon became seductive beyond endurance.[7]

---

*Oregon or Columbia River, 1810–1813* (Lincoln: University of Nebraska Press, 1986), pp. 120–1.

[5] For example, Peter A. Browne published in 1843 a set of lectures in which he maintained that "the soil is fruitful, the climate moderate, and the mountains . . . filled with mineral wealth. The mouth of the Columbia River is the finest site in the known world for a commercial city. It is within ten day's sail and six day's [sic] steamboat navigation of the Sandwich Islands, and within thirty days, over an unruffled ocean, of Canton. In the hands of a free and enterprising people there is scarcely any limit to the opulence of such a city." Peter A. Browne, "Oregon Territory" (Philadelphia: United States Book & Job Printing Office, 1843), p. 8.

[6] Hall J. Kelley, *A Geographical Sketch of that Part of North America called Oregon* (Boston: J. Howe, 1830), as printed in Fred W. Powell, ed., *Hall J. Kelley on Oregon* (Princeton, N.J.: Princeton University Press, 1932), pp. ix, 21.

[7] A bill authorizing land grants to Oregon settlers was introduced in the U.S. House of

The dream of a grand estate on the Pacific became a reality on September 27, 1850, when Congress, eager to reward Oregon pioneers and to accelerate settlement, passed the Donation Land Law. The law granted 320 acres to single persons and 640 acres to married couples who established residence in Oregon before December 1, 1851. It allowed Sublimity area pioneers like Daniel Waldo, George W. Hunt, and his neighbor Paul Darst to take legal title to the lands they had previously claimed. Hunt remembered that by 1854, when "there was scarcely a settler on every square mile of the best of the land, and on the poorest of the land no settlers at all, they thought the country was all settled up."[8]

Though they may have felt crowded by 1854, they in fact had plenty of elbow room. In 1857 the imposing, dour figure of Paul Darst rode from farm to farm assessing, for tax purposes, the property of the 104 men who paid taxes in the Sublimity area. Their average farm (median) was a commodious 292 acres (mean, 312 acres). The Donation Land Claim Act had greatly influenced the size of their farms. George W. Hunt owned 640 acres, and almost a third of his fellow taxpayers (30 percent) also owned land in either the 640- or 320-acre parcel that was their statutory right under the Land Claim Act. John Downing, with 682 acres, had the most land of any of Sublimity folk. He and George Hunt were among the 49 percent who had farms of 320 acres or larger. Eighty-one percent of all taxpayers owned at least some land, the smallest parcel, that of F. E. Caldwell, being twenty-three acres.

In contrast, the one-time neighbors of the Hunts, still in Wayne County, Indiana, had by that time much smaller farms, averaging 135 acres, as did the former neighbors of the Downings, in Davis County, Iowa, averaging 164 acres. Those who had come to the Willamette Valley commonly owned twice as much land as those who stayed behind.[9]

Representatives in 1824 by John Floyd of Virginia, a cousin of Sergeant Charles Floyd, of the Lewis and Clark expedition, and a good friend of General William Clark and of Senator Thomas Hart Benton. The bill failed, as did another introduced in 1827, but by 1842 bills were being introduced offering a square mile of land to American men over eighteen who settled in Oregon, the news certainly augmenting the large migration of 1843. See Charles Henry Carey, *History of Oregon* (Portland: The Pioneer Historical Publishing Company, 1922), pp. 307–11, 364.

[8] G. W. Hunt, "History of the Hunt Family," quoted in Steeves, *Book of Remembrance*, p. 107.

[9] Sublimity area holdings are from the manuscript tax assessment rolls for Marion County, 1857, Oregon State Archives, Salem. Oregon, Utah, and Idaho laws at the time mandated that property be assessed at full market value. Data on the size of average farms in Indiana and Iowa are calculated from U.S. Census, *Agriculture of the United*

In the typical migration from Virginia, Kentucky, or Tennessee to Indiana, Illinois, and Missouri, the yeomen and women had escaped a galling hierarchical social structure whereby a few planters controlled great tracts of land, leaving others little opportunity to increase their holdings.[10] In the Midwest they found more commodious tracts and relative social equality and independence.[11] On the Pacific they became at last proprietors of estates that bid fair to rival in size those of the planters whose privileges and position they and their parents had for generations viewed with longing from afar. It seemed that in Oregon the dreams of generations of poor whites from the Old South had found their ultimate fulfillment.

\* \* \*

The Mormons who settled in Alpine had likewise been driven west by compelling visions, but of an altogether different sort. Many had been industrial workers in their native England, tending the spinning machines and power looms that transformed into finished cloth the bales of cotton shipped across the Atlantic by southern planters (among whom many of Sublimity's founders had lived). Industrialization had largely severed for them the ancient nexus of family and land. More compelling than land was the hope of escape from "Babylon," which in the language of nineteenth-century Mormon missionaries meant the sins and corruption of a decadent world. But to these people, escape from Babylon meant more. It meant escape from the confusion and unpredictability that industrialization had thrust upon them.

The Mormon missionaries were shocked at the squalor of English industrial districts. They saw a resonance between sin and the living conditions of the English working classes and explicitly stated that their message offered escape from both. Repentance and baptism freed the convert from sin, and gathering with the Saints to the remote oases of Utah freed them from the cacophony of the industrial world. One

*States in 1860* (Washington, D.C.: Government Printing Office, 1864), pp. 42, 46, 198–9. The tax rolls for Sublimity, as for Alpine and Middleton, list, of course, only those obligated to pay taxes and often do not include the penurious. They do, however, report nonlandowners and thus represent a reasonably broad spectrum of the households in the area.

[10] Eugene D. Genovese, *The Political Economy of Slavery: Studies in the Economy and Society of the Slave South* (New York: Random House Vintage, 1965); Gavin Wright, *The Political Economy of the Cotton South: Households, Markets, and Wealth in the Nineteenth Century* (New York: W.W. Norton & Company, 1978), pp. 26–37.

[11] The most common farm size in Sugar Creek, Illinois, in the 1840s was eighty acres. John Mack Faragher, *Sugar Creek: Life on the Illinois Prairie* (New Haven, Conn.: Yale University Press, 1986).

Mormon elder attempted to counter the charge of a Manchester pastor that the doctrine of the gathering was not scriptural. "Now really it would seem when millions are either starving or slaving for a precarious subsistence in this country, it would not need much teaching or scripture to persuade them to go where provision and land are cheap and plentiful, and employment in abundance for millions of people." The Mormon periodical, *The Millennial Star*, underscored the point in "A Mormon Farmer's Song," to be sung to the tune of the popular "Life on an Ocean Wave":

> A life on my own free soil,
> A home on the Salt Lake sod,
> I'll never at labor recoil,
> But thankfully worship my God;
> For Babylon has not a charm,
> With its turmoil and noise and strife,
> O give me a flourishing farm,
> With a kind and endearing wife.

> Chorus:
> A life on my own free soil,
> A home on a farmer's cot,
> Among Mormons I'll labor and toil,
> And ask for no happier lot.

The song ended with an extra chorus that struck a deep chord among the Mormon converts from Lancashire and the surrounding counties:

> From the Yoke of the tyrant set free,
> his "rattle box bell" quite forgot
> A home in the valley give me
> and kings may well envy my lot.[12]

On the Mormon Farm they would be free from the tyranny of the foreman. Their lives would follow their own rhythms, not those set by the "rattle box bell," a device that marked shift changes and rest periods for industrial workers. As they sailed from Liverpool out into the Atlantic, bound for the "Mountains of Ephraim," the babel of factory work and life receded, and in its place came visions of an ordered, harmonious future among mutually caring fellow Saints in Zion.

In Utah most did, indeed, turn to farming, finding it necessary to abandon or relegate to marginality the trades they had mastered in their youth. Though Mormon church leaders were desperate to found

---

[12] *Millennial Star* I, No. 10 (February 1841): 252; I, No. 8 (December 1840): 210; XII, No. 1 (January 1, 1850): 48.

basic industries and made heroic efforts to do so, industrialization in Utah was slow in coming and progressed with fits and starts.[13] Incoming converts commonly made their way to one of the oases along the western edge of the Wasatch Mountains and there became Mormon farmers.

Alpine was one of nearly 500 such oases. It may have had some advantages over the working-class districts of Liverpool or Preston, but it offered farmers only the meanest, hardscrabble living. William and Julia Dyer Strong, already parents of William, seven, Don, four, and infant Julia, reported to tax assessors in 1860 that they owned fifteen acres of land. There were as many of their neighbors who farmed less than that amount as there were who farmed more. James and Mary Healey also had a young family – William, eight, Mary, four, and Elizabeth, two. James tilled seven acres, close to the minimum (six acres) for the community, but the Catherine Nash family, their property listed under the name of Catherine's oldest son, Worthy, had a forty-acre farm, the largest in the settlement.[14] There were altogether twenty-one taxpayers. Their farmlands lay outside the townsite (often non-contiguous parcels) and were on average just slightly larger (mean, 15.4) than William Strong's 15 acres. All but two of the Alpiners had at least some land, but only three had farms larger than the smallest in Sublimity, F. E. Caldwell's twenty-three acres. Clearly, the resources available to support a family were minimal. Households were nearly as large as those of Sublimity (5.7 to Sublimity's 6.1 persons per household; median for both, 6), yet average farms were less than one-twentieth the size of those in the Oregon district.[15]

Why were their farms so relatively small? Beginning their move to the Far West in 1846 as refugees from the United States, the Mormons had been drawn back into the net of U.S. jurisdiction through the Mexican War and the subsequent treaty of Guadalupe Hidalgo of 1848. U.S. officials, though welcoming an American presence in the region, were nonetheless ambivalent about this particular group of

---

[13] These efforts are the principal concern of Leonard J. Arrington's classic study of Mormon economic development, *Great Basin Kingdom* (Cambridge, Mass.: Harvard University Press, 1958).

[14] The household consisted of twenty-four-year-old Worthy, listed first; his brother Ephraim, twenty-two; their mother Catherine, forty-seven; and their cousin, Albert Marsh, then eighteen.

[15] The 1860 tax rolls for Alpine are, through some mysterious archival shuffling process, in the possession of the Special Collections Library, of Utah State University. I am indebted to a colleague, Charles M. Hatch, for calling them to my attention and making them available to me.

settlers and felt no need to offer them incentives to populate the West, as they had the Oregon pioneers. There was no Donation Land Claim Act for Utah. There was not even a federal land office until 1868, when a mining boom stimulated an influx of non-Mormons, whose property interests, federal officials determined, needed protecting. But the limited amount of arable land would have made tracts as large as those available to Oregon pioneers impractical even had the U.S. government chosen to offer them. The *total* amount of land divided among Alpine's twenty-one taxpayers was 323 acres – about the same as the minimum plot available to each farmer in Oregon under the Donation Land Claim Act. Thirty-four of the Sublimity farmers had more land than the 323 acres all of the Alpine farmers shared. In Utah, arable land had to be close enough to creeks or rivers for irrigation, level enough for water to flow evenly through ditch and furrow networks, and at an elevation not subject to late and early frosts. The quantity of land in the Great Basin meeting these essential criteria was severely limited. The Alpine town choir, at their Independence Day Celebration in 1863, must have sung with fervor the anthem "Give us Room That We May Dwell."[16]

But the austere character of the land is only part of the answer. There were for the Mormons, as for the Sublimity settlers, options. In the mid-1840s, while planning their move from Illinois, Mormon leaders considered possible settlement sites in Texas, northern Michigan, and Vancouver Island. One group traveled to San Francisco by sea in 1846, and had already founded a colony in the San Joaquin Valley before Brigham Young's advance party reached the Great Salt Lake. Their leader, Sam Brannan, met Young and his party in the summer of 1847 on the Green River in present Wyoming and urged them to join his group in Central California. Mormons recently discharged from service in the Mexican War arrived in the Salt Lake Valley that fall after traveling overland from San Diego and Los Angeles and spoke of opportunities for settlement in Southern California.[17] Thousands of other Americans (including the Hunts and Downings) were on the trail that year for Oregon, where it was widely known that huge tracts of prime Willamette Valley land were still available.

Brigham Young considered these and other options and rejected them. The fact was that abundant land was not the first priority for the Mormons. What they sought above all was refuge – a place where they would be left alone to build a society according to their own

---

[16] *Deseret News* 13 (July 5, 1863): 24.
[17] Eugene E. Campbell, "A history of the Church of Jesus Christ of Latter-Day Saints in California, 1846–1946" (Ph.D. diss., University of Southern California, 1952).

lights. As Brigham Young later put it, the Salt Lake area was "a good place to make Saints," by which he meant that the region was relatively free from material distractions and devoid of prior settlers, among whom in the Midwest the Mormons had always experienced opposition and conflict.[18] The principal qualities that the new home of the Mormons should have were isolation and remoteness. Beyond that, all that was needed was enough farm land to grow an adequate supply of food and fiber for the settlers. If they could subsist in the Great Basin, that would suffice.[19]

Hoping to provide a sufficiency for all Latter-day Saints who might wish to come to Zion, the Mormon leaders worked out their own land allotment system based on the principle of usufruct (one should have no more than one could till). In opening new settlements, they often distributed land by lot, in five-, ten-, or fifteen-acre parcels, with fifteen to twenty acres deemed sufficient for a thrifty farm.[20] The earliest Alpine settlers worked land in one large field, probably with separate parcels surrounded by a common fence on the outer perimeter. And though we have found no account of how or when they divided the "big field" into private holdings, the predominance of fifteen-acre plots in 1860 (one-quarter of the taxpayers farmed that amount of land) suggests that the initial allocation may have followed the common practice.[21]

Not one of the 1860 Alpine taxpayers reported undeveloped lands that could open the possibility of future growth, a fact eloquent in its implications for the many children being born to Alpine couples. The Mountains of Ephraim apparently offered the Mormon converts little material advantage over the sweatshops of Manchester, and it is abundantly clear that the Mormon Elders' promise of "cheap and plentiful" land was severely qualified by the actual circumstances in Utah. The Strongs and Healeys had good reason to question whether their children could be fed and clothed from such farms, let alone receive a patrimony.

[18] Sermon of Brigham Young, August 17, 1856, in *Journal of Discourses*, 26 vols. (London: S. W. Richards, 1857), 4: 32.

[19] See Arrington, *Great Basin Kingdom*, p. 41.

[20] The smaller parcels were closer to the town center; the larger were on the outskirts. An artisan might be granted only a five- or ten-acre plot. A farmer might have a closer five-acre and a more distant ten-acre plot or an even more remote fifteen-acre plot.

[21] Journal History, October 24, 1857, LDS Church Historical Department, Salt Lake City, Utah. On Mormon land distribution practices see Feramorz Y. Fox, "The Mormon Land System: A Study of the Settlement and Utilization of Land Under the Mormon Church" (Ph.D. diss., Northwestern University, 1932).

*   *   *

Middleton's settlers, like those of Alpine, did not see land as the principal attraction drawing them toward the Far West. Typical were Lewis and Harriet Spangler, of Kentucky origin, who had moved to Illinois and then in 1858 to Missouri. After a six-year sojourn there, "the tragedies of the Civil War drove us roaming again." Their son-in-law, John White, a Union sympathizer, returned to Illinois with his wife, Susan, and their children. The oldest Spangler son, Norval, enlisted in the Confederate cause. Their home was ransacked by militiamen demanding food, lodging, and firearms.

"We suffered many outrages by irresponsible soldiers," the next-to-youngest child, Mary, remembered, "most of them our own State militia, and several of them former neighbors, whom father had kept in food during several months." Lewis Spangler was eventually arrested for his Confederate sympathies, taken to Alton, Illinois, and imprisoned for several weeks before being released after being forced to swear allegiance to the Union. The second son, David, ran away to join the Confederate army during his father's absence, and his younger brother, Jim, tried to follow after having his life threatened by Union raiders.

Expecting their home to be burned by bushwhackers, they moved back in 1863 to Illinois, where they were living when they received the terrible news of Norval's death in the battle of Baker's Creek, near Vicksburg, Mississippi. In Illinois, they soon realized, John White and the eighteen-year-old Jim could be drafted into the Union army. "To escape the calamity of brother fighting against brother, the family decided to join the great tide of emigration that went West the summer of 1864 and to start before the draft caught us." Mary Luster surmised that the several families they traveled with "were probably impelled by the same motives. West of Missouri were mostly territories and it seemed like going to another country to leave the States and while we lived in the west we always spoke of going back to the states."[22]

In all this narrative, there is no mention of traveling to the West to realize unfulfilled hopes or dreams – no talk of free land or of gathering with like-minded people. Certainly for Sublimity and Alpine settlers, as for those who came to Middleton, the West was in some measure a place of refuge. Some of the Sublimity settlers had sought refuge from the rigid hierarchy and increasing limitation on opportunities for yeomen in the Old South. Alpine settlers hoped to escape the perils of life as industrial workers and to follow their faith without

[22] Mary R. Luster, *The Autobiography of Mary R. Luster* (Springfield, Mo., n.p., 1933), pp. 39, 54, and passim.

persecution. But accompanying their quests for refuge were alluring visions of becoming proprietors of huge estates or of gathering into a harmonious heaven-blessed community with other Saints. There is little of hope or promise in the Spangler journey. Their errand into the wilderness was expedient, not purposeful.

Passing through the Boise Valley in 1864, the Spanglers stopped to nurse a gravely ill daughter, Isabell. After her death and burial at Middleton, they settled down and laid claim to a piece of land. There Lewis Spangler farmed and took time to serve as a county commissioner and justice of the peace. Harriet and Mary, finding that eggs were a dollar a dozen and fryers a dollar apiece, "started in the chicken business."[23] Mary remembered that in the first summer "we cleared seventy-five dollars and had thirty hens to start our next year's business. . . . My three hills of water melons netted me seven dollars and I sold eight dollars worth of onions and radishes."[24] But in 1868, with the Civil War ended, the family decided, for reasons not evident in the narrative, to return to Missouri. They sold their land claim to a Thomas Woods, and with no apparent regrets left Middleton to complete their odyssey, returning to Cass County, Missouri, where they eventually bought a farm and spent the remainder of their days.[25]

The Spangler narrative echoes that of Junius Wright, a physician, who must have arrived in Middleton barely in time to tend the Spangler's daughter, Isabell, in her fatal illness. Both narratives make it clear that, with mining camps offering premium prices for vegetables, grain, and hay, farming proved to be as remunerative as mining. Mary called her raising chickens a "business." Junius remembered his growing vegetables as "profitable." Yet a decision to profit from a land claim did not shut out the possibility of striking it rich in the mines. The Spangler boys worked both on farms and in the mines, as did Junius Wright. Like the Spanglers and Wright, many Middleton farmers shuttled from farm to mine while working their land. And if the mines did not pay, the land claim could be worked for a profit or eventually sold to advantage, as both the Spanglers and the Wrights learned. Thus the deeper social and familial meanings of land own-

---

[23] Her reference to their enterprise as a "business" is significant. Memoirs from Sublimity and Alpine farmers use words like "raising" or "growing" in reference to farming activities, but never starting "a business."

[24] Luster, *Autobiography*, passim, and pp. 80–1.

[25] Mary Spangler Luster remembered that Thomas Woods was from Virginia. He is listed in the 1870 census as a native of Georgia, but her memory that he married Viola Kennedy is confirmed by the census. The quit claim deed that the Spanglers used to convey their land to the Woodses apparently proved invalid, as in 1870 Wood is listed as a farm laborer without real estate but with $600 in personal property.

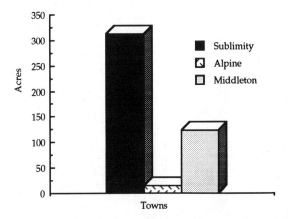

(For sources, see footnotes 9, 15, 27, and 28)

Figure 5.1 Mean size of farms, early Sublimity, Alpine, and Middleton.

ership, felt by their predecessors who came to Oregon, were gradually eroded and its possession was becoming in the minds of these people, like that of a shop, a store, or a mine, one of many equally acceptable means of making a living.

The dual-enterprise strategy for survival in early Idaho was widespread. Wright reported that when he arrived in the fall of 1864, "all available farm sites along the River from the Canyon nine miles above Boise to its union with the Snake fifty miles below was taken under the law of squatter's rights."[26] And though the first claims to Boise Valley land were without legal title, the Homestead Act had, by 1870, placed its imprint on the Valley as clearly as had the Donation Land Claim Act on Sublimity a decade earlier. The average size of the farms in Middleton in 1870 was (median) 151 acres (mean, 122.9). Thirty-one percent of the fifty-one taxpayers owned 160-acre parcels, their allotment under the Homestead Act. Yet, in the Boise Valley, land was less widely distributed. Whereas in Sublimity 81 percent of the taxpayers owned land, and in Alpine 90 percent owned at least a few acres, in Middleton but 72 percent were landowners. Those who claimed land, then, had substantial farms. Though one settler had but 8 acres, the next two largest farms were 80 acres each, and the largest was an extensive 400-acre spread.[27]

---

[26] "Our Honeymoon," p. 9, Junius B. Wright "Reminiscences," Idaho State Archives, Boise Idaho.
[27] The data are from 1860 tax assessment rolls for the part of Ada County that later

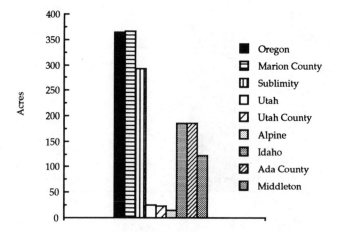

(For sources see footnotes 9, 15, 27, and 28)

Figure 5.2 Average (mean) acres per farm for states, counties, and towns, Oregon and Utah, 1860; Idaho, 1870.

We see then three different peoples drawn to the frontier between 1840 and 1870, each propelled into their arduous and dangerous journey by different dreams. Land filled the vision only of the Oregon bound. Those gathering to Utah wanted to be near others of their faith and to live under the tutelage of their prophet; those to Idaho sought escape from the ravages of war and hoped to find wealth in gold and silver.

Opportunities in the new lands varied greatly. The abundance of rain, the moderate climate, and the rolling Willamette countryside offered seemingly unbounded virgin farmlands, though some of the ridge and hill land was taken up by stands of pine and fir, especially

became Canyon County. The records were kindly made available to me by the County Commissioners of Canyon County, in Caldwell, and are now in the Idaho State Archives, Boise. In the accompanying Figures 5.1 and 5.2, mean rather than the more common median data on size of farms are reported to be consistent with the county and state-level data of Figure 5.2, which are calculated from aggregate statistics and therefore can only report means.

Idaho law throughout the period under consideration ordered that counties assess taxes at "full cash value." It was common at the time for counties to require assessors to post a bond as a surety against their full and honest assessment of property values in the county, thus enhancing the likelihood that the assessments represent full market values. See Section 11 of the Revenue Act of 1864, *Laws of the territory of Idaho, First Session* (1864), p. 399, and *Revised Statutes of the Territory of Idaho* (1887), p. 205. Judith Austin, editor of *Idaho Yesterdays* at the Idaho State Historical Society, generously supplied this information to me.

along the eastern edge of the valley. Utah was comparatively austere, dry and extreme in temperatures, the native plants being bunch grass, rabbit and sagebrush rather than forests. Most land level enough for the plow was too dry to farm. The climate in the Boise Valley was more moderate but nearly as dry, a deficiency compensated for by the spring flooding of Boise River bottomlands, where the first land claims were made. The river was lined with large cottonwoods and willow brush. Grass and brush-covered bottomlands extended for two or three miles on either side, and as one climbed up onto the benches, sagebrush became the predominant vegetation. Federal land laws opened or constricted the ambitions of those seeking farmland in the West, in Oregon making 640-acre family farms a reality, in Utah having little relevance, in Idaho keeping claims close to the 160 acres the Homestead Act permitted.

Yet, there was more at work in the building of new societies than the limits and opportunities of climate, topography, soil fertility, and land law. Prior aspirations and expectations affected powerfully what the people saw and what they built in the Far West. As Sarah Hunt Steeves suggested, cultural predispositions trailed with them the whole long way, leading them to settle certain places but not others, and once in place to shape their holding and use of land in a manner as compatible with their hopes and dreams as the limits of the places would allow. Thus, the Oregon families felt crowded on their 300-acre farms, the Alpine folk made do in their mountain haven with 15, and the Middleton people worked their 160-acre homesteads into efficient engines of material advantage – trucking and bartering their produce and then their land into profits before leaving for greener pastures elsewhere.

*     *     *

Though the settlers rarely spoke about the deeper meaning to them of owning a farm, much can be learned from examining how families in the three districts used the land.[28] George and Elizabeth Hunt's 640-acre farm was about two miles north of Sublimity and one of the most nicely situated in the district, its fields sloping gently to the north, where they ended along an east-west running county road. In 1865 they produced on their farm (for a family of five) some 100 bushels each of wheat and potatoes and 250 bushels of oats, and had already planted orchards yielding 300 bushels of apples. They also had a flock

---

[28] Though Oregon tax lists do not report production and the manuscripts of the U.S. Agricultural Census are lost, a state census, taken in 1865, gives us some sense of how the Oregon farmers used their lands and is the principal source for the ensuing discussion. It is in the Oregon State Archives, Salem.

of 80 sheep, producing a clip of 400 pounds of wool. In the mild coastal climate the twenty-five head of cattle, six horses, and twenty hogs they owned would graze most of the winter, so they put up only one ton of hay. In addition, they churned some 300 pounds of butter, and cut 200 board feet of timber. The census did not report farm machinery as a separate category, but Hunt reported that all of his property was worth $4,300, including $2,300 in personal property, part of which may have been machinery. The average Sublimity farm family was less productive than the George Hunts, producing (medians) 100 bushels each of wheat and oats, 30 bushels of apples, 10 bushels of potatoes and 4 tons of hay. They ran, in addition, twenty sheep, four hogs, four horses, and eight cattle, producing from their livestock, besides unreported meats, 60 pounds of wool and 100 pounds of butter. They owned property worth $1,470, including $500 in personal property, which apparently included farm implements.[29]

The six members of the William and Julia Strong household, like most Alpine families, lived in town rather than on their farm land. Julia tended a garden, chickens, and the three milk cows kept on their town lot, from the cream of which she churned fifty pounds of butter in 1860. William commuted out of the town to work their fifteen acres. He apparently farmed his land more intensively than did George Hunt, reporting a much greater yield per acre. Strong reported harvesting 100 bushels of wheat, 40 of corn, 15 of oats, and 60 of potatoes. The family of six owned, in addition to the three milk cows, a brace of working oxen, one additional head of cattle (perhaps a calf or a beef cow for slaughter), six sheep, and two hogs. They had farm implements worth $40 and paid no wages to farm workers. All their property was valued at some $440. Their production was close to the average for their community. Alpine farmers (median) raised eighty bushels of wheat, fifteen each of corn and oats, and forty of potatoes. They had two milk cows (hopefully, one would be always fresh), two other cattle (beef or calves), two draught oxen, and two hogs. They produced thirty-five pounds of butter and put up two tons of hay with an average $40 worth of equipment and no hired workers. The value of their farm, livestock, and equipment was $340.[30]

William Montgomery was the developer who had laid out the Middleton townsite in 1863 and gave the district its name. He had been a partner in Middleton's first mercantile store, and by 1870 he and his

---

[29] See 1865 Oregon State Census. The census does not specify ages or uses of cattle or other livestock.

[30] The data are from the 1860 tax rolls for Utah County, Special Collections, Utah State University.

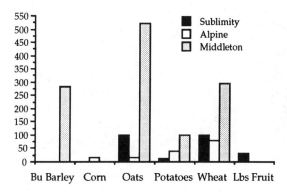

(For sources, see footnotes 9, 15, 27, and 28)

Figure 5.3 Field crops (medians), Sublimity and Alpine 1860; Middleton, 1870.

wife, Caroline, were apparently running a small hotel while farming their 160 acres. Besides the four family members, the household included two farm laborers and six others engaged in various trades and professions. Montgomery harvested 160 bushels of wheat and an impressive 600 of oats, specializing in the latter crop, which was used primarily as feed for horses. He put up ten tons of hay, which he likely used as winter forage for his two horses and four head of cattle. Apparently these were not milk cows, as the family reported producing no butter, and they had to buy from others any potatoes, corn, or pork that they may have needed. Montgomery paid $100 in wages to farm workers and had $50 in farm equipment. The average (median) 160-acre farm was remarkably productive, yielding 295 bushels of wheat, 524 of oats, 282 of barley, 100 of potatoes, and 8 tons of hay. The livestock commonly included three horses, two milk cows (which produced fifty pounds of butter), three other cattle, and two hogs. The average farmer usually had $100 in farm equipment and paid $150 in wages to farm hands. The entire farm was worth even more than those in Sublimity – some $2,000.[31] Figure 5.3 and 5.4 dramatically illustrate the concentration of Montgomery and other Middleton farmers on field crops. Sublimity farmers still harvested comparatively little grain, though they raised more livestock than farmers in the other districts.

[31] Middleton Centennial Book Commitee, *Middleton in Picture and Story* (Nampa, Idaho: Downtown Printing, 1989), p. 2; Boise *Tri-Weekly Statesman*, September 2, 1869. The Montgomery farm was close to the norm for early Middleton. U.S. Census manuscript for Ada County agricultural production, 1870, Idaho State Archives, Boise, Idaho.

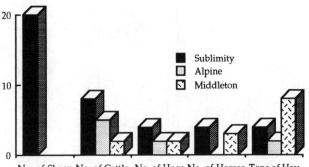

No. of Sheep  No. of Cattle  No. of Hogs  No. of Horses  Tons of Hay

(For sources see footnotes 9, 15, 27, and 28)

Figure 5.4 Livestock and hay (medians), Sublimity and Alpine, 1860; Middleton, 1870

Though farmers in all three districts raised crops common in communities with temperate climates across the United States, there are differences in emphasis, suggesting a variety of production strategies and clearly indicating dramatically different levels of affluence. For example, there were many horses on the Oregon and Idaho farms, and the oats needed to feed them were a major crop. The Utah farmers had few horses and raised little oats, but thirteen of the twenty-one farmers reported one or more teams of working oxen. The plodding, patient oxen were at the bottom of the hierarchy of desired draught animals of the period. Horses or mules were at the top, their prevalence in Oregon and Idaho attesting to the greater affluence of settlers in these districts as well as (at least in the case of Idaho) a drive toward greater efficiency. Horses were essential to the use of most field machinery because of their agility and brisk pace, and they could transport wagons, carriages, or riders far more rapidly than could oxen.

There were other notable differences. Alpine farmers, alone of the three groups, put a large part of their land into corn. They harvested more potatoes than Sublimity farmers but fewer than those of Middleton. Sublimity farmers raised more hogs per farm than did Alpiners, and those from the Oregon and Utah towns both exceeded the Idaho farmers in number of cattle.

Such statistics may at first glance appear to be random and meaningless, but a closer look reveals patterns that help us understand much about the three societies. A typical Sublimity farmer put much of his land in wheat and oats but also raised small quantities of barley,

potatoes, and corn.[32] He ran a number of sheep in the Cascade foothills to the east, and also kept a few head of cattle and hogs. He might
harvest some of the timber that crowned the hilltops of his farm. The
ownership of horses seems to have been a particularly important
source of pride and status, as the average farm had four, more than
would have been needed for draught animals, given the amount of
land actually cultivated. Some of the Sublimity families clearly grew
staple crops for sale to Salem, Oregon City, or for export to California,
Hawaii, or mining camps in the Northwest. John Downing threshed
out 800 bushels of wheat in 1865, and Henry Foster reaped a huge
harvest of 1,200 bushels of oats, obviously far more than would have
been consumed on their farms. But most of their neighbors raised
small quantities of a variety of crops, clearly aiming first at independence and survival. If God were to bless them with a surplus, so much
the better.

The crops and livestock that Alpine farmers favored – corn, potatoes, wheat, hogs, dairy cows, and oxen – all were staples of a family
farm. The corn, potatoes, and wheat were easily processed for consumption in the home and, in the dry Utah climate, readily stored for
winter use. The cows were a source of milk, butter, and fresh meat,
and the hogs provided storable meats – bacon, hams, and lard. Most
farmers raised at least some of these crops, but not large quantities.
Only two families did not have a dairy cow or hogs; all raised some
wheat, all but three some potatoes, all but four some corn. No farmer
in the Utah town had more than five cows or hogs. The largest wheat
crop was 160 bushels; corn 100; oats 85; and potatoes 200. Rarely was
a crop so abundant that it could not be consumed within the household before the next harvest.

In Middleton, barley, oats, and wheat tower in quantity above other
crops, all three in great demand in nearby mining camps – wheat for
bread, oats to feed the draught animals that hauled ore and commodities to and from the mines, and barley to supply the brewing industries that helped slake the thirst of mining crews in off hours. It is
thus no surprise that the Middleton farmers raised more of these crops
than the Utah farmers, but they also raised far more than their contemporaries in Oregon, who had much larger farms. The average (median) Middleton farmer reaped three times as much wheat (295

[32] With the largest part of the Sublimity population coming from the corn and hog
regions of the Old South and the Ohio River Valley, one might expect that the Oregon
settlers would have grown more corn. They soon learned, however, neither the moist,
relatively cool climate nor solid nutrients of the Willamette Valley were conducive to
corn culture.

bushels) as his counterpart in Sublimity (100) and 3.6 times as much as the average farmer in Alpine (80). The largest wheat crop from any one farm in Alpine was 160 bushels, that in Sublimity 800, and that in Middleton 1,600. Similarly the largest Alpine oats crop was 85 bushels; in Sublimity 1,200; and in Middleton 2,200. The largest potato harvests in Sublimity and Alpine were 200 bushels, hardly enough to see the average family of five or six through the winter; in Middleton it was 2,500 bushels, obviously, most of it bound for the market. There is a clear tendency in Middleton for farmers to specialize in the production of one or more staples and to be less concerned about raising the variety of crops needed to feed, clothe, and shelter the family.

One indicator of production more for the market than for household use is the variability among farms in basic crops grown. If a relatively few farmers raised cattle or hogs or wheat, it would suggest that their strategy of production was to concentrate on efficient production of one crop for market sale. They would then use the proceeds from the sale of their specialty crop to purchase for household use commodities in which other farmers specialized. The result of such a strategy would be to increase the activity of local and broader markets where goods were exchanged, and with it the number of commercial transactions taking place within the community. Production in such a district could be seen as tending toward commercial more than diversified agriculture. Perhaps most important, it increased the frequency of commercial and contractual interaction among the community's residents.

A comparison of commodities produced in both small and large average quantities and measured differently (hundreds of bushels of wheat compared to dozens of cattle) can be made by using the coefficient of variation (CV). The CV can vary from 0, when all farmers raised at least some of the same crop (e.g., barley), to 5, 6, or more if a few of the farmers in the district specialized in that crop and many raised none.[33] Four crops essential to farm households in all three districts and least likely to be affected by climatic variations or special economic situations were listed on production records for the Oregon, Utah, and Sublimity towns – wheat, hogs, cattle, and potatoes. In Sublimity the average CV for the four crops was 1.2 – a reasonably high value suggesting considerable but not dramatic variability among the crops grown. It would seem that the basic crops were common to many farms, but there was in addition some specialization, creating the possibility of exchange. In Alpine, the mean CV for the four basic

[33] The CV is calculated by dividing the standard deviation of a particular value by the mean, or average, of that value.

household crops was 0.7, indicating that specialization was far less common and that production for the market was less common. The Middleton CV, at 1.5, was almost a third higher than that of Sublimity and twice that of Alpine, suggesting that the Idaho farmers tended toward greater specialization and were more committed to a strategy of production oriented toward markets and exchange.

Though there is clearly a continuum, with some farmers in all three districts more market oriented than others and all farmers hoping to sell or barter some surplus, production for sale apparently was less central to people in Sublimity and Alpine. It was most common in the Oregon and Utah districts for each farm to produce the variety of crops needed for the family rather than the large quantities we would expect of a commercial enterprise.[34]

If we were to assume that Sublimity farmers fed their stock three months of the year at half the minimum currently recommended by agricultural agents for maintenance of healthy animals, they would have fed 145 bushels annually, 65 percent of the family grain production.[35] Thus the families and their stock were capable of consuming most if not all of what they produced. Some, such as the Downings

[34] In fact, the harvest of the average farm in the two latter districts was barely enough to feed the family and their livestock. If the Oregon farm families ate as much as southeastern Pennsylvania folk of the late eighteenth century, they would have required 200 bushels of grain, all they produced, along with much of their 30 bushels of apples and 10 of potatoes, just to feed the family for a year. Yet, the farm households included more than just family. Seventy-three of eighty-one Sublimity families had at least one cow (median, eight), that essential of subsistence households; seventy-two had at least one horse (median, four); and most had some hogs (median, four) and sheep (median, twenty). The livestock could easily have consumed as much as the family – an additional 205 bushels each year. Historian Bettye Hobbs Pruitt proposed much lower estimates of consumption for eighteenth-century New England farms, suggesting that an average annual requirement of forty-eight bushels of grains was sufficient for a family of six, including their animals, which would leave the Sublimity folk considerable room for marketable surpluses. Her conclusions, however, were reached by assuming household size, estimating an implausibly low requirement for feeding livestock, and accepting confirmation from one anecdotal observation by Ezra Stiles. See James T. Lemon, *The Best Poor Man's Country: A Geographical Study of Early Southeastern Pennsylvania* (New York: W. W. Norton and Company, 1976), esp. pp. 150–228. Lemon's typical farm is described on pp. 152–3 and 155. Bettye Hobbs Pruitt, "Self-Sufficiency and the Agricultural Economy of Eighteenth-Century Massachusetts," *William and Mary Quarterly* 41 (July, 1984): 333–64, esp. pp. 343–8.

[35] Minimum consumption levels for animals reported by Mark Nelson, Utah State University Agricultural Agent, as ten pounds of grain a day for horses and cattle and two for sheep; and thirty pounds of hay for large livestock and fifteen for sheep. Such nutrition would have been required when pasturage was minimal, as in winter months, or during periods of stress, such as pregnancy and lactation, making a three-month annual need a bare minimum. Interview with the author, January 29, 1989.

and Hunts, had substantial surpluses, and probably most sold sea-sonal surpluses of marketable goods, enduring lean periods until cows freshened, spring warmth encouraged their poultry to lay, or garden vegetables came in. The survival of such lean periods would have required considerable local exchange and barter, as Pruitt has pointed out. Yet their world, like that of Steven Hahn's Georgia upcountry yeomen, would seem clearly to have been "one in which production and consumption focused on the household, in which kinship rather than the marketplace mediated most productive relations, in which general farming prevailed and family self-sufficiency proved a fun-damental concern."[36]

As we have seen, Alpine families had to farm virtually all their land to achieve half the production level of those in Sublimity. There a family of six and their eight head of livestock had to live on 110 bush-els of grains, 40 bushels of potatoes, 35 pounds of butter, and 2 tons of hay. The average Middleton farmer, by contrast, wallowed in sur-plus production. He harvested 1,101 bushel of grains, 100 bushels of potatoes, and 8 tons of hay – far more than his family of five and their ten large farm animals could possibly consume.

Most striking in this entire picture is the varying degree to which farmers in the three districts exploited the land available to them. Thus far we have noted dramatic differences in the size of farms – the Sub-limity holdings averaging (median) 292 acres and the Alpine and Mid-dleton farms 15 and 151 acres, respectively. But the most critical aspect of production is the number of improved acres of land, the proportion of each farm that was actually under the plow. Astonishingly, Sublim-ity farmers, on average, farmed but 27 of their 292 acres, about 9 percent of all the land they owned. It is no surprise that the Alpine farmers reported cultivating all their arable land. An average Middle-ton farmer tilled 52 percent of his land, or 78 acres of a typical 151-acre farm.[37]

---

[36] Steven Hahn, *The Roots of Southern Populism: Yeoman Farmers and the Transformation of the Georgia Upcountry, 1850–1890* (New York: Oxford University Press, 1983), p. 29. The discussion of what constitutes sufficient production for subsistence and for mar-ket continues. See Pruitt, "Self-Sufficiency," and Carole Shammas, "How Self-Sufficient Was Early America?" *Journal of Interdisciplinary History* 13 (1982): 260–2; James A. Henretta, "Families and Farms: *Mentalité* in Pre-Industrial America," *William and Mary Quarterly*, 3rd Ser., 35 (1978): 3–32; Michael Merrill, "Cash Is Good to Eat: Self-Sufficiency and Exchange in the Rural Economy of the United States," *Radical History Review* 4 (1977): 67–8; and Lemon, *Poor Man's County*. Of course, the more central issue, at least in this author's opinion, is not whether farms were self-sufficient by any quantitative measure, but rather what the producers saw as the principal purposes of their labors.

[37] The acreage data for Sublimity and Alpine are from the 1857 Marion County tax list,

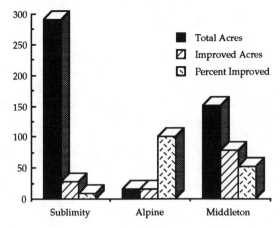

(For sources, see footnote 37)

Figure 5.5 Median acres, acres improved, and percentage improved, early Middleton, Alpine, and Sublimity.

How do we account for such striking differences in the use of the land? Sublimity's George Hunt bothered to till but 35 of his 640 acres, the Healeys and Strongs of Alpine worked every inch of their respective 7- and 15-acre farms, and William Montgomery put a full 100 of his 160 acres in the Boise River bottoms under the plow. For the Healeys, the Strongs, and their neighbors, the answer is clear. They had to put all the land they could under the plow or they would not survive. Had larger farms been possible, they very likely would have planted all they could manage to till, planning to sell as much as possible in the market. As artisans, tradespeople, and industrial workers in their native England, they had been fully initiated into a lifestyle shaped by capitalistic and commercial values. They thus would have had no difficulty seeing farming as a business. But severely limited supplies of land and lack of other economic options overwhelmed for them the cultural predispositions that might otherwise have come more strongly into play. After allocating their fields to the corn, wheat, potatoes, hay, and livestock needed to provide for the family, they had no land left to expand one crop's yield to marketable levels. Agrarian life for them was expedient, a way of making a living, with little deeper cultural meaning. They planted virtually every acre of their

as well as those from 1860 Utah County and 1870 Ada County. In the cases of Sublimity and Middleton, the proportion of acreage improved was calculated from the Oregon State Census of 1865 and the U.S. agricultural census for Ada County in 1870 and was then applied to the total acreage listed in the tax records, which in these two cases do not report acres improved.

Lilliputian parcels, but even then they harvested barely enough to keep body and soul together.[38]

The Middleton people put a smaller proportion of their land into production, yet each family still farmed five times as much land as the Alpine folk. Farming was to them what it would have been for Alpiners had their lands been more abundant – a business. Their major constraint on production was the paucity of farm workers. Junius Wright, a war refugee, stopped to winter in Middleton in 1864 and "expected to leave in the spring" but was persuaded by Moses Fowler to stay and help farm Fowler's land.[39] Jim and Gus, older boys of the Spangler family, hired on with a farmer a few miles upriver from Middleton.[40] All up and down the valley, young men on the move found work as farm laborers. In 1870 more than half of the 135 Middleton males over the age of eleven (54 percent) were listed by the census taker as farm workers. In Alpine no one was listed as a farm worker. The average Middleton farmer paid out $326 for hired help in 1870 and tried further to maximize production by investing $163 in farm equipment (means).[41] Alpine records on farm labor and equipment have not survived, but the average Utah county farmer paid out but $29 for help in 1870 and owned only $76 in equipment.[42] The heavy reliance upon hired help in Middleton, and the considerable investment in farm equipment suggest that commercial agriculture was the principal aim. For Middleton as for the Alpine farmers, land was primarily an instrument of livelihood, the principal difference being that on Middleton's 160-acre farms, one lived much better.

Certainly there were, as we have seen, farmers in Sublimity whose primary aim was production for the market. John Downing, a native of Pennsylvania, with a decade-long sojourn in Iowa, reported owning 960 acres in 1865 and cultivating some 150. He produced that year

---

[38] Indeed, Larry Logue suggests in his study of St. George, another Mormon community, that malnutrition was a major problem, especially for women, accounting for high rates of maternal mortality. See *A Sermon in the Desert: Belief and Behavior in Early St. George, Utah* (Urbana: University of Illinois Press, 1988).

[39] J. B. Wright Reminiscences, "Our Honeymoon," p. 11; "Our Honeymoon, cont." p. 9.

[40] Luster, *Autobiography*, p. 74.

[41] The Middleton data are from the manuscript of the agricultural census for 1870. Means are used to make the numbers more comparable with those from the Oregon and Utah communities. See footnote 42.

[42] See appropriate tables in Joseph C. G. Kennedy, Superintendent of the Census, *Agriculture of the United States in 1860"* (Washington, D.C.: Government Printing Office), esp. pp. 180, 220; and Francis A. Walker, Superintendent of the Census, *The Statistics of Wealth and Industry"* (Washington, D.C.: Government Printing Office, 1872), pp. 262, 364.

800 bushels each of wheat and oats, owned 21 horses and 25 hogs, ran 56 cattle and 350 head of sheep, and harvested 400 bushels of apples, obviously far more than he and his family could consume. But his nearby Hoosier-born brother-in-law, George Hunt, farmed just 35 of his 640 acres and produced only 100 bushels of wheat and 230 of oats. He put up a token one ton of hay, which meant that his eighty sheep, six horses, and twenty-five cows had little more to tide them through the winter than the forage they could scratch up, and were in most years scrawny by spring. His farm would have had some surplus for the market in apples, wool, and some grains, but certainly nothing approaching its potential. He in fact farmed but 5.5 of every 100 acres he owned.

Why this husbanding of hundreds of fertile acres by Willamette Valley settlers? Much of their land was wooded and thus could not be farmed without costly clearing of timber. Yet there were extensive tracts of prairies and open grasslands that had long been managed by the native Calapooia, Santiam, and Molalla peoples through the burning back of brush and forest vegetation before the Americans arrived. Daniel Waldo was originally attracted to the area north and east of Sublimity because there was little timber and "thousands of acres of rolling land stretching in every direction." One of the earliest Sublimity area settlers, Hadley Hobson, recalled that at the time of settlement, "there was very little timber in Sublimity, or near the town . . . [and that one] could see westward nearly eight miles without being hindered by any tall timber."[43] Though we do not know what proportion of Sublimity lands were in forest, the average Marion County farm in 1870 was 404 acres, with almost half reported as woodland (197 acres) and another 6 percent (22 acres) as unimproved for other reasons.[44] There is no reason to believe that Sublimity departed significantly from the county average in the proportion of farms wooded. Thus farmers like John Downing and George Hunt probably could have tilled nearly half of their land – the average Sublimity farmer

[43] See Richard White, "The Altered Landscape: Social Change in the Pacific Northwest," in *Regionalism and the Pacific Northwest*, ed. William G. Robbins et al. (Corvallis: Oregon State University Press, 1983), pp. 109–24. See also T. T. Geer, *Fifty Years in Oregon* (New York: The Neale Publishing Company, 1912), p. 219. Hobson is quoted in Mark Schmid, *Sublimity: The Story of an Oregon Countryside, 1850–1950* (St. Benedict, Ore.: The Library Bookstore, 1951), p. 51. In other passages, Schmid, who was not an early Sublimity settler, as Hobson was, suggests that some areas were heavily timbered (see pp. 38–9). Although it is unquestionably the case that east of Sublimity the proportion of timbered land increased, Hobson's account suggests that the area west of Sublimity town, which includes about a third of what I have defined as the Sublimity district for the purposes of this study, was virtually free of timber.

[44] Agricultural Census of 1870, *The Statistics of Wealth and Industry*, pp. 230, 361.

having something in the neighborhood of 143 nonwooded acres if close to the county average. Fences, roads, and buildings probably took another 6 percent, as suggested in the 1870 county figures, leaving 134 tillable acres. Yet, according to the 1865 state census, George Hunt farmed but thirty-five acres and his neighbors, on average, twenty-seven.

Had the Sublimity farmers been as prone as those of Middleton to maximize production for the market, there could have been but two additional constraints on the number of acres they farmed – lack of markets and lack of labor. The gold rushes spanning two mid-century decades affected both markets and labor supplies. They whipsawed Oregon's development, abruptly opening undreamed of markets while drawing off many of the young men needed to increase farm production and just as abruptly pouring the stream of men back home to increase production when markets were down. Hundreds of Oregonians headed out to beat the rush from the states as soon as they heard of California's American River strikes in 1848. Reuben Lewis and John Herron of the broader Sublimity area were part of the 1848 tide. In 1849 John S. Hunt and his son, George W., joined the rush, which eventually included Julius Howd, Moses Ira Smith (stepson of John S. Hunt), Elijah Smith, and, in 1851, George and Elizabeth Hunt's neighbor, Paul Darst. The Sublimity families remembered the California sojourns as reasonably profitable. William McKinney claimed $8,000 in earnings, Paul Darst earned $1,500, and George Hunt brought home enough to get his start in life, including three prized nuggets he saved as wedding gifts for his bride.[45]

By February 1849 the Rev. George Henry Atkinson, viewing the scene from his relatively comfortable Oregon City ministry could discern the impact:

> Those, who have obtained money will not work. Labor is from $2 to $5 per day. Common laborers will probably be $5 during the summer. Goods are scarce and very high in price. From 200 to 500 percent is made upon them. 1000 per cent and 2,000 are not uncommon in California. Gold dust is abundant. Its owners pay it freely to the merchants. Flour has risen here from $5 to $10 per bu. & were there vessels to carry it off it would be $15 or $20. . . . The merchants are reaping golden harvests with their few goods. All the goods in the nearest marts of Pacific have been directed to California. We are left nearly destitute.[46]

[45] Steeves, *Book of Remembrance*, pp. 10, 41, 96–8, 125, 132–3, 137–43, 220, 248–9.
[46] George Henry Atkinson to Josiah Little, February 2, 1849. George Henry Atkinson Collection, Huntington Library, San Marino, Calif.

The double bind of increased demand and decreased supply threw the market for farm goods into chaos. During 1849 prices rose locally both for labor and for commodities. Atkinson reported gold flowing freely and many returning to "do nobly by their wives," in building imposing houses and making other improvements on their farms. Reverend Atkinson feared that city folk would be importing flour from California to survive, as "the farmers have their pockets full of money and they do not intend to raise more than they need themselves."[47] With wheat sometimes used as a medium of exchange, the credit structure was buffeted by dramatic swings in commodity prices. Lucy J. Hall Bennet's father purchased land on the Tualatin prairie for a specified number of bushels of wheat, valued at $300. Attracted to the mines, he returned to find that the price of wheat had risen several times, the vendor demanding payment in wheat, as they had agreed. Hall convinced the seller to accept the $300, but many fared less well (and others very well) in such erratic markets.[48]

And, of course, this was just the beginning. The California mines created a strong demand for Oregon products that slackened in the mid-1850s but was discernible throughout the decade. As late as 1857, Elijah Bristow, who had a farm near Eugene, was delighted that the California market for Oregon goods was not only holding firm but increasing. "Stock and produce of all kinds are on the rise here," he wrote a friend. "There has been an immence amount of Stock driven from here to California during this Spring and Summer So that we . . . have some Show to make liquer money."[49] The next year, new strikes were made in the Fraser River district of British Columbia, drawing some 10,000 miners to the area by the fall of 1858 and prompting another tide of demand and diminished supply for Oregon harvests. A brief slack period followed in 1860, but a new strike on Orofino Creek in central Idaho that same year was the harbinger of a succession of rushes that led the frantic searchers to the Salmon River (1861), the Boise Basin (1862), and on to Grasshopper Creek (1862) and Alder Creek (1863) in present Montana.[50] Oregon argonauts and

[47] Atkinson to Josiah Hale, February 17, 1849 and December 27, 1849. George Henry Atkinson Collection, Huntington Library.

[48] Lucy J. Hall Bennett Memoir, in Frederic E. Lockley Collection, Huntington Library. She remembered that wheat had risen from $1 a bushel to $5 during her father's absence.

[49] Elijah Bristow to Wm. C. Hiatte, June 30, 1857, Elijah Lafayette Bristow Letterbook, Huntington Library.

[50] On June 22, 1860, Elijah Bristow wrote to H. G. Bristow that "Times are very dull here yet. Money is a great deal Scarser, than it was when you were here." Bristow Letterbook, Huntington Library.

Oregon produce were a substantial component of this turbulent flow, with continuing repercussions upon the farmers of the Willamette. Umatilla Landing, Walla Walla, and, far up the Snake River, Lewiston, Washington Territory, became thriving ports in the 1860s, receiving goods to be freighted by pack and wagon train along the famous Mullan Road and other trails to mining districts as far away as Virginia City, Montana.[51]

Elijah Bristow, though not from Sublimity, shared the experiences of many Oregonians in the Idaho and Montana mines. Propelled into a personal crisis by the death of his wife, he left his four children with a sister-in-law in the summer of 1862 and joined the throng, expecting to make a fortune through a dual enterprise of prospecting and marketing Oregon goods that a partner in Eugene shipped to him. There he was in constant association with "webfoot" friends from the Eugene area.

> Selton & Cathey are here, & in fact *nearly everybody and all their neighbors*. Skaggs & the Boys left here yesterday morning. Selton talks of going to Elk City. So does Jim Thompson & others. . . . Mr. Hazelton & Cathy got in yesterday. Mr. Jones & Guthry are pitching prospecting. There are *thousands* of men out every day prospecting. The hills are covered with tents as far as you can See, & men are going back every day. My advice to those that have not started, is to stay at Home, for the thing is overdone.[52]

Yet Bristow stayed, moving on from camp to camp, making his way in 1863 to mining camps on the upper Boise River supplied with foods by Middleton and other Boise Valley farmers. He remained until the next winter, working a claim and attempting to vend Oregon products in the volatile mining camp markets. Though he had made his way back to Eugene by January, he still planned to go "east of the mountains" (to the Montana mines) in the spring.[53]

Thus, while the once lucrative California market for Oregon produce had declined in the 1860s as Californians turned from mining to farming, other markets in British Columbia and then Idaho and Montana took up a good bit of the slack. This is indicated by "production

[51] The principal study of the impact of the gold rushes on Oregon is Arthur L. Throckmorton, *Oregon Argonauts* (Portland: Oregon Historical Society, 1961). See also G. Thomas Edwards, "Walla Walla: Gateway to the Pacific Northwest Interior," *Montana: The Magazine of Western History* (Summer, 1990): 28–43.

[52] Bristow to T. G. Hendricks from Florence, Idaho, June 1, 1862. Bristow Letterbook, Huntington Library.

[53] Bristow to Henry G. Bristow, January 31, 1864. Bristow Letterbook, Huntington Library. His letterbook ends with his promise to return to the mines after a visit with children and friends in Eugene.

unit ratios," a rough measure of regional self-sufficiency calculated by totaling the quantities produced of the nine most basic farm commodities and dividing these "production units" by the number of persons in the region (or, for other purposes, by the number of improved acres). The California ratio of production units to persons had climbed in the decade from 1860 to 1870 from 43.1 to 63.1, paralleling, in fact, Oregon's growth from 46.4 to 62.5 during the same period. Nevada, by contrast, clearly a food-importing state, had ratios of but 3.1 in 1860 and 17.9 in 1870.[54]

This measure does not permit us to draw with confidence a firm line separating food-importing from food-exporting states. It would appear, however, that California by 1870 was producing more than its own population needed and perhaps was competing with Oregon for sales in some external markets, such as Hawaii. Nonetheless, the Willamette Valley was far better situated than California to serve the new mining areas being opened in eastern Oregon, Idaho, and Montana, suffering competition only from Missouri Valley farmers, who shipped up the Missouri to Fort Benton, and from Utah farmers freighting north from the Wasatch Front.[55] The Missouri and Utah inroads into the mining district markets apparently were not major, however, as Oregon farmers continued increasing their products per

[54] These are calculated for northern states by adding the quantities produced in each state of corn, barley, wheat, oats, and potatoes (all reported in bushels), as well as the number of milk cows, other cattle (principally beef), sheep, and hogs. The total, combining, as it does, bushels of grain and head of livestock, is called "production units." The total of production units is divided by the number of persons in the state or region to derive an index of self-sufficiency and by the number of acres to derive an index of productivity. The ratio has the benefit of being comparable across time and regions because it is based upon quantities of product, not dollar value, which fluctuated greatly according to market conditions. It is not useful in comparing regions that do not have a common ratio of livestock to grain production, as those states or regions concentrating on livestock will have lower ratios, and it is obviously not a refined instrument. An adaptation for comparing southern and northern states would be possible by adding cotton, tobacco, rice, and other warm-climate crops. The data are from the appropriate tables in the 1860 Census, *Agriculture of the United States in 1860*, and the 1870 Census, *The Statistics of Wealth and Industry*.

[55] The Utah trade was important to the territory, as it brought specie into a cash-poor economy, but it seems unlikely that Utah could have shipped a large proportion of all farm commodities to the mines. The subsistence character of the Utah farm economy would have placed severe restraints on the quantities that could be exported without courting famine at home. Production units per person were but 18.8 in 1860 and had declined to 13.7 in 1870, less than those of Nevada. In major agricultural states, production unit ratios were commonly in the 60s and 70s and reached as high as Iowa's 109.4 in 1870. The Utah/Montana trade is described in Betty M. Madsen and Brigham D. Madsen in *North to Montana! Jehus, Bullwhackers, and Mule Skinners on the Montana Trail* (Salt Lake City: University of Utah Press, 1980).

person during the 1860s as well as their efficiency in products per acre, suggesting that they had by no means saturated the market and that there were outlets for the wheat, oats, potatoes, and pork of the Hunts and Downings. In short, it was not for lack of markets that they and their neighbors farmed so little of their land.

Could labor shortages have been the reason? The narratives do suggest that the mines strained the farm labor market in Oregon. Writing in February 1849 during the peak of the California rush, George Atkinson lamented that "Labor . . . cannot be obtained this year. . . . The flour mill may soon cease running. Ere long we shall have no wheat to grind. Few are raising any wheat." By July, however, many of the errant farmers had already returned. And despite Reverend Atkinson's fear that "The rage for wealth will destroy the morality of many," he was surprised to find them "generally active and industrious while at home." Though "a small harvest is expected," he attributed the dearth as much to the weather as to the lack of farm workers. "Much of the winter wheat was injured by the frost, & rains," he concluded, but nonetheless "we shall raise enough for our own use."[56] It was apparently the pattern for many to coordinate trips to the mines with crop cycles, leaving after planting and returning to harvest. Elijah Bristow reported that the Idaho mines "are fully as rich & extensive as I expected to find them. But it is just as I have always Said about mines in general, it is no use for a man to start out with the expectation of getting right into a rich claim, & make two or three thousand Dollars and go back Home in time to Help to Harvest."[57] His going out of his way to deplore such a strategy suggests that it was common. Indeed, already in June 1862, Bristow noted from Idaho that "men are going back every day," some presumably disappointed at their earnings but perhaps as many to be on hand for the harvest of winter wheat. And in fact in Idaho, and other areas where placer mining was common (since it depended upon an abundance of water), the drying of streams in summer often reduced the scale of mining activity, permitting the labor force to rotate from mines to fields in a seasonal cycle.

Young men between twelve and twenty-five were the likely pool from which farm laborers were drawn, a pool better stocked in Sublimity than in either the Idaho or Utah districts. There were seventy-nine youth of these ages in Sublimity, forty in Middleton, and six in

---

[56] George Henry Atkinson to Josiah L. Hale, February 17, 1849, and to Josiah Little, July 25, 1849. George Henry Atkinson Collection, Huntington Library.

[57] Elijah Bristow to T. G. Hendricks, June 28, 1862. Bristow Letterbook, Huntington Library.

Alpine, these representing 42 percent of the Sublimity male work force (men between twelve and sixty-five) but only 30 percent of those in Middleton and 33 percent of the Alpine male workers.[58] Thus, as many as twenty-two young men, or 28 percent of the Sublimity youth, could remain throughout the season in the mines and still leave a local labor pool as large in proportion to the whole labor force as that in Middleton and Alpine. Though certainly the labor supply was at times a problem, as it was throughout the West, it would not seem to be sufficient to account for the average farmer leaving 80 percent of his improved land idle.

It is possible, of course, that the yeomen of Sublimity were principally shrewd speculators, who had learned during their sojourn in the Midwest that new land, held long enough, can be sold for a considerable profit. This strategy was one that many ultimately followed. Yet the more important question is, did they acquire the land with speculation in mind? A good many of the Sublimity folk had come to the area in the late 1840s and early 1850s when land was either free, as became possible in 1850 under the provisions of the Donation Land Claim Act, or extremely inexpensive. In 1846 Henry Smith bought 640 acres from William Brown, with a cabin and ten acres fenced and planted in potatoes, for "one old horse and a gun."[59] George and Elizabeth Hunt began building their estate in the early 1850s when they took up a 640-acre donation land claim.[60] Of course, early land prices varied according to improvements and the quality and location of the tract. Lorenza Byrd's family remembered that in 1850 he sold his 320-acre claim at Victor Point, in the northern Sublimity area, together with the 14 by 14 foot log cabin he had built, to John M. Savage for $500 ($1.56 an acre).

Both the Hunts and the Savages were among the 44 of 104 in the area who were assessed taxes in 1857 and remained in Sublimity until 1871, for which a subsequent tax list is available. This list shows that

[58] Data calculated from the 1860 manuscript censuses for Sublimity and Alpine; from the first available (1870) census for Middleton. It is not uncommon for youth of eleven years to be listed as farm workers in the manuscript census. This status was for most related to life course, and by the mid-twenties they more commonly either owned or rented enough land to work as farmers in their own right. Thus the twelve to twenty-five males group as a proportion of the whole male work force, aged twelve to sixty-five, seems a reasonable means of comparing available labor pools. Alpine, of course, was much smaller in 1860, and a change of one or two could have significantly changed the percentage in the labor pool. Women worked on the farms, particularly in poultry, dairy, and vegetable gardening, but I have not found one account of farm women leaving to work in mines and so have not included them in this calculation.

[59] Steeves, *Book of Remembrance*, p. 89.

[60] Steeves, *Book of Remembrance*, p. 99.

George Hunt increased his holdings during the fourteen-year interval from 640 to 830 acres and John Downing from 682 to a staggering 1,275. Some, such as James Anderson and Isaac Coy, sold part of their land, and John Greenstreet, John Taylor, and John Stanton sold all of theirs. Altogether, eighteen Sublimity farmers (41 percent) sold part of their holdings, parting with 123 acres (median) on average (mean 193), leaving them with a still commodious 229 acres (mean, 218) – 200 acres more than the average they had actually tilled in 1865. But the majority followed the Hunts and Downings, either keeping their lands intact or adding to them over the years. Four did not change their acreage at all. Twenty-two (50 percent) increased their holdings. The median farm stayed virtually unchanged – 317 acres in 1857 and 316 in 1871. The average farm increased from 323 to 364 acres.

Moreover, the Sublimity people were remarkably prone to stay, considering the very high mobility that characterized both rural and urban Americans in the second half of the nineteenth century.[61] Elijah Bristow, trying in 1857 to convince a friend to come to Oregon, still thought of the society as unsettled and restless. Explaining that nearby half-sections sold for as little as $400, he concluded, "This country is like all other new country settled up with characters who will never be contented in any one place very long at a time."[62] Yet, despite the still unsettled character of the region, the Sublimity farmers seemed content to hold on to their land. Thirty-eight percent of the 1860 heads of household remained there until 1870. Forty-two percent of the 1857 taxpayers were still paying taxes there fourteen years later, in 1871. Given that many of the settlers came in the late 1840s and early 1850s, their grip on their land was strong and enduring, hardly the behavior we would expect of speculators. Though there was, as always, buying and selling during the period, more was bought than sold. And both those who sold and those who bought ended the decade of the 1860s with very large farms, far more than they had under the plow in 1865 – the average farm larger at the end of the decade than at the begin-

---

[61] In the classic study of rural persistence rates, James C. Malin found that 51 percent of farm operators in eastern and east-central Kansas stayed between 1885 and 1895. Wisconsin farmers during the same period had a persistence rate of but 21 percent, and other studies show most farm districts falling within these two extremes. See James C. Malin, "The Turnover of Farm Population in Kansas," *Kansas Historical Quarterly* 4 (November 1935): 339–72, esp. 366; and Peter J. Coleman, "Restless Grant County: Americans on the Move," *Wisconsin Magazine of History* 46 (1962): 16–20. See also a listing of persistence studies of rural areas in Stephen Thernstrom, *The Other Bostonians* (Cambridge, Mass.: Harvard University Press, 1973), p. 226.

[62] Elijah Bristow to Zachary C. Fields, April 3, 1857. Bristow Letterbook, Huntington Library.

ning. Though one could hardly say that land values skyrocketed during the 1857–71 period, average prices did increase by 56 percent, from $2.59 to $4.05 an acre, probably enough to induce a speculator to tire of waiting, sell, and move on. The evidence is eloquent in describing a population uncommonly devoted not only to land ownership, but also to owning tracts far larger than they could reasonably cultivate themselves. We are still left with the question, why? What did all this land mean to these people?

Though not incontrovertible, the evidence is persuasive that a good many of the settlers of Sublimity were saving land as a patrimony for their children. It would appear that they were doing so because their understanding of the meaning and purposes of land ownership was similar to that described by Hector St. John de Crévecoeur, who on the eve of the American Revolution expressed himself as an "American Farmer":

> This formerly rude soil has been converted by my father into a
> pleasant farm, and in return it has established our rights; on it is
> founded our rank, our freedom, our power as citizens, our
> importance as inhabitants of such a district.[63]

There are numerous clues that suggest the presence of such an attitude in Sublimity. The Sublimity farmers chose to farm only enough of their land to fill their basic needs so that they could conserve the rest for their children.[64] Maximum present use of the land was less important to them than saving a portion for their progeny. The Rev. George Atkinson, it will be recalled, feared in 1849 that city folk would be importing flour from California to survive, as "the farmers have their pockets full of money and they do not intend to raise more than they need themselves."[65] Moses Ira Smith remembered that "There was no keen competition in the exchange of farm products for cash, by commission merchants. Those early settlers only raised what they needed for their own family and for the help of the needy."[66] Bemused by such practices, city dwellers, often New Englanders steeped in a different ethic, saw the rural farmers as lacking in industry and the spirit of progress.

---

[63] J. Hector St. John de Crévecoeur, *Letters from an American Farmer* (New York: Penguin Books, 1986), p. 54.

[64] As we have seen, this contentment with a reasonable subsistence had long been characteristic of their ancestors. See Hahn, *Southern Populism*, p. 29; Faragher, *Sugar Creek*, p. 98.

[65] Atkinson to Josiah Hale, February 17, 1849 and December 27, 1849. George Henry Atkinson Collection, Huntington Library.

[66] Steeves, *Book of Remembrance*, p. 118. Steeves has drawn from a memoir written by Smith about 1876 that was not available to the author.

Data we have seen on the use of the land support these anecdotes. Early Sublimity farmers, although selling some of what they produced, nonetheless had a sense that a certain level of production was enough and chose not to push all their land into production, even when there was a strong market and apparently sufficient labor. For such persons, land ownership had complex and deep layers of meaning that, as Crévecoeur eloquently suggested, related to family rights, rank, freedom, and power. So, although twenty or thirty acres were enough to farm, no amount of land could be too much to own, as realization of their deepest aspirations depended upon husbanding enough to provide all these blessings to future generations. Sublimity farmer Allan Simpson argued in 1873 against planting entirely to one crop. "Of course," he said, "those who expect or intend to emigrate as soon as they have exhausted the soil, will care little for the future, but those of us who expect to make Oregon our permanent abiding place and bequeath the soil to our posterity, will look with abhorrence upon such a foolish and suicidal system of agriculture."[67] Apparently the early settlers of Sublimity had not yet fully imbibed the more commercial and capitalistic mentality that greatly diminished the cultural meaning of land ownership for Alpine and Middleton founders.

The stress upon the dignity of family among Sublimity people is consistent with the placement and style of their homes (their domestic hearth). Though like most frontier people they first built log cabins, they moved as soon as possible to tall frame houses, often with substantial porches and porticos, and carefully sited so that, even when modest in size, they seem imposing. In these homes Sublimity people socialized, held church services, bore children, christened and wed them, and bid their earthly farewells. Sarah Hunt Steeves praised T. L. Davidson because he "loved his home and took great enjoyment in the building of the beautiful home in its sightly location in the midst of grove of fine oak trees, where it has stood for so many years and gives promise of many years service yet to come." Lorenza Byrd, she reported, had "built a very good, substantial house, much better than the average." Paul and Cinderella Darst, neighbors of the Hunts and Downings, "built one of the most substantial houses on his own farm of any in the county. This old home is still in use by his family, after a lapse of over fifty years since his death."[68] Elijah Smith settled midway between Sublimity and Silverton, "where a very commodious

---

[67] *The Willamette Farmer*, January 11, 1873.
[68] A family that had bought the farm from the aged Parthena Darst still lived in the home in 1992. Parthena, born in 1868, was the last living child of Paul and Cinderella Darst.

house was built." Though the original home of Jesse and Ruby Looney was of the common log type, Steeves seemed pleased that their son, Norris, built "a commodious farm home" for his parents. Phillip and Delilah Glover built their log home "amid tall oak trees on a knoll overlooking the surrounding country.... In later years [he] erected a large, commodious farmhouse, where he and his good wife lived in peace and plenty," and from which he presided at times as justice of the peace and constable.

But the grandest home of all was that of John S. Downing, a central character in the Hunt/Downing/Darst neighborhood of Whiteaker. Virtually all the Marion county pioneers, Steeves wrote, had at some time "enjoyed the hospitality of 'Uncle' John Downing, at his fine old Colonial mansion near Sublimity." He was the very image of a country gentleman,

> a tall, spare man with black hair and beard slightly streaked with gray and he had a way of holding his head proudly back, making a sort of double chin. Uncle John always wore a white shirt and collar.
>
> It is hard to think of one without the other; they were so well suited, the man to the house and the house to the man. The fine old home was built in a setting of tall fir trees, ... [It had a] full two stories, ... wide, low gables, and faced the setting sun. You entered the front of the house across a wide veranda, with great octagonal columns supporting a portico above.... The main house was divided into a living room and parlor, both of ample proportions, separated by a wide hall containing the only spindle staircase the country could boast of for miles around.
>
> At the end of each of these two large rooms was [a] wide fireplace and at one side a bookcase and desk combined; at the other side a cupboard with glass doors, where were kept the wonderful silver water pitcher and other family heirlooms which we children could admire but not handle. The woodwork in this room was of curly Oregon maple, very finely polished....
>
> There was the good store carpet with its bold, conventional design ... and the center table upon which rested the family album and daguerreotypes all so precisely set.... There were the haircloth sofa, the walnut whatnot and lastly, the only square, grand piano that we thought existed outside cities, and over this the oil portrait of the beautiful adopted daughter, Mary, who had passed on many years before....
>
> The room was seldom used, except for gala days, weddings, and funerals, and seemed sacred to me.... Back of the living room was the large dining room that could seat all the heads of families for

miles around, while the young folks waited for the second table. We gathered here at game dinners, when the men of he neighborhood hunted for a week before; at oyster suppers, wedding dinners and on Sundays to dinner after church at Rock Point school house.[69]

The identification of man with house; of classical proportions and comfortable elegance; of artifacts of family heritage prominently displayed (the pitcher, the album); of weddings, funerals and dinners after the hunt and after services; and, most eloquently, the designation of the place as "sacred" all attest to the power of the farmhome in the iconography of Sublimity settlers.

There was more. The symbolic center of family life was the home. Yet many families and small neighborhoods made, in addition, space on the land for the family dead. One of the first tasks of Jesse Looney after his arrival in 1850 was to plat the family cemetery. His brother, William, drowned in the Santiam River, was the first to be buried there, and Jesse and his wife, Ruby, as well as other family members were eventually interred in the "little cemetery . . . located on a sunny knoll in sight of the family home."[70] Phillip and Delilah Glover were likewise buried "on a sightly hill on the old homestead they both loved so well." When in 1850 a hired man of John S. Hunt was killed in a logging accident, the patriarch designated a "little knoll" on his land for a family cemetery. Shortly thereafter, his wife, Temperance, died and was buried there. Eventually he, a son, two daughters, two daughters-in-law, two sons-in-law (including John Downing), and numerous grandchildren and neighbors were buried at the site. Theirs was just one of perhaps a dozen small family burying grounds that dot the landscape around Sublimity, often, as Steeves suggested, on

[69] Regarding the Davidson home, see Steeves, *Book of Remembrance*, p. 149; on Byrd, p. 135; on Darst, p. 132; on Smith, p. 250–1; on Looney, p. 23; on Glover, pp. 185–8; on Downing, pp. 92–3. The Downing home had been built in 1859 by a local craftsman named John Goff. The piano had been willed to the Downing family by Mary C. Riches, who lived with them until she died in May 1875 at age twenty-two. In her will she left the piano, valued at $300, first to Temperance Downing for her lifetime and then to Alice I. Downing, who at the time was fifteen years old. It was, of course, Mary's portrait that hung over the piano. See Marion County Probate Records, File 551.

It is interesting that four of the references to these homes place them in groves of oak or fir trees, the reference suggesting a sacred character to the setting of which the houses, in the minds of Sublimity folk, perhaps partook. That is to say that the house and grove together constituted a place sacred to the family – that the home, set amid the grove, comprised the center of their world.

[70] Looney in Steeves, *Book of Remembrance*, pp. 23–4. Glovers, pp. 185–8.

hills overlooking the family home and fields.[71] The inclusion of a family burying ground completes the primary physical world of Sublimity settlers. The fields, homes, and graveyards constituted a material setting and visual metaphors for the very concept of what it meant to be a Hunt, Downing, Darst, or member of another Sublimity clan – a people who in this, their place, played out the transcendent spiritual acts of union, generation, affinity, and death.

Sarah Hunt Steeves explained that her parents and grandparents had come to the Willamette with their families because they wanted land upon which to build their homes and opportunities for their sons. In the family, land, and generational succession were contained the central purposes of being. Thus the land should remain in the family. And ideally, the family would stay together on the land across generations. The narratives collected by Steeves affirm again and again the importance to these people of family continuity on the land. Towner Savage had to come to Oregon because "farms upon which his several sons could settle, formed quite an inducement for making the journey." Abijah Carey had settled east of Salem, "where a permanent home was made and the old home place is still in the hands of the Carey family." Catherine Pugh of Salem outlived her husband, David, and was "surrounded in her later years, . . . by her sons and adoring grandchildren and on to the fourth generation of grandchildren." Virgil and Phernie Tabitha Pringle, also of Salem, "lived to a ripe old age and . . . celebrated their sixtieth wedding anniversary, surrounded by children, grandchildren and great-grandchildren." Jesse Looney had "in the years that past, by dint of hard labor and good business insight, . . . added to his original claim until at the time of his death, at the age of 69 years, he was able to give each of his children a fine farm and almost all the land is still in the hands of his descendants." Polly Frazier Lewis "lived to a ripe old age, much beloved by her large family of children and grandchildren, who reverence her memory, and are proud to be descendants of this fine, courageous woman."[72]

On April 22, 1890, George Washington Hunt, age fifty-nine, and Elizabeth, age fifty-six, made out their wills. They provided that each of their five surviving sons and daughters would receive a specified plot of land – a commodious 160 acres. Moreover, a portion of their daughter Sarah's land was to remain a family cemetery. George wrote:

> I do hereby set it apart and dedicate it as a family burying
> ground forever for the heirs of my body and all descendents of my

[71] Steeves wrote an entire piece on the Mt. Hope cemetery in *Book of Remembrance*, pp. 103–4.

[72] Steeves, *Book of Remembrance*, pp. 11, 24, 27, 46–7, 66, 69, 79.

Photo 10 Sublimity area cemetery and adjoining fields. (Photo by the author.)

> body and they shall have ingress and egress to and from said
> burying ground for the purpose of burial and repairing said
> grounds and fences and doing such other acts around or about
> upon the premises necessary . . . and may at all reasonable hours
> enter upon said grounds for the purpose of doing honor to the
> dead and cherishing their memory or decorating their tombs.

George Washington Hunt could hardly have hoped for more. But he did. For the farm was to nurture the descendants of George and Elizabeth throughout their mortal lives before it received the dust of their dead bodies.

> It is my desire and will that the lands heretofore devised herein to
> M. W. Hunt and Jeptha T. Hunt and Sarah F. Hunt shall descend
> to the heirs of their bodies only and in case there shall be no heirs
> of any one of their bodies the land of that one without said heirs
> shall revert to the other heirs of my body.[73]

The power and meaning of Hunt's attachment to his Oregon lands is hardly comprehensible to Americans of the twentieth century. Even his contemporaries in Utah and Idaho could not have fathomed the dimensions of his vision. In Alpine land could serve few enduring social and familial functions. The five- or ten-acre plots were often in noncontiguous parcels and, following Mormon practice, outside of a platted townsite and hence out of sight. William and Elizabeth Strong could picture a house on a village street as the hearth of their family, but not one set amid an extensive family plantation, as the Hunts could. Moreover, their fifteen acres could at best support but one of the ten children they would eventually bring into the world. The others would have to seek a livelihood elsewhere.

Middleton farmers certainly built homes on their land, sometimes imposing and enduring, but more often "sagebrush" houses, the walls one board thick. They frequently traded and bartered their land, and simply sold out when opportunities presented themselves elsewhere. Rarely do we see among them the association of land, family independence, honor, and continuity that is common in Sublimity. The Spanglers returned to Missouri after their Middleton sojourn. Junius Wright sold his original claim, remained in the valley as an entrepreneur and developer for a time, and then moved on to Oregon. Land, for the Middleton as well as for the Utah people, was not encumbered with powerful associations. It offered a way for the present generation to make a living. In Sublimity it was laden with cultural burdens that touched the most fundamental perceptions of identity and the very purposes of life itself.

---

[73] Probate Case Files, No. 2168, Marion County Court House, Salem, Oregon.

# 6 *The place where we lived*

This is Alpine's chapter. Settlers in the Mormon town participated in a dizzying round of church-sponsored voluntary activities that brought them into daily contact with others in their community. Years of such contacts built strong bonds that attached them and their children firmly to the place. Middleton people were far less likely to meet and work together. Forming few bonds within the area, they had little to hold them if opportunity beckoned elsewhere. In Sublimity there was an intensity of community as strong as or stronger than that in Alpine, but the sphere of interaction was confined mostly to neighbor/kin groups.

Religion, of course, played rather different roles in the three societies. In Sublimity, religious observance at first took place in the home among neighbors and kin, with both men and women participating. This changed, however, as missionaries began to evangelize the district and build churches. Sublimity people became consumers of religious observance, not initiators. Alpine's people found religion entering in some measure into almost all that they did. It was for them a principal source of community identity and cohesiveness. In Middleton many were for a time distant from religious observance, their more atomistic social structure failing to sustain common worship, whether in family or in community. But as nearby towns were founded, ministers there extended their pastoral care to the rural district. Still, neither in Sublimity nor in Middleton is there evidence that religion was a major agent in forming a sense of community.

Different modes of production and exchange also helped strengthen or dissolve community ties. Informal borrowing and lending, characteristic of early Alpine and Sublimity, created unspecified feelings of future obligation and connection. Exchange mediated by cash and contracts, as in Middleton, minimized such obligations. Only in Alpine did community remain powerful enough to attach future generations to the place.

185

Alpine's William Johnson and Julia Dyer Strong, natives of Warwickshire, England, brought ten children into the world between 1853
and 1872. Somehow both made time, while rearing their family, to
meet and work with their neighbors in volunteer activities. William
was an organizer and stalwart in the ward (church) choir. Julia sang
with him and in the Relief Society (women's organization) choir as
well. He, in addition, served on the city council and the board of
directors of the Alpine Cooperative Store, was a director of the City
Library Association and of the Lehi and Alpine United Orders (attempting economic communalism), president of the Sunday School,
and for seventeen years a counselor to the bishop of the local Mormon
ward.

Catherine Nash, who had come to Alpine as a single parent from
her native Wiltshire with three sons and a nephew, was an officer in
the Relief Society, as were fourteen other women of the town prior to
1880, including two of Catherine's daughters-in-law and the wife of
the nephew she raised, Albert Marsh. Her son, Ephraim, was in the
choir and held a volunteer civic office; her other son, Worthy, was in
the militia. Isaac had been killed at age eighteen in a fall from a
wagon. Catherine's nephew, Albert, drilled with his cousin in the militia, but in addition helped direct the Sunday school, presided over
the Young Men's Mutual Improvement Association, was on the board
of the local church corporation, and of the town council, and in 1863
took a full summer to drive a team and wagon 1,000 miles to the
Missouri and back, helping to bring incoming immigrants to Utah.

Their experience was common in Alpine. The range and intensity
of community interaction are suggested in the journal of William Goforth Nelson, an early settler. He wrote that on December 3, 1851, the
ten or twelve Alpine (then called Mountainville) families met at the
home of William Wordsworth "to consider building a school house."
They decided to do so and had it finished in less than a month. On
February 10, 1852, they met in their new building to organize a branch
of the Latter-day Saint Church, a clerk recording the event with the
observation, significant to Latter-day Saints, that "such organization
was duly affected according to the laws and order of the church."[1]
The new branch president, Charles S. Peterson, appointed Nelson a
"Teacher," charged with fellow Teacher Thomas B. Nelson to visit the
homes of the citizens and monitor their spiritual and economic well-
being. By that September the central church leaders had organized the

---

[1] In Chapter 2 I have described the preoccupation with order in the Mormon faith and
its possible appeal to the English working people who comprised the largest part of
the population of Alpine.

Photo 11 The William Johnson and Julia Dyer Strong family. Standing are Davis, Julia, Don Carlos, Eliza, and Samuel. Seated are Estella, William Johnson Strong, Julia Dyer Strong, and Frank. The photograph was probably taken in the mid-1890s, when William and Julia were in their sixties. (Used by permission of Rulon McDaniels.)

group into a full ward, or congregation, with Isaac Houston appointed to preside as their first bishop.

Two weeks later, in early October, tragedy struck the little settlement when twenty-month-old James Lemon, Jr., was reported missing. Within a fortnight his body was found, mutilated, all assumed, by Ute Indians, who had long inhabited the area.[2] The trauma of this event, together with regular loss of stock, led to a decision to move their log homes, originally built along creeks, together, so that the back walls would form an enclosure. William Nelson and William Faust "each owned a good ox team and wagon, and we hauled nearly all the houses into the fort where the owners put them up again." During this period the able-bodied men of the town were organized into a militia, in case of armed conflict with the Indians. The next summer, with tensions mounting in what was called "Walker's War," they built a twelve-foot-high mud wall around the perimeter of the fort some thirty feet beyond the houses.[3]

They also "planted a few acres of land in wheat and garden just outside the fort wall. These little farms were all fenced with brush and poles and when the grain was ripe our lieutenants, William Wordsworth and Charles S. Peterson, called on some of us to do the harvesting, which was all done with cradles." Finally, with the level of hostility subsiding, "we were all released from further military duty and commenced work on our farms."

A disastrous winter followed, the deep snow and severe cold killing "nearly all the cattle and horses owned by the people of Alpine."[4] Yet the settlement not only survived but, following the advice of church leaders in Salt Lake City, built yet another enclosure out from the first,

[2] Later, according to local lore, a Ute Indian known as Squash Head claimed to have kidnapped the child and then killed it because of its crying. The event may have happened as remembered, but the memory is perhaps most important in the image of Native Americans it perpetuated for the Alpine people. Though never directly the object of Indian attack, Alpine's elaborate defenses, consisting of three different enclosures to surround the community, were costly and speak eloquently of the peoples' fears. The Squash Head story is in the Manuscript History of Alpine Ward under the year, 1852, LDS Church Archives.

[3] "Walker's War" was a series of confrontations in 1853 among Utah Valley Indians and whites, instigated by the Ute chief Wahkara's anxieties concerning white encroachment on tribal ranges and efforts to stem the slave trade, from which Wahkara had long profited. Some twenty whites and an unknown number of Indians were killed before the signing of a formal peace treaty in May 1854. See Howard A. Christy, "The Walker War: Defense and Conciliation as Strategy," *Utah Historical Quarterly* 47 (Fall, 1979): 395–420.

[4] William Goforth Nelson, "Autobiography," typescript in LDS Church Archives, Salt Lake City.

this one fourteen feet high, with wooden gates at the center of the
north and south walls. The project cost $4,300 and the labor of forty-
eight men. The territorial legislature granted a charter early in 1855,
giving the village the ambitious name of Alpine City. Later in the year
an influx of British-born Saints, including the Waltons, the Healeys,
the Nashes, Albert Marsh, and the Carlisles, augmented the population.

As the chronicle continues, we see a succession of challenges met
by community responses. All hands fought grasshopper infestations
that destroyed much of their crops in 1855 and 1856. John W. Vance
and William J. Strong found time to organize a Sunday school, which
supplemented weekly Sunday meetings of the ward membership and
Sunday afternoon meetings of a Quorum of Seventies. In 1857 the
bishop appointed several of the leading men "to go into the mountains to meet Johnston's Army," the Mormon term for the Utah Expedition that President James Buchanan had sent to install a new
territorial governor and put down a rumored rebellion against U.S.
authority. The Alpine men did their part to confirm the rumor, joining
a territorial militia that harassed the federal army, fired grasslands to
deplete forage for their animals, burned supply trains, and successfully forced the troops to winter at a makeshift camp in Wyoming. In
the meantime, the rest of the Alpine population was opening their
homes to fellow Saints being evacuated from the Salt Lake Valley in
order to facilitate a scorched-earth policy should the negotiations between the Mormon leaders and the U.S. officials fail.[5] Among those
sojourning in Alpine during the "move south" were the Moyles, the
David Adamses, and the Richard Booths. All decided that they liked
the settlement and eventually returned to cast their lot with the Alpine
folk.

Thus, before 1860, when a sizable settled population is first identifiable through civil records, the Alpine settlers had frequently met and
worked together to build a meeting house, organize a congregation,
search for and mourn a child, found a militia, build a city wall, move
houses into it, dig a rudimentary canal system, fence, plant, and harvest crops, enlarge the city wall, form a city government, fight grass-
hoppers, found a Sunday school, send representatives to counter
federal troops, and house refugees from the conflict. In all these activities, the people were forced out of their houses to meet and interact
regularly with others in their town. Moreover, in their efforts to
counter both the native Utes and the federal government, they were

---

[5] Still the definitive study of the Utah Expedition is Norman F. Furniss, *The Mormon
Conflict, 1850–1859* (New Haven, Conn.: Yale University Press, 1960).

united to form a broader community of Latter-day Saints fighting against perceived common enemies, which drew them out from personal and familial loyalties toward those of town and society.

And that was just the beginning. During the years 1861 through 1864, James Freestone, Albert Marsh, and James Hamilton joined others in contributing teams, wagons, oxen, and a full summer of their time, driving east to the Missouri or the advancing rail head, loading immigrants into their wagons, and transporting them and their effects to Utah. The townspeople built a new meeting house in 1863, this one of stone, replaced in 1872 by a still larger one. During the decade, meetings held under church auspices proliferated. George Clark became superintendent of a revitalized Sunday school in 1865, working with William Johnson Strong, George Freestone, and Albert Marsh. By 1867 the youth had organized a Mutual Education Society that met two nights a week "and engaged in various exercises, such as reading, criticism, writing, arithmetic, English grammar, etc." In 1867 the organization was renamed the Alpine Literary Society, which continued until 1875, when its functions were taken over by the Young Ladies Mutual Improvement Association and the Young Men's Mutual Improvement Association, the two groups meeting weekly and joining the last Sunday evening of the month in a common activity. Throughout the 1870s, the two organizations required the regular meeting and interaction of officers Albert Marsh, Robert Booth, Margaret McCullough, Ann Devey, Maria Adams, Clara Strong, Angelia Vance, Julia Strong, Margaret Booth, Eliza Carlisle, Alice Healey, Martha Adams, and others.

As we have seen, the women in 1868 founded their own organization, the Relief Society, with the bishop's wife, Margaret McCullough, as president. She worked in the Relief Society with Elizabeth Carlisle, Mary Watkins, Elsie Booth, Alice Freestone, Anne Walton, and Angelia Vance. Together they planned social occasions for women in the settlement, carried out welfare and assistance activities, promoted economic growth through the purchase of a community loom, attempted sericulture, and built a granary to store the wheat they gleaned for the poor after regular harvests. They also organized a women's choir and appointed ladies to visit homes to determine where assistance might be needed. Margaret McCullough presided over these activities for thirty-four years until 1902.

Elsie Booth was chosen first president of the Primary organization in 1879, providing religious instruction and social activities for young children, working during her seventeen-year tenure with Eliza Houston, Rhoda Vance, Martha Healey, Ann Devey, Rhoda Vance, Fannie E. Moyle, and others. William Johnson Strong organized a choir that included among its singers some thirty-four men and women. There were, in addition, theater companies, frequent dances, elaborate celebrations of national and local holidays, community projects to build and maintain canals and ditches, a city council, a cooperative store, and, in the 1890s, a hand-written newspaper, consisting of news and homilies, written by Alpine folk and circulated from house to house.[6]

The adult (over age seventeen) population of Alpine was 36 persons in 1860, 93 in 1870, and 171 in 1880, averaging 100 over the entire period. And during the period, at least 111 men and women staffed 172 volunteer offices. Seventy (63 percent) of the volunteer workers were men, and forty-one (37 percent) were women. The volunteer women, on average, held 1.4 offices, most of them in the Relief Society, the Young Ladies Mutual Improvement Association, the Primary, and the choir. The men, on average, held 1.6 offices, filling all civic positions but one, militia duty, and all Mormon priesthood offices, which were reserved for men. No one in the community held more than five positions over the period, several men and women held four or three, and the choir and militia involved a number, such as Julia Strong, who otherwise did not engage in public service.[7] One cannot but be struck by the extent of involvement of both men and women, a condition of life in early Alpine that brought most to interact with others outside of their immediate families on almost a daily basis. Eleven

---

[6] "Alpine Monthly Gleaner," 1898–1914, LDS Archives, Salt Lake City, Utah.

[7] Obviously, I am here using rate of participation in voluntary leadership positions as a surrogate for frequency of interaction among the whole population. The two are not the same, but it seems reasonable to assume that a high rate of voluntary service would correlate with a high rate of community interaction. It is also possible, as we shall see in the case of Sublimity, to have high rates of interaction that occur in settings where records are not kept. Thus the counting of incidence of voluntary service is clearly an imperfect instrument, but surely better than an intuitive guess, particularly when the numbers are consistent with anecdotal evidence.

These data represent a minimal listing, as they are gathered from various sources, including principally the Manuscript History and *Alpine Yesterdays*, cited in previous chapters. The bishops and presidents of organizations tended to have very long tenures in office, whereas their counselors (usually two in Mormon practice) changed fairly frequently. The list includes some elective civil offices that were not remunerative, but it does not include paid officials, such as police officers or marshals. Nor does it include teachers and non-office-holding members of organizations, except for the choir and militia, for which people volunteered and made extraordinary commitments. The period of office holding considered here extends from founding through 1880, with many offices being filled several times by successive office holders, whereas the whole adult population that was available to fill these offices ranged each year during the period from 36 in 1860 to 171 in 1880. In other words, I am saying that at least 111 officers filled 172 positions over some twenty years when an average of 100 adults was available to fill offices. I am not saying that 100 of 111 persons in the town held offices at any one time.

more persons filled voluntary positions over the three decades than the average number of adults in the town.

\* \* \*

Junius Wright, from southern Iowa, summing up his first summer of farming in Middleton, was pleased that

> I had no trouble selling all we could spare at a good price.... We forgot about our honeymoon trip and return to Iowa. We came in contact with people from all parts of the country, formed new acquaintances, and friendships and became familiar with the geography and resources of the great west and realized that we were cutting a conspicuous figure in making the desert blossom as the rose.[8]

His memory of making new friends among the diverse pioneers of the Boise Valley tells only a part of the tale. It is true that Middleton's settlers, like pioneers to any new land, felt the need for human association and found occasions where they met and worked together. Upon his arrival late in 1864, Wright "was fortunate in finding a little nook unclaimed at the lower end of the Canyon."[9] During the search he met a stock dealer, Joe Payne, "who wanted to stop with us." The Wrights built a cabin and partitioned off the west end for sleeping rooms, they on one side and Payne and a new arrival, Joel Richards, apparently also looking for winter lodging, on the other. During the winter, Wright occupied himself with a number of activities that involved association with other settlers. He persuaded a hauler, "Mr. Gates," to market a ton of hay for him (for $80) in the mining town of Idaho City in exchange for medical services. Being a physician, Wright treated Boise Valley neighbors suffering from malaria and other ailments. He brewed vinegar, which he sold in the Boise market for $2 a gallon. He and Richardson trailed some cattle south to better pasturage along the Snake River, sharing their cramped wagon bed one night with a Missourian, Thomas Graham, who was caught away from home at night looking for stray cattle.

It is remarkable that Wright remembered many years later the names of those he met that winter. He formed enduring associations with none of them, and indeed seemed to see their meeting as one of circumstance only, sharing company and mutual assistance through what proved to a hard winter before going their separate ways. Over the next two or three years the placer mines were worked out, prices

---

[8] Junius Wright Reminiscence, "A Summer with the Fowler Family," pp. 5–6, Idaho State Archives.
[9] Wright Reminiscence, "Our Honeymoon," p. 9.

for crops fell, and most moved on, so that "the influx of permanent population just about balanced the outflow of transients."[10]

The Lewis Spanglers arrived in the Boise Valley at the same time as the Wrights and, according to the narrative of young Mary, were lucky to find "two bachelor ranch men" who were willing to share their cabin with the family that winter. The next summer they claimed a piece of land near the canyon close to "Mr. White," husband of an older Spangler daughter, Susan. There they built a cabin of cotton-wood logs patterned after the one the Whites had already built. Lewis Spangler became a justice of the peace, his duties occasionally bring-ing strangers to their cabin, and "we also had preaching in our home." In 1866, at age thirteen, Mary was invited to the first party of her life, "an event in which the entire family was interested." That fall she attended school for the first time. Thereafter she accompanied her brothers to dances and socials, enjoying the attention brought by being one of the two "large girls" in the valley. She remembered a summer with her brother George, guarding their wheat and corn patches from free-grazing stock, the two lone teenagers amusing themselves by making rafts of bundled tulle reeds to float in the Boise River. A cat-tleman named Gates (the same who hauled hay for Wright?) visited the family from time to time, and on one occasion entrusted them with the care of saddlebags filled with $5,000 in gold dust.

Clearly, the Wrights and Spanglers enjoyed the company of others they met during their sojourn in the Middleton area. They and their neighbors welcomed occasional "preachings" in homes, put up trav-elers, attended home schools, and enjoyed dances, parties, and other gatherings. Yet, compared to Alpine, their social interaction seems thin and sporadic. The "new acquaintances" J. B. Wright found in Middleton were fewer, the time together shorter, the contexts of meet-ing different than in Alpine. So infrequent were such meetings that, decades later, both Wright and Spangler could remember the names of people they had met on only one occasion. It would seem that such human contacts loomed so large in memory because they were so rare.

The surviving record of community interaction is eloquent. There were enough settlers in the Middleton area by 1863 to lead William Montgomery to plat a town site. Nonetheless, for a considerable pe-riod, community gatherings were rare. In 1866, two years after the arrival of the Spangler family, Mary was invited to her first party. Pioneer farmer John Eggleston held a ball in November 1868 to cele-brate the completion of a new house "costing over four thousand dol-lars," taking particular pride in a large room where neighborhood

[10] Wright, untitled section beginning "The Gold Mines of Boise Basin," p. 1.

dances could be held.[11] In 1870 a music teacher, Fred Dunagan, sponsored a picnic to honor his scholars, after which a dance was held at the Eggleston home.[12] These were the only generally attended social gatherings reported in the area for a full decade after the platting of the town, though Mary Spangler's account indicates that there were other, less formal dances and parties.

Spangler mentioned occasional home worship, and there are reports of a circuit preacher visiting a schoolhouse in the village on a monthly basis to hold services as early as 1869. Yet it was six years later, in 1875 or 1876, that the group of Methodists built a church three miles east of the town, in a district called Central Park, assisted with funds provided by the Extension Service of the Methodist Episcopal Church.[13] This little congregation was active and committed to their faith, organizing a Sunday school in 1880 that lasted for two years and hosting in the 1880s Quarterly Conferences of the Boise Valley Middleton Circuit and the Grande Ronde and Boise City Districts. The members served on mission, Sunday school, temperance, tract, education, and other church committees.

The first regular services in Middleton town were another decade in coming, and still another eight years passed before the group of Baptists gathered enough resources to raise a building – the first in the town, completed in 1893. In December 1881, the Central Park Rev. G. W. Gramm had been optimistic about Middleton. "The outlook at Middleton is very good. There are many good people living in the vicinity of Middleton whom I trust ere many days shall be added to the church such as shall be eternally saved." Yet the Methodists did not extend their activities to Middleton proper until 1895. The newly arrived Rev. G. O. Richardson was shocked at the impiety of Middletonians when he began to evangelize the town. "Its earliest inhabitants were infidels," he reported,

> they had gathered unto themselves large numbers of people of like opinions. They had withstood every effort of evangelism for thirty years. Their social activities centered on a racecourse, a dance hall and a liquor saloon. Sunday was a day of recreation and revelry.[14]

---

[11] Boise, *Tri-Weekly Statesman*, November 21, 1868.

[12] Boise, *Tri-Weekly Statesman*, May 11, 1870.

[13] The Idaho State Archives contain a copy of a letter dated June 24, 1876, which reports a resolution of the Third Quarter Conference of the Boise Valley Circuit thanking the Church Extension Society of the Methodist Episcopal Church for help in building the Central Park Church.

[14] See Morris Foote, comp., *One Hundred Years in Middleton* (Middleton, Idaho: *Boise Valley Herald*, 1963), p. 33; and Rev. G. O. Richardson to Mrs. Grace Bixby, 1938, copy in records of the Middleton Methodist Church; also C. A. Quinn letter, undated

Though the good reverend's evangelical fervor no doubt tempted him to hyperbole, we still cannot help noticing that religious activities in the area were relatively late and sporadic. The first churchhouse in the larger community was eleven years in coming, and the first in the village was built twenty-eight years after settlement. A new minister in 1895 regarded the town as almost totally unchurched.

Middleton settlers built a twenty-four by fifty foot schoolhouse as early as 1869. Some thirty to fifty pupils attended classes there during the first decades, though we do not know how regular and consistent schooling was before extant records of the school district commence in September 1885. Citizens organized a Grange in 1874, with J. B. Wright as its first master. The Grangers shortly made efforts to acquire the flour mill James Stephenson had built in 1871, but within two years the organization had fallen apart. Efforts to reactivate the Grange in 1908 and the 1920s also failed before a permanent reorganization was made in 1935, which has continued. The Farmer's Alliance, founded in 1894, did not persist. The first fraternal lodge, the IOOF, did not come until 1899. Incorporation of Middleton Village was not until 1910, almost a half century after first settlement.

The Middleton settlers felt no need to organize a militia, in spite of occasional conflicts with Indians, as the U.S. garrison at Fort Boise, some twenty-two miles upriver, provided military protection. An Indian scare in 1877 led several of the settlers east of Middleton to build a log fort, and perhaps as many as thirty families sought refuge there for a brief period in 1878, but after a few days all returned to their own farmsteads. Middleton people were not entirely isolated, but clearly their efforts to launch one or another organization or program came late, were infrequent, rarely touched more than a few of the settlers, and none, with the possible exception of the school, endured long enough to provide frequent occasions for social interaction or a focus for volunteer community life in the district.[15]

There were 170 adults in Middleton in 1870, 158 in 1880, and about

and without addressee, Idaho State Archives, in which he reports that Middleton's first services were in 1895 and the church was dedicated in 1896.
[15] Boise *Tri-Weekly Statesman*, September 2, 1869; November 4, 1876. Early school records are in the possession of Mrs. Marguerite Foote of Middleton. The Farmer's Alliance organization is described in the *Idaho Daily Statesman*, April 25, 1891. The piece mentions, significantly, that "such clubs are attractive for the reason that there is so little else in the way of recreation or amusement which varies the monotony of ordinary farming life." Information on the IOOF was made available to the author by present officers of the lodge; on Middleton's incorporation see *Caldwell Tribune*, July 13, 1907 and Foote, *Middleton*, p. 40. Fort Schindler was mentioned in several accounts. See esp. Middleton Centennial Book Committee, *Middleton in Picture and Story* (Nampa, Ida.: Downtown Printing, 1989), p. 169.

172 in 1890, making an average over the period of 167. An exhaustive search of every available source shows that during the period from founding to 1890, there were as many as twenty-three men and women staffing thirty-one volunteer positions in civic organizations, the Grange, and the church.[16] Nineteen were men. The four women included Cordelia Foote, who organized the first Baptist Sunday school in 1885, as well as Emmaroy Fowler, C. Newton, and Bell Dodd, all active in the Central Park Methodist Church east of Middleton. The woman filled 1.2 positions on average, all in their respective churches. The men held 1.4 offices, including all civic posts, Grange offices, and fifteen of twenty church positions. One man, Moses Fowler, held three offices, all with the Methodist church, including work as a lay pastor. Six other persons, including his wife, Emmaroy Fowler, held two offices and all the rest one.[17]

[16] I here use the end date of 1890 in order to consider social interaction over about the same span of time as I consider in Alpine and Sublimity.

[17] As with Alpine, these data represent a minimal listing, as they are gathered from various sources, including principally the two local histories by Morris Foote and by the Middleton Centennial Book Committee, cited in footnote 15, and the J. B. Wright and Mary Spangler Luster reminiscences. They include as well Jennie Cornell's extensive biographical files on early Middleton folk, from which information for the centennial volume was extracted, newspaper stories, records of Middleton Baptist and the Central Park and Middleton Methodist churches, IOOF records, and school records. Jack Keith, pastor of the First Baptist Church (Conservative) of Middleton, kindly shared their earliest extant records, as did the pastor of the Middleton Methodist Church. Mrs. Marguerite Foote had the earliest school records in her custody at the time I used them, and the early IOOF records were made available by the present officers. As in Alpine, the list of volunteer positions includes some elective civic offices that were not remunerative, but it does not include paid officials such as police officers or marshals.

The period of office holding considered here extends from founding through 1890, as Middleton was founded about ten years after Alpine. As with Alpine, the data represent only roughly the extent of office holding in the community, and in both cases there were probably many more offices filled that were not recorded or for which records have not survived. Failure to record offices or loss of records probably affected our understanding of Middleton's social interaction more than that of Alpine. Yet I carried out equally careful searches in the same types of archives and sources, and through any contacts I could manage with local historians in both towns. Indeed, having been raised in Middleton and having attended Middleton public schools, I had better contacts in the town than in Alpine. It seems unlikely that the Middleton information imbalance could be so extreme as to account for the enormous disparity in frequency and (as we shall see) character of social interaction. Moreover, whatever propensity there may have been for Middleton people not to record activities or not to preserve their records to the extent seen in Alpine is in itself an artifact of considerable importance. When a community has less concern about retaining a written record of its past, that fact may say a good deal about the meaning of that community to those who lived there.

The contrast with Alpine could hardly be more striking. There, with an adult population 60 percent that of Middleton, five times as many men and women filled five times as many voluntary positions and offices. Alpine women were far more visible in public life, filling 37 percent of the offices, whereas Middleton women filled 18 percent. Fourteen percent of the average number of adults in Middleton during the period held at least one volunteer position. Of the adults in Alpine, 111 percent held at least one volunteer position.

It is obvious that serving in volunteer associations was easier in Alpine, where all lived in a compact settlement. Moreover, in the Utah town, all were brought under the umbrella of one faith, whereas in Middleton two different faiths contended for communicants, and there were many of no faith, which diminished the critical mass needed to sustain voluntary association. Still, the differences between the two communities are so dramatic as to suggest that there were real and fundamental variations in their patterns of human association. The Utah community drew nearly all adults into some type of voluntary activity that caused them almost daily to talk to, work with, contend with, and in time form enduring ties to others in the settlement. Some then, and many now, would see such closeness as a stifling imposition on personal time and space. The Idaho community left the great majority of adults (86 percent) free to carry out their personal agendas. They could pick and choose whom they would associate with, how often, and in what contexts (and readily ignore those whom they wished not to associate with). Personal time and space were for them largely unfettered by broader human ties. For them the pronoun "we" came most often to mean the immediate family.

\* \* \*

In some senses, the Oregon settlers likewise were accustomed to considerable control over their time and space. They differed from the Middleton folk in one important respect. They used the word "we" in a broader sense to include a cluster of kin and neighbors. Alternatively, one could say that they differed from Alpiners in one very important respect. For them "we" had a more narrow meaning, including principally kin and close neighbors. Whichever perspective one chooses, the Sublimity pattern appears to be a vestige of a social order that had been common in the Old South, and perhaps in other early European settlements in the Americas as well.

George and Elizabeth Hunt, for example, settled on the 640 acres they had acquired and made it something of a community center for themselves, the Darsts, Downings, and other neighbors, though Sublimity town lay just two miles to the south of them. Their district, called Whiteaker, included the cemetery Hunt mentioned in his will, as well as three neighborhood enterprises he built next to his home during the 1860s and 1870s – a small store, a blacksmith shop, and an armory, which served a local militia he supported and encouraged. Hunt also found space on his place for a minister to preach on Sundays before he joined the United Brethren Church in Sublimity. His neighbor, Paul Darst, provided schooling for some thirty neighborhood children of all ages in a schoolhouse erected (apparently with $100 in county tax funds) on Hunt's property in 1856. George Hunt's sister, Temperance, and her husband, John Downing, lived a short distance to the west of the Hunt place. Their imposing, well-appointed Greek Revival home was a favorite gathering place for Sunday dinners, weddings, funerals, fox hunts, and other neighborhood events.[18]

Such self-contained communities dotted the landscape in the Sublimity area. Some, located at crossroads (Hobson's Corner, named Sublimity in 1856) or near streams (Stayton, on the Santiam River) grew eventually into full-fledged commercial centers, but the kin/ neighbor clusters remained for a considerable period the primary social spaces for Sublimity area people and persisted in the memory of their children, who identify their ancestors with Whiteaker, Victor Point, Macleay, or Fern Ridge more than with Sublimity.[19] There is evidence to suggest that the citizens of these tight-knit communities met often for worship, schooling, exchange, defense, and socializing. Beyond their networks, interaction with others was rare, occurring at the county level more than in the nearby towns, as leading citizens took up county offices that involved them in building roads and bridges, keeping land records, providing neighborhood schools, assessing and collecting taxes, marketing surplus crops, and politicking.

Thus it is virtually impossible to construct an overview of the early history of the area, as each neighbor/kin cluster had in essence its own story – stories that, alas, though persisting in folk memory, were rarely written down or shared with others. There are nonetheless several fragmentary accounts, especially those collected by Mark Schmid and Sarah Hunt Steeves, that share common themes. Most mention the ancestral home in the Midwest or South, the sojourn in the Midwest, the decision to take the great leap to the Pacific, and the trials of the overland journey. They pay homage to pioneer Daniel Waldo, originally from Indiana and Missouri, who, while exploring prospects

[18] Sarah Hunt Steeves, *Book of Remembrance of Marion County, Oregon, Pioneers, 1840–1860* (Portland, Ore.: The Berncliff Press, 1927), pp. 96–101, 131–2, 90–3.

[19] Mark Schmid, *Sublimity: The Story of an Oregon Countryside, 1850–1950* (St. Benedict, Ore.: The Library Bookstore, 1951), pp. 12–21.

along the Willamette in 1843, learned from a trapper he had known in Missouri of "thousands of acres of rolling land stretching in every direction, covered everywhere with native grass, knee high." Delighted with the new site (now near the town of Shaw, northwest of Sublimity), Waldo built a cabin and settled in.[20] Others made claims nearby, forming a community very much like the later settlement at Whiteaker, complete with schoolhouse and other local institutions. The sternly practical Waldo became "by common consent, the acting squire for the neighborhood," helping to litigate civil disputes throughout the district.[21] The broader district, including the northern reaches of the area I have defined as Sublimity, shortly became known as Waldo Hills.

Waldo's venture seems to have been the common pattern, and within a decade such communities proliferated across the Waldo Hills. Pioneers of the various districts gave prominence in their recollections to the process of choosing their home sites. They refer to the acquiring of land that made the family farm possible and frequently mention prominent oak or fir trees, sometimes groves of them, that drew them to the spot they chose for their home (the trees symbolically sanctifying the future family hearth). They describe early weddings and funerals (especially crucial events for the neighbor/kin groups) that always took place in the home.

The memoirs honor in general terms particularly charitable people, such as Sarah Brown Condit of Aumsville, "the good woman sent for in the community in every time of need."[22] They speak of early deaths in Oregon and the opening of family cemeteries. They remember preachings, again usually in the home, and schooling, naming preachers, teachers, and pupils. Visits to neighbors and kin recur frequently. Sarah Hunt Steeves remembered that "As I had no grandparents and was sort of a relative to Reverend [George] Ashby, I was privileged to call him and his good wife grandpa and grandma, and I loved them as my own kin. . . . Grandma was an excellent cook and . . . nobody's fried chicken or dried apple pies tasted quite so good and permission to visit these interesting old people and remain over night, snugly tucked in the featherbed, was one of the joys of my childhood."[23]

---

[20] Waldo was well established by 1844, when the famed Rocky Mountain trapper James Clyman made a special point of commenting on Waldo's excellent herd of cattle. James Clyman, *Journal of a Mountain Man*, ed., Linda M. Hasselstrom (Missoula, Mont.: Mountain Press Publishing Company, 1984), p. 164.

[21] T. T. Geer, *Fifty Years in Oregon* (New York: The Neale Publishing Company, 1912), pp. 217–21.

[22] Steeves, *Book of Remembrance*, p. 289.

[23] Steeves, *Book of Remembrance*, pp. 302–3.

In these accounts many claim a role in the "Abiqua War," in March 1848, when local militias were called out to subdue itinerant bands of Klamath and Molalla Indians who were stirred by the Cayuse War to harass white settlers in the Willamette Valley.[24] Others were involved during the Rogue River Wars of the mid-1850s. Surprisingly, except for these encounters, the native inhabitants seem to have been invisible to the American settlers. Though the contact between native and white cultures elsewhere in the West altered that of the white settlers in substantive ways, there is little evidence that this happened in the Waldo Hills districts.[25] Rarely do the settlers mention the Molalla, Klamath, Calapooia, or Santiam peoples after the Abiqua War.[26] When Oregon Indians were confined to reservations during the 1850s, they seem to have disappeared from white consciousness, except as a source for stories of the heroism of the pioneers.

Strongly embedded in local memory was the discovery of gold in California, the Fraser River, or Idaho and odysseys to the mines, returning, after many trials, with enough gold to buy more land, make needed improvements on their farms, and settle happily into arcadian life. Hadley Hobson had come originally from Missouri to California but was disappointed, explaining to his parents that he "found such a mixed multitude of people from all parts of the world and the society was so bad that I could not bear the idea of raising a family in such a wicked country, so I steered for Oregon." Though he hoped to get to newly discovered mines in southern Oregon, he explained, "I have not had the chance to go to them yet. I have been improving my

---

[24] George W. Hunt wrote a brief description of his role in the affair in his *A History of the Hunt Family* (Boston: MacDonald, Gill & Company, 1890), pp. 33–7.

[25] James Axtell wrote a stimulating essay stressing the importance of cultural interaction, "Colonial America without the Indians: Counterfactual Reflections," *Journal of American History* 73 (March 1987): 981–96. Elizabeth A. H. John persuasively describes such interaction in *Storms Brewed in Other Men's Worlds: The Confontation of Indians, Spanish, and French in the Southwest, 1540–1795* (College Station: Texas A & M University Press, 1975). It may be significant that the most compelling accounts of cultural exchange were most often written during periods of initial or very early contact between European and Native American cultures. The English had been in the region since 1825, and the character of contact between the two groups had become to some extent routinized by the time American settlers began to come in the 1840s. This may have made it easier for the Americans to deal with the native peoples from a considerable distance, minimizing the degree of influence upon their own culture.

[26] Diplomacy between the Native Americans and representatives of the Territory of Oregon and of the United States continued throughout the 1850s, resulting in the cession by various tribes of most Willamette Valley lands to the Anglo settlers by the end of the 1850s and in the removal of the Indians to several reservations. See Charles Henry Carey, *History of Oregon* (Portland: The Pioneer Historical Publishing Company, 1922), pp. 576–629.

farm so as I could raise my own support."[27] The mines were alluring
to Oregonians, but their principal appeal lay in the promise of quick
cash that could be applied to improving farms. Many Sublimity men
followed the path of William John Humphreys, who mined in southern Oregon, California, and Idaho, "but always retained possession of
his Waldo hills farm, . . . still held by the children and heirs."[28]

Sublimity town began at a crossroads where entrepreneurs in the
early 1850s saw an opportunity to serve the district's farmers by lo-
cating a dry goods store, a blacksmith forge, a gunsmith shop, and
two saloons. The hamlet was just north of Hadley Hobson's land claim
and so at first was called Hobson Corner. The need in 1852 to submit
a formal name for a post office led James Denny to suggest "Sublimity" because of the sublime view from his hilltop cabin. The name
loomed large in 1860 because census officials applied it to a vast precinct, but the kin/neighbor clusters were clearly the real communities
and became more visible in the 1860s and 1870s as each established
its schoolhouse, cemetery, post office, and Grange.

Sublimity thus had no more claim as a name for the surrounding
country than did Whiteaker, though in 1857 the United Brethren established a school there called Sublimity College. The school at first
was partially supported by state funds, providing a primary and a
rudimentary secondary education for those in the immediate vicinity,
and serving as a social and recreational center. Sublimity College declined during the Civil War but was revivified in 1865 and bravely
continued until the early 1870s, when it became a victim of competition from an improved public school system and dwindling support
from United Brethren churches in the East.[29]

Some Sublimity folk remember that the Civil War caused bitter di-
visions. Local historian Mark Schmid reported that so many returned
east to support their respective sides in the conflict that "Sublimity
was soon deserted, houses became vacant and neglected, money was
scarce and prices exorbitant. It seemed as if the wilderness was again
going to creep down from the hills and engulf the lately cleared lands
on every side."[30] In fact, 38 percent of Sublimity's 1860 household
heads were still there in 1870, a high persistence rate for a rural population at any time. Thirty-nine percent of the 1860 Sublimity house-

[27] Hadley Hobson to his parents, June 15, 1851, in *Oregon Historical Quarterly* (Spring,
1992): 65–72.

[28] Steeves, *Book of Remembrance*, pp. 285–6.

[29] *The Oregon Statesman*, October 6, 1862, has an ad for a "permanent" school established
by W. W. Beach "in the building formerly known as 'Sublimity College,' offering to
pupils superior advantages for acquiring a *Good English Education*."

[30] Schmid, *Sublimity*, pp. 18–20, 55–6.

hold heads born in slave states were there in 1870, as well as 37 percent of those born elsewhere. The Civil War surely caused rancorous debates and perhaps some departures, both permanent and temporary, but hardly depopulation.

For the old settlers, mostly Protestant and American born, the trauma of the war may, in fact, have been less than that created by an influx of German-speaking Roman Catholics during the 1870s and 1880s. In 1860 only one head of household, Francis Henline, was from a German-speaking country. Another joined the population by 1870. But by 1880 there were ten families headed by a parent born in Germany, Bavaria, Prussia, Austria, or Switzerland, including a Catholic priest, Father Stampfl. Six other families from Luxembourg, Belgium, and Bohemia were probably Catholic and spoke German or Flemish. (All but the Belgian-born Peter Thomas and Nicholas La Croix had German names.) Seven of the new arrivals bought homes in Sublimity town, where they were highly visible because of their concentration there and their acquisition of the Sublimity College facilities for a religious center. The new arrivals caused considerable consternation among a people who considered all faiths but Protestantism suspect.[31] Thus the community was strained by both regional and religious differences during the 1860s and 1870s.

But, of course, to speak of such a community strain is to misrepresent the social character of the Sublimity area. There was in fact no extended sense of community or "we-ness" to be challenged by either the Civil War or the arrival of the Catholics. The neighbor/kin clusters remained largely intact, and each was fairly uniform in religious and political conviction. They had in any case never interacted to any great extent with those outside. If Sublimity town suddenly seemed to have been taken over by Catholics, that was a matter of some concern to the people of Whiteaker but ultimately did not cause any significant change in their own society. The remarkable intensity of communal attachments within the neighbor/kin clusters diminished the practical effects of changes taking place outside.

Although the existence of these tiny communities can hardly be

---

[31] French Catholic trappers had been among the earliest European settlers in the Willamette Valley, and Catholic churches and schools were founded on the French Prairie, at St. Paul and Gervais, well north of Sublimity, but there had hitherto been none in the Sublimity area. Descendants of the earliest settlers a century later seemed to think of the Catholics of Sublimity as a separate people and recall their arrival as something of an alien invasion. Sharing one religious and educational center and one cemetery in Sublimity town, they were sharply different not only in religious inclination but also, perhaps more important, in social organization from their country Protestant neighbor/kin clustering predecessors.

doubted, it is extremely difficult to document the level of interaction within them. Indeed, the intimacy of their connectedness obviated any need to formalize and thus record patterns of association. A kindly deed done for a cousin or in-law – a gift, a loan, lending a hand at harvest time, the boarding of a child, the hosting of a preaching service or wedding – was done informally and rarely became a matter of record. Nonetheless, some evidence of voluntary service in the Sublimity area survives and offers at least tentative insights. Sublimity district had a much larger population than Alpine or even Middleton, with 258 adults in 1860, 313 in 1870, and 402 in 1880. During the period to 1880, I have identified forty-four men and women who worked in sixty-seven volunteer positions in civic organizations, militias, the Grange, schools, lodges, and the church. All but five were men, and four of the five women filled offices in one organization, the Pomona Grange, which had a countywide membership. The other, Delilah Glover, did not have a formally appointed position but was highly regarded as a nurse and midwife and may well have been compensated for her compassionate service. Each of the women filled just one position. The men held 1.2 offices on average, but a few filled a disproportionate number of offices. Six of the men (14 percent of the total number of volunteers) – George Hunt, William Porter, George and John Downing, Paul Darst, and Elijah Strong – served in twenty-four offices, 36 percent of the total number of offices held.[32] Altogether, the forty-four persons who served in volunteer activities represented 13.5 percent of the average adult population during the period to 1880.

What can we make of the overall picture of voluntary association in the three districts? Most dramatically, Alpine people were far more

[32] As indicated in the text, because of the highly localized community structure of Sublimity, these data represent an even more minimal listing than for Middleton and Alpine. They are gathered from various sources, including principally the local history by Mark Schmid and Sarah Hunt Steeves's collective biography of Marion county pioneers. They include as well information taken from minutes of the Pomona Grange of Marion County; scrapbooks kept by the Patton and Downing families, which contained numerous clippings of obituaries and other vital events; typescript histories of the Victor Point district by Bernita J. Sharp, and of the Stayton Church of Christ by Mathilda Siegmund Jones; and the William Porter diary for the year 1848, all made available by Daraleen Wade. Copies of letters from 1878 written by W. H. Daugherty and John C. Peebles that describe some of the curriculum and list the board of directors of Sublimity College were made available to me by Addie Dyal of Salem. As for the other communities, the list of volunteer positions includes some elective civic offices that were minimally remunerative, such as clerks of local school districts, but does not include paid persons, such as school teachers, tax assessors, police officers, or marshalls.

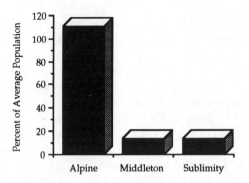

(For sources see footnotes 10, 20, and 32)

Figure 6.1 Percent of the average adult population holding volunteer positions during first two decades.

likely to engage in voluntary service than those of Middleton and Sublimity. Of the average adult population of Alpine over the first three decades after settlement, 111 percent can be identified as having at least one voluntary position in the community, compared to 14 percent for Middleton and 13.5 percent for Sublimity, though in Sublimity, but not Middleton, there is much evidence to suggest a much higher unrecorded level of activity at the kin/neighbor level.

Variations in the relative types of voluntary association in the three societies are suggestive. Alpine women were much more likely to hold voluntary positions than their sisters in Middleton or Sublimity, bringing them often out of their homes and into the public sphere. Yet none of the forty-one women held church positions related to worship, but rather directed and served in organizations providing social welfare assistance for the community, in social activities and moral instruction for other women or children, or sang in one of the choirs. In contrast, the core of responsibility for all five of the Middleton women who held voluntary positions was purely religious – organizing Sunday schools or serving on missionary and other church committees. And if the church provided the principal opportunity for women in public service in Middleton, the Grange did so in Sublimity, where four of the five women in voluntary service held Grange offices. Only one woman, Margaret Booth of Alpine, held civic office.

Civic offices were more important in Middleton and Sublimity than in Alpine, accounting for 25 percent and 19 percent of the voluntary positions held, compared to 15 percent in the Utah town. Both Sublimity and Alpine had many opportunities for service in primarily social organizations (16 and 15 percent), but Middleton lagged well

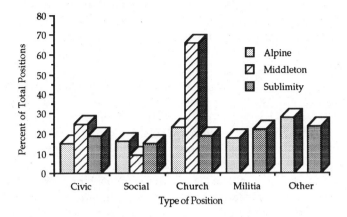

(For sources see footnotes 10, 20, and 32)

Figure 6.2 Allocation of voluntary positions in Alpine, Middleton, and Sublimity by type of activity.

behind with but 9 percent, again evidence of the relative paucity of social life in the Idaho town.

Militias were also important in the Utah and Oregon towns, involving 22 and 18 percent of voluntary work, respectively, whereas the Idaho people were quite willing to let professional soldiers handle military concerns. Of course, Oregon and Utah were settled earlier than Idaho, and at a time when the U.S. army rarely assumed responsibility for defense of far western settlers. But in addition, the earlier settlers were influenced by an older American tradition, when the risks of war seemed remote, and militia drills and position in a hierarchy of named offices served important social functions.[33] The Middleton folk, refugees from the Civil War, shared a darker perspective on war and military maneuvers and, since a number were likely draft resisters or even deserters, perhaps had good reason not to have their names entered on militia rosters.

It would seem significant that the variety of opportunities for volunteer activity was much greater in Alpine and Sublimity than in Middleton. Religious and civic positions made up nearly the whole tiny sphere of opportunity for social interaction in the Idaho town, whereas in Alpine and Sublimity there were militias, choirs, school

[33] A useful overview of the role of the militia in American life is Marcus Cunliffe, *Soldiers and Civilians: The Martial Spirit in America, 1775–1865* (Boston: Little, Brown, 1968); see also Robert Utley's *Frontiersmen in Blue: The United States Army and the Indian 1848–1865* (New York: Macmillan, 1967).

committees, and a greater number of largely social and recreational organizations, such as Granges and debating societies, that were sustained by the local people. In Middleton, if one was not religious or did not aspire to public office there were fewer opportunities to form friendships and ties beyond the household.

In Sublimity and Middleton a relative few held most of the voluntary positions, suggesting a hierarchy of community leadership heavily weighted at the top. Ten percent of Sublimity adults held 82 percent of the volunteer positions; the same group in Middleton held 78 percent. People in the Sublimity kin/neighbor groups understood well their own informal, ordered hierarchy and long-held patterns of deference, with the result that most did not consider seeking the community leadership positions that the few occupied. In Middleton it is more likely that indifference more than deference was at work. Most demurred not because they assumed that those who had always sustained the community would take the lead but because they were not interested in or concerned with a broader community. In Alpine the hierarchy of priesthood office was the driving force in the community. Yet, though all adult men and women had a place in that hierarchy, a very few filled the top leadership positions through the end of the century.[34]

Thomas Jefferson McCullough was bishop of Alpine from 1867 until his death in 1893 and mayor from 1867 to 1882. His wife, Margaret, was Relief Society president from 1868 to 1902. The couple for over a quarter century headed Alpine society, holding high status, power, and wealth – commonly seen as the hallmarks of those at the top of a hierarchical order.[35] Yet they used their place not to foster an oli-

---

[34] The question of whether adult Mormon women "hold" the priesthood (are given priesthood power) is a matter of debate and discussion, with the present church hierarchy often suggesting that they do not. Yet, as we have seen in Chapter 5, Mormon ritual and doctrine for a century and a half have clearly indicated that in the temple "endowment," which is normally given at or shortly before marriage, women are given the priesthood. This may be rather a fine distinction, however, as it is equally clear that they are not ordained to priesthood *office*, as men are, which denies them entry to the leadership track that may lead to presiding over wards, stakes, or the church generally. They can and do, however, preside over some organizations at all of these levels, including the Relief Society, which the founder of Mormonism said was the women's counterpart of the priesthood office. See Linda King Newell, "A Gift Given, a Gift Taken: Washing, Anointing, and Blessing the Sick Among Mormon Women," *Sunstone* 6 (November/December 1981): 16–25.

[35] McCullough first appears on the tax rolls in 1860 with 30 acres, nearly twice that of others in the town (mean, 15.4), and he was the second most wealthy man after Catherine Nash's son, Worthy. By 1870, two years after he became bishop, his acreage had increased to fifty-one and his total wealth had more than doubled, from $1,350 to $2,740, whereas the average of the community had increased but 53 percent, from

garchic structure of leaders who out of noblesse oblige or by default gathered unto themselves a lion's share of community offices, as in Sublimity and Middleton. Rather, they distributed responsibility and thus, in great measure, power by issuing "callings" broadly among the citizens of their town to take up the manifold tasks they felt essential to general well-being.

In fact, though we have spoken of "voluntary offices" in this chapter, the term is something of a misnomer in the Alpine context if understood as spontaneous discerning and voluntary filling of community needs by the rank and file. The bishop and Relief Society president were principal agents in the task of discerning community needs, in convening community councils at various levels to discuss possible means of filling those needs, and then in asking citizens to implement the means decided upon. Citizens thus were called to the various tasks. They did not volunteer. Indeed, one who volunteered might have been seen as ambitious for office. Even the McCulloughs were not always the prime movers, for in many matters, such as in the building of the fort walls, the calling of young men to take wagons east, or the organizing of the Relief Society, they were asked to do so by the general church leaders. The Alpine system, clearly hierarchical, gained its vitality from the shared sense of the people that the McCulloughs had been divinely called to their positions and hence held legitimate authority to lead the community.

*    *    *

Perhaps the most striking fact relating to the allocation of voluntary positions is the seeming predominance of religion. This would seem consistent with a discussion, begun by Frederick Jackson Turner in 1893, that has focused on the question of what religion did or did not do "to regulate the frontier." Turner concluded that "a moving frontier must have had important results on the character of religious organization in the United States. The religious aspects of the frontier make a chapter in our history which needs study."[36] Don H. Doyle, studying townsmen rather than farmers, found that in Jacksonville, Illinois, "The church provided one of the most potent instruments for

---

$480 to $735. In the subsequent decade, the first full decade since he had become bishop and one plagued by economic distress, his wealth declined by 22 percent, whereas the average wealth of Alpine's taxpayers decreased by 16 percent. The central point is that he was one of the wealthier men in the community before he became bishop in 1868 and remained so, though his share of total wealth declined from 7 to 5 percent in his first full decade as bishop.

[36] Frederick Jackson Turner, "The Significance of the Frontier in American History," the 1893 essay printed in Frederick Jackson Turner, *The Frontier in American History* (New York: H. Holt and Company, 1920).

organizing the diverse and fluid population of the new community."[37] John Mack Faragher concluded that camp meetings held in the Sugar Creek, Illinois, area during the second decade of the nineteenth century "transferred the fervor and commitment of revival Protestantism into communal institutions. At the camp meeting not only individuals and churches, but whole communities got organized and were provided with a mystical, sanctified genesis." The churches, Faragher concluded, were "forces of order" that "reinforced basic cultural assumptions" and were "a bulwark of support for the national imperial enterprise that brought Americans to Sugar Creek."[38]

It is certainly true that religious activities accounted for a large proportion of association in all three of our districts – 23 percent in Alpine, a commanding 66 percent in Middleton, and 19 percent in Sublimity. Yet for Middleton at least, the church bell resounded so loudly because the social space was otherwise so empty. The 66 percent represented twenty-one of thirty-two leadership positions known and 16 adult men and women of 167 in the community – about 1 in 10. This suggests that the power of religion as a cohesive force in the Boise Valley could not have been great. A comparison of the role of religion in three societies helps clarify the matter.

In 1889 two Boise ministers, one a Methodist the other a Baptist, combined their talents in a protracted crusade against the forces of evil. Their urgent sermons led sixteen souls to the anxious bench. M. S. Cobb, a devout Baptist, wrote that when facing the hard question of which pastor would gather in the newly saved, "it was thought that a majority of the converts would choose to become members of the Baptist Church." Some of the converts were farmers in the valley west of Boise, so on March 16 the Boise City pastor, the Rev. L. W. Gowen, preached briefly at the Cox schoolhouse and then asked "all present . . . who wished to be organized into a church to rise to their feet." Three men and five women "rose and joined hands and received

---

[37] Don Harrison Doyle, *The Social Order of a Frontier Community: Jacksonville, Illinois, 1825–70* (Urbana: University of Illinois Press, 1978), pp. 157, 164.

[38] John Mack Faragher, *Sugar Creek: Life on the Illinois Prairie* (New Haven, Conn.: Yale University Press, 1986), pp. 164, 168. For a brief review of these issues, see also John Mack Faragher, "Open Country Community: Sugar Creek, Illinois, 1820–1850," in Steven Hahn and Jonathan Prude, eds., *The Countryside in the Age of Capitalist Transformation: Essays in the Social History of Rural America* (Chapel Hill: University of North Carolina Press, 1985), pp. 233–58.

Robert V. Hine noted that in the West "religion was the bearer of the town's values, and the Protestant churches their physical reminders." Yet he concluded less optimistically that "in general the more churches in a town the greater the social cleavage." Robert V. Hine, *Community on the American Frontier: Separate But Not Alone* (Norman: University of Oklahoma Press, 1980), pp. 144–5.

a hand of welcome to the denomination." Another of those present, William Huckleby, then "rose and stated that he believed God had forgiven him for his sinful wandering and wished again to become a member of the Church of Christ. He was unanimously received."

Such scenes were repeated hundreds of times throughout the West in the nineteenth century as the pious, long severed from their home congregations in the States, began gradually to coalesce into like-minded bodies in the new setting. Yet a close reading of the account suggests that we are not seeing in the Boise Valley a replication of the Baptist congregations these folk had left in the Midwest or the Old South. First, and most obviously, there had been for many a long period of what Brother Huckleby called "sinful wandering" between the fragmenting of the old congregation and the gathering of the new. The Breshears family, mainstays of both the Boise Valley and, later, the Middleton Baptist churches (the latter founded in 1895), were already present in the valley in 1880, giving them ample wandering time before the Middleton congregation was founded. Something of the general state of religious activity in early Idaho is suggested by C. DeWitt Smith, a Methodist, who wrote from the Territory in 1865, "Little church here. We did have services for several days (Sundays) but that is now ended. I read my bible. No Methodists here. Nearly everyone looks upon religion and piety as a weakness. Men, women, and children."[39] No doubt every member of the new Boise Valley Church had spent several years apart from organized religion, and some had been wandering for a quarter century or more.

Second, it does not seem to strain Brother Cobb's intent to suggest that a need for community was an important motivation of those gathering into the new church. He stressed that the members "would feel more at home to join a church in the neighborhood than in the city," enjoying "more of a home feeling in a local church." The joining of hands at the inaugural meeting bespoke a deep hope that the ties left severed through long separation from old communities would now be bound anew. Yet their few numbers suggested that the time between leaving the old communion and entering the new had had its erosive effects.

In fact, Cobb frankly recognized that maintaining a church in the West would be a struggle. A neighborhood church would have the positive effect of causing the communicants to "take greater interest in its work and welfare." He expected that in the local group "there

[39] Pamphlet titled "A Brief History of Idaho and Western Montana as Settled and District Organized by the Church of the Brethren (n.p.: Church of the Brethren, 1914), p. 8 in Idaho State Archives.

would [be] a more decided feeling of responsibility financially and otherwise for the maintenance of the church." Even so, he had to recognize the fluidity of religious connections and convictions on the frontier. In the smaller rural congregation, he maintained, "members could be received or dismissed with greater facility and in case any disciplinary work was ever needed . . . it could be more wisely done."[40]

The clerk of the Boise Valley Church would seem unwittingly to have articulated the principal problems facing established religion as it sought to spread its influence in the Far West. Many had wandered for years, with only minimal churching. In the process, the perceived need for close human association beyond family and a few trusted friends had diminished. Rural people, in any case, were uncomfortable with the character of urban pastors and worship practices. And moving about inhibited the forming of close ties generally and of congregations in particular. These problems were not unique to Middleton, however, and are evident among the first Anglo-American populations in the Far West – those that settled in Sublimity and other rural districts in Oregon.

In Sublimity the culture of the settlers, the scattered settlement pattern, and the topography combined to inhibit organized religion. Extant records and the memory of old-timers can substantiate the building of but one church in the Sublimity area before 1889, the Mill Creek Church of Christ, built in 1858.[41] There were by 1878 at least six neighborhood schoolhouses scattered throughout the district, and church services and other local gatherings were often held in them.[42] Though Sublimity College lasted for less than a decade, its building served as a center for the United Brethren, one of the two or three religious congregations known to have been founded within the area, and became a convent for Sisters of the Precious Blood between 1885 and 1891. The St. Boniface Parish Church was built there in 1889.[43]

Early Oregon missionary George H. Atkinson faced the problem of unfixed religious conviction when he opened a ministry for the Congregational Church in 1848. In Astoria he noted with apparent dis-

---

[40] Record Book of the Boise Valley Baptist Church, Idaho State Archives, Boise.

[41] The group organized a Church of God congregation that met monthly in a sixteen by twenty foot schoolhouse on Mill Creek between Sublimity and Aumsville and built a building in 1858. They moved to Aumsville in 1868 as the Aumsville Church of Christ. Mathilda Siegmund Jones, "Chronological History of the Church of Christ, Stayton, Oregon," unpublished manuscript in possession of the author.

[42] *Historical Atlas Map of Marion & Linn Counties* (San Francisco: Edgar Williams & Co., 1878), pp. 44–5, 48–9.

[43] Schmid, *Sublimity*, pp. 82–6.

appointment that "no one professes religion . . . except Mr. McClure, a catholic." However, in Clatsop he was informed that Oregon settlers represented a variety of denominations. "The Campbellites occupy large portions in the southern counties. Catholics are popular because they are building and spending large sums of money among the people. The Methodists . . . hold the highest influence among the people. The Baptists have three preachers." Yet he went on to note that a Baptist church and a Presbyterian church consisted of eight and twelve members, respectively. "Difficulties impede the Gospel in this territory. Yet I feel that God will give aid to all who trust him and seek his glory. Though they begin with few and feeble means he will raise up sons and daughters to his chh. and fill its treasuries and build its temples."[44]

A decade later the treasuries were still empty, the temples unbuilt. Writing in 1857, Atkinson felt "deeply grieved that so little has been done, that so few have been converted, and that so few attend meeting." That year he gave up his peregrinations into the surrounding rural districts "because the people attended so little." By June 1858 he lamented that after ten years of labor "we have yet no revival, no spiritual change for the better unless it be in this clearer view of Christ wh. I feel glad to confess & wh. I trust one or two others feel. O that my faith may be strong & unwavering."[45] Catherine Blaine, working with her husband for the Methodists in 1853, was no more optimistic. "Quite a number of our neighbors were in the states members of churches but are now Universalists or infidels in theory and in practice no better."[46]

The 1860 census confirmed the pessimism, reporting in all of Marion County, Oregon, but nine persistent and formally organized churches (most of them likely in Salem), the lot of them capable of accommodating but 1,900 persons, about 26 percent of the county population. Three were Methodist and two each were Episcopal, Presbyterian, and Roman Catholic.[47] The situation had changed but little in 1870, with

---

[44] E. Ruth Rockwood, ed., "Diary of Rev George H. Atkinson, D.D., 1847–58," *Oregon Historical Quarterly* 40 (1939): 172, 177–8.

[45] Atkinson Diary, *Oregon Historical Quarterly* 41 (1940): 301–3.

[46] Catherine Paine Blaine to unknown correspondent, December 22, 1853, and May 8, 1854, in David Edwards Blaine and Catherine Paine Blaine Collection of Letters Written 1853–62 from Oregon and Washington to Relatives in New York, Huntington Library, San Marino, California. The letters cited were written from Seattle.

[47] *Statistics of the United States . . . in 1860* (Washington, D.C.: Government Printing Office, 1866), p. 433. Population from *1900 Census Reports*, Vol. I, *Twelfth Census of the United States taken in the Year 1900: Population, Part I* (Washington, D.C.: U.S. Government Printing Office, 1901), p. 36.

eight churches reported in the county, capable of accommodating some 2,300 worshippers, now 23 percent of the population.[48]

This does not imply, as we shall see, an absence of religious sentiments and feelings among the rural people, but it does suggest that their religious activites were mostly local, involving them, rarely if at all, in any broader community. With churches able to accommodate but a quarter of the county population (and no doubt fewer in rural areas like Sublimity), it would not seem possible that organized religion could have played a significant role in regulating this frontier or organizing whole communities, as John Mack Faragher and Don H. Doyle found for the areas they studied.

The content and character of this local religion are very difficult to ascertain. Sublimity people left no diaries or journals that have been made available to me. Sarah Hunt Steeves gathered brief biographies of thirty-six persons who settled and founded families in the Sublimity area. In nineteen of these the persons indicated a denominational preference, and eight reported that they were devout members of one or another denomination. This and other sources lead to several observations. Most settlers considered themselves to be Christians (if only Universalists), and observed rituals in the home and neighborhood that underscored that identity. George W. Hunt wrote that "not long after our marriage we commenced holding family worship; and this alter, with more or less faithfulness, has been kept up ever since."[49] Bibles in which were recorded vital family events were common. Blessings on food, prayers, prayer meetings, hymn singing, and exhortations were held in homes and schoolhouses for gatherings of families and close neighbors, with frequent but ephemeral organization into local bodies of believers. George Hunt's father, John S. Hunt, organized the Lebanon Baptist Church in his home in 1851 with five members, and the group held services in homes as well as in the local school.[50]

The content of their worship is illusive. The central themes, judging from hymns and reminiscences, were comfort and hope. The trials of mortality were explained as God's will, which His people must patiently endure. Through Jesus Christ the poor could find forgiveness of sins and hope that in a better world loved ones would again be seen, and pain, poverty, hunger, and privation would be no more.

---

[48] *Statistics of the United States . . . in 1870* (Washington, D.C.: Government Printing Office, 1876), p. 552.

[49] G. W. Hunt, *Hunt Family*, p. 74.

[50] Steeves, *Book of Remembrance*, p. 95.

One hymn, remembered by G. W. Kennedy, an 1853 pioneer, promised:

> There is a happy land, far far away,
> Where saints in glory stand, bright, bright as day;
> Lord we shall live with Thee, blessed ever more.

Kennedy recalled that "Our cabin, being large, was for years the preaching place for the neighborhood. And that fervent preaching, heart stirring singing and Godly worship, warms my whole soul as I recall it to memory." In the home, he remembered, "There was religion there without formalism; fervent worship, without fanaticism; bible reading, song and prayer attended the coming and going of the day, and made the home an embryo church. There could be no better type or prefigure of it." On a tour of rural districts in the Willamette Valley in July 1848, Reverend Atkinson found many families holding services in their home. Pastors of the Disciples of Christ described in the 1850s "little country organizations here and there over the land" and estimated that in Oregon there were "about 1200 disciples, but in a most disorganized condition."

The West Union Baptist Church began in 1844 with five Baptists meeting in the home of David T. Lenox on the Tualatin Plains. "We gave each other the hand of fellowship, and . . . the tears flowed from every eye. . . . We hope to be directed by the Lord in the choice of one to take the charge of the church, and to baptize, . . . we know of no other course to pursue than to attend to all the ordinances of the church. We are few and weak, and are placed in a community where we must do our duty." The group met monthly in private homes and schoolhouses until they built their own church in 1853. They first heard a sermon by an ordained minister nearly a year after their organization and had no regular minister until the 1870s.[51]

Atkinson found, in his visits to rural homes, that most would readily name a denominational preference, but in fact commitment was not strong, many recounting a succession of groups that they had affiliated with over the years. John S. Hunt was a Baptist. His son, George W., joined the United Brethren but late in life experienced a powerful conversion to a "holiness" persuasion. Nancy Hunt's father was a Presbyterian; she a Methodist; her last husband a Baptist. Ordained pastors of any denomination were frequently sought to officiate at weddings and other vital events such as serious illnesses,

---

[51] See G. W. Kennedy, *The Pioneer Campfire* (Portland: Clarke-Kundret Printing Co., 1914), pp. 52, 159, 156; Atkinson Diary, vol. 40: 348, 350, 354; C. F. Swander, *Making Disciples in Oregon* (C. F. Swander, 1928), p. 40; Orin Oliphant, ed., "Minutes West Union Baptist Church," *Oregon Historical Quarterly* 36 (1935): 246ff.

christenings, and funerals. Lewis C. Griffith was married to Susan Savage by the Rev. John Stipp, a Baptist, though they were devout Presbyterians.[52] Except on such occasions, daily exercise of religion required no ordained ministry and relied on individual application of Bible teachings to personal lives. Revivals and camp meetings were occasional events. The people preferred informal, intuitive preaching at such gatherings, as well as participatory worship, including speaking in tongues and other manifestations of the spirit. Such preferences probably indicate the character of the family and personal worship that predominated in their lives. Accounts of camp meetings usually indicate a few conversions, but the meetings were sporadic and there is no evidence that they altered the home religion in any significant way or the highly localized orientation of the population.[53]

Thus deep chasms separated the pastors sent to Oregon by various East Coast mission societies in the 1840s and 1850s from the people they hoped to serve. Many of the missionaries were a northeastern urban people who found themselves ministering to a largely southern rural folk. They were educated and polished, working among a people often illiterate and unkempt.[54] Mrs. Blaine, a New York native, assisting her missionary husband in Seattle, found that "most of our residents are from the western states and I find them different from our people. We are engaged this evening to visit with a Mr. Smith from Rochester. His is the only family in town from our state. I feel very differently toward him and those who know nothing of our part of the world."[55] Moreover, they failed utterly to understand the character of rural religion. Their training in a more rational, formal mode of worship made them uncomfortable with frontier excesses. Reverend Atkinson wrote that at a camp meeting "Some women spoke. Two screamed very loud and grasped hands, uttering many things incoherently. . . . Old tunes are changed. Very few are sung as nearly correct as in country churches at home. Some are barbarously altered.

---

[52] Steeves, *Book of Remembrance*, pp. 95, 193–4.

[53] Numerous passages in the Atkinson Diary attest to these circumstances, as does the correspondence of Baptist Minister Ezra Fisher, *Oregon Historical Quarterly* 16–17 (1915–16): 209ff. See also Kennedy, *Pioneer Campfire*, esp. pp. 147–227.

[54] The classic study of the missions, done under the tutelage of Frederick Jackson Turner, is Colin Brummitt Goodykoontz, *Home Missions on the American Frontier* (Caldwell, Idaho: The Caxton Printers, Ltd., 1939). Also important are T. Scott Miyakawa, *Protestants and Pioneers: Individualism and Conformity on the American Frontier* (Chicago: University of Chicago Press, 1964), and Ferenc Morton Szasz, *The Protestant Clergy in the Great Plains and Mountain West, 1865–1915* (Albuquerque: University of New Mexico Press, 1988).

[55] Catherine Paine Blaine to unknown correspondent, December 22, 1853, Blaine Collection, Huntington Library, San Marino, Calif.

Other tunes are framed apparently for the occasion. I suppose many sung daily here never were expressed as notes."[56]

The seeming incoherence of religious organization vexed the home missionary society preachers even more than ecstatic utterances. Since they equated organized religion and piety, their mission became in large measure one that aimed as much to organize as to convert. In such a task, the principal measure of their success was to be able to report progress in establishing formal, enduring congregations whose members could be counted.

The stakes were great, for the organization of religion in the West would have important consequences for the whole society. Josiah Strong, a Congregationalist, warned America, in writing of the West, that "Communities and commonwealths, like men, have their childhood, which is the formative period. *It is the first permanent settlers who impress themselves and their character on the future."* He contrasted two settlements on the Western Reserve. One was founded by a man committed to "a well-organized and well Christianized township, with all the best arrangement and appliances of New England Civilization." The other was founded by an infidel, "who expressed the desire that there might never be a Christian church in the township." From the former township came educators, pastors, professionals, and legislators. None from the latter attended college, and of the few who entered professional life, "none . . . has gained a wide reputation." Quoting Edmund Burke, he warned that in the West, "society is still chaotic; religious, educational and political institutions are embryonic; but their character is being rapidly fashioned by the swift, impetuous forces of intense western life."[57] In so arguing, he made the same mistake as dozens of the pastors evangelizing the West – assuming that the kin/neighbor organization of religious and communal life was in fact no organization. Until the cords of communal life were stretched out enough to sustain permanent congregations and build churches, they were invisible to the missionary pastors. Religion in any setting other than an established congregation was to them hardly religion at all.

The situation pitched the ministers into an all-out war of each against each. For if the rural folk were not strongly attached to particular denominations, the missionaries were, and were determined to make the folk so.[58] In early Oregon the supply of people willing to

[56] Atkinson Diary, vol. 40: 270, 272.
[57] Josiah Strong, *Our Country: Its Possible Future and Its Present Crisis* (New York: American Home Missionary Society, 1885), pp. 144–53.
[58] Dorothea R. Muller saw Josiah Strong's Congregationalist ministry in Cheyenne, Wy-

identify with a large congregation was perennially insufficient to meet the demand. Mission diaries are filled with evidence of tough competition for souls, not only with the "papists," but with other Protestant denominations as well. Atkinson wrote:

> There is evidently a combination of sectarians. The Methodists are determined that all should be Methodists. . . . The Baptists use all means to increase their own sect & private interests, feeling that they only have all the truth. The Presbyterians are determined to take their element out of our churches & to turn over as many Cong'l churches as possible. We have felt all these opposing & distracting agencies. We know not what to do. . . . Shall we then go in for our sect? Shall we make it the great object? Shall we defend it on all occasions & try to bring others to it?[59]

Most did, indeed. In the process they became more tolerant of the folk religion, some consciously seeking to make their sermons ever more attractive to their flock. Atkinson moved from written sermons to notes and extemporaneous speeches, making organized religion less formal and more accessible to the country people, all in an effort to enhance his ability to attach as many as possible to his particular cause. Thus, driven by earnest and well-intended motives, the ministers altered the nature of their own worship in their attempt to extend the bounds of family and neighborhood community, teasing out strands labeled Baptist, Congregational, Methodist, or Catholic. To the extent that they succeeded, they tore at the unities of family, religion, and social life that had defined those communities. Seeking community expressed as an institutional church they wounded old communities, and by their wish to gather the converted to them alone they inhibited the founding of new.

The 1890 census indicated progress in Marion County, if progress it was. In two decades the number of congregations visible to census takers had increased eightfold, to seventy-two, with some 6,018 persons, 26 percent of the population, avowing that they were communicants of one or another religious body. There was, however, by that time more than twice as much seating capacity in churches and halls

---

oming, between 1871 and 1873 as fostering institutions other than the church that benefited the whole community. Strong left Cheyenne, however, partly because he felt that there was a surfeit of denominations in the frontier town and that there was a greater need for his services elsewhere. Moreover, some of the reforms he advocated had caused severe divisiveness among the citizens. "Church Building and Community Making on the Frontier, a Case Study: Josiah Strong, Home Missionary in Cheyenne, 1871–1873," *Western Historical Quarterly* 10 (1979): 191–216.

[59] Atkinson Diary, vol., 41: 289; see Atkinson Diary, vol. 40: 265–7, 270–1, 275, 278, 282, and 357 for other examples of denominational rivalry.

(14,760 places) as there were communicants, the churches capable of
seating 64 percent of the county population.[60] There were apparently
a good many who, like the old Mountain Man, Osborne Russell, concluded that "Having found the Savior alone he wishes to serve Him
alone, yet he is willing to assist the cause. He will do all he can to
obtain a school house for the meeting."[61] The home mission effort
succeeded wonderfully in building churches but failed to fill them
with the rural folk they had come to gather in. They had raised up
from the rich lands along the Willamette the structure of community,
but not its substance, which for a time, at least, continued obstinately
to reside in the neighbor/kin districts.

*   *   *

Obviously, the settlement and social pattern of Alpine, unlike that of
Sublimity, favored organized religion. Formal organization took place
within a year of first settlement in Alpine, but not until a meeting
house, the visible symbol of the community, was built. That structure
was built as a cooperative endeavor in less than a month. It was replaced in 1863 with a larger building, and this with a still larger one
in 1872. No Sublimity group felt the need for such a structure until
six years after the post office was organized, when the Mill Creek
Church of God was built by some fifteen or twenty of the ninety-seven
families in the area. In contrast to the Sublimity area, Alpine community leadership was highly visible and centralized. There was an
officially designated church leader from 1851 on, with one man serving as church leader for thirty-seven years and as mayor for twenty-
seven. In Alpine the church, rather than being one of several
competing voluntary associations, was the motivating and driving
force behind politics, as well as a plethora of cooperative endeavors,
such as stores, libraries, choirs, militias, and public works projects,
and was withal the center of social life. Neighbors and kin in Alpine
likely met more often in the meeting house than in their parlors, the
favorite meeting place of Sublimity folk. Yet both the communal and
kin/neighbor orientation of relationships in the society were successful in creating strong bonds.

The census of religion in 1860 indicates that in Utah county there
were six churches, all Mormon, capable of accommodating 3,475, or
42 percent of the population of 8,248. The 1870 data show little growth
in "sittings" – 4,300 in twelve organizations – now capable of accom-

---

[60] *The Miscellaneous Documents of the House of Representatives for the First Session of the
Fifty-second Congress, 1891–1892*, vol. 50, part 7 (Washington, D.C.: Government Printing Office, 1895), p. 77. Population from *1900 Census Reports*, p. 36.
[61] Atkinson Diary, vol. 40: 351.

modating 35 percent of the 12,203 inhabitants. The 1890 census for the first time shows numbers of members, totaling 19,547, or 82 percent of the population (23,768).[62] The same figures for Sublimity were 26 percent, 23 percent and 26 percent. Moreover, as noted previously, churches in Marion county were overbuilt by 1890, their capacity more than double the reported number of members; those in Utah County underbuilt, with nearly twice as many members as spaces in the churches (12,063), the churches capable of seating but 62 percent of the churched population.[63]

One possible reason for this disparity is that in Marion County the population, being accustomed to a more personal religion, was, like Osborne Russell, willing to support ministers in building churches but still preferred family or neighborhood to church worship. In Utah County organized religion was much more intimately tied to the community, so that those who did not attend church or were not religious still reported themselves as members, and thought of themselves as Mormons, by virtue of their being citizens. It was very nearly a patriotic duty to be a Mormon. The pressure to identify one's religion was not as strongly felt in Sublimity. Yet the fact remains that organized religion was successful in touching, in some sense only a quarter of the population of Marion County by 1890 but four-fifths of the population of Utah County. These data are even more impressive when we note that in Mormon society children are not counted as members until after the age of eight. In this very pro-natal society, 20 percent of the population were under the age of eight, leaving virtually no one unchurched.

These data raise very interesting questions concerning the relationship of belief to behavior in Utah. Public belief is very well documented, with hundreds of sermons by church leaders published and available. They are filled not only with the calls to repentance and salvation through Christ that are found in the sermons of other Christian faiths, but also with much discussion of practical, secular concerns related to the problems of settling a new land. Certainly the call to

---

[62] It is difficult to estimate the population likely to become official church members. Oregon and Utah had similar age structures in 1870, but Mormons did not baptize and officially count children as members until the age of eight. In Oregon the practice varied according to the congregation, with Baptists not counting youth as members until baptized as young adults but most other congregations counting them shortly after birth. In light of this, a crude rate comparing members with the whole population is appropriate, particularly when striking differences are seen.

[63] *Statistics of the United States . . . in 1860*, p. 455; *Statistics of the United States . . . in 1870*, p. 535; *Miscellaneous Documents of Congress, 1891–1892*, p. 84. Population from *1900 Census Reports*, p. 42.

"flee Babylon" – to come to Utah and help build a cooperative, communal society – is there. Apostles Erastus Snow and Franklin D. Richards traveled in 1852 to the remote frontier town of Cedar City to see why an ambitious effort to start an iron industry was floundering. "We found a Scotch party, a Welch party, an English party and an American party," they reported, "and we turned Iron Masters and undertook to put all these parties through the furnace, and run out a party of Saints for building up the Kingdom of God."[64] Also present is an almost distinctive distrust of outsiders ("Gentiles") and frequent recital of the persecutions the Mormons had endured in the Midwest.

Since building the Kingdom of God was equated with establishing a cooperative, prosperous, settled society in Utah, personal belief became less an index of commitment than public behavior. What the Mormons *thought* about religion, beyond a fundamental faith in Christ and in Joseph Smith and Brigham Young as His designated spokesmen on earth, was less an issue in the society than what Mormons *did* about it. The finer points of Mormon theology, then as now, are filled with much speculation and interpretation, and there is no creed or catechism to resolve differing views. Acquiring true religion, in the Mormon view, was rather like learning a skill. It was a process, not an event, a practicum more than a lecture course.

Thus Alpiners rarely write of sermons in their reminiscences and folk histories, but they take great pride in their support in the 1860s of the volunteer effort to drive to the Missouri River to bring immigrants back to Utah. James Freestone wrote in his journal, "In the year 1861 the Bishop of Alpine called me to take my young yoke of oxen and go back to the states for emigrants, which I did. . . . In the year 1863 Bishop asked me if I would go again." Again, he did. Brigham Young asked James G. Hovey in 1850 to help establish a new colony in southern Utah. He wrote in a consciously biblical style,

> The President Called out some Hundred to go and make a
> Settlement in Iron County on the Little Salt lake. I Joseph being
> caled to go also not withstanding my harde labours since I have
> been in the valley. I am willing to forsake all and go build up the
> Kingdom of God. . . . I had my mind made up this winter to rest a
> litle and enjoy my labours hence there seams to be no stoping
> place for a man but he must do the will of God.[65]

[64] *Deseret News*, December 25, 1852; sermon of Brigham Young, August 17, 1856, in *Journal of Discourses*, 26 vols. (London: F. D. Richards 1855–86), 4:32, 23.

[65] James Freestone Journal, quoted in Wild, *Alpine Yesterdays*, p. 10. Joseph Grafton Hovey Journal, November 6, 1850, LDS Church Archives.

Yet there was even in so close a society some room for private beliefs. Bishop McCullough, preaching at the funeral of Richard T. Booth, acknowledged that the townspeople were known to speak their mind. "I don't know of a man who will be missed as much as Brother Booth and I don't know of anyone who has been grumbled at so much except myself."[66] Although many responded to church calls, some did not. A churchwide effort to organize a cooperative economy in the 1870s was short-lived and in most communities of little economic consequence. Certainly in many instances, as Larry M. Logue concluded in studying a farming community in southern Utah, "Individuals and families continued to guard their ability to ultimately decide their own fate within a culture of mutual cooperation and supervision.[67]

Nonetheless it is clear that, in Alpine, religion was a powerful unifying and organizing force for the society. We have seen that religion need not be so. Religious people in Oregon found satisfying expression for their faith in very small kin/neighbor groups that did not favor a sense of broader community. Those in Utah, however, could hardly imagine a viable faith except as expressed in the broader community. Curiously, the Utah population, in this view, was at one with the home missionaries to Oregon.

The home missionaries who came to Utah had a dramatically different task than did those in Oregon. In Oregon they worked with a friendly and even supportive people, who nonetheless remained indifferent to organized religion. In Utah they encountered a structure much like the one they hoped to build – close-knit communities with religion as their central and animating force. Episcopal Bishop Daniel S. Tuttle remembered of his ministry in Utah an occasion when he visited the "not very refined" Mormon Bishop Edwin D. Wooley, who was also county recorder, to record a property deed. When he asked the cost of the transaction, Bishop Wooley put his hand on Tuttle's shoulder and said, "O nothing, nothing; we bishops, you know must try to favor each other." The rustic Mormon saw the Episcopal bishop as an ecclesiastical peer, an unsettling experience for Tuttle that could not have happened in Oregon except when meeting fellow clerics.

Home missionaries saw the Oregon settlers as irreligious because

---

[66] "Richard Thornton Booth," by niece Rolva Booth Ross in "Builders of Alpine," a collection of reminiscences gathered by the Mountainville Camp of the Daughters of the Utah Pioneers and in the possession of Jennie Adams Wild.

[67] Larry M Logue, in a study of a rural Mormon society in southern Utah, has documented considerable correspondence between sermons and private beliefs, though he notes some areas of personal dissent with public doctrine. See Larry M. Logue, *A Sermon in the Desert: Belief and Behavior in Early St. George, Utah* (Urbana and Chicago: University of Illinois Press, 1988).

their society was structured in a way that inhibited organized religion. They saw the Utahns as irreligious because their highly cohesive society, centered on an alternative religion, was even more resistant to their ministry. The missionaries' special animus toward Roman Catholics in Oregon derived from some of the same considerations, though in Utah, unlike in Oregon, the alternative religion held a commanding position in the society. Bishop Tuttle concluded that "God has given three Divine institutions for the help and guidance of mankind, the Family, the State, the church. Whenever an ecclesiastical organization sets itself up as supreme, swallowing either or both of the other coordinate powers, then it becomes a despotism to be resisted and a danger to be resolutely fought. . . . Mormon priestly domination is un-American and anti-American."[68] The type of structure Tuttle found in Utah, especially the overlay on a broad, communitywide level of religious and secular planes, was, of course, unique in the American West. Yet it provides an extreme example of a particular type of social organization that was attainable under certain circumstances and against which we can fruitfully compare other societies.

    *   *   *

Bishop Tuttle had worked in the burgeoning mining center of Boise prior to coming to Salt Lake City, noting that his ministry there included the Boise Basin and Silver City mining areas, as well as "Boise City . . . and the farming district up and down the river."[69] Down the river some twenty miles was the Middleton district, already well established when Bishop Tuttle arrived in 1867. As we have seen, these were a people whose roots were more like those of Sublimity than of Alpine. Yet twenty momentous years had passed since the first stream of Oregon settlers headed West, and those who left the same places in the mid-1860s to come to Middleton were much changed. Middleton was peopled by wartime and immediately postwar migrants, who were attracted in part by the quick wealth promised by mines and the scarcity prices for foodstuffs. The connection with the mines gave the farmlands of the early Middleton area their raison d'etre, probably accounts for the founding of a gristmill there by 1871, and tied the Middleton economy to the mining camps. More than that, however, the profile of Middleton's early population suggests that the town, as it appeared in 1870, can profitably be understood not just as a farm town supplying a mining town with its products, but in some measure as an extension of the mining town. In several essential ways, early

---

[68] The Right Rev. D. S. Tuttle, *Reminiscences of a Missionary Bishop* (New York: Thomas Whittaker, 1906), pp. 314, 354.
[69] Tuttle, *Reminiscences*, p. 148.

Middleton was very much like a mining town. The Middleton sex ratio was very high (186.7; Alpine, 105.8; Sublimity, 99.4) – higher, in fact, than those of Silver City town (139) and the mining town of Orofino (151) at the time. The figure includes a high proportion of unmarried young men, so it is not surprising that we find a saloon-keeper listed in the census but no minister. In fact, according to Junius B. Wright's account, the second business in the town was J. T. Flippin's saloon, opened in 1865, hard on the heels of Montgomery and Fuller's general store.

J. B. Wright, a Methodist, and his close neighbors built a school-house in 1864, which he remembered also served as a church, though he made no mention of what services were held there.[70] The members were apparently the nucleus of the Methodist group that built a church three miles east of the town in 1875 or 1876.[71] There are reports of a circuit preacher visiting a schoolhouse in the village on a monthly basis to hold services as early as 1869. Mrs. A. H. Paul remembered that there were at the time "spells of preaching" in that and other schoolhouses, and Mary Spangler also reported preachings in the homes.[72] Cordelia Foote, a Baptist, began holding Sunday school in her home in 1886, but another nine years passed before a congregation was officially formed in 1895. Their church – the first in Middleton village – was completed in 1897. A historian of Methodism in the area concluded that "For a long time there were no religious services of any kind. It is said that some of the inhabitants made the boast that there was no religion in Middleton, nor was there need of any."[73]

This paucity of organized religion was in part a result of an interface between Protestant missionaries and local residents that followed a different pattern in Idaho than in Oregon. The missionaries in Idaho, perhaps learning from the Oregon experience many of them had, con-centrated more on urban areas. As a result, the towns of Caldwell and Nampa, founded in the 1880s, had thriving congregations of most faiths shortly after founding. The established ministers in these towns then took upon themselves the task of organizing members in the older rural districts, some of the groups eventually growing suffi-ciently to form their own congregations. The Boise Valley Baptist Church was clearly an offshoot of a Boise congregation. The Breshears

---

[70] Wright, Reminiscences, "Our Honey Moon, Continued," pp. 10–11.

[71] Letter of June 24, 1876, reporting a resolution of the Third Quarter Conference of the Boise Valley Circuit, Idaho State Archives.

[72] Annie Laurie Bird, *Boise; The Peace Valley* (Caldwell, Ida.: Caxton Printers, Ltd., 1934), p. 241.

[73] H. I. Miller, undated historical account of Methodism, in Idaho Conference Papers, MS 456, Idaho State Archives.

family helped to found that congregation in 1889 and then the Middleton Baptist Church, farther down the river valley, in 1895.

Until churches were organized in the rural areas, the urban ministers continued, as in Oregon, to officiate at vital events as requested by local people – especially weddings but also christenings and funerals. The diary of the Presbyterian Rev. J. T. Boone in Caldwell shows in the 1890s a regular peregrination to conduct afternoon services for portions of his congregation (they were not seen as separate groups) living in nearby towns, including Middleton, and frequent visits to perform at their weddings or preach at their funerals. The ministries in the larger towns, rather than those sent out by the home missionary societies, mothered the rural churches into being. Even then, as the minutes of the Middleton Baptist Church indicate, getting off the ground was a hard struggle. The five or six families that formed the core of the congregation struggled constantly to raise funds sufficient to build and maintain churches and compensate ministers. Frequently they shared pastors with other congregations, hearing sermons monthly or bi-weekly.[74] Many of the pastors who were willing to preach for the minimal wages offered by rural Idaho churches in the '90s had served in the dwindling Utah mission effort.[75] In Oregon, on those occasions when local groups evolved into organized congregations, it was more common for a spontaneous gathering of the like-minded to seek a minister, who was supplied by the home missionary society. In Idaho the rural settlers were long in place, with little worship at home or elsewhere, when settled ministers of established congregations in nearby towns began to gather them.

But could it be that what we are observing, as at Sublimity, is a society that shunned organized religion and preferred to exercise its religiosity in more private settings? The evidence is fragmentary, but it suggests that this was much less the case than with the Oregon settlers. In reminiscences of Sublimity folk there are frequent references to the religious persuasion of early settlers (twenty of thirty-six), in spite of only occasional examples of successful organization. In one set of forty-one capsule biographies of early Middletonians, the religious persuasion of but thirteen is mentioned. Whereas in Sublimity a strong folk religion is evident, though rarely expressed in formal congregations and meeting houses, in Middleton that religion seems to

[74] J. T. Boone diary, typescript, Idaho State Archives. Original in the College of Idaho Library, Caldwell, of which Boone was the founder and first president.
[75] Records of the First Baptist Church (Conservative), Middleton, Idaho. Also Letter of Transferal, Idaho Conference of the Methodist Church Papers, MS 456, Idaho State Archives.

have faded almost from view. The pious in Middleton waited in a near religious vacuum until a critical mass was reached which then proceeded to established organized, formal religion. This long wait may have accentuated changed values, a reordering of priorities among the people as to what types of human association they preferred.

Ada County reported seven churches in 1870, most if not all in Boise City, providing 900 sittings for the county population of 2,675 – space for a promising 34 percent of the population (26 percent in Marion County, 42 percent in Utah County). This capacity may well reflect the relative affluence of the population in the early days of mining, which favored the efforts of the first ministers to build churches, if not congregations.[76] By 1890 the census reported only 1,365 communicants in the county, 16 percent of the population (26 percent in Sublimity, 82 percent in Alpine). Churches and halls in the county at the time could accommodate 3,865 worshippers, which means that if all members attended they would have been but one third full.

We see, then, in Sublimity, Alpine, and Middleton, three strikingly different patterns of religion and religious activity in the early settlement period. The traditional notion of a monochrome agricultural people in the Far West is hardly adequate in helping us to understand the society brought by the emigrants and how it was modified in the new physical and social setting. The religious beliefs and practices of early Oregon settlers, still insufficiently understood, were expressed for the most part in close informal gatherings characterized by intuitive, often emotional worship and observance. Protestant missionaries, different from the people in regional background, educational level, and religious experience, competed with only indifferent success in an effort to draw the rural people into a multiplicity of more structured, formal religious societies and patterns of worship. To the extent that they succeeded, they tore at the narrow but personally affirming pattern of social organization and in some instances altered their own pattern of worship in the effort to compete successfully. In any case, they can be seen as but one of a number of voluntary associations

---

[76] Bishop Tuttle found people in Silver City in 1867 willing to raise $2,800 a year for a minister. G. W. Kennedy preached at a saloon in a Grant County mining town, and at the end of the sermon one of the miners got up and said, "Now boys, you know . . . I am not much on religion. . . . I can take up the collection; now out with the coin, and don't keep me waiting." The donation was a liberal one. But Middleton Baptists struggled in 1910 to raise an $800 annual salary for a minister. Tuttle, *Reminiscences*, p. 153; Kennedy, *Pioneer Campfire*, pp. 219–20; Middleton Baptist Records, November 22, 1908.

altering the social habits of the people as the century progressed, touching by 1890 only a quarter of the population.

Most Alpine people came directly from England, a fact that might have encouraged to some degree their acceptance of the highly structured, hierarchical society and communal values found in the Mormon villages. Yet they were not, for the most part, from rural areas of England, and there were many other Mormon villages similar in character peopled by American-born persons or Scandinavians. More likely, their rapid socialization stemmed from the powerful ideological commitments their conversion to Mormonism entailed. In any case, their society was one where unities of space, religion, and other associations combined to create as integrated a society as North America has seen outside of small, closed communes such as those of the Hutterites. Protestant missionaries found such a society to be much like the one each would have liked to build in Oregon. Yet they condemned the Mormons as un-Christian and un-American because a competing religion was at the center of most associations and institutions. The social identity of Alpine folk extended beyond close neighbors and kin to include the whole of the broader community. Partly in consequence, by 1890, four-fifths reported themselves to be members of a church, and counting children under eight, 100 percent of Alpine's Utah County was churched.

Middleton seems to have been in some ways more like Sublimity, and its population came from roughly the same parts of the states. Yet, the intervening war and the increasing commercialization of the American rural economy combined to put a distinctive stamp on the society. Religious practice was neither highly localized nor broadly communal, but rather diminished. Home missionaries were less active among the rural people, preferring to organize the larger towns, where the social character of the population in many respects was more compatible with their own. Once founded, the urban congregations began to incorporate rural believers into their membership and in some instances eventually helped the country people form their own churches. Yet in 1890, only 16 percent of their population was churched.

Certainly historians may differ on what proportion of a locality might be needed to provide a core of community. But the 16 percent churched in Ada County by 1890, and even the 26 percent in Marion County, would have faced an uphill battle. Only the 82 percent in Alpine could have been a "potent instrument" for organizing "whole communities." There may well have been integrating forces at work in Sublimity and Middleton, but religion was not chief among them. If Middleton does indeed offer a glimpse of a progression in the broader society between the 1840s and the 1860s, we see an acceleration of a secular trend of great importance.[77] Large portions of the society moved from highly localized nodes of intense community, with close and commanding mutual obligations, toward a pronounced individualism whereby persons acted on their own, involving their lives with others principally in transactional and commercial meetings that had personal aggrandizement as their central motivation. Josiah Strong lamented, and some celebrated, the direction in which the West was heading. Yet except, perhaps, in Alpine, all were powerless to alter its course. Nonetheless, without the churches, social life on the farming frontier would have been dramatically diminished, especially in Middleton, where most of the few voluntary offices held in the community were church related.

Thus Alpine's Catherine Nash, or William and Julia Strong, spent many hours meeting and working with others of their village, not because of family obligations so much as a sense of obligation to a broader community – the Mormon ward and village – and to the religious movement they were assured was to usher in the Kingdom of God on earth and establish Zion. The Wrights and the Spanglers of Middleton certainly at times worshipped and socialized with other settlers of the Boise Valley. But their contacts outside their immediate family were few. Their social world was limited nearly to their own household. The Hunts and the Downings hosted frequent gatherings of neighbors and extended kin for worship, militia drills, fox hunts, weddings, and funerals. Their society reached beyond the immediate family, but not far beyond it, gathering nearby kin and neighbors into a powerfully affective net of community attachment. It would be pointless to maintain that one of these societies had more or less of something called community, but certainly the *dimensions* of community varied greatly – Alpine's reaching out to include many of the 300 persons who lived in their town;[78] Middleton's confined to close kin,

---

[77] Among recent writers who feel that the secular trend has continued and become destructive in our time are Christopher Lasch, *The Culture of Narcissism* (New York: W. W. Norton, and Company, 1979); and Robert N. Bellah, Richard Madsen, William M. Sullivan, Ann Swidler, and Steven M. Tipton, *Habits of the Heart: Individualism and Commitment in American Life* (Berkeley: University of California Press, 1985).

[78] There is, of course, a long-standing debate on what we are really talking about when we use the word "community." Indeed, one scholar has catalogued than no fewer than ninety-four different meanings of the word. Thomas Bender has offered a useful, brief definition: "A community involves a limited number of people in a somewhat restricted social space or network held together by shared understandings and a sense of obligation. Relationships are close, often intimate, and usually face to face. Individuals are bound together by affective or emotional ties rather than by a perception of individual self interest. There is a 'we-ness' in a community; one is a member.

the 5 or 6 other persons who lived in the household; and Sublimity's to the 40 or 50 people who comprised their family, nearby kin, and neighbors.

While the range and frequency of social interaction are important in building a sense of mutual concern and obligation, the nature of the interactions – the context of the meeting – are at least as important.[79] Singing together builds different kinds of attachments than bidding against one another at an auction. We have thus far considered voluntary association – getting together to worship, learn, sing, celebrate, or mourn. Yet it is important as well to understand the manner in which people of the three communities conducted the vital tasks of feeding, clothing, and housing themselves, for there also we see patterns that seem to emerge naturally from the traditions and habits they brought with them to the West.

\* \* \*

By 1870, when a U.S. census taker made the Alpine rounds a second time, there were eight in the William and Julia Strong household: the couple, aged thirty-eight and thirty-four, and six children ranging from Don, thirteen to baby Estella, not quite a year old. The family farmed thirty acres, twice as much as they had in 1860. They also kept a garden lot in town and had a team of horses, three milk cows, two oxen, four calves or steers for beef, twelve sheep, and two hogs. Their granary stored 240 bushels of wheat, 200 of corn, and 80 of oats. They kept 250 pounds of potatoes in the root cellar behind the house and Julia had churned 100 pounds of butter that year and worked 20 pounds of wool into socks and sweaters against the hard Alpine win-

---

Sense of self and of community may be difficult to distinguish." See Thomas Bender, *Community and Social Change in America* (New Brunswick, N.J.: Rutgers University Press, 1978), pp. 7–8; George A. Hillery, Jr., "Definitions of Community: Areas of Agreement," *Rural Sociology* 20 (1955): 118; and Joseph R. Gusfield, *Community: A Critical Response* (New York: Harper and Row, 1975).

[79] Ferdinand Tönnies, perhaps the most dominant voice in the considerable sociological literature on community, emphasized this point in turgid Germanic prose. "Living together is a continuous exchange of . . . aid and assistance and . . . the degree of its intimacy depends upon its frequency. However the character of these relationships is determined by the underlying motives involved, which motives will manifest definite differences." Ferdinand Tönnies, *Community and Society*, trans. Charles P. Loomis (New York: Harper Torchbooks, 1957), p. 244. Much of the subsequent literature relating to Tönnies's famed ideal types of *Gemeinschaft* and *Gesellschaft* is skillfully analyzed by Pitirim A. Sorokin, Rudolf Heberle, Charles P. Loomis, and John C. McKinney in the introduction to this translation of Tönnies's principal writings on community. The quoted material is from an essay written in 1931, toward the end of the German sociologist's career and originally printed in *Handwörterbuch der Soziologie* (Stuttgart: Ferdinand Enke Verlag, 1931).

ter. The family no doubt had other commodities not reported – chickens, eggs, carrots, onions, and other garden vegetables. They were much better off than in 1860, having more than doubled their total wealth, from $440 to $1,000.[80] Yet, after contributing 10 percent of their harvest to the bishop's storehouse and saving enough for their own needs, they had very little to trade. Indeed, they may have had to draw upon the storehouse in April or May to make it through until clumps of pie plant (rhubarb) began to push through the wet soil, followed in a few weeks by the radishes, lettuce, beets, peas, new potatoes, and the bloom of apricots that would bring color and variety once again to their bland winter diet.

By 1870 the Spangler family had left Middleton to return to Missouri. Junius and Elizabeth Wright were living in a house in Middleton and apparently renting their land. Moses Fowler, who had invited Wright to stay and help him farm in 1865, was still on his farm. Moses and Emmaroy, thirty-nine and thirty-six years old, had no children but had taken in her mother, Matilda Douglas, her blind brother, William, and Moses' sister Elizabeth. Their farm appeared to be a successful commercial operation. On 160 improved acres they harvested 1,600 bushels of spring wheat, 2,000 of oats, and 200 of barley and produced 400 pounds of butter from the milk of their seven cows. Of course, Fowler needed help in running so extensive an operation, and had purchased $300 in farm equipment and paid out $1,500 in wages to the young men who helped him. The Fowlers, however, produced no hay, pork, wool, corn, potatoes, or garden vegetables.[81] They apparently sold their grain for cash at nearby mining camps and used the proceeds to buy the food and clothing needed for their household.

That same summer there were six in the household of George and Elizabeth Hunt. The Hunts were about the same age as the Strongs and Fowlers, thirty-nine and thirty-six, and had a daughter and two sons – Georgianna, twelve; Melanchthon, ten; and Jeptha, eight. A twenty-two-year-old hired hand, E. F. Perkins, lived with them. They farmed 35 of their 640 acres, harvesting 100 bushels of wheat, 250 of oats, 100 of potatoes, and 300 of apples, a ton of hay, 200 board feet of lumber, and a clip of 400 pounds of wool from their eighty sheep. They also kept twenty hogs, six horses, and twenty-five head of cattle, churning 300 pounds of butter from the cream. They harvested less

---

[80] Sources are the U.S. Manuscript Census for 1870 and the Utah County tax lists for the same year.

[81] Sources are the 1870 U.S. Manuscript Census for Ada County and the manuscript of the U.S. Agricultural Production Census for Ada County for the same year. The Idaho tax lists, unlike those in Utah, do not contain production information for field crops.

wheat and potatoes than the Strongs, but had two fewer mouths to feed and could make up any deficiencies by selling or bartering surplus hogs, cattle, wool, apples, and timber.[82] By relying on beef, hams, and bacon, they could feed themselves well enough through the mild Oregon winters. If flour became scarce in the spring, Elizabeth could readily borrow from her sister-in-law, Temperance Downing, who lived on the next farm and would have saved a good winter's supply from the 800 bushels of wheat John had harvested that year.

The Strongs, Fowlers, and Hunts each typify the predominant mode of production in their districts – the first meanly subsistent, the second expansively commercial, the third aiming first to provide for the family, though with a clear intent to grow a surplus of certain crops for market sale. These patterns of production imply differing attitudes toward the land and its uses and different roles for women within the three societies, as suggested in Chapters 4 and 5. But they may also define different contexts for human interaction more generally within the three societies.

Alpine people met, discussed, planned, and worked with one another in voluntary associations on a daily basis. Yet the subsistence character of their economy meant that they seldom met at the marketplace. Most families had little to buy or sell. The variety and paucity of crops produced on each farm indicate that their main aim was to produce enough to provide until the next harvest. When exchange took place, it was most often a cup of flour for an egg, a skein of yarn for a hen, or a mess of beans for a pan of potatoes, not 500 bushels of wheat for $1,000.[83] In time of need, they could seek assistance from the bishop's storehouse or the Relief Society granary, where a variety of the commodities donated as tithing were kept for redistribution to the poor. But the contexts of material exchange were most commonly neighborly borrowing and lending among households (done principally by women) or contributions to or assistance from the tithing house, which, being administered by the bishop and the Relief Society president, was sanctified and removed from worldly bargaining and seeking of advantage.

---

[82] Sources are the U.S. Manuscript Census for 1870 and the Oregon State Census for 1865. Oregon tax lists contain no information on field crops, and the manuscript of the U.S. Agricultural Census has apparently been lost or destroyed.

[83] The $2 per bushel price is from a list of standard prices for farm commodities published in 1863 at the central tithing office in Salt Lake City under Brigham Young's endorsement. This attempt to introduce stability into an often erratic price structure may have been unique to Utah. Bishops were to pay out and receive commodities from their local tithing office at the administered price, which thus set levels of prices within the economy generally.

The significance of this is profound. If it were possible to peer in on Alpine on a Saturday afternoon in the 1870s and observe each meeting of the townspeople, we would find a striking pattern. William Strong might be soliciting books from Albert Marsh for the Alpine City Library Association. Julia, noted for her fine voice, would perhaps be rehearsing a song to sing at the funeral of the Devey baby, Albert, who had lived just three months. Ten or fifteen other women of the Relief Society choir might also be rehearsing and others preparing a luncheon for the Devey family. Bishop McCullough would be seeing that the meeting house was draped in white and making last-minute preparations before conducting the funeral. Some would be shopping at the Alpine Cooperative Store for needles, thread, or tea. A few with some surplus – John Moyle, Angelia Vance, Thomas Carlisle, or James Wiley – might be hauling vegetables, milk, butter, or eggs to the rail station at American Fork for shipment to Salt Lake City or mining camps up American Fork Canyon or in the Salt Lake Valley. The youth of the Alpine Literary Society could be enjoying a canyon outing. Elsie Booth might have organized an activity for the smaller children, while Richard T. Booth and John Vance discussed plans for a future Sunday School picnic.

We would see that people were interacting with others outside their household almost everywhere we looked and that most were engaged in or planning voluntary activities. Certainly some household members would be carrying out the tasks necessary for physical survival – producing, feeding, clothing, housing, and exchanging – but these occupied a relatively small part of person-to-person contacts outside the household. And each time people met and talked – when the Deveys asked Julia to sing at baby Albert's funeral, when Albert Marsh allowed as how he could give a half-day's work to the library fund, when Elsie Booth took twenty or thirty children on a canyon walk, teaching them to identify shooting stars, or Indian paintbrush, or to make oboe-like whistles from joint grass beside the streams, or even when the men and women of the town sang together weekly in a choir – each time these encounters took place, strands of vaguely defined outward obligation and connection were being teased out, twisted, and in time securely tied. The obligations were never made contractual or explicit, and in their very indeterminate quality lay their power. For who can say when debts owed to one who took time from life-sustaining activities to teach embroidery, literature, or that the meadow lark sings "Alpine is a pretty little place!" are repaid? The Alpine people, without quite willing or realizing it, were constructing a web of obligation and attachment that held most emotionally and physically to the town.

Photo 12 Alpine children of the 1870s in front of the Old Rock Church, which also served as their schoolhouse. Standing on the right is Ephraim Healey. (Used by permission of Jennie Wild.)

Yet, Alpine was no utopia. In this hardscrabble corner of the Rockies, resources were scarce and valuable. There were conflicts and bitter feelings over water, land, timber, and what songs should be sung at the Fourth of July celebration. Living cheek by jowl, as the Alpiners did, and cajoled into offices and organizations that made them work together on a daily basis, their contact turned abrasive at times. There were neighbors whose blood no doubt boiled when William Johnson Strong swore or kicked at their dogs. He, in turn, was infuriated when Ephie Nash, Billy Hammett, Dick Carlisle, and Jed Wilkin wildly raced their horses up Main Street, then ducked under James Healey's fence to escape successfully his wrath.[84] Some took offense when released from a church calling or not called to one they coveted. There was hurtful gossip about who had a drinking problem, or was lazy, or had fornicated, or never cared for their yard. And there were, of course, those who refused calls, did not attend church, and obstinately resisted the persistent effort to tie them into the web of community. Alpine was not a comfortable place for the lone eccentric, and its pattern of association limited individualism and privacy.

It may, in fact, be that, were it possible to count incidents of conflict, we would find more in Alpine than in Middleton or Sublimity.[85]

---

[84] William Johnson Strong was known to dislike dogs (a sentiment reportedly reciprocated by the canine population of the town). His irritation at horse racing on Main Street is recounted by Betha Strong Ingram in Bill and Carolyn B. Strong, *A Proud Heritage: The Ancestors and Descendants of Clifford Oscar Strong and Fern Paxman Miller*, vol. III (np., nd.), pp. 294–5.

[85] A Yale anthropology student, Michael Raber sought to do precisely that in a Mormon town similar to Alpine – Spring City in Utah's Sanpete Valley. His conclusion, from noting many incidents of conflict, was that the communal character of the Mormon village has been greatly overstated. In so stating, he failed to understand that the kind of conflict he observed may be characteristic of the closeness of community rather than a refutation of it. The more people interact, the more occasions for conflict will arise. A communal people, in spite of conflict, find some means of accommodation and continue to live together and to interact as a community. A society where all lived in isolation from one another would have no conflict. See Michael Scott Raber, "Religious Polity and Local Production: The Origins of a Mormon Town" (Ph.D. diss., Yale University, 1978). The classic work on the Mormon village is by Lowry Nelson, *The Mormon Village: A Pattern and Technique of Land Settlement* (Salt Lake City: University of Utah Press, 1952). The book is a compilation of several sociological case studies of Mormon villages conducted by Lowry Nelson during the 1920s and 1930s. Also of importance is Evon Z. Vogt and Ethel M. Albert, eds., *People of Rimrock: A Study of Values in Five Cultures* (Cambridge, Mass.: Harvard University Press, 1966). This is the summary volume of the "Comparative Study of Values in Five Cultures" project conducted between 1949 and 1955 by the Harvard University Laboratory of Social Relations and supported by grants from the Rockefeller Foundation. The personnel, from several disciplines, included Clyde Kluckhohn and Talcott Parsons. One, Thomas F. O'Dea, became one of the leading scholars on Mormon society, and an-

Clearly, the more people interacted, the greater the chances that they would disagree on some matters. When this happened, the church had its own set of courts for resolving civil conflicts among Mormons. If a dispute could not be resolved by informal negotiation, the litigants would bring the matter to the "Teachers," who would try to help resolve it or who might refer it to the bishop, whose calling designated him as a "common judge in Israel." When it was brought to the bishop, he would set a date for a trial and issue summonses to the disputants and relevant witnesses. At the appointed time all parties would assemble, pray, sing a hymn, and read a passage of scripture together. The bishop would then urge the parties to repent and resolve their differences themselves. If they could not, the trial would continue, the bishop and his two counselors hearing testimony from the aggrieved parties and witnesses. Then the bishopric (the bishop and the two counselors) would consult together, after which the bishop would propose a resolution, and if at least one counselor concurred, the decision was given to the disputants. It was expected that they would part friends and abide by the bishop's decision.

If neither of the counselors agreed with the bishop, or if one of the parties still felt that justice had not been done, he might appeal to the high council court. This court, consisting of a body of high priests, would convene and follow similar procedures in deciding the case. If hard feelings remained, the parties might appeal to the first presidency of the church or risk community opprobrium by bringing their case to a civil court. Justices of the peace and members of the county courts, however, were often the same persons who staffed the church courts, so that only in a federal court might a different set of attitudes be brought to bear on the matter.[86]

other, Robert N. Bellah, a principal student of individualism and community in the United States more generally. See Thomas F. O'Dea, *The Mormons* (Chicago: University of Chicago Press, 1957), and Bellah et. al., *Habits of the Heart.* For an extensive bibliography of studies of Mormon values and community, see Dean L. May, "The Making of Saints: The Mormon Town as a Setting for the Study of Cultural Change," *Utah Historical Quarterly* 45 (1977): 75–92, esp. p. 78.

Jennie Adams Wild, Dennis Smith, and Rulon McDaniels, Alpine natives, took the time to teach me what meadow larks sing there, how to tell when it will be a bad water year (by noting on July 24 if there's still snow in the "Sleigh Runner," a ravine on a nearby mountainside), and what the ditches, nearby canyons, and cemetery at the edge of town mean to old Alpiners.

[86] As noted earlier, those in Mormonism's "lesser," or Aaronic, priesthood held the offices of deacon, teacher, or priest and, with bishops, had special responsibilities for temporal matters in the church. The higher Melchizedek Priesthood holders usually held the office of elder, seventy, or high priest and were more responsible for spiritual administrative work. An excellent study of the Mormon legal system is Edwin Brown

Though court records in Utah Valley are not complete, those that have survived indicate the types of disputes brought to civil courts. In the year 1859 only nineteen cases came before the probate court from all of Utah County. Over half (ten) were divorce cases. It appears that most, if not all, were brought to the court in order to give civil sanction to decisions already made, perhaps in the bishops' courts. All the divorces were routinely granted, most on the grounds of incompatibility, though in some cases adultery was the complaint. Occasionally the judge proposed a specific division of property, but more commonly he merely affirmed an informal understanding the couple had already agreed upon. When children were involved, the judge always gave custody to the woman.

There was one case of assault, Nathaniel Williams bringing charges against Josh Hunt for shooting his son, Arch, in the thigh. After subpoenaing and taking testimony from several witnesses, the judge dismissed the charges on the grounds that the boys were drunk and the shooting was an accident. James N. Pettit accused James N. Cole of assaulting him and robbing him of $75. As the case continued, Pettit admitted that he could not remember what happened, as he was drunk at the time. The judge found Cole guilty of assault and of profaning the name of God, and fined him $5 and court costs. Perhaps the most sensational controversy occurred when Joseph Holly accused Joseph Sanchez of poisoning a horse so that it could not win a race upon which Holly had bet a pair of pants. After several witnesses testified, the judge dismissed the case for lack of evidence.

There were two suits brought to the court for assistance in collecting debts, the larger to secure payment of $147 owed on a $500 dollar note, and the other over ownership of a pair of oxen that was later withdrawn. Two cases of guardianship were determined by the court. None of the nineteen cases involved Alpine people. Indeed, extant records through 1874 contain cases brought from all the surrounding towns, but none from Alpine. Probably some combination of the town's small size, the homogeneity of the place (all but three families were Latter-day Saints), and confidence in the bishop and his court kept disputes from reaching the civil court.[87]

Firmage and Richard Collin Mangrum, *Zion in the Courts: A Legal History of the Church of Jesus Christ of Latter-day Saints, 1830–1900* (Urbana: University of Illinois Press, 1988). See esp. pp. 29–37 for a description of the various church courts and their procedures. Regrettably, minutes of Alpine bishops' courts have apparently not survived.

[87] I was able to locate three record books of early probate courts from Utah County. Probate Docket 1, December 27, 1852–59; Probate Docket Book A, March 1861–April 1874; Letters and Bonds Record, Book G, 1875–1900. All are in the Utah State Archives, Salt Lake City, though I used microfilm copies in the Latter-day Saint Family History

Church courts litigated disputes over allocation of irrigation water, disturbing the peace, or compensation for damages done by a stray animal, matters that other Americans would have considered purely secular. The procedures of these courts were invested by the community with sacred authority. Thus, though the level of bickering and murmuring may have been considerable, even that was turned into an agent of cohesiveness by sanctifying it through the process of resolving the matter face-to-face in front of the bishop after prayers and scripture reading. Though Alpiners, like people of Sublimity and Middleton, found occasion for mutual confrontation and hostility, the powerful fact remains that these incidents did not greatly diminish their commitment to the community. Despite the minuscule farms, the paucity of irrigation water, and the continuous opening of expansive new lands throughout the West under the Homestead Act, creating opportunities elsewhere, 31 percent of the men, women, and children who lived in Alpine in 1860 were still there a decade later (twenty-seven of eighty-six).

Middleton's Moses Fowler would hardly have noticed the nuisance of neighborhood dogs so vexing to William Johnson Strong. There, all but a few lived in homes on their land, where the nearest neighbor would be a half mile or more away, far enough to mute the yapping. The expansive distribution of homes in the Middleton district diminished not only neighborhood friction and petty irritation, but also convivial socializing. As we have seen, in the Idaho district, it was relatively rare to meet and work together in voluntary association.

It is thus no surprise that, were we to peer in on their society in the 1870s, Middleton would be strikingly different from Alpine. We would see dozens of freight wagons going to and from the mill (at the time north of the village center), laden with grain they brought from the farms of Fowler and his neighbors, and with barrels of flour as they left to make their way to the Boise Basin or the Owyhee mines. Each stop of a wagon involved contact and negotiation. Fowler might frown a bit when the miller, Sam Foote, told him that the price paid for wheat at the mill had dropped. John Eggleston and Dan Jury would be arranging to ship their abundant barley harvest to a brewery in Boise. John Kerr would be hauling potatoes to Silver City or con-

Library in Salt Lake City.

In 1851 the territorial legislature of Utah gave probate courts an unusual grant of power, making both criminal and civil cases subject to their jurisdiction. Thus, the dockets are a mix of probate inventories, criminal cases, and civil cases. Gustive O. Larsen recounts the circumstances that led to the increased responsibility of Utah's probate courts in *The "Americanization" of Utah for Statehood* (San Marino, Calif.: The Huntington Library, 1971), pp. 7–18.

tracting with William Hemingway to do it for him. A cluster of men waiting their turn to unload might be discussing whether wheat or oats would be best for planting this season. Who has horses to sell (James Thomas), or milk, butter, and cheese (G. Wooten), or beef (Jacob Plowhead)? Has the water gone down enough to let us bypass Perry Munday's ferry (and save $3.00 per wagon on a round trip to the Owyhee mines)?[88]

There was a good deal of other exchange taking place as well. Since it was common for farmers to specialize in one or a few crops for commercial sale, many households had to purchase or trade with others for eggs, butter, vegetables, and other goods. No doubt much of this exchange took place informally between households, as in Alpine and Sublimity. But merchandising seems also to have played a considerable role in Middleton. In 1865 William Montgomery and V. R. Fuller opened a store in the village. In 1870 there were two stores, one run by Perry Munday and the other by James Stevenson and Abner Packard. Edward Shainwald came to Middleton about 1877 to open yet another mercantile business. Trucking and bartering from farm to market, from home to home and from store to home, were the common activities that brought Middleton people into contact with one another.

We would, of course, see amusements and recreation. Here and there across the valley, and surely at John Eggleston's fine home, there would be occasional evening dances, Moses Fowler's blind brother-in-law, William Douglas, perhaps setting the pace with his fiddle. On Sunday there would be horse races, with much good-natured banter, a few bets placed, and occasional detours to J. H. Holland's saloon for a beer or shot of whiskey.[89] Also, on some Sundays, four or five Methodist families would worship together at Central Park, and in homes and schoolhouses elsewhere in the district, others listened to sermons by itinerant or visiting city pastors. On almost any day, we would see men chatting about local politics, commodity prices, and social events in the saloon, the mill, the two stores, the blacksmith shop and the butcher shop.[90]

---

[88] The names given are of those who reported harvesting large quantities of the commodities mentioned to the marshalls taking the U.S. Agricultural Census for 1870. Perry Munday advertised his ferry in the *Boise Semi-Weekly Democrat* on December 19, 1868.

[89] Eggleston's facilities are described in the *Idaho Tri-Weekly Statesman*, November 21, 1868. The musical talents of Will Douglas are mentioned in Jennie Cornell, "Pioneers of Canyon County," Book 2. Judge Milton Kelly of Boise described a visit to the J. H. Holland saloon in the Boise *Tri-Weekly Statesman*, November 4, 1876.

[90] Thomas Carlisle operated a small store in his Alpine home as early as 1867, and the

Yet it may be significant that the settings for this socializing were principally commercial and male. We find no record of library associations, literary clubs, children's organizations, women's societies, choirs, or militias. Almost everywhere we look in Middleton, production and marketing constitute the content and setting of social interaction. These contacts were no doubt amiable, not mean-spirited or grasping, and the nexus of each was mutual, not just personal, advantage. Yet every man weighed his own strength in the negotiation and tried to maximize his profit in the deal that was struck. Moreover, once the exchange took place and the accounts were settled, that was the end of the matter. The ties that might bring them together again were expectations of future opportunity, not unbounded strands of past obligation.

Given this setting, it is not surprising that most disputes had to do with contracts and exchange. The small-town irritations of Alpine appear less commonly in the court records of the Middleton area. Ensuring that the intense, lively commercial activity of the Idaho town took place smoothly was the principal task of the legal system. Disputes in Ada County courts had less to do with getting along with neighbors than with getting and spending. Cases were numerous, and all but a few were suits to collect unpaid debts. Only six divorce petitions appeared in court records from 1865 through 1870, and divorce settlements remained uncommon until the 1880s.

I have been able to find in the voluminous Ada County dockets extending throughout the 1880s fourteen cases that involved Middleton people – eleven for debt collection, one for unspecified damages, and two petitions for divorce. Among the litigants was J. M. Stephenson who between 1867 and 1870 sued John Groff, S. L. Peasley, Daniel Jury, and even the prominent sponsor of local dances, John Eggleston, for debts ranging from Groff's $228.38 to Eggleston's $650.50. Mary C. Fuller divorced merchant V. R. Fuller in 1869, gaining custody of their one son, Charles; and Lucinda Daly was granted a divorce from Michael J. Daly in 1880, the settlement giving her custody of the children but reserving for him visiting rights and ordering that she not take the children out of the territory.[91] The court records affirm the

Alpine cooperative store was opened in 1868. Except for the stores, Alpine had no other businesses that could serve as a setting for local talk and gossip.

[91] Ada County Judgment Book A, District Court, Third Judicial District, esp. pp. 80, 106, 168, 179, 291, 292, 336, and 494; and Book B, p. 1142. The Ada County District Court was, of course, not the precise counterpart of the Utah County Probate Court, making more precise comparisons of numbers of cases by type problematical. Because of the broad jurisdiction of the Utah court, however, the two judicial bodies may be closer to the same level of appeal, and hence more comparable, than would be the case

prevalence of concern over contractual financial obligations in the society. The routine of daily life in Middleton was preoccupied with activities of specified obligation and short duration. There were relatively few fuzzy strands of voluntary human interaction to snag and hold one to the place. Of the whole 1870 population, only 19 percent was still there a decade later.

The Sublimity economy was much more like that of Alpine, though by custom more than hard necessity. While the people took much pride in having a fine home and a thrifty farm, and were alert to markets, mines, and other means to better themselves, the first aim of each family was independence. They grew a variety of crops on their farms, and at first only a few, like John Downing, native of Pennsylvania, moved aggressively into production of staples. Most of the others were content to farm only enough of their great tracts of land to feed themselves and provide a modest surplus to sell. They resisted the tendency of growth and progress to steal the leisure from their lives. Theirs seems, from the reminiscences we have, a convivial society, a people who enjoyed getting together for family events and holidays. They valued neighbors more than profits and tried to keep a reasonable balance between them.

George Hunt told his daughter a morality tale that says much about his values. An early family, the Fieldses, found a tract of land to squat on and set up camp under a great fir tree that stood beside the pioneer road. The family raised a few sheep, kept to themselves, and let neighbors know that they wanted to be left alone. One day passersby noticed no signs of life and, investigating, found every member of the family dead or sick from a fever. The rescuers discovered $1,500 in cash sewed into the pillow ticks – the probable reason for their unfriendliness. The family, Sarah Hunt Steeves concluded,

> would not make friends, for fear they would be robbed.
>
> Thus this family, supposed to have been poor, except for their sheep, starved to death or died of neglect, with plenty of funds for their needs, right in camp.
>
> For years the old fir tree stood guard over the place of this ill-fated camp, when a fire laid it low and then this old fallen monarch was still pointed out and the story told of the pioneer folk who lost their lives, probably because they refused their neighbors' friendship.[92]

elsewhere. The Ada County records are in the Idaho State Archives in Boise, though I used microfilm copies in the Latter-day Saint Family History Libary, Salt Lake City.
[92] Steeves, *Book of Remembrance*, p. 70.

The story is powerful and eloquent, the sacred fir tree initially offering promise in spite of the family's aloofness. Yet, alas, it, like the Fields family, was burned and wasted after they chose money over neighborliness, the profane over the sacred. Worldliness had destroyed the once proud "monarch," and its rotting hulk became a warning to those who passed that way.

Yet the sin of the Fieldses was their aloofness from *neighbors*, not from all who came by. If there is a single word that best captures the social mentality of the Sublimity folk, it is "clannish." They had a strong sense of common identity within the neighbor/kin group (they were often, after all, blood relatives). And they dotted the Waldo Hills with small, powerful communities that provided admirably for the social, moral, and physical needs of their members. Like the people of Alpine, they interacted principally in social, volunteer settings that spun threads of connection and obligation. But the span of these threads was short. And while it was imperative to offer hospitality to all, those not of the clan were rarely given access to their small world. Relations with the outside were formal, contractual, and commercial.

If we were to look in on the Sublimity people, then, in the 1870s, we would see two main levels of interaction. First is a number of small communities spread across the landscape. Within each there would be frequent, close familial, human contact. Georgianna Hunt, sixteen, might well be helping for a day at Cinderella Darst's, whose husband, Paul, had died suddenly of "apoplexy," leaving her with two daughters and an infant son, Charles, born shortly after his father's death. Elizabeth could be tending the family store, selling needles, tea, or tobacco to Margaret Downing, wife of John's brother, James, or to another neighbor lady, Elizabeth Shanks. Or she might be attending her sister-in-law, Temperance Hunt Downing, whose chronic illness led to her death in 1876. On a Saturday or Sunday, George would be drilling the local men in a militia exercise. Or there might be a Sabbath service at the Rock Point school that many of the neighbor folk would attend. For at least a few months each year the Whiteaker children, representing perhaps ten or fifteen families, again most of them kin, would attend the school at Rock Point, their parents boarding the teacher, each for a few weeks at a time. In any given household one might find members of a neighboring household assisting with a barn raising, helping thresh the wheat, canning, knitting, or simply passing the time.

There certainly were occasions, as in Alpine, where neighbors called upon one another to borrow a cup of flour, a dozen eggs, or other things they found suddenly in short supply. Yet the effort each household made to be independent of all others minimized such exchanges.

As in Alpine, the people met each other far more often in the voluntary, sociable activities and settings that fostered indeterminate, and hence enduring, feelings of mutual affection and obligation.

There existed within this structure an informal credit system whereby neighbors built up, through many small transactions, complex networks of credit and debt. The diary of F. Wilbur, who lived north of Sublimity, in the Silverton area, details the everyday life of rural people of the area. One set of entries begins in November 1859:

> 11/11 Did chores. Went to Silverton Bot of A. Coolidge a pair of overalls $.75.
>
> 11/12 Went & looked up a stick for Sled Tongue cut & brot it home & worked on it some. Rainy.
>
> 13 Drew a load of wood. Put in Sled Tongue & etc. Rainy.
>
> 11/17 Killed Hogs. H. C. Small, B. Geer, & Grover Leonard helping. Killed 15. Rainy.
>
> 11/18 T & B went to Silverton & took 13 of the hogs to Coolidge. Rainy.
>
> 11/19 Attended Division. Paid to Dues $1.25.
>
> 11/21 Tim Came down. T & W and we run out my land and examined some of Wilcox's lines. Went to Silverton & carried a couple of letters.
>
> 11/26 T. J. Wilcox T. H. Small, F. Cox, John Cox, Sam'l Cox, T. W. Porter went a hunting & killed 3 deer. Next day they cut up and divided the deer.
>
> 12/2 Laid up fence for Benjamin Davenport.
>
> 12/5 Very cold cut wood fed hogs & c. Settled with Timothy and found I owe him $37.88 for which I gave my note.
>
> $37.88[93]

As the diary continues, Wilbur carefully records where he went, whom he lodged with, whom he worked for, who worked for him, what he bought where, and for how much. It shows a range of friendships and associations concentrated on the Smalls, Davenports, Kings, Coxes, Wilcoxes, and others in his immediate neighborhood, but certainly extending beyond in some instances. It has nothing to do with recording his private thoughts or expressing his philosophy of life. In fact, one cannot read the diary without concluding that he intended it to be a memory prompter, helping him keep track of the countless little obligations that living in such a community engendered.

Wilbur recorded in the right-hand margin of his diary debts of a specific cash value, and, as in the case of Ai Coolidge of Silverton, these most often involved persons outside his kin/neighbor group.

[93] F. Wilbur, Diary, MS 408B, Oregon Historical Society Library, Portland.

But for many activities – the help he received killing hogs or "laying" fence for Benjamin Davenport – he specified no value, though these clearly were debts to be kept in mind. The diary thus is a guide to the complex relationships that tied him to the community.[94] Yet one of the striking aspects of Wilbur's diary is that it is almost unique for the region. Very few were as attentive to the recording of their life's obligations as he. The diary displays the tip of a submerged mountain of similar life obligations that were not written down but nonetheless performed in a personal way many of the functions that banks, credit cards, currency, lawyers, judges, unskilled laborers, debt collectors, motels, and restaurants now do with more finality and privacy, and thus with different social consequences. Even the settling of one's estate in such a society became a matter of community concern, for it involved the collection and payment of all debts involving the deceased, a clearing of monetary accounts, and, at the same time, a deeply and widely felt clearing of the many more unspecified emotional accounts that years of living in Whiteaker, Maccleay, or Victor Point had accrued.[95]

Within the neighbor/kin group there were incidents that caused friction and anger. John Downing, neighborhood squire, devout Campbellite, and Prohibition Party member, was furious that a gang of neighbor boys, including young Francis and Charles Henline (Charles was no more than thirteen), and F. T. Perkins, George Hunt's hired hand, had celebrated the 1874 winter holidays in drunken revelry. He no doubt gave them a tongue lashing they would long remember. Yet, paradoxically, in this setting the processes of confrontation and then reconciliation probably added to the already stout ties that attached the people of the neighborhood to one another. When Downing filed charges, they were not against the boys for public drunkenness or disturbing the peace but against M. Haupert, not of their group, who had sold them the liquor.[96] In consequence, the peo-

---

[94] Laurel Thatcher Ulrich made brilliant use of Martha Ballard's similar diary, reconstructing the complex relationship of a Maine midwife to her society in *A Midwive's Tale: The Life of Martha Ballard, Based on Her Diary, 1785–1812* (New York: Alfred A. Knopf, 1991).

[95] The probate records of Marion County, which we will examine in more detail in Chapter 7, make this point very clearly.

[96] The case was heard on February 3, 1875, and since Haupert refused to speak in his defense, the judge, Judge W. H. Powell, levied a separate fine of $50 for each youth involved, totaling several hundred dollars. According to Downing's complaint, Haupert sold liquor to Valentine Caldwell, eighteen; Charles Henline, thirteen; Francis Henline, eighteen; E. F. Perkins, a seventeen-year-old farm laborer, working for George Hunt, William Smith, nineteen; and William Davey. Marion County Justice Court Case Files, 90A-16, 84/16, 1866–67, Folder 17, Oregon State Archives, Sublimity.

ple of Sublimity formed ties that held them at first nearly as firmly to the place as did those that kept the Alpiners from wandering. Thirty percent of the 1860 Sublimity area dwellers were still there in 1870.

As the Downing/Haupert incident suggests, there is evidence that a different ethic prevailed when dealing with those outside the family-kin group. And though these dealings occupied only a small proportion of the total encounters with others, they were of great portent. We see in early Sublimity a primary set of relationships that in the close neighbor-kin group was like that prevailing in Alpine village, and a secondary set outside the group like that prevailing in Middleton. Relationships in the first group were characterized by personal, indeterminate networks of affection, obligation, (or even irritation) that during the course of a person's life bound him or her to others; those in the second, by markets, cash, contracts, and civil law that minimized such bonds and kept one free. As the century wore on, the primary sphere was diminishing, making Sublimity folk ever more attracted to the Middleton mentality.

Nor was Alpine free of such temptations. Most Alpiners had been born among the factories, trading houses, and wharves of Lancashire, England, and surrounding counties – the most commercialized, capitalistic region of the world at the time. They had grown up there and had been steeped in those values. Yet part of the reason they had chosen the message of Mormonism was that it offered an escape from that world. Countless sermons taught that happiness and safety could be found not in material possessions, but in living in a unified and harmonious society. Powerfully etched in their minds through a common sacred ritual was the image of a genial Satan, dressed in a dark, conservative business suit, promising that they could have anything they wanted (in this world) for money. Rejecting his tempting offer, the ritual taught, would lead to life under inspired guidance, with fellow Saints, comforted by close human relationships that provided safety "through these last days of trouble and gloom." Once set on this course, they were willing to endure poverty and even scorn, if it came to it, for the promise in their hymn that "no longer as strangers on earth need we roam."[97] Yet most did not see a disjunction between their embracing a communal social ethic and involvement, to the extent that their resources permitted, in a commercial, capitalist economy like the one that they had known in England. Middleton was in the back of their minds as well. Catherine Nash profited from making

---

[97] "Now Let Us Rejoice," no. 118 in *Hymns: Church of Jesus Christ of Latter-day Saints* (Salt Lake City: Deseret Book Company, 1975).

and marketing butter and cheese in the Alpine area, helping her household, by 1860, become the wealthiest in the town.[98]

Nonetheless, for a time, faith, fear of Babylon, and hard poverty kept the Utah folk in place. Their incessant interaction in voluntary associations helped to diminish a sense of self or even family. It drew them out and beyond into what they saw as a community of Saints, a City of God on earth, represented in their experience by the life they knew in Alpine. Catherine Nash's descendants affirmed an identity even more important to them than the family name when they wrote the history of their clan. They called the book *Alpine: The Place Where We Lived*.[99]

---

[98] This helps explain the failure of the United Order of the 1870s as an economic reform. See Leonard J. Arrington, Feramorz Y. Fox, and Dean L. May, *Building the City of God: Community and Cooperation Among the Mormons*, 2nd ed. (Urbana and Chicago: University of Illinois Press, 1992); and Dean L. May, "Brigham Young and the Bishops: The United Order in the City," in *New Views of Mormon History: A Collection of Essays*, ed. Davis Bitton and Maureen Ursenbach Beecher (Salt Lake City: University of Utah Press, 1987).

[99] Merma G. Carlisle, ed., *Alpine: The Place Where We Lived* (Nash family publication, n.p., n.d.).

# 7    Our paths diverged

The last chapter belongs to Middleton. As the century continued, the three districts converged in some respects. Sublimity's people became less stable, their tendency to remain in place declining to Middleton levels. Alpine diverged in this regard, its people becoming even more attached to the place. Sublimity farms became smaller, those of Middleton and Alpine larger. Sublimity farmers moved toward full use of their land to grow staple crops for the market, and even in Alpine there was a trend in that direction. The sphere of public concerns shrank, and nuclear families relied increasingly on banks, attorneys, or funeral parlors to take care of matters now thought of as private. Though some differences endured, modernization ultimately moved Sublimity and Alpine in the direction of Middleton.

The Spangler family left Middleton in 1868 to return to Missouri. There they bought a farm in Cass County, near the town of Pleasant Hill, where the younger children grew to adulthood. Mary, the next-to-youngest daughter, recalled that her father "never recovered from the hardships, losses and humiliations of the war." The son-in-law, Mr. White, was not content in Missouri and took his family to his native Illinois, but after his wife, Susan Spangler, died, he remarried and moved back west to Washington State. Two of the Spangler boys, Gus and Jim, tried to make a go of a forty-acre farm adjoining their parents, but eventually gave up on it and went south and east to Henry County. Another boy, David, married and began to farm the eighty acres his bride owned, while the youngest, George, stayed for a time to help his parents. Mary lamented that "from the year 1871 our paths diverged. The home ties were broken. Only mother, father, and George were permanently there." Toward the end of her long life she regretted not knowing her kin better, explaining that "I have lived in a town remote from the other members of the family most of my

Photo 13 Mary Spangler Luster in her later years. (Used by permission of the Springfield, Missouri, Historical Society.)

life. . . . The line has extended to the fourth and fifth generations. They live in all parts of the Middle West and West and will only know each other by tracing their kinship in this story."[1]

[1] Mary R. Luster, *The Autobiography of Mary R. Luster* (n.p.: Springfield, Mo., 1933), pp. 99, 100, 101, 191. Mary R. Spangler Luster was in part regretting a life course change as the children began to leave the parental home and make lives of their own. Yet her

Mary told her story as a tragedy culminating in the loss of family coherence and identity. She seemed to understand that the "losses, hardships and humiliations of the war" had profoundly affected not only her father, but all of them. Many Middleton people shared their experience. There were 114 different surnames represented by males living in the district in 1870. Forty years later nineteen families remained (17 percent of the original set) that bore one of those names.[2] Few found continuity in the place. They had not come in extended family groups, and they left after a brief sojourn to go elsewhere.[3] If the Spangler family is representative, most were never able again to pick up the threads, as they had been before the war.

Sublimity had begun differently. The Hunts and Downings had come to the Willamette Valley before the war and with their kin – indeed, because they wanted to perpetuate their families on the land. Yet, surprisingly, after forty years, not many more of the Sublimity families stayed in place than in Middleton. Of 109 different surnames among males there in 1860, twenty-four families remained with those same names in 1900, or 22 percent. During the forty-year interval, the Sublimity people had lost much of the family coherence with which their society had begun in the West, a denouement of their original dream that had its own elements of tragedy.

For Alpine's founders, especially the English born, such as the Strongs, the Nashes, and the Healeys, the processes of industrialization, conversion to Mormonism, and migration to Utah had pruned the structure and functions of family to a nub. Of necessity, the family in the Mormon town had been secondary to the community as the central unit of society and the core of identity. Yet the persistence of the families in Alpine over forty years, even with economic oppor-

---

narrative makes it clear that she was also conscious of a systemic breakdown of family coherence that went well beyond the maturing of her parental family.

[2] The source is, of course, the U.S. Manuscript Census for the years indicated. For a forty-year span, the persistence of surnames seems a reasonable index of the degree to which families perpetuate themselves in the place. In forty years many of the original settlers die, and children and grandchildren are beginning to form households, making precise tracing dependent upon full family reconstitution and name-by-name linkage, which have not been possible in this study. The percentages represent the upward limit of family persistence, since a number of common surnames are likely to be present in both census lists without a family connection. I have in each instance taken the whole set of surnames of males in the locality at the beginning of the period, considering them all likely to form families of that name, and then compared them with the number of families in the districts bearing those surnames after forty years. The interval for Sublimity and Alpine is 1860 to 1900; for Middleton, which was founded later, it is 1870 to 1910.

[3] Only four of fifty-three founding families had shared surnames with others.

tunity so limited, is astonishing. In 1900, nineteen families remained in the town bearing one of the fourteen surnames present in the founding population – 136 percent (Middleton, 17 percent; Sublimity, 22 percent). In 1860 there had been one household each of Healeys, Nashes, and Strongs. In 1900 there were twelve households in the town with these names – seven of Healeys, three of Strongs, and two of Nashes.

How did the one society hold its families so tightly as the others began to disintegrate? It is impossible to account for all the factors that might have kept the Alpine families rooted in place for so long. Certainly one was that they wanted to live among others of their faith. In the entire territory between 1850 and 1900, 87 percent of the people whose first child was born in Utah remained until their last child was born. In the northern Utah region, 69 percent remained for the approximately twenty-year span of their childbearing years; and in Lehi, next to Alpine, 61 percent.[4] It would seem that the Latter-day Saints found satisfactions in living among other Mormons sufficient to counter the clear economic disadvantages of the Great Basin.

The nether side of this wish to live with other Saints was a fear of living elsewhere. Mormons invariably saw the conflicts they had had with others in New York, Ohio, Missouri, and Illinois as persecution, and these experiences had become a central theme in the ritual retelling of the Mormon past. In painting, poetry, song, and story, Mormons portrayed the "mobbers" as cruel, implacable enemies of the Saints, and the Gentile world generally as corrupt and hostile. The experience of even recent converts seemed to affirm the validity of those images. Distinctive political, economic, and social practices, including especially plural marriage or polygamy, made them objects of ridicule and suspicion when they traveled or lived outside of Mormon country.

Episcopal Bishop Daniel S. Tuttle told of registering at a San Francisco hotel under the name of "Bishop Tuttle and Wife, Salt Lake City." He later found that some wag had crossed out "wife" and written "wives." On another occasion he and his party, registering at a Monterey hotel as from Salt Lake City, "were at once eyed askance by our fellow guests, and were quite avoided as being Mormons, until some one happened on the scene who knew our true position and corrected the mistake." He found the incidents amusing and did not

---

[4] Dean L. May, Lee L. Bean, and Mark H. Skolnick, "The Stability Ratio: An Index of Community Cohesiveness in Nineteenth-Century Mormon Towns," in Robert M. Taylor, Jr., and Ralph J. Crandall, eds., *Generations and Change: Genealogical Perspectives in Social History* (Macon, Ga.: Mercer University Press, 1986), pp. 141–58, esp. p. 152.

seem to realize that they represented expressions of prejudice and stereotyping that could inflict real pain on Mormons and encourage them to avoid traveling or moving away from their own settlements.[5] Having sacrificed much to gather with the Saints, and fearing emotional or even physical assault elsewhere, they were loath to leave. Alpine youth might have had better prospects in western Idaho, Oregon, or California. But removal to these places was not an option because there were few Mormons there. Opportunities among the Saints elsewhere in the Great Basin were limited as well. Tillable land was severely limited and, as we have seen, quickly divided into tiny parcels by the tide of immigrants coming to Zion. There were few options outside of Alpine for those who chose to stay with the Saints.

Perhaps even more important, the ties of mutual affection and obligation formed over the years by intense voluntary association could not easily be severed. It was critical that the cement binding their community flowed not from a mystical expectation that the land would sustain and perpetuate the family or from the alchemy by which land was made to produce gold. As the economy changed toward trades, services, and manufacturing characteristic of urban life, the sense of community in Alpine was hardly ruffled. Brigham Young's efforts notwithstanding, the sense of belonging in Alpine had never rested upon a particular economic ethos. The connectedness arising from a plethora of voluntary associations was not tightly keyed to economic change. It continued throughout the century to affirm the sense of order, harmony, and, above all, belonging that had assuaged the discontents the great majority of Alpiners had known in England.

Over the first full decade after settlement, attachment to the broader community of Alpine held the people more firmly to the town than attachment to a kin/neighbor group alone, as in Sublimity.[6] In 1860–70 Alpine, where farmers reported that most tillable land had already been taken, five of fifteen heads of household remained throughout

---

[5] Mormon artist C. C. A. Christensen painted a series of large canvases that, between 1865 and the turn of the century, he took on tour to Mormon towns and villages. An assistant unrolled the paintings as a script was read portraying the persecutions of the Mormons. See Carl Cramer, "A Panorama of Mormon Life," *Art in America* 58 (May/ June 1970): 52–65. Numerous poems, and especially hymns, referred to the need to flee from Babylon to a place of safety. And as converts in Europe, who had not been present during the Midwest period, began to attach their identity to the new faith, the ritual retelling of the Mormon past recounted again and again the unjust sufferings of the Saints. The Tuttle anecdotes are in Daniel S. Tuttle, *Reminiscences of a Missionary Bishop* (New York: Thomas Whittaker, 1906), pp. 262–3.

[6] Alpine was not founded and Sublimity is not identifiable in the 1850 census. Thus, for both districts, the 1860–70 decade is the first for which we have reasonably reliable records.

the decade. In Sublimity, where the family was the central unit of society and little more than a tenth of the available land was being cultivated, 38 percent of the heads of household (thirty-seven of ninety-seven) stayed. Middleton, economically the most prosperous, but with weaker ties of both kin group and community, held but 23 percent of its families (twelve of fifty-three).[7] Thus, as we would expect, nearly four of each ten founding Oregon families remained on their land for the first decade, and a third of the early Alpine families lasted out the decade as well. By contrst, little more than a fifth of Middleton's founding families were present at the end of its first decade.

The second decade, however, brought important changes. In Alpine, neither completion of the transcontinental railroad nor the depression that followed the Panic of 1873 was unsettling enough to reverse a growing attachment to the place. Seventy percent of the 1870 families (twenty-six of thirty-seven) were there at the end of the decade. At the same time, the proportion remaining in Sublimity was rapidly declining, indeed dropping to Middleton levels. There 20 percent of the families (24 of 119) stayed in place over the decade from 1870 to 1880. Persistence of Middleton folk in their second decade cannot be determined because of the loss of the 1890 census, but during the two-decade period to 1900, some 7 percent of the families persisted (five of seventy-three).

Of great portent was the flight of youth from Sublimity. Twenty percent of the young men who had been between the ages of ten and twenty in 1860 remained until 1870. Over the next decade the proportion remaining dropped by almost half, to 11 percent, and only one young man found a niche that permitted him to start a new household in the district. Fifty-five percent of Alpine's young men (seventeen of thirty-one) were there a decade later, half of them marrying and forming their own households within the community.[8] In

---

[7] The appropriate manuscript federal censuses provided the information from which these data were calculated. None of the town data account for deaths. Reports in the 1900 census on deaths of children born to women over fifty (who had thus completed their childbearing by about 1890) show that those in Middleton and Alpine in 1900 had experienced rather high and similar rates of child death. Thirty-three percent of all the children born to the Alpine women died by 1900 and 31 percent of those born to Middleton women. Twenty-two percent of the children born to the same cohort of Sublimity women died before 1900. Since the founding populations had similar age structures, child death is a reasonable surrogate for overall deaths. The higher incidence of deaths in Alpine and Middleton should have suppressed their persistence rates compared to the rate in Sublimity.

[8] In both cases, I have included families that persisted in spite of the death or absence of the head of household. I consider only young men from ten to twenty years of age,

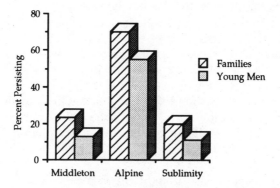

(Source: U.S. Manuscript Census for 1870 and 1880. See also footnote 8)

Figure 7.1 Persistence, 1870–1880 in Middleton, Alpine, and Sublimity families and young men aged ten to twenty.

Middleton 8 percent of the young men through age twenty (seven of eighty-eight) remained between 1880 and 1900.

Given the atomistic, success-driven tendencies in the Middleton society, the moving of many to take advantage of other opportunities is not surprising. But the disintegration of the close, kin-oriented Sublimity society during its second decade *is* surprising and requires further explanation. It is important to note that there were in the community from the outset both Hunts and Downings. The Hunts, and many others like them, were Hoosiers, or from the southern portions of the old Northwest and, though well off by local standards, were in the early years not as given to commercial farming as John Downing, of Pennsylvania background, was. The marriage of Temperance Hunt to John Downing seemed to portend a union of more than just families. Sarah Hunt's admiration for her uncle John's "fine old colonial mansion," with its imposing facade and its elegant fur-

because this was the age group most likely to form households over the next ten years, and because young women who married changed their names and thus are virtually impossible to trace.

For Middleton we have only the one decade (1870–80) that we can compare directly in Figure 7.2 with Alpine and Sublimity, which were in their second decade since founding. Also, the larger population of Alpine in 1870 makes persistence rates between 1870 and 1880 reasonably stable and reliable. The loss of the manuscript of the U.S. Census for 1890 makes the next period a twenty-year span. The Middleton population seems not to have gotten more stable with the passing decades, however, having between 1880 and 1900 a persistence rate of 7 percent for families (five of seventy-three) and 8 percent for young men through age twenty (seven of eighty-eight).

nishings, suggests, in fact, that the Hunts emulated the Downings. In essence, the Hunts were yeomen, and their kin/neighbors, the Downings, represented for them a planter tradition. It was nonetheless evident to the Hunts that in Oregon, where there was land aplenty, elevation to a planter's estate was not a distant dream but a very real possibility. John Downing's success came not from how much land he owned (many of his neighbors had nearly as much) but from the way he used it. Farming all tillable land, employing labor-saving machinery, and concentrating on raising marketable staples of grains and wool, he was by 1865 the most affluent and influential farmer in the neighborhood. Others in the neighbor/kin group – the Hunts, Carters, and Darsts – could hardly avoid seeing that, and as the years passed, they began to strive for similar measures of success, losing their original vision of cultivating only the amount of land they needed to sustain themselves and husbanding the rest for their descendants. The few commercially oriented farmers from the Northeast and the Mid-Atlantic states were a powerful leaven in the rural districts of the Willamette Valley.

There was leaven in the cities as well. When the *Willamette Farmer* began publication in Salem in 1869, it reinforced the momentum toward commercial farming that rural people were gaining from association with more progressive neighbors.[9] The eight-page weekly newspaper published local market reports and some local and national news. It aggressively promoted the latest models of plows, seed drills, mowers, and reapers. And in dozens of pieces on how better to farm, it relied heavily on copy lifted from agricultural journals of the Northeast and Midwest, where the Civil War had greatly accelerated the trend toward farming as a business. Again and again these articles stressed the importance of efficiency, economy, and keeping an eye on profits. A poem written by a farmer from Middlebury, Vermont, pithily summarized a principal message of the *Farmer*.

> The cash that from his acres came,
> Each year was something grand,
> And yet no schemes to spend the same
> By him were ever planned.
> For it was clear to every eye, he kept a steady hand.

[9] William E. Bowen found that Oregon cities tended to have a much higher concentration of people from the Northeast and Upper Midwest than did most rural districts. Of the seven printers in Salem in 1870, five were from the Northeast or Mid-Atlantic states, though two of the three known to have been connected with the *Willamette Farmer* were natives of Tennessee and Kentucky. See William A. Bowen, *The Willamette Valley: Migration and Settlement on the Oregon Frontier* (Seattle: University of Washington Press, 1978), p. 43.

. . . . . . . . . . . . . . . . . . . . . . . . . . . . . . . . . . . . . . . . . . . . . . . . . . . . . . . . . . . . . . . . . . . .

And o'er the mishaps on his farm,
He suffered no remorse,
But set down all that came along,
To profit, or to loss.
One day the Husbandman of all,
Called in for his amount,
He found the Farmer on his couch, and low ran nature's fount;
Accounts adjusted, he was borne
Up to his last account.[10]

Stressing the (here) eternal importance of cash, profit, loss, and close accounting, the newspaper told rural folk of the valley how to make a success of their farms. John Downing was the correspondent to the *Farmer* from his district, a perfect model for the values the journal promoted. His brother-in-law, George Hunt, came by the 1870s in some measure to follow his lead, reporting to the *Farmer* in December 1872 that "land is looking up, and rapidly changing hands. I notice that those taking the place of the old settlers, are wide awake; so we will rather gain than lose by the change. . . . Our [farmer's] club consists of fourteen of as wide awake members as you can pick out in any neighborhood, and I am told our office takes the largest number of *Willamette Farmers* for the population, of any office in the State."[11]

This changing perception of the purposes of land ownership commonly led Sublimity farmers to one of two courses of action, both with the same ultimate consequences. Some followed Downing's lead, putting all the land they could into commercial production, and thus preempting the formerly virgin land originally held for the children to take up as they came of age. Others began selling the land they had been saving, paring their holdings down to a manageable size while converting the surplus into capital that could be used for machinery, houses, and outbuildings. In the first case, most young men coming of age felt they could not wait until their fathers relinquished their land; in the second, there was too little land per son to wait for. Many youth were thus propelled away from their neighbor/kin groups, and in many cases away from farming altogether. The intended nexus of family and land was diminished, in part because the

---

[10] "The Thrifty Farmer," by S. E. Rockwell of Middlebury, Vt., in the *Willamette Farmer*, November 12, 1871.

[11] The *Willamette Farmer*, March 2, 1872. Hunt's contrast between "wide-awake" new settlers and the old settlers obviously shows an understanding that a new mentality is infusing the district. He equates this new mentality with joining the Farmer's Club, an early local manifestation of the broader national movement represented in the Grange and Farmers' Alliances, and with subscribing to the *Farmer*.

parents' wish to better themselves seduced them away from the expectations that had driven them to acquire their vast farms.

As Sublimity's founders came to see that land could be converted
into cash and comforts, their fundamental purposes of life gradually
shifted from perpetuation of the family on the land to acquisition of
wealth (which most, no doubt, expected would in any case one day
be passed on to their descendants). As that shift proceeded, the land
lost its magic and became, as in Middleton, simply one of many possible ways to make a living. Perhaps underlying this shift was the
transformation in values that the Civil War had accelerated and the
triumphant North had disseminated throughout the United States.
The neighbor/kin groups proved vulnerable to the great transformation sweeping rural America. Before the founding generation died,
they had disintegrated into an atomistic structure barely distinguish-
able from that established by the Middleton folk, who had fled the
carnage to come West in the 1860s. Mary Spangler's lament for her
family might as well have been for them.

* * *

Junius B. Wright, another of Middleton's early citizens, did not share
Mary Spangler's dark sense of declension. When news of gold and
silver strikes in Idaho captured his attention, he decided to leave
southern Iowa and head west. From that day he did not look back.
He recounted no tearful farewells in his memoir, as George Hunt had
done. Not once in a long, rambling reminiscence did he hint that he
and his wife missed old haunts, friends, and family. And if, as he
maintained, the poorer people he had known in his youth were de-
ficient in having "no individualism to incite to effort or gain renown,"
he himself was not wanting in this regard. Once in Idaho, he devoted
his talents and energies to gaining his own share of both the wealth
and status that in the burgeoning Boise Valley were up for grabs.

After a profitable first season in 1865, farming with Moses Fowler,
Wright combined his practice of medicine with farming and began to
claim and buy up land in the district. By 1870 he had acquired 400
acres, more than any other Middleton area resident. In total wealth
he ranked third, next to the store owner and ferry operator, Perry
Munday, and Wright's erstwhile partner, Moses Fowler. In 1874 he
was promoting a yellow clay he had apparently found on his land as
a possible resource for a crockery industry. That failing to materialize,
he moved the next year to Boise, where he opened a drug store. There
he was elected twice to the state legislature and served as school trus-
tee for three terms.[12]

---

[12] Biographical information on Wright is from Wallace W. Elliott, *History of Idaho Ter-*

Photo 14  Junius B. Wright of Middleton. (Idaho State Historical Society, Photo 900B. Used by permission of the Idaho State Historical Society.)

By the end of the decade he had sold 126 acres of his land in the Middleton area but retained the rest, perhaps hoping to profit from a rise in values as the Oregon Short Line railroad approached. The line was built well south of the Boise River, however, bypassing Middleton and making the towns of Nampa and Caldwell the new commercial centers of an invigorated lower Boise Valley. Sensing opportunity in Caldwell, Wright moved there in 1883, the year the rail line was completed, opening another drug business. By 1890 he had sold all of his Middleton holdings and moved to a farm nine miles west of Caldwell, where he lived until the turn of the century, when he finally severed his connection to the area and moved to Portland.[13]

The pattern of Wright's association with Middleton was a common one. At first, with Boise Basin and Owyhee miners creating a strong demand for food, land was a good investment.[14] Yet, mining was notoriously unstable, and economic success in a rapidly changing environment required a varied repertoire of entrepreneurial strategies, at which Wright excelled. Even during a local recession at the end of the 1870s, he held on to most of his land and pursued the main chance wherever it might lead. Yet in the end he did not find it hard to abandon the place. This search for a livelihood beyond farming is suggested in the changing occupational structure of Middleton. Whereas in 1870 some 93 percent of the fifty-three household heads reported themselves to be farmers, by 1880 the number of farmers had dropped to 58 percent (of seventy-three).[15]

Yet the commercial character of the region remained as evident in farming as in running a pharmacy. The average farmer in 1880 (medians) owned 199 acres, paid out $201 for hired hands, had invested $203 in farm equipment, and produced crops worth $1,488. He marketed 770 bushels of wheat, 198 of oats, and 202 of barley. The median wealth was $895 in 1870, dropped to $517 in 1880, but tripled after completion of the railroad in 1883, to reach $1,605 by 1890, very close

---

*ritory* (San Francisco: Wallace W. Elliott & Co., 1884), pp. 258–9; Junius B. Wright, Reminiscences, Idaho State Archives; Boise, *Tri-Weekly Statesman*, June 17, 1874; and Jennie Cornell Files, "Pioneers of Canyon County, Idaho," Book II.

[13] Data on Wright's holdings are from the tax assessment rolls for Ada County. They are presently in the Idaho State Archives, Boise.

[14] The population of Boise and Owyhee counties, the nearest to Middleton, with a predominantly mining population, declined by 16 percent between 1870 and 1880, from 5,547 to 4,640. It rose considerably during the next decade, however, to 7,978, though the new population included a good many ranchers, who were competing with Middleton farmers in the stock industry but probably provided markets for some animal forage grains, such as oats. See the printed reports of the U.S. Census, 1870, 1880, and 1890.

[15] Occupations are from the manuscript of the U.S. Census for 1860 and 1870.

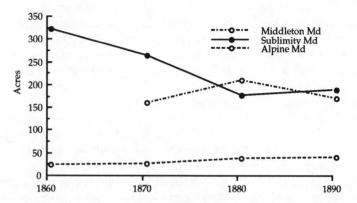

(Source: Tax assessment rolls for Sublimity, 1857, 1871, 1880, and 1889; for Alpine, 1860, 1870, 1880, and 1890; for Middleton, 1870, 1880, and 1890. Sublimity and Middleton rolls are in the Oregon and Idaho State Archives in Salem and Boise; those for Alpine are in the Utah State University Library, Special Collections, and the Utah State Archives.)

Figure 7.2 Median size of farms, 1860–1890, Middleton, Sublimity, and Alpine.

to that of Sublimity farmers.[16] Those of means in Middleton did very well. The wealthiest third of Middleton's families claimed 62 percent of all the community's assets in 1870, 78 percent in 1880, and 67 percent in 1890. Except for 1880, those in the middle third had a reasonable share for their numbers – 28 percent, a dismal 18 percent, and again 28 percent at the beginning of each respective decade. The poorest third had 10 percent of all the wealth in 1870, dropped to but 3 percent in 1880, and recovered only to 6 percent in 1890. Their average was 6 percent, the lowest of the three communities. Middleton was a good place to be if one were lucky enough to be among the top two thirds. If not, one might do better to join the many moving on.

Though Middleton's first farmers had tilled river bottomlands that did not require irrigation, many soon began to divert water from the river to raise crops on the dry, higher benchlands.[17] The 6,270 acres

[16] Size of farms and production data, such as cost of labor, farm equipment, and crops produced, are from the manuscript of the U.S. Agricultural Census for 1880. Wealth numbers are from the Ada County tax assessment rolls for 1880. Both sets of records are in the Idaho State Archives, Boise.

[17] The first applications for water rights from the Boise River were made June 1, 1864. Forty-eight were made prior to 1870, another twenty-five the next decade, forty-one during the 1880s, and another fourteen before 1900. See Edwin B. Karn, "Report on Canal Deliveries from the Boise River and Different Features affecting these Deliveries for the Irrigation System of 1949" (n.p., n.d.), Chart 24.

they farmed in 1870 were increased to 9,127 by 1880 and remained stable at that level through 1890. Yet, the increased acreage, as we have seen, was not made available to new settlers or youth, but rather was used to increase the productivity and profitability of already established farms. Sixteen men under thirty headed households in 1880. Six listed themselves as farmers or farm workers. Three had been there in 1870, sons of Robert and Sarah Clark. Mr. Clark died in 1875 and Mrs. Clark remarried, leaving the land to the boys.[18] Average holdings for the six young men who listed themselves as farmers (medians) were 80 acres, the mean 115. The typical (median) farm in the whole district had risen by 1880 from 151 to 199 acres, and that of farmers over twenty-nine to 220 acres (mean, 242).[19] Clearly, newly opened lands were being consolidated into existing farms, and when early settlers sold out, their lands were purchased by older men whose wealth made such a large investment possible.

As in 1870, Middleton farmers used their augmented fields to specialize in one or another crop. Moses Fowler harvested 3,000 bushels of oats in 1880; Reuben Breshears and Thomas Norris each threshed 1,500 bushels of wheat. Daniel Dodd ran 140 head of cattle; Pleasant Latham had 300 chickens. The average CV of the four basic crops – wheat, potatoes, hogs, and cattle – indicates the degree to which these crops tended to be grown by a few specialists rather than by most farmers. The CV for Middleton was stable from 1870 to 1880 at 1.5, remaining also the highest of the three districts. Agriculture in the Boise Valley had begun principally as a commercial venture and remained so through the ensuing decades.

Middleton farms gradually increased in size throughout 1890, and though ownership changed, it was a new incoming population, with considerable capital, that took up the established farms, rather than the children of parents who had pioneered the place. The newcomers' commitment to making a success of a commercial farm was at least as strong as that of the Fowlers, the Wrights, or the Montgomerys, and the completion of the railroad in 1883 stabilized prices for their crops while ensuring a predictable demand. Many of Middleton's farmers by 1890 were wealthy, not only in land, which accounted for 42 percent of their assets, but in personal property, perhaps a better

---

[18] The land was listed in the tax rolls as the property of George and James Clark, their brother William claiming no land. James W. and William had sold their interest to the others by 1880. See Ada County Probate Records, Book D, pp. 8ff. Another young man, Andrew Reagon, was the third landowner.

[19] The acreage data are from the manuscript of the US Census of Agriculture, considering only those who were heads of household and listing their occupation as farmers or farm workers.

indicator of standard of living – livestock and other possessions acquired over the years in a volatile commercial climate where alert,
ambitious individualists like Wright did very well.

Alpine began with an agricultural economy of niggardly subsistence, and over the early decades its citizens, although making some
gains, still remained far below the levels of Middleton and Sublimity
folk. During Alpine's first decades, from 1860 through 1880, total farm
land increased and farms became larger. Nonetheless, the paucity of
land and water, and the determination of the people and their children
to stay in the place, kept farms small and inevitably forced many out
of farming. Whereas all of the heads of household had been farmers
in 1860, that number dropped to 66 percent in 1870 and to 63 percent
in 1880, only slightly more than in Middleton.[20] Still, farming remained the base of the economy, and niches were opened to agricul-
turists as the Alpine people built canals to water higher lands
previously thought useless and claimed grazing areas in the foothills.

All the land farmed in Alpine in 1860 had totaled but 324 acres. In
1867 the principal streams and springs flowing into the area were
formally claimed by the city for community use, and over the next
few years the town fathers oversaw the building of a network of dams
and canals for distributing the water.[21] Alpiners' expansion into areas
previously thought marginal doubled their agricultural land by 1870
to 649 acres. The next decade saw a five-fold increase to 3,127 acres.
Thus, though we might have expected that virtually all the younger
men coming of age would have been forced to leave the community
or to seek occupations outside of farming, the opening of new lands
through extending irrigation ditches and the claiming of marginal
foothill tracts made farming or stock raising a possibility for many.
William and Julia Strong's oldest surviving son, Don, was twenty-
three in 1880, working twenty acres and claiming another forty-three
of unimproved land. Hyrum Healey, oldest son of John and Mary
Hemingway Healey, was twenty-eight, farming twenty-five acres,
with another five unimproved. Of the nineteen heads of household
under thirty in 1880, eleven listed themselves as farmers in the census,
the group averaging (medians) twenty acres of land each, somewhat
but not impossibly behind the average thirty-one-acre farm of those
over thirty.

Alpine had a much smaller pool of wealth than Middleton. The
median wealth reported in 1860 was $400, rising to $564 by 1870 but

[20] Manuscript of the U.S. Census for the years indicated in text.
[21] Jennie Adams Wild, *Alpine Yesterdays: A History of Alpine, Utah County, Utah, 1850–
1980* (Salt Lake City: Blaine Hudson Printing, 1982), pp. 207–10.

dropping again to $450 by 1880. Yet the town's meager assets were more evenly distributed than those of the Idaho or Oregon communities. The richest third of the population claimed 60 percent of the total wealth in 1860 and even less, 58 percent, in 1870. The 1870s, however, saw a considerable sharpening of differences, with the upper third claiming 64 percent at the end of the decade, though the average still remained 61 percent, well below the proportion controlled by the wealthy in Middleton and Sublimity. The middling people held fairly consistently to their portion, 28 percent in 1860, 29 percent in 1870, and 26 percent in 1880, their mean of 28 being the highest of the three localities. There were poor among the Alpine folk, the lower third claiming 12, 13, and 10 percent of the wealth at the beginning of each successive decade, with an average of 12 percent for the entire period, faring again much better than their peers in the other towns.

Between 1860 and 1880, Alpiners added new lands and consolidated older 15- and 20-acre plots, bringing the average farm to a somewhat more viable 28-acre size, still far behind the 199-acre Middleton farms. Alpine's farmers still tilled their land in a pattern that suggests that providing for the family was their first priority. The average (median) farmer in 1880 had no machinery, paid no wages, and told census takers the total value of production on his farm was $200 (mean, $307). He harvested but seventy-five bushels of wheat, twenty-three of oats, virtually no barley, and but twenty bushels of corn, still barely enough to feed the family and livestock throughout the Alpine winters.[22] A few farmers, nonetheless, were breaking into production for the market. Bishop McCullough paid out $400 in wages in 1880. William J. Strong raised $300 bushels of oats, John McDaniel 200 of corn, and Ephraim Nash 450 of wheat. Thomas Carlisle farmed 160 acres of improved land, four times the size of the largest farm in 1860, owned by Ephraim Nash. The CV shows a move toward specialization in certain crops on the part of Alpine farmers, rising from 0.7 in 1860 to 1.04 in 1880, still well below that of the other districts but suggesting a trend toward a more commercial orientation.[23]

In the 1870s Brigham Young had urged Alpine's folk, with other Mormons, to enter a communal "United Order of Enoch" that would make most assets community property and reduce extremes in wealth. William Johnson Strong served for a time on the board of directors of the Alpine United Order. Yet the movement proved divisive, and

---

[22] The medians in 1860 had been eighty bushels of wheat, fifteen of oats, and fifteen of corn.

[23] Production data are from the manuscript of the U.S. Census of Agriculture for Utah County, in the LDS Church Archives, Salt Lake City, Utah.

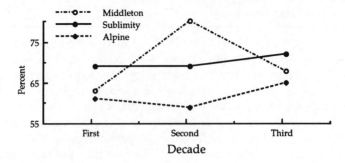

Figure 7.3
(A) Percent of total wealth owned by wealthiest third of household heads.

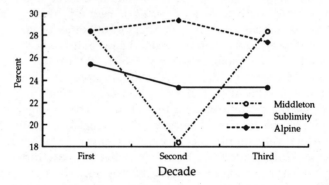

(B) Percent of total wealth owned by middle third of household heads.

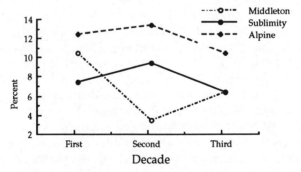

(C) Percent of total wealth owned by the poorest third of household heads.

(Sources: Marion County tax assessment rolls for 1857, 1871, 1880; Ada County tax assessment rolls for 1870, 1880, and 1890; and Utah County tax assessment rolls for 1860, 1870, and 1880. The total of heads of household at the nearest census rather than the number of taxpayers was used in determining the proportions of the population in each category.)

many participated only reluctantly. In most settlements the United Order did not last more than a season or two and had no long-term effect on economic patterns. And when Young died in 1877, his successors backed away from communalism.[24] Private ownership of property and production, insofar as possible, for markets reasserted themselves. Though the general poverty of Alpine people still kept them very much in a world apart, they were beginning by the end of the decade to move toward an economy like that of Middleton and Sublimity.

Most Sublimity farmers had raised only a modest surplus during the 1860s, but a few were already moving toward commercial farming. In 1865 John Downing cultivated 150 of his 960 acres and harvested large surpluses of wheat, oats, wool, and apples. George Hunt farmed only 35 of his 640 acres but grew marketable quantities of oats, apples, and wool. There are no surviving agricultural censuses for the district until the Marion County Census of 1895. The less informative tax list of 1871 shows that whereas Downing and Hunt were increasing their holdings to 1,275 and 843 acres, respectively (the most they would own in their lives), the average farm in the area was declining somewhat to 253 acres (mean, 268 acres).[25]

The trend continued throughout 1880, with Downing's holdings still a commodious 1,070 acres and Hunt's 800, but the median for the district dropped rapidly to 167 acres, less than in Middleton. The 1870s were, as George Hunt expressed it to the *Willamette Farmer*, a time when land was "rapidly changing hands." Increasing numbers of the original settlers were choosing to sell part or all of their farms. Nor was the land passing on to their heirs, as Sublimity's founders had once hoped. Only 11 percent of the young men present in 1870 were still there in 1880, and only three of these had formed their own households. They were among the twenty-two young married farmers there in 1880, who averaged 136 acres each, somewhat smaller than the norm for the community, but nonetheless parcels the most affluent Alpine farmers would have coveted.

Sublimity farmers were wealthy throughout the entire period compared with those from Idaho and Utah. Median wealth was $1,325 per taxpayer in 1860, dropped to $895 in 1870, but doubled during the 1870s to $1,652. Yet their abundance tended to be almost as unevenly

---

[24] See Leonard J. Arrington, Feramorz Young Fox, and Dean L. May, *Building the City of God: Community and Cooperation Among the Mormons*, 2nd ed. (Urbana: University of Illinois Press, 1992).

[25] The surviving tax assessment roll closest to the decade change is for 1871. It is in the Oregon State Archives, Salem.

divided among the population as in Middleton. The wealthiest third steadily maintained their share at 68 percent in 1860 and 1870, increasing it to 71 percent by 1880 (averaging 70 percent throughout the period). The poorest third did somewhat better in Sublimity than in Middleton, though not as well as the poorest in Alpine. They held 7 percent of the wealth in 1860, rose to 9 percent in 1870, then dropped to 6 percent by 1880 (mean, 7 percent) at a time when general wealth was increasing rapidly. The middle group did, on average, less well than in Alpine and Middleton, their 25 percent share in 1860 dropping to 23 percent in 1870 and remaining at that level throughout 1880 (mean, 24 percent).

The dominant share enjoyed by the top third in Sublimity at first seems surprising. We would have expected Middleton, always strongly commercial, to have the most uneven distribution of wealth. Yet the Donation Land Claim Act made it possible for Sublimity farmers, who wanted enough land to provide viable farms for their children, to take up huge tracts. And in Sublimity the supply of land was less elastic compared to the Utah and Idaho communities, where irrigation could substantially increase the total land available for agriculture. In the Oregon district, increases in the number of households occurred largely by breaking off part of larger tracts, but these newer farms were small compared to the farms still held by those who had acquired Donation Land Claims. Thus, with land comprising 69 percent of all wealth, total assets were increasingly ill distributed.

George Hunt was sixty-four when the Marion County Census of 1895 gives us another glimpse of production in the district. He had apparently retired from active farming. His son, Jeptha, was busy transforming the 160 acres that his father had given him into a profitable commercial venture, specializing in wool, oats, and wheat. John Downing's son, Albert, also had a farm in the district, but he perhaps was renting most of his land, as he reported producing only twenty-six hogs on the 183 acres he owned. The trend in the district is nonetheless clear. Farms were becoming leaner and more efficient. The median farm was 115 acres by 1890, 37 percent of what it had been in 1865. Almost half of the land claimed was now tilled, whereas in 1865 less than a tenth was under the plow.

Average production per farm was notably increased. George W. Hunt's brother, John A. Hunt, clipped 1,400 pounds of wool for market in 1895. Jeptha Hunt, his son, raised 1,500 bushels of wheat. Jeptha's harvest of 3,500 bushels of oats far surpassed that of any other farmer in a district that clearly favored oats as a staple that season. Median production of most basic crops was close to what it had been in 1865; ninety-six bushels of wheat, forty pounds of potatoes, ten hogs, eight cattle, and five tons of hay. However, this does not suggest stable or declining productivity per farm, but rather indicates how specialized Sublimity farms had become in the intervening years. By 1895 it was less common for farmers to produce the variety of crops needed to sustain their families throughout a season. Mean wheat production had increased from 128 to 177 bushels per farm, though the median actually dropped by 4 bushels. The mean clip of wool rose from 158 to 405 pounds, whereas the median dropped to 0. Oats was clearly the cash crop of preference in 1895, the median farm producing 600 bushels, (mean, 884 bushels).[26]

The change in the CV underscores the trend toward more specialized and commercial farming. In 1865 it had been 1.2. By 1895 it had risen to 1.4, almost the level of Middleton. George Hunt had something to say about that when, in 1873, the Oregon State Board of the Farmer's Clubs considered asking all farmers to contribute to the building of producer-owned warehouses and freighting vessels so that they could control the marketing of their crops. Hunt opposed the plan, maintaining that the majority in his district "was not in favor of going in to that kind of business – as they followed a mixed husbandry – instead of making wheat-raising a specialty."[27] That had been, of course, his ideal and, indeed, his practice in 1873. But by 1895 his son, Jeptha, had moved dramatically toward the Middleton model, laboring from sun to sun, tilling all of his 160 acres, stuffing his granaries and sheds with oats, wheat, and wool.

Hunt no doubt took pride in his son's increasing wealth. After all, he himself had been an advocate and officer of the State Fair, had supported the Farmer's Clubs and the Grange, had been an avid subscriber to the *Willamette Farmer*, and in the 1870s had heralded the arrival of a new breed of "wide-awake" farmers to the Sublimity area. Nonetheless, as the century drew to a close, he may at times have looked askance at the frenetic pace of activity, the relentless teasing of product from every available acre, the shipping of ton upon ton of food and fiber down the river to the Portland markets. He had good cause to wonder if all the changes had been for the better and to lament much that Junius Wright celebrated in the new West.

      *   *   *

---

[26] The median being the value of the middle case, it is possible for a few at the top to raise very large quantities, making the average considerable, while the middle farmers raise none, making the median zero.

[27] The *Willamette Farmer*, April 5, 1873.

George Washington Hunt thought deeply about how he might influence his family after his passing. In 1890 he and his wife, Elizabeth, made out their wills, through which they intended to entail their property to their descendants and establish a family cemetery. The same year, he published in Boston his "History of the Hunt Family From the Norman Conquest, 1066 A.D., to the Year 1890."[28] Both wills and history were brave attempts to tilt against the mills that had transformed their world. When the Hunts wrote their wills, all the surviving children but nineteen-year-old Sarah were already married and on their own. Only Jeptha, the youngest son, lived on the family estate – he, his wife, Myrtie White, and their four children, finding in Hunt lands their domicile and livelihood.

Elizabeth Hunt died in 1891. Before George died in 1902, he had moved to Salem and turned the farm over to his son. By that time the oldest child, Temperance, lived in Albany with her husband, Robert Ashby. Georgianna had died in 1893. Sarah had married B. L. Steeves in 1893 and moved with him to Weiser, Idaho, not far from Middleton. Only Jeptha never strayed from Sublimity. The Hunts – five households in 1860, three on contiguous lands – had only one household to represent them there in 1900.

There had been twelve family clusters scattered across the rolling Sublimity countryside in 1860, containing thirty-one households. By 1900 two identifiable kin groups remained from that pioneer stock. The founders had not perpetuated their social world to the next generation. A number of early names were still there, and more were found in neighboring districts and towns. There were still Darsts, Hunts, Downings, Geers, and Phillipses in Sublimity country. But typically, if a descendant remained on the family land, it was one family, not a cluster. The transformation was profoundly important. For these people family coherence had been sundered, and with it their social world. Outmigration and death had narrowed the small, intense neighbor/kin communities to single families of husband, wife, and children. The changes diminished the little communities that had once been the setting of most social activities – of worship, weddings, holidays, births, and funerals. They severed the networks that had ex-

---

[28] Marion County Probate Records, Case 2,168, filed November 26. 1902. Hunt left 160 acres each to Melancthon, Jeptha, and Sarah. He explained that the reason he did not give land to the older daughters, Temperance E. Ashby and Georgianna I. Hunt, was that their mother had given each of them 160 acres in her will, "which will is a counterpart of this." I assume from this statement that the same wish that the land remain in the hands of the "heirs of my body" was expressed in his wife's will as well, which I have not been able to find. See also G. W. Hunt, *A History of the Hunt Family* (Boston: McDonald, Gill & Co., 1890).

changed food, fiber, credit, and labor – that had shared the burdens of the handicapped, poor, and enfeebled. And although the core families that remained certainly formed friendships and worked often together in common causes, they could not sustain the neighborhood community in the form their predecessors had known.

Most did not miss the old ways. As rural people began more and more to be linked to urban networks, institutions proliferated that accomplished for them what the neighbor/kin groups had once done. A death, for example, once made waves that rippled out, washing many in the community. Where credit and exchange took place mainly through personal rather than institutional transactions, people accumulated petty debts and credits that they carried throughout their lives. The process of settling the accounts of a lifetime was one that involved the neighbor/kin group as well as the immediate family.

William B. Logan, for example, died on March 1, 1861. The probate court appointed a son-in-law, George Schriver, executor. Commonly, because their duties affected many in the community, the probate judges asked executors and appraisers to post a bond to ensure the honesty and competence of their performance (though in this case, none is mentioned). W. W. Brooks promptly presented Schriver with a petition asking that he be granted a deed for ten acres of land he had purchased from Logan in 1858 for $100. John P. Anderson, a close neighbor, appraised the land and considered the petition of Brooks, together with Hadley Hobson and Solomon Alberson's attestations of the validity of the sale. During this process, Schriver was collecting debts that neighbors owed to Logan, as evidenced by handwritten notes or vouchers Logan had saved. Schriver himself was obligated for three notes totaling $8.50. A close neighbor, John Brown, owed $6.00; and Abraham Ollinger and William B. Simpson each owed $10.00. It was later discovered that Charles Kirkpatrick owed Logan an additional $27.50.

The court asked three other neighbors, John Downing, John P. Anderson, and George Downing, to appraise the rest of the estate. They estimated that Logan's remaining land, some twenty acres, was worth $60. Logan also had an iron wedge and spade worth $7.00, a turning lathe and tools valued at $20, a "white Indian mare" worth $40, a "clay bank colored" mare at $50, and a "red cow with some white in the face" valued at $12.00. Against these assets John P. Anderson and John Downing charged $3.00 each for appraising the estate, Downing $4.30 for "halling lumber for the grave," and David Simpson $4.75 for making a coffin. They submitted an appraisal listing assets, valued at $252, on July 13.

Schriver then sold Logan's personal property, perhaps (as was often done) at a public auction attended by all the close neighbors and kin. The appraisers had been optimistic. Bills of sale of personal property belonging to the estate of William B. Logan listed one dun mare, $30; a lot of tools, $5; one gray mare, $18.50; one cow, $9.50; another lot of tools, $5.50; and one coat (that the appraisers had missed), $6, for a total of $74.50. When Schriver deducted expenses, the estate was finally settled with a positive balance of $181.45 for Logan's heirs, the whole process completed some ten months after he had died.

Logan's death was not just a family affair. The process, even with so small an estate, had involved directly twelve of Logan's neighbors and kin. Some no doubt had seen his death as a worrisome signal that now they must scratch up the cash to pay debts contracted years before; others saw that it would require them to collect deeds (and, more often, debts owed by the deceased). Neighbors would be asked to administer the estate or appraise it; to build a coffin, or dig a grave; to auction Logan's effects or purchase them, including the coat Logan had once worn. And, of course, there remained, with it all, the sense of personal loss felt most directly by the next of kin, but also by the many more whose lives had become intertwined through a thousand unnoted acts of association with William Logan, whose life estate was now settled.[29]

John Downing died a quarter of a century later, on September 16, 1887. His first wife, Temperance Hunt, had preceded him in 1876, leaving $3,500 in land and a $2,500 policy with the Aetna Insurance Company. A year later he married Jennie Carpenter, and they had one son, Everett, born in 1878. When John died twelve years later, he left no will. Ten days after his death, his widow and his second son, Albert, petitioned to be appointed administrators of the estate. They had apparently paid any debts and funeral expenses, as none are listed in the probate records. The executors appointed a brother-in-law, John A. Hunt, and neighbors L. C. Griffith and W. J. Humphreys, to appraise the property. Their inventory listed 135 items, including real estate, livestock, machinery, household furnishings, and commodities on hand, totaling in value $20,956.02. Nothing was sold at auction or otherwise separated from the estate. There were in the entire inventory, the largest in the area between 1855 and 1905, only three notes, one from a nephew, James T. Downing, and one each from D. F. Campbell and C. H. Daly, none apparently close neighbors. The probate was completed within three months of Downing's death, the process involving principally his wife and children.[30]

[29] Marion County Probate Records, File 211.
[30] Marion County Probate Records, File 1040.

The Downing probate illustrates important changes that were taking place. Retail storekeepers, banks, and savings institutions were taking over a greater share of the lending and borrowing done in the district. Insurance companies, attorneys, and undertakers were helping to formalize and smooth out the duties related to death. Fewer estates required the calling in and paying of petty debts and obligations, as such debts became concentrated in the estates of a handful of businessmen who were making a living lending to local people. The process was becoming more private, more routine, and more costly, less personal and less involving. Death was becoming a concern principally of the immediate family and of institutions with which the deceased had made contractual arrangements. It was no longer a community matter.

The shrinking of the family/kin group did not necessarily signal a diminishing of human ties and associations. Sublimity people had always taken political tasks as a duty of citizenship – serving on juries or road committees or running for political office. These often involved interaction with others beyond their immediate neighborhood, especially at the county level. [31] The Farmer's Clubs, begun in Oregon in the late 1860s, were initially meetings of neighbors and kin, but by 1873 were organizing into county and then state clubs and beginning to plan common marketing procedures in order to keep profits high during a time of sagging prices.[32] The Grange began in Oregon in 1873, and following a national pattern, local organizations quickly proliferated into county and state Granges. The State Fair, sponsored by the Oregon Agricultural Society, annually brought farmers from throughout the state to Salem for an occupationally based "camp meeting" of social events, entertainments, exhibits, and shop talk. George Hunt's daughter, Sarah, remembered that in the 1870s "there were not so many diversions, fewer places to go and less entertainment," and that May Day, Independence Day, and the State Fair were the three main events of the year. It was common for families to have their own shanties at the fair grounds, those of neighbor/kin groups close to one another, in which the whole family annually camped while attending the event.[33] For men, women, and children, acquain-

---

[31] These duties were considerable and involved a good many Sublimity people. See Marion County Commissioners Court Journals, State Archives, Salem.

[32] *Willamette Farmer*, all of 1873, a remarkably innovative year for Salem area farmers; see esp. February 1 and 8, March 22, and April 10.

[33] Sarah Hunt Steeves describes the compound her family shared with others from Whiteaker in her *Book of Remembrance of Marion County, Oregon, Pioneers* (Portland: The Berncliff Press, 1927), pp. 303–8.

tances and experiences were being broadened beyond the neighbor/ kin group through all of these processes.

Activities that drew people away from their neighbor/kin group proliferated as the century drew to a close, becoming less related to civic duty or to occupation and often centered in Sublimity village or in Stayton rather than Whiteaker or Macleay or even the county seat, Salem. The *Stayton Mail* began publication in 1896, and immediately reported half a dozen lodges and organizations that commonly met in Stayton on a weekly or biweekly basis. A debating club considered such issues as "Resolved that from a moral standpoint, the world is growing better." The trend was away from neighbor/kin to town or village associations and even from occupationally defined gatherings to those stressing general brother- and sisterhood.

The people of Whiteaker found themselves more and more in a world where they socialized with those they chose to be with, and less with those to whom they felt obligated through kinship or the chance of being next-door neighbors. The spectrum of obligations to their new communities was narrowed, no longer demanding personal involvement in material and other matters that increasingly were the private concerns of the nuclear family. A new set of self-selected communities, which people could enter or withdraw from at will, and which demanded relatively little of their members, was replacing the older inclusive community of neighbor and kin.

Farm women were taking the initiative to lessen their burdens and enlarge their sphere of activities. Some, wishing to limit the size of their families, responded to advertisements in the *Stayton Mail* for compounds such as Dr. Martel's French female pills, the latter promising that particulars and testimonials would be mailed free "in [a] plain sealed letter."[34] The younger women had attended neighborhood schools and were more literate. They were hence more comfortable in public, going out of the home to do the buying that a more commercial economy required for maintenance of the household, and to attend town churches with regular weekly services, ladies' aid societies, and even literary clubs.

Most people were finding that formal contracts, the terms neatly delineated and negotiated through persons representing banks, milling companies, or retailers, now mediated a greater share of the obligations they incurred in the course of their lives. The personal networks of debit and credit occupied an increasingly smaller sphere. One of the great virtues of such contracts was that unlike personal obligations, the terms by which the relationship could be ended were

[34] The ads appear frequently in the *Stayton Mail*. See esp. the March 10, 1899, number.

clearly indicated, and once those terms were met, the interests of both parties in one another were terminated.

Most Sublimity folk seemed to welcome the changes, for they made association a matter of personal preference and choice, and reserved to the private intimacy of the nuclear family a range of concerns that had once been shared but now were increasingly regarded as nobody's business but their own. Yet some may have had misgivings. At the age of fifty-five, George Hunt had a remarkable experience. He had been a Christian since his conversion in his early teens and had always lived a pious life, holding family services in his home, superintending and teaching Sunday school, and otherwise supporting the Christian faith. Yet, in the mid-1880s he became increasingly troubled and anxious.

> Sometimes, during this period, it would occur to me, "Is there not a better experience for Christians than they seem to have?" I would cry from the depths of my soul, "Lord, give my soul rest!." I would wander up to the banks of Jordan, but hearing the report of the spies, would turn back into the wilderness, discouraged.

Moved by a sermon on "Christian perfection" preached in Whiteaker by T. H. Organ, a "holiness evangelist," Hunt determined to attend a holiness camp meeting at the town of Philomath, some 35 miles from his home, in Benton County, near Corvallis. There

> after a few hours of testing I received the baptism of fire and the Holy Ghost. Jesus swept out of the temple all the money changers and those that sold doves, and took up His abode in the temple, and I realized I had a pure heart and was sanctified wholly. . . . I can compare my forty years of wilderness life to a sort of serving the Lord as the son of the bond-woman (legal service), for we are bought with a price; while "if the Son hath made you free, you are free indeed."

Four years later, he and Elizabeth made out their wills and he published his family history, reserving to its final pages the story of his rescue from the sins of money changing and selling doves – his salvation from a material and commercial world. "I now follow the Lord with a free, joyous, gladsome service, and my peace floweth like a river. Glory to God and the Lamb forever. Amen."[35] His book, and the will he made out the same year, were clear attempts to save his descendants, as he had been saved, from materialism and fragmentation. He had sinned in moving their world toward that of Middleton, but he had repented, done what he could to make restitution, and in faith had found his peace.

[35] Hunt, *History*, pp. 76–9.

The faith of Alpine's William Johnson and Julia Dyer Strong had always laid more stress on practice than profession. They may have read Brigham Young's advice on Christian perfection:

> Remember that it is the trifling things of life which make up our experience, and that a small number of great and important events transpire without them. They are, however small, the important little duties of life, upon the daily practice of which much depends to fit a people for the coming of the Lord Jesus, or to prepare them for exaltation in the Kingdom of Our God.
>
> Therefore, give heed unto the teachings of those we have sent among you, and let all strife, animosity, and contention cease in your minds. Live your religion, and let peace, faith, charity and good works abound.[36]

Perhaps chief among the teachings the Strongs were admonished "to give heed to" was the charge to "build up Zion." The task, as seen by nineteenth-century Mormons, had many dimensions. Building up Zion had required that they gather with the Saints and stay aloof from the Gentile world. Julia left their native England in 1851; William, longing to be with her, made a dramatic escape from his apprenticeship as a tinsmith the next year. They were reunited in St. Louis and married there on their way to Utah, where they arrived in September 1852. After a time in Provo, they settled in Alpine, where they remained for the rest of their lives. He died in Alpine in October 1904, she the next February.

They were to bring as many children into the world as the Lord should send them. A church patriarch, Emer Harris, promised William that his progeny "shall be numerous upon the earth and they shall bear off the priesthood after thee." Julia bore ten children between 1853 and 1871, seven of them growing to adulthood. William did not, like many of his contemporaries, marry a second or plural wife, an omission contrary to the counsel of church leaders, which nonetheless did not keep him and Julia from receiving in 1899 their "Second Anointing," a ritual reserved for only a select few.[37] The two of them had not done badly. They were the only Strongs in Alpine in 1860. By 1910 there were thirty of their direct descendants living in the town.

The faithful were pledged to contribute all their time and talents to

---

[36] From the 13th General Epistle of the First Presidency, October 22, 1855, LDS Church Archives, Salt Lake City.

[37] A copy of the patriarchal blessing and the reference to the second anointing are in Bill and Carolyn B. Strong, *A Proud Heritage: The Ancestors and Descendants of Clifford Oscar Strong and Fern Paxman Miller*, vol. III (np., nd.), pp. 294–6.

the task of building Zion. In addition to the bearing and raising of children (which especially occupied Julia's time), the Strongs accepted numerous voluntary service positions in the community. As we have seen, both sang in various choirs throughout their lives. He directed the church choir in Alpine for twenty-one years. He was a counselor in the Alpine Ward bishopric for seventeen years and president of the Alpine coop, as well as of the city council. He was superintendent of the Sunday school and a director of the Alpine City Library Association and the United Order. In their last years, both William and Julia devoted much time to Latter-day Saint temple service, participating in ceremonies that were to "seal" individuals into families that would endure throughout the eternity.

The Zion visible to William and Julia Strong – the one in which they carried out all the "trifling things" of their lives – was not an imposing farm home, a stretch of orchards, woodlands, fields, and a family cemetery. It was the community of Alpine, some 300 to 400 people, living in adobe or brick homes in a square-surveyed, compact village, with a common cemetery on a hill at the north edge of the town. The people there held up as a model the ancient prophet Enoch's city of Zion, where all were "of one heart and one mind, and dwelt in righteousness; and there was no poor among them."[38] Yet perfection eluded them. They were not all of one heart and mind. Though we have little direct evidence, because disputes were usually mediated in bishops' courts, the minutes of which have not survived, there was grumbling and complaining, and conflict over water, land, and other matters, all common in a community where people lived so close upon one another. Still, as we have seen, the level of their cooperation in meeting the challenges of living in so inhospitable an environment was impressive.

Not all lived righteously. Bishops' courts were convened to deal not only with civil disputes, but also with apostasy and with breaches of moral and ethical conduct. There can be no doubt that, as in most small communities, privacy was not easily preserved. Sinners and reprobates, independent thinkers and lone eccentrics, were isolated and shunned. There was for a time, in fact, a special lower part of the cemetery where dissidents found their last resting place.

There were poor among them. Though in the mid-1870s William Strong was on the board of directors of the economic cooperative called the United Order, by 1880 the Strongs owned fifty-three acres of land and $1,290 in taxable property, making theirs the sixth wealth-

---

[38] The quote is from the Book of Moses, a Latter-day Saint scripture revealed to Joseph Smith in June 1830, chapter 7, verse 18.

iest household in the town. They were solidly among the top third that claimed 64 percent of the wealth. Population pressures on the limited available land had brought average prices to $14.40 an acre (mean, $19.00) when it was $10.44 in Sublimity ($9.79) and $2.28 ($3.60) in Middleton.[39] Poverty was evidenced in many unkempt homes and yards, broken fences, and underfunded schools.[40] It is true that their poverty was in large consequence a result of the meager resources of the district and the people's refusal to move away from Zion. Church-sponsored organizations, especially the women's Relief Society, worked hard to open new opportunities and to set up institutions to care for the poor. And wealth was demonstrably more evenly distributed among them than among their contemporaries in Sublimity and Middleton. Nonetheless, in the mid-1870s they rejected Brigham Young's plan for a communal economy, despite strong and persistent counsel to adopt it. When the United Order proved controversial and divisive, they opted for a community of persons over a community of property and saw no necessary connection between them. At the beginning of the 1880s, differences in wealth were increasing, while more and more of the population edged into the worlds of private property and commercial capitalism, in farming and in trade, worlds alien to their fundamental belief that all belongs to God and that men are but temporary stewards over material goods.

Yet, to the extent that a sense of belonging – of attachment to a community and place – is a worthy social aspiration, they succeeded wonderfully, at least for a time. As we have seen, at the end of the third decade after settlement, and while the coherence and stability of Middleton and Sublimity were disintegrating, those of Alpine became more tightly joined. Economic opportunities were severely limited compared to those in the Idaho and Oregon districts. Yet, between 1870 and 1880 the community retained 70 percent of its adults and 55 percent of its maturing young men. It was their hope, expressed in a popular hymn, that one day man could walk "beyond the power of

---

[39] Middleton, as we have seen, was experiencing a localized economic downturn in 1880. Average land prices doubled over the next decade but still were $5.39 (median, $5.33) in 1890.

[40] Brigham Young and his successors preached often about the need to paint, fix up, and tidy the Mormon communities. Taxes in Alpine were just over 1 percent of the assessed value of property. In Middleton they were 2.8 percent. Though we do not know how much of the tax yield went to schools, it likely would have been far less per child in Alpine than in Middleton. If we were to assume that in both localities half of the tax yield went to schools, Alpine would have spent $0.55 per pupil compared to $5.79 in Middleton. Sublimity tax lists for 1880 and 1889 do not record the amount of tax assessed.

mammon" – that as Zion was built up, the earth would "afford the Saints a holy home, like Adam-ondi-Ahman."[41] It would seem that these refugees from the Industrial Revolution had found in Alpine the home they sought, one they would cling to tightly despite the pain of poverty and the temptation of better opportunities elsewhere. It was not sermons or powerful conversions that had accomplished this. It was the daily exercise of denying self – of paying tithes and offerings, accepting voluntary positions within the community, working day in, day out at leading choirs, teaching children piety, sewing quilts, gleaning grain, or taking teams to the Missouri. In fact it was, as Brigham Young said, the "trifling things" of everyday life that attached these people so firmly to their Zion.

Middleton folk were not at any time so firmly attached to the place they found in the West. But that did not matter to them. Certainly they loved and cared for their spouses and children, found friendships among their neighbors, and scrambled to make a living on a rapidly changing frontier. Whereas Alpine people fought vainly to combat "the feeling of mine," those of Middleton welcomed such a sentiment as an important agent of general progress. To be tied to a particular people and place could only inhibit the ability to do well for self and seed. There were few social disciplinarians in Middleton – no hortatory assaults on private property or impositions on personal privacy. Merchants were honored and emulated, and making a farm into a profitable business was the smart thing to do.

In the volatile, free-for-all economic climate of the early Boise Valley, some won and some lost. Junius Wright managed his affairs well, farming and running a hotel in Middleton in the late 1860s. He held on to his land there when in the mid-1870s he moved to Boise to open a drug store. Then, with the coming of the railroad, he sold it, no doubt for a good price, and moved to the new town of Caldwell, opening a drug store there. He settled finally on a farm nine miles west of Caldwell, where he lived comfortably until he moved to Portland late in life.[42] William Montgomery, who platted the original Mid-

---

[41] Adam-ohndi-Ahman is a place sacred to Mormons near the Grand River, in Daviess County, Missouri, where Joseph Smith said Adam called his descendants together just prior to his death to bestow upon them his last blessing and where he one day shall again visit his descendants. See the Mormon scripture called the "Doctrine and Covenants," a compilation of revelations and instructions by Joseph Smith and his successors, Sections 78:15; 107:53; and 116. The hymn "Adam-ohndi-Ahman" is in *Hymns*, No. 389.

[42] Biographical information on Wright is from Elliott, *History of Idaho Territory*, pp. 258–9; Wright, "Reminiscences"; Boise, *Tri-Weekly Statesman*, June 17, 1874; Cornell Files, "Pioneers of Canyon County, Idaho," Book II; and Ada County tax assessment rolls for 1870 and 1880.

dleton town site, claimed 350 acres in 1880, which with other assets was valued at $1,475. Yet, he mortgaged his property in the early 1880s and in 1888 lost it all for failure to pay a $5,000 note. He and his family left Middleton and were not heard of again in those parts.[43] Moses Fowler, Wright's early partner in farming, though not increasing his fortune greatly, kept his holdings above 200 acres all his life and died in Middleton at the turn of the century with 210 acres and an estate worth $3,305.[44]

It would not be exactly accurate, however, to say of these three, as Mary Spangler did of her father's family, that their "paths diverged." Certainly they knew each other in Middleton, and there they dealt and worked with one another. But in the deepest sense, their paths never had converged. Their common meeting places were Sam Foote's mill, the Stevenson and Packard store, or J. H. Holland's saloon, all businesses, where the main work was the selling and buying of commodities. Certainly there was talk and conviviality in these settings, but little giving of self to others in ways that required long-term commitments. Death in Middleton was a family matter from the outset, with fewer notes of petty debit and credit, and with spouses and the nuclear family of the deceased, rather than the neighborhood community, taking over the duties of settling the estate.[45]

There were hundreds of personal, noncommercial exchanges taking place over decades within Sublimity's neighbor/kin groups and in Alpine town, and these had supported, at least for a time, a significant social convergence among the people there. In Middleton such exchanges were relatively rare. Divergence was the Middleton norm from the beginning. Over the three decades from 1870 to 1900, 4 percent of the Middleton population remained (11 of 281), compared to 32 percent of Alpine's people (73 of 210).

Still, lest Sublimity or Alpine folk take too much comfort from the contrast, we must acknowledge that their visions of what they were building in the West ultimately were not fully realized. Had we asked George Hunt and many of his Sublimity neighbors what they would expect to find there 100 years hence, they would have imagined a

---

[43] See Abstract of Title No. 58134, property of Lee Moberly, Middleton, Idaho, in Jennie Cornell File, "Pioneer Homesteads East of Middleton." The abstract shows an action of February 29, 1888, against Montgomery by Cyrus and Richard Jacobs, attaching some 308 acres of his property for refusing to pay his debts to them of $5308.96 and $28.75, plus interest at 10 percent from January 7, 1880.

[44] Fowler data from Ada County tax assessment rolls, 1870, 1880, 1890, 1910.

[45] Ada County Probate Records, State Archives, Boise. There are notes listed in a number of the estates settled in the Middleton area, but they are relatively large and concentrated in a relative few, who obviously were recognized as lenders.

mosaic of extended family groups, living independently and comfortably on adjoining thrifty farms, bound to the land and to one another by a common family heritage. In fact, a family descended from George Hunt does still live on part of his land. But the rest are scattered. The cemetery on Sarah's quarter section, which George Hunt said was to be "a family burying ground forever for the heirs of my body and all descendants of my body," is lost, its hallowed ground plowed and built upon. Hunt himself is buried in an Odd Fellows cemetery in Salem. His repentance was too little and too late to repair the breaches that the drive he had led to prosperity and profits was causing.

Alpiners also had a dream, and though driven by religious faith, it was as centered in this world as were the dreams of their contemporaries in Oregon and Idaho. They chose to flee from the Babylon of industrial capitalism to "the mountains of Ephraim," where, led by God's anointed, they could build a society that was harmonious, orderly, unified, and compassionate – a people fit "for the coming of the Lord Jesus," as Brigham Young put it. It was their deepest desire to find community, so that "no longer as strangers on earth need we roam." Alpine still exists. Strongs and Healeys and Nashes still live there in considerable numbers. There is indeed much rootedness and much mutual care and sharing there. In one sense, it may not matter much to old Alpiners that their fields are now covered with expensive homes, for the land never had for them the magic that it had for George Hunt and his neighbors. It was, as for Middleton folk, a way to make a living. Yet old-timers speak with regret of the day the ward was divided. They look askance at subdivisions that flout the orderly line of the old streets, with their predictable names, and they regret that their children no longer can afford to live there. Real estate developers and wealthy urbanites have pushed values beyond the reach of Alpine's children. People can now buy almost anything they want in Alpine for money.

Junius Wright found his first summer in Middleton "pleasant and profitable," and so determined to stay for a time. "Agriculture and allied enterprises soon established a foundation for progressive prosperity," he remembered. In fact, he and other Middleton folk had no particular social vision beyond "progressive prosperity" when they came. They were fleeing from a war and seeking comfort from its ravages in the promise of riches. They found good land free, and farmed it fully and profitably. Though there were hard times (those in the 1880s costing William Montgomery his place), many prospered. If they did very well, like Wright, they moved on. If they did poorly, like Montgomery, they moved as well. Those who stayed found it hard to found and maintain institutions that would free them from their world of getting and spending. Each person, each family, made it on their own, and in the end took satisfaction in having done so. They were beholden to no one. They could turn the rich resources of the unsettled West to their own ends, and it was no one's business but their own.[46] They were among the thousands who built the New West of the 1860s that is with us still.

The men and women who founded Sublimity and Alpine had dreamed dreams and seen visions. Their stories are poignant and powerful for what they dreamed and for where they failed. As the paths of individuals within Sublimity, Alpine, and Middleton diverged ever more, the societies they built moved together – first Sublimity, then gradually Alpine, turning towards Middleton's call – to live for the moment; to comfort and plenty; to privacy, and to self.

---

[46] It is interesting that political scientist Robert Blank sees Idaho as having a political culture that is unusually individualistic. Robert H. Blank, *Individualism in Idaho: The Territorial Foundations* (Pullman: Washington State University Press, 1988).

# *Coda*

History should enhance our understanding of how change took place in the human past and suggest how the past has shaped our present. These have been my purposes in this study. The project has led me to several conclusions that may in some respects alter the way we have looked at the American West.

Since the founding of the Republic, when Hector St. Jean de Crève-coeur wrote his *Letters of an American Farmer*, it has been common to think of the frontier areas of North America as places where European societies were transformed through the process of settling places where few of their kind had lived. Frederick Jackson Turner formulated the most eloquent and influential statement of this idea a century ago in a speech he gave at the 1893 Columbian Exposition in Chicago. His purpose was to propose that the settling of North America had hitherto led to a uniformity of political and cultural values that had given Americans a distinctive stamp, freeing them from the heritage they had acquired in the eastern United States or in Europe. His was the testy assertion of a native and dedicated midwesterner that the East doesn't count for much, and that the true American society was formed and perpetuated as part of the westering process.

He furthermore suggested that there were different kinds of frontiers, based partly, as Crèvecoeur had proposed, on stages of settlement and keyed to occupational preferences of the settlers – a trapper's frontier, a miner's frontier, a rancher's frontier, a farmer's frontier. Some years ago, looking at the historical literature about the settlement of the West, it seemed to me that there were studies of trapping, mining, and ranching societies in abundance but very little about farmers. Perhaps my own upbringing, on a western Idaho farm, helped persuade me that there might be a story there. Finding most community studies to be discrete and isolated, I wanted to be able to compare agrarian societies in different parts of the West, and I ultimately focused on the Sublimity, Alpine, and Middleton districts.

In choosing to study only farmers, I encountered a good many "ho

277

hums" from colleagues in the profession. They thought farmers to be a staid and uniform people, pale in comparison to trappers, ranchers, or miners. A comparison of different farming districts, they opined, would be as interesting and enlightening as a comparison of apples and apples. Of course, as any connoisseur of apples knows, apples exist, or once existed, in rich and fascinating variety. So too, I found, did agrarian settlers of the Far West. The three peoples I studied brought with them markedly different sets of goals and aspirations that had been shaped by their place of departure from points east and the time of their parting. There was diversity among Anglo settlers, even the Anglo farmers, of the Far West, just as there was diversity among the Native Americans and Hispanics who had long inhabited the region. To see all European or English western settlers as avid perpetrators of a common culture, either heroically "winning" the West or conquering and exploiting it, is to see them only superficially.

I have been impressed in this study with the continuity of cultures brought to the Far West. Indeed, in these instances the frontier did not greatly alter the people who went there, but rather made it possible for them to realize the deepest aspirations of the cultures from which they came. The West was a place where dreams could come true, dreams that perforce had arisen from their past. They built in the West what they would have built in the East had it been possible. In the way they ordered their families, in their uses of the land, and in their relations with others in the new setting, they followed the practices they had followed or wished to follow before they left.

This observation extended and complicated my task enormously, for it led me to the Missouri, the Mississippi, and the Ohio river valleys, and beyond them to Virginia and the Carolinas. It took me back across the Atlantic, in fact, to the first industrialized region of the world, the counties in west central England, and to Mormon missions among the English working classes. And it thrust me into the terrible conflagration of the Civil War as I tried to understand how it had affected the people who fled it.

Within all my peoples there was variety, but there were dominant groups, whose shaping of the new societies at first seemed to overwhelm the minorities among them. Moreover these first peoples of European descent to come to their places in the West established habits and traditions to which latecomers for a time accommodated themselves. For a generation or more the founding majority dominated not only the minority cofounders, but also most of those who came later. They left an imprint that, though altered by subsequent events, still is evident in all three societies today.

Nonetheless, change came, as it always does. One agent of change

was the frontier in that it provided a setting where different cultures
would come together. In none of my three societies, however, was the
encounter principally between Northern Europeans and Native Americans. Though there had been Indians in all three districts, and continued to be some interaction, the most common practice of the
Northern Europeans was simply to ignore those dramatically different
from themselves – to bracket them out of sight and out of mind. Cultural borrowing took place among the Northern European groups
more than between them and other groups. The dominant founders
eventually saw within their societies alternative customs and practices
that caused some to shift their goals, in some cases to the point where,
without quite expecting or realizing it, their original dream was subverted and they found themselves, often with misgivings, hurtling
down a new and different track.

Such was especially the case with those who settled the Willamette
Valley. There the dominant group were yeoman farmers of southern
ancestry. Starting west in the 1840s, most after a sojourn in the Ohio,
Mississippi, and Missouri river valleys, they brought a set of attitudes
toward family, land, and community that subsequent generations
would find remote and alien. They moved and settled in neighbor/
kin clusters. They claimed enormous tracts of land, enough, they
hoped, so that their children and children's children would be able to
remain on their land. They opened neighborhood cemeteries so that
they and their children would be together in death as in life. They
built imposing frame homes that seemed distant echoes of the plantation houses they and their ancestors had known in the Old South.
Their social world was narrow but intense, fulfilling, and mutually
supportive.

They were at first conservative in their use of the land. Though
hardly environmentalists in our modern sense of the word, they were
conservationists. They saw themselves as holding the land in trust,
reserving it for the day when a future generation might need it. If it
was not their aim to follow the biblical injunction to "replenish" the
earth, neither were they eager to deplete it quickly, for they had the
long view and were concerned for those of their stock who would
follow them. They farmed but a tiny portion of the land they owned,
and though selling at market any surplus they could, their first aim
was to make sure that the land provided for family needs. Sufficiency,
not unbounded wealth, was their goal. When they went to the mines,
it was to return with enough gold to buy more land or improve their
farms.

This was the disposition of George Washington Hunt of Indiana (of
North Carolina ancestry) and of the many settlers in the Sublimity

district of similar descent. It was not the view of John Downing of Pennsylvania. The marriage of Temperance Hunt to John Downing seems in fact a metaphor for what was to happen in broader Sublimity. Neighbors and kin by marriage, they lived and worked side by side throughout the 1850s and 1860s. But whereas Hunt farmed but a tenth of his land, growing little more than his family needed, Downing worked night and day, plowing, harrowing, and seeding all his acres into profitable production of staple crops. Downing became the wealthiest man in the district.

In the 1870s Hunt was won over to Downing's model, joining his brother-in-law in pursuing farming as a business – a commercial enterprise. In the heat of this pursuit he forgot for a time his original vision, that this land was to be forever the sacred center of the Hunts, the guarantor of their independence, their power, and their rights as citizens of a free republic. The whole future of the race was to have been assured by their possession of this soil. And now he, George Hunt, in the pursuit of the moment, was putting it all into production, while his children, suddenly uncertain of their claim, were moving off to other callings. A powerful religious conversion persuaded him to drive the "money changers" from the temple. He wrote a book intended to impress his heirs with the power of their family heritage. He willed that his land be divided among them, intending that it should always be in the hands of his descendants. But it was all in vain. Markets, contractual relationships, and the pursuit of unbounded wealth had compromised his original dream beyond recovery. The nexus of family and land was severed, the tight-knit communities of neighbor and kin disintegrated, and the Willamette moved toward modernity. The yeoman vision was unable to withstand modernization because it was built on a limited set of social relationships and was tied to a particular economic notion, the sense that family and land were mutually supportive and inseparable. The Downing model had subverted the yeoman vision.

The settlers of Alpine were already part of the modern world when they came to the West. They were converts to Mormonism, and were among the first in the world to see the old order shattered by the mines and mills of industrial Britain. Mormon missionaries taught of a haven in the West where they could escape working-class poverty and dislocation, joining themselves to a community of Saints. Their conversion and migration fragmented families and led them to form new ties to church leaders and ultimately to fellow citizens in the Utah villages where they settled. Neither land nor family, in the broadest sense, were as important to them as community. Usually not farmers before they came to the West, they did not invest land with special meaning but saw it as a way to make a living. The small fields they farmed outside the town yielded barely enough to survive on, and providing the essentials for family survival became their first priority. If they were lucky enough to realize a surplus, they would sell it for what they could get. Yet, in spite of relative poverty, their intense interaction with others in a plethora of church-sponsored voluntary activities created a rich social life that helped form enduring bonds to the place. Their social world was more inclusive than that of the Sublimity people and extended beyond kin to include a broader town community.

Yet they, like the Sublimity people, were not immune to modernization. Though church leaders tried to impose a communal economy upon them, they resisted, seeing no necessary connection between their economic and their social/religious lives. Thus, when railroads, mines, and smelters came to the area, they were quick to take work off the farm and to squeeze from their land any surplus possible in order to enhance their meager living. They welcomed commercial activity and capitalist endeavor, and would gladly have turned their farms to staple production had the land and water been sufficient to do so. Their leaders had originally preached a doctrine of stewardship that would make them custodians of the land, obligated to turn it over intact to their descendants, but the message did not endure. Their social ties did, however, and kept them and their children in place despite promising prospects elsewhere. As the kin/neighbor communities of Sublimity began to unravel, the community of Alpine became knit ever tighter. People like Catherine Nash and William and Julia Dyer Strong lived to see their children and grandchildren filling niches in the town. Most eventually were buried in the one cemetery on the north edge of Alpine.

The Alpine people and their heirs still feel a strong attachment to the place. Family reunions draw them back, and descendants of the pioneers, long since removed to Salt Lake City or Idaho or Oregon, come home to reminisce, some to be buried with their people on the hill. There is nonetheless a new Alpine, built by wealthy outsiders on fields the Alpiners broke up and sold for subdivisions. It appears that Alpine may in time follow Sublimity in failing to perpetuate its original dream.

Middleton represented from the outset a new society, one that was wholly and unabashedly modern. The Junius Wrights and Lewis Spanglers who settled there were fleeing the ravages of the Civil War and seeking to assuage their pain with the gritty balm of material things. Though they were mostly from the same stock as the Sublimity folk, the intervening years had changed them. They had participated in a rapid turn to market production and caught a glimpse of gold. Their new acquisitiveness combined with the terrible dislocation caused by war to change attitudes toward family, land, and community. They fled the East helter-skelter, not as kin groups, but rather as individuals and nuclear families. When the Boise Valley lands seemed to promise as much wealth as the mines, they were quick to stake a claim and devote it to marketable crops.

Exploiting their lands fully, they seldom thought beyond the moment, and were quick to sell if they found that the soils were being depleted or if a new opportunity beckoned elsewhere. Selling in the market was their first priority. They could meet family needs through exchange. Contracts and exchange mediated most human relationships, activities incapable of forming the enduring ties that the people in Sublimity and Alpine had known. Economically wealthy, Middleton was poor in human relationships. Churches and other social activities were slow to come and hard to perpetuate. The cemetery was out of town on a sagebrush flat. The many who left seldom came back. Ambition, wealth, and individualism characterized their world, and minimized the number and strength of human ties. Their social world did not encompass family/kin groups or larger town communities, but only their spouses, children, and selves.

If this description of these three societies is close to what was there, then the implications for us in the late twentieth century are considerable. The Sublimity and Alpine folk, after all, built pioneer outposts in the Mountain and Pacific West. They were the Pilgrims of the Pacific, content to pursue homely errands of their own. Though they set distinctive cultural patterns that endure in some measure, the great tide of settlement came to the Far West during and after the Civil War and is best represented by Middleton's people, vanguard of a whole new race. Leaving a society powerfully transformed since the 1840s by Yankee acquisitiveness and brutal war, the newcomers brought a culture that in its quest for self-fulfillment conquered and exploited with little restraint, and ultimately made even Sublimity and Alpine into approximate images of itself.

Several social critics, including the late Christopher Lasch and Robert Bellah, have suggested that the great malaise of the United States in recent decades is that we have become narcissistic and selfish, obsessively devoted to material well-being. We seem incapable of the long view or of forgoing personal gratification for the good of a broader community. These critics have observed that leaders at the very highest levels of political and social authority sustain and encourage this condition. Alexis de Tocqueville thought he saw in the 1830s the direction of things:

> Thus not only does democracy make every man forget his
> ancestors, but it hides his descendants and separates his
> contemporaries from him; it throws him back forever upon
> himself alone and threatens in the end to confine him entirely
> within the solitude of his own heart.

The founders of Sublimity and Alpine in their own ways fought
that tide. Those of Middleton swept it along.

# Notes on sources

I have attempted in this study to understand the most fundamental values of three peoples who settled different regions of the American West more than a century ago and to suggest how those values influenced the character of the societies they built. Why did they come? How did their understanding of family, of land and its uses, and of community shape their societies? Are there discernible patterns in the cultures of these peoples, all pioneers of what Frederick Jackson Turner might have called the farmer's frontier?

Of course, these questions, involving received traditions, attitudes, and unspoken (perhaps even unconscious) assumptions as to what human society should be like, are not easily answered. The problem is particularly difficult when studying rural people who seldom wrote about their lives and who almost never reflected in writing on the character of the errands they undertook in helping to settle Oregon, Utah, and Idaho. I have found a few statements and observations from the period. The minutes of Farmer's Clubs meetings reported verbatim in the *Willamette Farmer* in the early 1870s helped me to capture the thoughts of several farmers in Sublimity and surrounding districts as of that time. George Hunt's will, written in 1890, is a remarkable document, expressing clearly and unequivocally his feelings about his land as it related to his family. His *History of the Hunt Family*, written at about the same time, offers revealing and important insights into his thought and values. But during the decade I have spent collecting information for this study, such discoveries have been rare. More commonly, I have either had to piece together fragments of the documented past that were not intended to express values or reveal mentalities – such humdrum sources as census lists, tax assessment roles, or probate records – or attempt to interpret texts created after the fact – memories of the past left by at least a few of the people who lived in Sublimity, Alpine, and Middleton.

In short, the nature of my study has forced me to glean understanding from sources that are concentrated at opposite sides of the range

284

of document types historians normally use to gain insights into the minds of past people. The broad and rich middle ground of diaries, letters, public speeches, or pronouncements and other narratives created at the time is minimally represented among what I have presumed to call "my" people. More commonly I found, on the one hand, bits of information about them gathered by civil officials or, on the other, narratives written years later for filiopietistic or autopietistic purposes.

Of the civil records, I have relied heavily on the manuscripts of the U.S. Census, available for each decade except 1890 through 1920. They name the persons in each household and provide additional information that varies somewhat from census to census but that, during the period of this study, includes occupation, birthplace, age, sex, race, schooling, literacy, and wealth. The 1900 and 1910 censuses also gathered information on parents' birthplaces, relationship of each person to the head of household, number of years married, number of children born, number of children living, farm or home ownership, physical debilities, and naturalization. The State of Oregon took elaborate censuses in 1865 and 1895 that gathered a wealth of detail about farm production, voting eligibility, and even the height, weight, and complexion of the heads of household, though not of all household members.

The information from these censuses is rich, and close scrutiny reveals patterns in how the societies were structured that make it possible to see changes over time and to compare the three societies at a given point in time. There has been much study of the manuscript censuses and their reliability as sources for social history. In cities, young men, the homeless, people who moved often, and persons of Asian, Hispanic, or African ancestry were often undercounted. This was much less the case in the rural districts I have studied. There were few among the rural population who fit these categories. The districts were sparsely populated. Their people were mutually watchful. Strangers stood out, and the census marshals most often found them. I therefore see the census as reasonably reliable for the populations and period included in this study.

The manuscripts of the U.S. Census are available on film at most major libraries and at virtually all genealogical research centers. I have used those in the Latter-day Saint Family History Library in Salt Lake City, the Oregon State Archives in Salem, the Oregon State Library in Salem, and the Marriott Library of the University of Utah in Salt Lake City.

Tax assessment rolls have also been vital to this study. Unlike the national census, these vary from region to region in the type of information they contain; they can also vary from year to year. Though remarkably detailed in the 1850s, they become more general and less complex toward the end of the century. They are nonetheless enormously useful. In all three localities, tax assessors were required by state or territorial law to assess all property of household heads at full market value for purposes of taxation. Tax assessors, such as Sublimity's Paul Darst, went from farm to farm and asked farmers for information about their wealth. They usually reported the number of acres owned, value of the land, value of farm machinery, amount of wages paid, number of farm animals and their value, and types of crops produced and the value of each. Sometimes they included the township, range, and section of the land, the number of clocks or musical instruments, or the proportion of land being tilled. These tax assessment rolls are supplemented at some points in this study by the manuscript of the U.S. Agricultural Census, which is available for the Idaho and Utah districts, but not for Oregon, and which provides valuable additional information, especially on farm productivity. This and the tax assessment rolls detail patterns in uses of the land, production decisions, and wealth, in this study revealing dramatic differences among the three societies.

The differences arise from numerous contingencies – the overall amount of land available, its condition (flat or hilly, forested or brush-covered), climatic conditions, labor supply, and market accessibility. These do not tell the whole story, however. It seems clear, as I have indicated in the text, that cultural predisposition was an important factor in the patterns of land use, and so I have presumed to infer from such data what meanings the land had for these people. There are problems with this type of source. When Paul Darst asked George Hunt to give him detailed information on his wealth, Hunt clearly would have given off-the-cuff estimates of his various assets and their value. And, given that the amount of wealth would determine the level of taxes, he was likely to underestimate the value of his possessions. Yet these factors should have affected all three societies in a similar way, making comparisons valid and instructive. Still, I have chosen to interpret only strong differences, feeling that the reliability of the records may not be sufficient for fine points.

The tax assessment rolls I used were in various repositories. Those for Marion County, Oregon, were in the Oregon State Archives. I found the earliest Canyon County, Idaho, rolls stacked in the county garage, in Caldwell, Idaho, littered with banana peels and lunch papers of the garage workers and splattered with oil and battery acid. They have since been moved to the safe haven of the Idaho State Archives in Boise, where, with the earliest Ada County records, they document the wealth of Middleton's people from founding through the turn of the century. The tax records for Utah Valley are in the Utah State Archives in Salt Lake City and in the Utah State University Library in Logan.

Probate court records have also been helpful in revealing the character of the three societies. These consist of wills, documents appointing executors to settle the estates of deceased persons, documents appointing appraisers, inventories prepared by the appraisers, reports on estate auctions, and final reports of the net worth of the estate. They contain valuable information, the earlier ones sometimes describing even the clothing or books of the deceased. The process varied somewhat from community to community, with early Sublimity probates involving a fairly broad network of kin and neighbors; Alpine probates being relatively infrequent, suggesting that conveyance of property to descendants was done more informally; and Middleton probates tending to involve principally the spouse and children of the deceased.

Sublimity has the fullest collection of probate records, housed in the Oregon State Archives and in the Marion County Courthouse. Because Utah probate courts had both criminal and civil jurisdiction, documents relating to the settling of estates occupy a small part of Utah County records and occur infrequently. These records are located in the Utah State Archives. A substantial number of probate records have survived from Idaho's Ada and Canyon counties and are in the Idaho State Archives.

Helpful in understanding the variety and character of conflict within the three districts were the records of civil and criminal courts. Most revealing in the Sublimity area were the justice courts, which carried a considerable burden of litigation at the grass-roots level of fairly petty matters – "using boisterous, obscene and profane language in a public place," assault, and collection of small debts. The circuit court heard similar cases, including some brought by appeal from the justice courts, the cases often relating to crimes, civil disputes, or other matters of a more serious nature. The Judgment Book of the District Court of Marion County offered brief abstracts of the judgments rendered in that court, but little information as to the nature of the disputes or complaints. The County Commissioner Court Journal provided valuable information on persons appointed to juries, appointment of road supervisors, regulation of ferry fees, and other administrative work of the county. All these records are in the Oregon State Archives.

Court records that would have contained information on disputes in Alpine are not as abundant or informative as those documenting disputes in Sublimity. Since the court of first resort in Alpine was the bishop's ecclesiastical court, the Utah County probate court there represents about the same level of juridical responsibility as the justice courts in Sublimity. No Alpine cases and very few Utah Valley cases reached even the level of the probate court. The records of this court contain the same types of complaints and criminal acts brought to Sublimity area justice courts, though with divorce dominating the dockets much more than in Sublimity or Middleton. All these records are in the Utah State Archives.

For the Middleton area, I have been able to locate only the *Ada County Judgment Book,* which documents lawsuits, civil complaints, divorces, and criminal cases at about the same level as Sublimity's justice court and Utah Valley's probate court. The several volumes of records from this court are in the Idaho State Archives. The level and character of the court records varied sufficiently from locality to locality to make any kind of quantitative comparison highly tentative, but the records nonetheless suggest patterns that reinforce impressions gained from other sources about the three societies.

The censuses, tax rolls, probate records, and court cases are the principal classes of civil documents I have used in my attempt to understand the values that drove the people of Sublimity, Alpine, and Middleton. Though intended only to facilitate the administrative work of public institutions, they reveal an astonishing amount of information about the character of the societies and the individuals who made up those societies.

I could not have been nearly as confident that I have understood these people, however, were the patterns in the civil records not sustained by narrative sources, most written well after early settlement. For the Sublimity area, the principal narrative source has been Sarah Hunt Steeves's *Book of Remembrance of Marion County Pioneers, 1840–1860* (Portland: The Berncliff Press, 1927). It contains biographies and reminiscences of dozens of early Marion County settlers, including many from the Sublimity area. These were gathered by Mrs. Steeves during the first two decades of the century, usually through personal interviews with the persons represented, many of whom were her neighbors and friends. The book also contains short vignettes about life in early Marion County, such as attending the fair or the colorful crowd at the Whiteaker store, often describing the appearance and personality of early Sublimity people in some detail. In some instances, Mrs. Steeves had access to memoirs and journals that I have not been able to find. One cannot help feeling, in reading her father's autobiography and her own works, that the Hunts had taken upon themselves the burden of being the shamans of the Sublimity area, called to remember for the community their collective past, to discern

its lessons, and to recite them for the benefit of subsequent generations. That task has since been taken up by Daraleen Wade, a great-
granddaughter of John Downing, an uncle of Sarah Hunt Steeves.

Alpine has a somewhat similar set of narratives, the manuscript
memoirs collected by the Daughters of the Utah Pioneers under the
direction of Jennie Adams Wild and collectively titled "Builders of
Alpine." These are often not as immediate as the Steeves materials,
representing second- or third-generation memories, rather than those
of the founders themselves, but nonetheless they provide very useful
insights. The local history, *Alpine Yesterdays: A History of Alpine, Utah
County, Utah, 1850–1980* (Salt Lake City: Blaine Hudson Printing,
1982), distills much that is in these narratives and adds valuable details. Collected and published by Jennie Adams Wild and other Alpine people, it is an authentic folk history and thus communicates
clearly the character and values of the society that produced it. Vern
W. Clark's "A Historical Study of Alpine" (M.S. thesis, Brigham
Young University, 1963) contains much useful information as well.
William Goforth Nelson's memoir, in the LDS Church Historical Department, documents the earliest settlement period. The Manuscript
History of Alpine, in the LDS Church Historical Department, a
chronicle compiled from a number of sources, provides much useful
information. Several family histories have been enormously fruitful,
including especially Bill and Carolyn B. Strong, *A Proud Heritage: The
Ancestors and Descendants of Clifford Oscar Strong and Fern Paxman Miller*, vol. III (np., nd.); Betha S. Ingram, ed. *The James & John Healey
Family History* (Provo, Utah: privately published, 1963); and Merma
G. Carlisle, ed., *Alpine: The Place Where We Lived* (Nash family publication, n.p., n.d.).

Middleton is represented by the remarkably revealing memoir written by Junius B. Wright in 1934 at the request of local members of the
Daughters of the American Revolution. Wright was in his ninety-
ninth year when he wrote the memoir, consisting of nearly 100 pages
of manuscript, but his memory, wit, and essential character come
through clearly. The memoir is in the Idaho State Archives. Also useful has been Mary R. Luster, *The Autobiography of Mary R. Luster*
(Springfield, Mo., n.p., 1933), in which she wrote about her family's
sojourn in the Middleton area in the 1860s. Two local histories have
been written by Middleton folk: Morris Foote, comp., *One Hundred
Years in Middleton* (Middleton, Idaho: *Boise Valley Herald*, 1963), and
Middleton Centennial Book Committee, *Middleton in Picture and Story*,
(Nampa, Idaho: Downtown Printing, 1989). The files of the late Jennie
Cornell supplement these folk histories with anecdotal accounts of
Middleton people and institutions collected from various sources over

many years. She was until her death a shaman for Middleton, just as Jennie Adams Wild was for Alpine and Daraleen Wade for Sublimity.

Some might question the usefulness of such memoirs and folk histories, produced after the fact by people of no special talent or training to praise their ancestors and predecessors in the locality. Historians have often been contemptuous of such documents, finding them prone to factual error, chaotically structured, and lacking in narrative flow. My experience has been that when read deeply and carefully, they are enormously valuable, particularly to a study such as this. Though written to honor the pioneers, it is clear from close reading that they vary in which particular qualities they praise. There are differences in what the authors choose to place first or last, what they emphasize or ignore, the descriptive adjectives they employ, the segments of the society they include or do not include. Even the titles of their books are often enlightening. When prepared by descendants of the settlers, these sources unconsciously reveal the most fundamental values and character of the societies from which they arise and of which they are the product.

Though I was initially disappointed to find virtually no diaries kept by my people during their lives, I feel that their descendants have done much to make up for the loss by telling the story of their parents with ingenuous eloquence and discernment. When read deeply, the memoirs and folk histories seem at times distillates of how these communities defined their purposes and what they valued over time. Their message does much to explain and reinforce the patterns contained in the civil sources. Taken together the civil sources and memoirs are consistent in offering what is, to my mind, compelling evidence that these societies were close to what I have here described; that could we talk to George Hunt, Catherine Nash, or Junius Wright about the things they valued most, they would tell a similar story.

Finally, the environment built by Sublimity, Alpine, and Middleton people offered many insights. Visiting these places, looking at houses and outbuildings, walking through their streets and fields and cemeteries, I felt my empathy for their world enormously enhanced. Indeed, one bitter cold, foggy November day, while exploring the Sublimity area with Daraleen Wade, I experienced something of what economist Joseph Schumpeter called a "preanalytic vision" – that moment when the welter of collected evidence is magically transformed in the mind from seemingly unassailable chaos to a comprehensible pattern.

It was the cemeteries that did it. As we drove along the roads and byways of the Sublimity countryside, we visited cemetery after cemetery, often small enclosures, perhaps fifty yards across, atop a wooded hill, overlooking the fields and houses built by those buried there. I thought of the one Alpine cemetery, a prominent hill on the north edge of town. Alpiners take pride in showing a stranger the graves of the founders at the summit, and many can from their front porches spy the markers of their ancestors and relatives, buried, as the years have passed, ever lower on its sloping sides. And I remembered Middleton, where I had grown up, with one cemetery up on a bench, out of sight of the village, in my youth hardly tended and surrounded by sagebrush flats. I recalled that Mark Twain had once said in *Roughing It* that "in order to know a community, one must observe the style of its funerals." And then the epiphany struck me, and I began to see in the placement of the cemeteries the very image of these societies in life. That vision, as Schumpeter explained, was modified and amended as I read further and as I teased data from my files, but the core of it remains.

# Appendix

Tables on representative towns, and proximity of farm and mine towns from Chapter 3.

Table A.1. *Mountain-to-Pacific Corridor, 1870: representative towns*

| Town | No. of Twns | Year Founded | Pop. | Hse holds | Persons /HH | Sex Ratio | % For'n | % Farm | % Mine | % Serve | % Other | No. Employd |
|---|---|---|---|---|---|---|---|---|---|---|---|---|
| Allton | 667 | 1862 | 383 | 85 | 4.5 | 180 | 31 | 24 | 31 | 32 | 13 | 156 |
| Utah | 174 | 1859 | 499 | 99 | 5 | 105 | 36 | 44 | 2 | 33 | 21 | 124 |
| Alpine | 1 | 1852 | 208 | 38 | 5.5 | 108 | 43 | 63 | 0 | 24 | 13 | 38 |
| Nevada | 117 | 1864 | 363 | 84 | 4.3 | 342 | 45 | 9 | 34 | 49 | 92 | 230 |
| Montana | 79 | 1866 | 261 | 89 | 3.7 | 348 | 38 | 15 | 49 | 29 | 7 | 178 |
| Idaho | 60 | 1864 | 250 | 68 | 3.7 | 588 | 52 | 14 | 58 | 21 | 7 | 181 |
| Middleton | 1 | 1863 | 252 | 59 | 4.2 | 196 | 14 | 85 | .8 | 15 | 0 | 133 |
| Oregon | 237 | 1852 | 384 | 78 | 4.9 | 122 | 10 | 45 | 0 | 34 | 21 | 129 |
| Sublimity | 1 | 1850 | 726 | 121 | 6 | 103 | 2 | 70 | 0 | 10 | 20 | 126 |

| Town | RE/ Prs ($) | PP/ Prs ($) | Wlt h/P ($) | RE/ HH ($) | PP/ HH ($) | Wlth /HH ($) | RE/ Emp ($) | PP/ Emp ($) | Wlth /Emp ($) | Yr of RR | RR Dst (mi) | Elev (ft) | Prec. (in.) | Temp. | Lat degr. min. | Long degr. min. |
|------|------|------|------|------|------|------|------|------|------|------|------|------|------|------|------|------|
| Allton | 242 | 229 | 471 | 1091 | 1034 | 2125 | 595 | 564 | 1159 | 1880 | 12 | 4667 | 14.5 | 47.8 | 42°01' | 114°14' |
| Utah | 104 | 82 | 186 | 527 | 412 | 939 | 421 | 330 | 751 | 1878 | 12 | 4950 | 14.4 | 49.0 | 40°09' | 112°10' |
| Alpine | 120 | 78 | 199 | 657 | 428 | 1085 | 657 | 428 | 1085 | 1872 | 6 | 5490 | 16.8 | 48.8 | 40°27' | 111°47' |
| Nevda | 415 | 317 | 732 | 1787 | 1365 | 3151 | 656 | 501 | 1157 | 1878 | 12 | 5256 | 8.6 | 49.3 | 40°23' | 116°49' |
| Montn | 202 | 535 | 737 | 590 | 1561 | 2151 | 297 | 784 | 1081 | 1883 | 37 | 4596 | 12.1 | 43.1 | 46°20' | 122°06' |
| Idaho | 159 | 278 | 437 | 581 | 1015 | 1597 | 219 | 383 | 602 | 1892 | 23 | 4130 | 33.0 | 45.2 | 44°26' | 115°27' |
| Middn | 337 | 325 | 663 | 1440 | 1393 | 2833 | 638 | 618 | 1256 | 1883 | 10 | 2838 | 25.3 | 43.6 | 42°30' | 116°37' |
| Oregn | 315 | 252 | 567 | 1549 | 1238 | 2786 | 935 | 747 | 1682 | 1871 | 5 | 226 | 40.6 | 52.4 | 45°01' | 122°06' |
| Subity | 779 | 219 | 998 | 4709 | 1319 | 5990 | 4488 | 1266 | 5753 | 1871 | 10 | 548 | 41.0 | 52.3 | 44°50' | 122°48' |

*Note:* The data are arithmetic means of each value for the entire dataset, as in Allton, or the subsets as indicated. Percent occupation is based on total occupations recorded. "Wlth/Emp" refers to wealth per person reporting an occupation to the census that would make that person likely to possess real estate or personal property. "RE" and "PP" refer to the reported assessed dollar value of real estate or personal property, adjusted according to county practice to what census takers called "true valuation." "Wlth" refers to total wealth, that is, RE plus PP. "Hseholds" or "HH" is the same as "Family" as entered in the census. Percent "For'n" is percent foreign born.

*Source:* Manuscript U.S. Census for 1870 and geographical dictionaries, place name books, early histories, and climatological guides for each state or territory.

Table A.2. *Proximity of farm and mine towns by state or territory, 1870*

| | Utah | | Nevada | | Montana | | Idaho | | Total | |
|---|---|---|---|---|---|---|---|---|---|---|
| | Lat N | Long W | Lat N | Long W | Lat N | Long W | Lat N | Long W | Lat N | Long W |
| Farm | 40°16' | 112°12' | 39°02' | 116°14' | 46°16' | 112°16' | 43°14' | 114°24' | 40°55' | 113°57' |
| Mine | 40°00' | 112°05' | 39°46' | 116°27' | 46°16' | 112°32' | 44°16' | 115°40' | 43°42' | 114°35' |
| Farm re mn | 16' N | 7' W | 44' S | 13' E | 0' | 16' E | 1°2' S | 1°16' E | 2°47' S | 38' E |
| Miles | 19 mi. | 6 mi. | 51 mi. | 11 mi. | 0 mi. | 14 mi. | 73 mi. | 63 mi. | 195 mi. | 32 mi. |
| Min miles | 20 mi. | NNW | 52 mi. | SSE | 14 mi. | E | 96 mi. | SE | 198 mi. | SSE |

*Note*: The arithmetic mean of latitudes and longitudes for all farm towns and for all mine towns in each state or territory was calculated for rows 1 and 2. From these the direction and distance of the average farm town from the average mine could be determined (Frm re mn [Farm town in relation to mine town]) for row 3. In row 4 the minutes or degrees are converted to miles, scaling miles from the grid of degrees of latitude and longitude in extreme northwestern Utah (close to the mean for the entire set of towns). For row 5 the shortest airline distance (Min[imum] miles) was calculated as the hypotenuse of the right angle of which the east-west and north-south mile distances were the other sides.

Table A.3 *Proximity of farm and mine towns in Salt Lake, Carson City, Virginia City, Montana, and Boise areas, 1870*

| | Salt Lake area 40–41° 111–113° | | | | | Carson area 39–40° 118–120° | | | | |
|---|---|---|---|---|---|---|---|---|---|---|
| | N | Pop | Fnd | Lat | Long | N | Pop | Fnd | Lat | Long |
| Farm | 34 | 653 | 1854 | 40°33' | 111°45' | 11 | 245 | 1861 | 39°12' | 119°31' |
| Mine | 3 | 191 | 1864 | 40°32' | 112°03' | 4 | 2996 | 1862 | 39°00' | 119°21' |
| Farm re mn | +31 | +462 | −10 | 1'N | 18'W | +7 | −2779 | −1 | 12'N | 10'W |
| Miles | | | | 1 | 15 | | | | 14 N | 8 W |
| Min miles | | | | 15 mi. W | | | | | 16 mi. NW | |

| Virginia City area 45–47° 111–113° | | | | | Boise area 42–44° 115–117° | | | | |
|---|---|---|---|---|---|---|---|---|---|
| N | Pop | Fnd | Lat | Long | N | Pop | Fnd | Lat | Long |
| 12 | 194 | 1866 | 45°57' | 111°49' | 6 | 237 | 1864 | 43°33' | 115°48' |
| 34 | 331 | 1867 | 46°19' | 112°17' | 19 | 302 | 1864 | 43°32' | 116°01' |
| −22 | −137 | −1 | 22'S | 28'E | −13 | −65 | 0 | 1'N | 13'E |
| | | | 26 S | 23 E | | | | 1 N | 11 E |
| | | | 35 mi. SE | | | | | 11 mi. E | |

*Note:* Values are based upon arithmetic means of those for all towns in the areas by type. From the means for latitude and longitude, the direction and distance of the average farm town from the average mine could be determined (Frm re mn [Farm town in relation to mine town]) for row 3. In row 4 the minutes or degrees are converted to miles, scaling miles from the grid of degrees of latitude and longitude in extreme northwestern Utah (close to the mean for the entire set of towns). For row 5 the shortest airline distance (Min[imum] miles) was calculated as the hypotenuse of the right angle of which the east-west and north-south mile distances were the other sides. The central question the table addresses is how far and in what direction need one go to get from the average mine town to the average farm town in 1870? The answer, clearly, is "not far" – in no case being greater than one day's drive for freighters. With the exception of the earlier settled Utah rural areas, farm and mine towns were founded at the same time and in close proximity to one another.

# Index